MANAGING
PERSONALITY

MANAGING PERSONALITY

Donald W. Fiske

ALDINETRANSACTION
A Division of Transaction Publishers
New Brunswick (U.S.A.) and London (U.K.)

First paperback printing 2009

Library of Congress Catalog Number: 2009000364
ISBN: 978-0-202-36260-1
Printed in the United States of America

Library of Congress Cataloging-in-Publication Data

Fiske, Donald Winslow, 1916-
   [Measuring the concepts of personality]
   Managing personality / Donald W. Fiske.
       p. cm.
   Published in 1971 under title: Measuring the concepts of personality.
   Includes bibliographical references and index.
   ISBN 978-0-202-36260-1 (pbk. : acid-free paper)
       1. Personality assessment. 2. Psychology--Methodology. I. Title.

BF698.4.F58 2009
155.2'8--dc22
                                                                2009000364

Contents

Foreword   xi
Preface   xv

PART ONE. WHAT DO WE MEASURE?   1

Introduction   3

1. The Roots of Personality Measurement   4

   Development of Procedures   5
      The clinical approach   5
      The inventory approach   6
      Systematic observations   7
      Other approaches   9
      Progress or productivity?   9
   Theory and Measurement   10
      Target concepts   11
      Theory and data must interact   13
   Summary   14

2. Orientations and Themes   16

   Setting the Stage   16
      Personality   16
      Basic research and other settings for measurement   17
   The Orientation of This Book   19
      "The Two Disciplines of Scientific Psychology"   19
      Some axiomatic propositions   24
      Some pervasive themes and theses   28
   Summary   35

3. Personality, Process, and Systematic Observations   37

   The Content to Be Observed and Measured   37
      Defining personality   37
      The general process   38
      Implications of the process concept   41

Extracting Order from Chaos   43
    The subject and his state   48
    The setting, the conditions for measurement   50
    The task set for the subjects   51
    The stimuli   52
    The responses   55
    Measurement as experimentation   56
    Caveat   58
    Summary   59

4. The Observational Data of Personology   61

    The Natural History of Personality   61
    Perspectives   62
        One or several perspectives?   63
        Perspectives and theories   65
    Summary   66

5. The Modes of Measuring Personality   68

    The Prior Behavior Mode (Mode 4)   73
    The Capabilities Mode (Mode 3)   76
    The Current Experiencing Mode (Mode 2)   76
    The Self Description Mode (Mode 1)   77
    The Observation of Behavior Mode (Mode 5)   77
    The Psychophysiology Mode (Mode 6)   79
    Perceptions of the Measuring Process   79
    The Modes and Their Differentiation   81
    Contexts   84
    Subject and Observer Variables   85
    Modes, Perspectives, and Other Classifications   86
    Method Variance   88
    Summary   89

6. The Specification of Constructs   90

    Guidelines for Conceptualizing a Variable   92
        What is a variable?   94
        The setting for a working definition   96
        The core of the construct   98
        Modes to be used   101
        Facets and elements   103
        Conditions   106

Necessary and desirable characteristics of conceptualizations   106
Other orientations   107
The empirical alternative   109
From Construing to Measuring   110
A glance ahead: processes in measuring   110
Three test designs   113
Summary   117

PART TWO. MEASURING   119

Introduction   121

7. Some Fundamentals of Measurement   122

Ideal Measurement   122
A fantasy   122
Reality   124
Measuring in a testing situation   127
Ideal testing   129
The isolated construct and interactions among constructs   130
The Single Datum   131
The measurement decision   131
The response attribute recorded   132
Potential indices   133
Summary   135

8. Indices: Their Models and Their Evaluation   137

Measurement Scales   138
Psychometric Models   140
Models with undifferentiated stimuli   140
The cumulative homogeneity model   142
Other models   146
Scaled scoring of observations   147
The measurement scales and the psychometric models   148
A critique of the psychometric models   149
Psychometric models and qualities of responses   150
Generalizability for a Single Test   150
Internal consistency   151
Stability   152
Generalization over producers   152
Indices of homogeneity   153
Computing the Homogeneity Indices   157
Variances   157

Homogeneity coefficients   160
  Other comments on the homogeneity indices   162
Generalizability Beyond the Single Test: Approaches to Validation   163
  Convergent and discriminant validation   164
  Criterion-related validity   166
  Construct validity   167
  The unity of generalizability   171
The Role of Expert Judgment in Personality Measurement   172
Summary   175

9. Behaving and Changing   177

The Stability of Behavior from a Short-Term View   177
  The stream of experiencing   177
  State vs. trait   180
  Consistency of behavior over repeated observations   180
  The stability of measurements   183
  Factors affecting the stability of test responses   186
The Long-Term Stability of Personality Measurements   189
The Study of Change   191
  Measuring experimental effects   191
  The measurement of therapeutic treatments   194
Measuring Change   197
  Initial level   197
  Indices of change   198
  Effects of unreliability   199
  Substantive considerations   200
Summary   201

10. A Human Being Takes a Test   203

The Layman's View of Testing   204
The Psychology of the Subject Taking a Test   206
  Three kinds of stimuli   206
  The motives of subjects   209
  The examiner's relationship to the subject   212
Dimensions of Test-Taking Behavior   213
  Response sets   213
  An overview of response sets   217
  Other subject variables   220
Ambiguity in Questionnaire Items   221
The Process in Responding to an Item   222

The Rights of the Subject   224
The Need for a Positive Approach   225
Summary   226

11. The Specificity of Behaviors and of Measurements   228

Specificity in Behaviors   229
  Complexity of stimuli   229
  Multiplicity of determinants   230
The Specificity of Instruments and Their Scores   232
  Specificity in Guilford's measures of intelligence   233
  Specificity in other tests of intelligence   236
  Specificity in measures of personality   237
  Specificity in personality tests within a single mode   238
  Specificity in personality tests from different modes   240
Other Views on Test Specificity   246
Implications of Test Specificity for Construct Validation   247
Summary   248

12. Measuring a Personality Construct Today   250

Criteria for Measurements of Individual Differences   250
  Meeting the criteria   252
  Fully adequate measurements   253
Feasible Programs of Personological Research   255
Methodologies   257
  Empirical approaches   257
  Psychometric techniques   260
The Measurement of a Construct   261
  Constructs, perspectives, and modes   261
Steps in Developing and Evaluating a Measuring Procedure   264
    1. Content validity   265
    2. Process validity   265
    3. Interjudge agreement   266
    4. Homogeneity   266
    5. Stability   267
    6. Convergence over measuring conditions   267
    7. Convergence over format   268
    8. Convergence within mode   268
    9. Convergence between modes   268
   10. Discriminant validation with constructs from the same
       substantive area   269

11. Discriminant validation with constructs of other kinds 269
12. Construct validation 270
Summary 272

13. Prospects and Issues 274

"What's Past Is Prologue" 274
Prospects 275
Indirect measures 278
Collaborative measurement 278
The experiencing and behaving subject 279
Issues 281
The target constructs for personality measurement 281
Personality constructs in cultural settings 284
Multiple determination and resultant specificity of scores 284
Is trait a false concept? 286
A more modest strategy 287
Is the single-variable approach viable? 288
Some Possible Strategies 290
Summary 292
Glossary 294
References 300
Index 314

Foreword

It is ironic that the personality which every one of us subjectively experiences as a solid reality reasonably open to scrutiny should prove so elusive to the research psychologist. It is even more ironic that a very large number of trained psychologists are completely unimpressed by the demonstrated difficulty of confirming propositions advanced by personality theorists or of reliably and validly assessing personality characteristics.

From one standpoint, such obduracy is understandable: if it were impossible to predict with some confidence how significant others will behave, our lives would be unbearably insecure. Since, in fact, the behavior of most individuals seem to be reasonably consistent, we are inclined to credit ourselves with a degree of understanding of their internal processes and overt behavior that is unwarranted. In other words, we *need* to believe that we can comprehend human behavior and, therefore, we *do* believe we can— empirical evidence to the contrary.

A more obvious basis for resistance exists for those psychologists whose professional prestige and livelihood depend on their putative ability to assess the personality of clients and predict their future behavior. It is always difficult to acknowledge, particularly to oneself, that a valued technical activity lacks adequate scientific support.

From another viewpoint, however, the resistance of many professional psychologists to accepting the somewhat discouraging findings of personality researchers is not comprehensible. Training in the methods of science is supposed to discipline the student to accept the outcome of properly conducted research whether the results please him or not. Moreover, the well-disciplined scientist does not permit himself the luxury of rationalizing away results which are contrary to his theoretical projections. This seems not to have occurred among many of those applied psychologists in whose work the concept of personality is important.

Perhaps many psychologists and laymen alike believe observations on personality functioning are too close to everyone's heart—and therefore too important—to be constrained by scientific protocol. Other psychologists sincerely believe that research methods must be far more sophisticated than they now are to capture the complexity they perceive in clients who consult them. Consequently these psychologists are well pleased with their elaborate speculations about personality functioning as working tools— even though it is more intuitive "feel" than confirmed fact on which they rest. Since social and behavioral scientists who attempt to apply their knowledge to the solution of practical problems must fly most of the time by the seat of their pants, freehand theorizing is not to be condemned. At the same time, if unconfirmed theory is confidently presented as fact, such misrepresentation can be highly detrimental to scientific progress.

This book, because of its meticulous statements on the current theories, methods and findings in the area of personality measurement will, no doubt, be most enthusiastically welcomed by those psychologists who are already persuaded of both the utility and difficulty of pursuing personology as a science. One hopes, however, that it will also attract the attention of those who are uneasy at the thought of having to live their entire professional lives in a "context of discovery" and, hence, seek informed advice on how to proceed to confirm or disconfirm their theoretical viewpoints.

One even dares to hope that some psychologists who have spurned much of the contemporary personality research will find in the book much to reassure them regarding methodological advances which do permit access to complex processes (albeit at considerable cost in effort).

Indeed, this is a book which one can recommend even to psychologists whose primary interest is not in personality theory or research. Most psychologists are concerned from time to time with measuring some facet of behavior as a dependent variable in research but many are perhaps rather more casual about it than they should be. While the author has quite deliberately not included technical directions for test construction (which he believes are available in other readily accessible texts), he does provide the theoretical rationale for adapting measurement procedures to the various problems research psychologists face.

Finally, in introducing this volume in the Concepts of Personality series I would like to echo a wish of the author that a much larger area of collaboration be established between measurement specialists and personality theorists. Experts in measurement have tended to view critically the ambiguity of concepts advanced by theorists and the theorists have tended to view with skepticism the capacity of the research psychologists to appreciate and cope with the deeply penetrating understanding they ascribe to their speculations. Thus, these two kinds of contributions essential to advancement in the scientific study of personality are only infrequently available at the same time in the same place. The author clearly favors an ecumenical movement to which the editor heartily subscribes.

RALPH W. HEINE

Preface

Some people have devoted their lives to understanding people and personalities. Writers portray characters with individual personalities and yet with universal traits and problems. Clinicians seek to know the personalities of those who come to them in trouble. Some scientists have identified personality as the focus of their theorizing and experimentation, and it is for these investigators that this book is intended. Its purpose is to contribute to the scientific study of personality.

The book is grounded on my basic conviction that scientific understanding requires measurement in order both to delineate the phenomena and observations in an objective, systematic fashion and to test our theories. As Lord Kelvin phrased it: "When you can measure what you are speaking about, and express it in numbers, you know something about it; but when you cannot measure it, when you cannot express it in numbers, your knowledge is of a meager and unsatisfactory kind: it may be the beginning of knowledge, but you have scarcely, in your thoughts, advanced to the stage of science, whatever the matter may be." (See Kaplan, 1964, p. 172.) Many others have also argued that science progresses with refinement of its mensuration, with improvement in its instrumentation and methodology. The critical issue, however, is not the adequacy of the measuring operations as evaluated internally, but rather the adequacy with which they provide an index for an explicit construct, broadly or narrowly conceived. Conversely, each construct (concept or theoretical term) must have its representation in measuring procedures that can be specified and publicly observed. At this time, the ideas, concepts, and variables of personality theories cannot be well coordinated with measurement operations. This book is concerned with tactics and strategies for improving these relationships between ideas and observations.

The general plan of this volume is to consider exactly what we want to measure, to examine the nature of measurement with particular reference to measuring personality, and to explore the actual process of measuring. We shall be constantly asking: What is the present state of affairs, in what respects is it unsatisfactory, and what can we do about it?

The book was written for two groups of people. It is intended to present the status quo to those who want a picture of personality measurement today. Such people may have some general interest in the field or may be interested in it because they intend to work in such related areas as clinical practice. The second audience includes students of personality (apprentices or journeymen) who are concerned with evaluating the measurement of personality in current research studies and especially people who are conducting such research or are preparing themselves for such work.

The text should be understandable to the serious upper-class undergraduate and to the graduate student in his early training. Fortunately, it does not have to build on a great deal of technical sophistication. It assumes that the reader has some knowledge of general psychology and has had at least one course on personality theory so that he is familiar with representative components of personality theories, such as traits, motives, dynamics, and other constructs. A rudimentary knowledge of basic descriptive statistics must be assumed: the reader must know about means, standard deviations, and variances; he must also have sufficient familiarity with the basic measures of association, for example, the Pearson product-moment correlation coefficient, sufficient acquaintance to have some intuitive feeling for the meaning of an r of .32 or .78, and some awareness of the several kinds of specific interpretations of such values. Although a course in test theory or tests and measurements would be of considerable value to the reader, it is not necessary, since the basic concepts of test theory required for the exposition will be presented in the text.

This book is intended to be a textbook in the old tradition: it is not primarily a pedagogically oriented presentation of what is known about personality measurement, but rather is a treatise on the topic from an individual viewpoint. It seeks not only to inform but also to persuade, even to convince.

This brief volume cannot have the comprehensiveness of a handbook. Much material must be expounded tightly or omitted. While studying it, the reader may wish to read other sources to make sure he understands the fundamental technical topics or to pursue subject matter that could not be included here. On measurement, he may consult the introductory essay by Hays (1967) on *Quantification in Psychology* or the recent textbook *Psychometric Theory* by Nunnally (1967). For a broader perspective, the section on measurement (Chapters 20–24) in *The Conduct of Inquiry* (Kaplan, 1964) is highly recommended. Pertinent descriptive statistics, including *r*, are expertly presented in *Psychological Statistics* (McNemar, 1962).

A concise introduction to the *Assessment of Human Characteristics* has been prepared by E. L. Kelly (1967). Two volumes with a viewpoint congenial to my own have been published by Vernon; *Personality Assessment: A Critical Survey* (1964) and *Personality Tests and Assessments* (1933). While one might think the latter must be quite out of date, the pertinence of its critical evaluations to the present scene is an indictment against the field. More contemporary and more oriented toward operationalizing theoretical concepts is Wiggins' *Personality and Prediction: Principles of Personality Assessment* (in preparation). It is also recommended for its treatment of important technical problems that could not be included in this volume. A critical survey of the current state of affairs in personality measurement, from a different viewpoint and to some degree complementing this book, can be found in the first part of Mischel's *Personality and Assessment* (1968).

This book differs in several ways from these and other volumes in the general area of personality measurement. Many texts limit their scope to the exposition of psychometric or basic test theory and to the examination of standard measuring instruments now available, topics that are only touched on here. In contrast, this volume takes a more comprehensive view of measurement, of the measurer and his intentions, and of the person being measured as he interacts with the measuring procedure. It stresses the necessity for intensive analysis of each concept being measured and the need for thorough examination of the rational and empirical links between such a concept and the measuring operations directed toward it. A related emphasis is on the nature of personality phenomena in general, and more particularly on the subject's experience and behavior while being measured. It presents my approach to measuring an attribute of personality for purposes of basic research, but does not attempt to be a cookbook or manual of detailed instructions.

Little attention is paid here to the many applications of personality measurement: personnel selection, counseling and guidance, clinical diagnosis, etc. These and other topics involving the prediction of later performance or adjustment have been the concerns of many other authors. One objective of this book is to complement their work by focusing on issues and problems they do not emphasize sufficiently.

By contributing to the advance of personality measurement, this book seeks to further the progress of personology, the science of personality. It assumes that the field is past the stage of naturalistic observation, although admittedly we have not reached agreement on any taxonomic classification of the phenomena being studied. It expresses the conviction that we must be concerned now with concepts, variables, and dimensions applicable to all people, rather than with the personality of the individual person. The case study of the individual has contributed much to our knowledge of personality, and it is an important method (see Bolgar, 1965) which will continue to be needed for insights into the ways in which the various aspects of personality may fit together and influence each other. Although such work on personality structure is necessary for efforts to help individuals in the clinic, the delineation and measurement of common personality attributes is a more pressing requirement for progress in personology.

The chapters of this book consider a variety of topics. While I have sought to build each chapter on the preceding ones, the reader may find that some chapters plunge into topics that are quite unfamiliar to him. When this happens, the reader may prefer to read the summary at the end of the chapter first, to gain an overall view of its contents, before reading its pages consecutively. (A cursory overview of the whole book appears in the introductions to Parts One and Two.) To assist the reader, a glossary is provided at the end of the volume, with both technical terms and words given particular meanings in the context of this account.

I owe much to many people. My scientific personality was influenced by Robert W. White, John J. Jenkins, E. Lowell Kelly, Clyde H. Coombs, and other early mentors. My current thinking has been aided by interactions with John M. Butler, Raymond B. Cattell, Lee J. Cronbach, W. Grant Dahlstrom, Lewis R. Goldberg, and many others. The approach developed here was built on preliminary formulations that were often generated in and always refined through stimulating discussions with a number of students and associates: Pamela Pearson, Thomas Tyler, Mrs. Ruth Boutin Kuncel, Castellano Turner, Dorcas Susan Butt, and others have contributed more than they probably realize. In particular, a number of the concepts in this book emerged from collaborative thinking with Miss Pearson and Mrs. Kuncel's tactful criticisms and incisive comments were of great value to me in my struggle toward clarity and consistency. Additionally, all these fellow workers and a number of others carried out empirical studies and analyses that have kept this book in contact with the realities of data.

I am also indebted to Fred Damarin and Eric Klinger for their critical suggestions on much of the content, to Ralph Heine for his encouragement and helpful reactions, and to Barabara Fiske for her thorough editorial critique. Mrs. Dorothy Ford typed and retyped the manuscript with great care and skill. Her valuable assistance is much appreciated.

Grateful acknowledgment is also made to the National Institute of Mental Health and to the National Science Foundation, whose research grants (MH 06582, GS 1060 and GS 1998) supported the empirical and conceptual examination of the perplexing problems in personality measurement, work on which the substance of the following chapters is based.

What Do We Measure?

Introduction

After sketching the sources of personality concepts and measuring operations, the first part of this book indicates the orientation toward measurement in basic research and introduces the chief themes and theses running through the later content. Then personality is defined as the way a person interacts with the world outside him and the world within him. These interactions are described as processes with distinct phases, processes that can be observed from several perspectives. In each perspective, an observer views and interprets some of these phenomena in a distinctive way. Systematic observations or measurements fall into several classes, depending on characteristics such as who provides the data and who produces the score.

The phenomena of personality are a wealth of complex material varying according to where the person is, how he feels, and what is stimulating him. The student of personality looks for regularities in the behavior observed under restricted conditions—a given situation with particular stimuli. The resulting systematic observations are guided by concepts of traits and other variables. Each concept refers to some one phase in the processes occurring in people. The concept must be spelled out so that we know what we want to measure and have some guidance in developing ways of measuring it. Each class of observations provides one general way to measure the concept, these several ways being more or less distinct from each other. Even within such a class, measurements of a concept may differ with the particular format of the measuring procedure used. The objective is to measure each subject in the same manner so that the measurements of the several subjects can be compared. Any one set of measurements should be getting at a relatively pure dimension of personality.

3

CHAPTER ONE

The Roots of
Personality Measurement

In the biblical story of Gideon, warriors were selected for a special mission by two screenings. The first considered their motivation; those who did not wish to participate were allowed to withdraw. The second involved observations of the way they drank from a body of water; those who put their heads down to the water were eliminated and those who brought water up to their mouths in their hands were chosen. The presumed rationale was that the latter were more alert and watchful.

Over the centuries, men have often been selected for special roles on the basis of their performance during rigorous training. This method was used to identify the elite Spartans and, centuries later, to determine those qualified for knighthood. On the other side of the world, there were formal procedures for examining candidates for office at least by the beginning of the Chan dynasty in China, three thousand years ago (DuBois, 1970). The tests were job samples, demonstrating the candidates' proficiencies. Even today there is no better way of selecting promising applicants than the properly devised and administered work sample. Today, however, the careful personnel psychologist makes an empirical study to establish the validity of all selection procedures he recommends, both predictive tests and work samples.

Thus applied psychology began much earlier than psychology as a basic science, which came into being only during the last century. The measurement of concepts of personality for purposes of pure research is even younger, beginning only a few decades ago.

4

Development of Procedures

The history of modern personality measurement dates from about World War I, when procedures were devised to obtain observations under somewhat standardized conditions or to collect data economically. Hermann Rorschach (1942) published his *Psychodiagnostik* in 1921, a year before his untimely death. In this volume, subtitled "A Diagnostic Test Based on Perception," he reports his observations on the responses to his famous inkblots as given by the 405 subjects he tested, and he tabulates the frequencies of some scores for each of several diagnostic categories. This is one of the earliest landmarks in clinical psychological testing as we know it today. While literally thousands of papers have been published about his test, vastly extending the available data on it, it is noteworthy that a large part of what Rorschach wrote is still accepted by clinicians today.

The other early landmark is the development of the Woodworth Personal Data Sheet, first published in 1919. (Woodworth is better known for the integrative texts on experimental psychology which he wrote in later years.) Designed to take the place of an interview, this inventory asked questions to determine whether the subject was poorly fitted for military service because he possessed certain undesirable characteristics or symptoms. Also developed for use during World War I were rating methods and some group tests of intelligence. In this national emergency, as in World War II, considerable technological development occurred within psychology. During the subsequent decades, several approaches contributed innovations and advances to the measurement of personality.

THE CLINICAL APPROACH

Although many new scoring categories and composite scores have been devised since Rorschach's book, inkblot testing remained essentially in its original form until Wayne Holtzman and his colleagues (1961) devised a new procedure with two series of forty-five blots each. The aim was to provide more systematic and comparable protocols. The subject gives just one response to each blot, so that differences in number of responses are no longer a problem. A comprehensive scoring manual enables scorers to obtain high levels of agreement with each other. The scoring categories are construed in dimensional form. Thus the Holtzman Inkblot Technique is a better psychometric instrument for basic research than the less structured and more judgmentally interpreted test on which it is based.

Another commonly used projective test is the Thematic Apperception Test (TAT), devised by Morgan and Murray (1935). In this test, the subject makes up stories based on a number of drawings. These stories can be interpreted or scored in innumerable ways, from identifying qualitative themes specific for the particular subject to rating the strengths of the subject's dispositions, as in Murray's "needs." Like the Rorschach, the TAT is in common clinical use; perhaps more than the Rorschach, it is also employed for empirical studies of normal persons.

The interview is the most widely used method for assessing personality. It is used in the clinic and in personnel selection for applied purposes; personology and social psychology also use it in basic research. Its popularity stems from its naturalness, simplicity, and flexibility. While it seems intuitively valid, many psychologists consider this face validity to be illusory, since much research has found no predictive validity for it. Although many guides for interviewers have been prepared, there is no standard form. Perhaps the most structured and objective type of interview is that developed for surveys of opinions. (In this context, "objective" means that the protocols themselves and the data derived from them are relatively free from influences associated with the particular interviewer.) Such interviews were used in a survey of views of testing, to be discussed later (Chapter 10). Standardized interviews have also been developed for epidemiological studies of mental disorders.

THE INVENTORY APPROACH

Following the example of the Personal Data Sheet, many inventories were published during the 1920s and 1930s, and the proliferation still continues. The early ones were often intended to measure maladjustment or neurotic tendencies, but tests were gradually developed for other attributes: dominance, Jung's introversion, etc.

The most widely used inventory today is probably the Minnesota Multiphasic Personality Inventory (MMPI). It is used not only in clinical psychology but also in personnel selection and in research investigations. In its original form in 1943, it consisted of a series of cards on each of which was printed a statement, which the subject sorted into two piles, one for true and one for false, as he considered they applied to him. A booklet form came into vogue a few years later. The original clinical keys and many later ones were developed empirically, by identifying responses given more frequently by a particular clinical group than by normal people. Thus a key for Hypochondriasis was developed from the responses of patients diagnosed as relatively pure cases of this tendency, uncomplicated by other pathologies; keys for Hysteria, Depression, Paranoia, etc., were constructed in the same way.

Values and interests are also measured frequently by paper-and-pencil instruments. One of the first was the Allport-Vernon Study of Values, which yields scores for Theoretical, Economic, Aesthetic, Social, Political, and Religious values, a classification first proposed by Spranger. This test was created *a priori* and later subjected to psychometric analysis and refinement.

Another well-known interest test was developed empirically, like the MMPI. Dating back to 1927, the Strong Vocational Interest Blank consists of several hundred items (recreational and work activities, school subjects, etc.) for which the subject indicates his liking or dislike. His responses are then compared with keys for a number of vocations, each key developed by comparing the responses of those who have been in that occupation for a number of years to responses by people in general. The rationale is obvious: if a subject's interests resemble those of people who have entered and remained in a vocation, it is more likely that he will enjoy that vocation. The rationale has been supported empirically.

Many dozens of inventories for traits or interests have been devised. Texts on tests and measurements usually describe in some detail a number of these. For comprehensive listings, data on publishers and prices, and critical reviews, see the *Mental Measurements Yearbooks,* published every few years by Oscar Buros (1965). His *Tests in Print* (1961) is another valuable reference. (Examples of items from various kinds of tests are given in Figure 5.2.)

SYSTEMATIC OBSERVATIONS

Another approach tries to capitalize on more naturalistic situations and realistic tasks. A favorite research method of developmental psychologists is observation of nursery-school children on the playground. Systematic techniques for standardized recording and rating yield scores for many characteristics. Less naturalistic but still compelling contexts have also been devised for measuring personality, often without the subject knowing that he is being measured, or at least without his knowing what attribute is being measured. During the late 1920s, Hartshorne, May, and Shuttleworth (1930) studied character in children. For example, they contrived procedures in which children would be tempted to cheat and would believe that such cheating would not be observed. (They report rather low relationships between the scores for the various procedures, a typical kind of finding that will be analyzed intensively in Chapter 11.)

World War II saw the introduction of new approaches to observation, this time in the service of selection for special purposes. These involved fairly realistic work samples (as in speed in completing an obstacle course), the use of informal observations as well as structured testing, and final judgments reached by first having each judge pool his ratings for various procedures into a composite rating and then having several such judges discuss and decide on a group judgment.

The earliest applications of these approaches were made in Germany in the years just before World War II. While not much is known about this work or its adequacy, it seems to have involved observations of performance on standard military tasks as well as effectiveness under stress.

Rather similar intensive testing procedures were developed in England for the War Office Selection Boards and for Civil Service Selection Boards after the war.

Shortly after the United States entered the war, the Office of Strategic Services set up "assessment schools" under the direction of Murray and MacKinnon to screen candidates for such special work as espionage, sabotage, and propaganda. This work was reported in *Assessment of Men* (OSS Assessment Staff, 1948). The candidates were tested for ability to maintain security (e.g., by not giving away their true identity), practical intelligence (as in solving an engineering problem with crude materials), verbal intelligence (as shown in discussion problems), leadership (in leaderless groups and when assigned the role of leader), functioning under stress (such as cross-examination), and ability to get along with others. In addition to taking the situational tests mentioned above, the subjects were interviewed, given projective tests, intelligence tests, and tests for special abilities, and required to fill out a long life-history form. Other procedures included observations at meals and when socializing with liquor, and sociometric reports of the impressions they made on fellow candidates.

Practical necessity made it impossible to obtain adequate data to test the validity of the judgments made by the OSS Assessment Staff. To determine the validity of such an assessment approach and to try to develop procedures for selecting potential clinical psychologists, a research program was instituted after the war at the University of Michigan (Kelly and Fiske, 1951). The design allowed the determination of the incremental contribution of various procedures; e.g., how much did an interview add to information available from various basic application materials? The procedures included more standard paper-and-pencil tests and fewer situational tests than the OSS program.

This research encountered considerable difficulty in its subsequent efforts to assess clinical performance. The measurement of professional competence is always a hard problem. Given the assumption that the various criterion measures were adequate, this study demonstrated that paper-and-pencil measures could predict clinical competences about as well as more expensive and judgmental procedures, such as projective tests, interviews, and situational tests. But none of the predictive coefficients were very high. Furthermore, the ratings of surface traits made during assessment had only modest correlations with subsequent ratings of the same traits. As we shall see later, these findings are fairly consistent with those from many other investigations. Personality measurements tend to be rather specific, varying with the conditions under which they are obtained, with the particular task given the subject, and also with the content of the items or stimuli to which the subject reacts.

At about the same time, a group at the Menninger Foundation started research on the selection of psychiatrists (Holt and Luborsky, 1958). This investigation was restricted essentially to clinical methods: interviews, projective tests, an intelligence test, and several tests devised for the particular purpose.

Stemming more directly from the OSS assessment work, the Institute for Personality Assessment and Research was set up in Berkeley under the direction of MacKinnon. This institute has been more interested in theory than were early assessment programs. It has studied adequacy of functioning in various vocational fields, with particular attention to the optimal functioning found in creative persons (MacKinnon, 1965; Barron, 1968). The emphasis has been increasingly placed not on scores from particular procedures, but on human judgments based on diverse observations, judgments made by the assessors, by the subjects about themselves, even by the subjects' parents.

OTHER APPROACHES

Clinical psychologists have always used observations of the way a subject goes about a task as one basis for judgments about his personality. In taking an intelligence test, for example, does the subject show caution by making few errors, especially careless ones? More recently, psychologists have studied cognitive styles—the way a person categorizes his perceptions, his ability to perceive something independent of its field or context, his ability to ignore distraction, etc. A quite different orientation is the study of the person's social stimulus value, of how he is perceived by others. Is he socially visible, is he liked, is he rejected, is he seen as a good leader? Finally, personality variables have been approached by measuring psychophysiological reactions. Everyone has heard of lie-detector tests, which assume that a subject will react differently when suppressing the truth than when telling it. Similar techniques are employed to study reactions to stress. Quite recently, careful experimentation has been done on the size of the pupil: with the intensity of illumination held constant, the pupil enlarges with positive interest in a stimulus and may contract with some negative reactions (Hess, 1968). (For a longer history of personality and other psychological testing, see DuBois, 1970.)

PROGRESS OR PRODUCTIVITY?

Does the history of the development of personality measurement show much progress? Many psychologists would say that such progress has been quite limited. What it does show is the creation of many new approaches, the refinement of old methods, and the invention of many varieties of specific instruments. There is little convincing and definitive evidence that

we are now measuring the concepts of personality appreciably better than
we were two or three decades ago, in part because of the many obstacles
to determining the adequacy with which any one construct is indexed by
one or more procedures. There certainly have been major technical advances in methods for analyzing quantitative measurements. The problems
in personality measurement are being more sharply delineated, but we do
not have the consensus required for scientific progress toward solutions.

If we dip into the journals published several decades ago, we can see
some evidence of progress. Earlier articles are often more literary and less
technical than recent ones. While they may be more readable, their use of
everyday language makes their message less precise. Of course, in earlier
years, there were fewer theories and technical concepts available.

The reports of research rarely tested propositions derived from theories.
The few theories existing at that time (such as Freud's and Jung's) were
not well systematized and did not present explicit definitions of terms, definitions that might have provided some guide for their objective measurement. (Current theories of personality are only somewhat better in these
respects.) The typical research study at that time was frankly and appropriately exploratory. The modern reader is also struck by the fact that none of
the specific instruments used in those studies is in common use today. In
part, many earlier procedures have been discarded because they were aimed
at concepts that we recognize today as being too broad and comprehensive
and usually too loose to be of much value in characterizing an individual;
e.g., introversion.

We can also see that the earlier literature was of value in its demonstration that certain approaches held little or no promise. There was enough
work on the study of handwriting, for example, to justify the current view
that graphology is not an effective approach to measuring personality. We
must, of course, be careful about reaching definitive conclusions from experiments conducted forty or fifty years ago, because the methodology of
experimentation, as well as the measuring procedures, was much less sophisticated at that time.

Theory and Measurement

What may be needed today is not the invention of instrumentation that
would be for psychology what the microscope was for the natural sciences,
but rather the insight of a Mendeleev, leading to an integrative periodic
table for components of personality. Measurement has developed technically
without sufficient interaction with conceptualization. While measurement in
basic research is used in the service of theory, theory has not provided
adequate guidance for measurement and theorists may not have recognized
the mutual interdependence between theory and systematic observation.

Everyone wants to understand other people and also to understand himself. Everyone has some of this understanding— he must have, if he is to interact with people in his daily life. Many theorists have tried to give us more of this understanding. They have often concentrated on the study of malfunctioning, as in psychopathology, where the phenomena are striking and extreme. This emphasis has also stemmed from the obvious facts that many people badly need all the help that can be given to them, and almost everyone could use some assistance toward reducing the frequency and extent of his discomforts and psychological tensions.

While many of the theoretical insights during the last eight decades seem to further our understanding, many people still lead unhappy lives and many find themselves in vocations or jobs that they do not like. Technical developments in personality measurement have also made some contributions to understanding and to applied problems. At one time, it looked as though the invention of assessment programs might be a major breakthrough: such programs might combine the best from unstructured and structured procedures of all kinds, integrating the information from all available sources. But hopes were disappointed. Perhaps human judgment was too limited for the task. Perhaps even experts cannot fit together the many pieces of the jigsaw puzzle of each personality. Perhaps the subject could not be completely natural under the strange and stressful conditions of being evaluated. Today we can gain much information about what makes a person unhappy and why he acts in unusual ways, in order to help him cope with his problems. We can also determine with modest success whether a person can perform a particular job. Yet many major questions are still unanswered. We have only the barest rudiments of a science of personality from which to derive any applied science or engineering. To advance that science, we must learn how to make systematic observations from which we can obtain dependable empirical generalizations. Such generalized findings can be used to test and refine existing theory and to form new inductive inferences, both uses contributing to conceptual progress.

TARGET CONCEPTS

In basic research, the targets of personality measurement are obviously the concepts of personality. These concepts have come from several sources. (See Hall and Lindzey, 1970.) A major source is the clinic. The problem of trying to understand and help people with psychological difficulties has been the origin of most dynamic concepts. Many psychoanalytic concepts were created from Freud's experience with psychopathology, and some of them have been the targets of measuring procedures. There are many scales for anxiety; there are Byrne's Repression-Sensitization Scale (1964) and Barron's Ego-Strength Scale; several measures of guilt have been devised by Mosher (1966). Jung's concepts of introversion and extraversion have been approached by various scales, although these concepts and measures are not in common use today. From his studies of brain-injured soldiers, Goldstein developed the concepts of abstract and concrete behavior, associating the latter with brain injury. He and his colleagues then developed several clinical tests for assessing these ways of functioning—for example, tasks requiring the sorting or classifying of familiar objects (Goldstein and Scheerer, 1941). Carl Rogers built his theory upon his psychotherapeutic work. Specific tests have been developed for very few of his concepts (but see Pearson, 1969). In addition to these instruments, many rating procedures have been devised and used to obtain judgments about behaviors or attributes related to clinical concepts.

Curiously, little in the way of comprehensive personality theory or general concepts has emerged from other kinds of applied psychology, such as vocational guidance or industrial work on personnel selection, although there are numerous scales for assessing interests and preferences, and for obtaining reports of job satisfaction. Perhaps the clinician has the advantage of being able to observe the experiences and behaviors of people in more extreme, more clear-cut, and possibly simpler form.

Gordon Allport (1942) investigated life histories as presented in autobiographies and examined personal documents, such as extended correspondence (1965). His individualized approach led to views about personality structure and organization rather than to the identification of common dimensions (1937, 1961). Four decades ago, however, he did participate in the development of the Allport-Vernon-Lindzey Study of Values, a device for assessing the relative strength of Theoretical, Aesthetic, Economic, and other values, based on Spranger's typology. In *Explorations in Personality,* Henry Murray and his colleagues (1938) utilized a variety of techniques for research on normal subjects, the integration being provided by his comprehensive taxonomic system of needs and other dispositions. Their questionnaire for self-report of these needs has been the basis for such standardized inventories as the Edwards Personal Preference Schedule and the Jackson Personality Research Form. In addition, Murray's "need for Achievement" has been the target of several instruments and the focus of considerable research.

A third source of concepts has been other parts of psychology. Hull's conceptualization of learning has been extended to personality by Dollard and Miller. Mowrer, Sears, Rotter, and many others have developed their thinking about personality with assistance from the massive literature on learning. Few standard procedures for assessing individual differences in personality have emerged from this work; one exception is Rotter's scale for determining general expectancies for internal as opposed to external control of reinforcements (1966). Kurt Lewin's field theory stemmed from his early training in the *Gestalt* approach, which was originally concerned with perception and cognition. Skinner's behavior theory, with its emphasis on reinforcement, is currently being extended to provide the orientation for behavior therapy.

THEORY AND DATA MUST INTERACT

In contrast to the theoretical work coming from these sources, little conceptualization has been based on systematic experimental data in the personality domain. Unlike other, more advanced sciences, the science of personality has not involved sufficient interaction between concepts and empirical findings. As opposed to the considerable body of investigations that are intended to be exploratory, which are searching for facts, there is a relatively small proportion of studies attempting to check on the accuracy of theoretical formulations. In part, this unfortunate state of affairs stems from the looseness of such theorizing; in part, it is a consequence of the large gap between the general abstractions in personality theory and the concrete observations in the research. Whatever the reasons, it is difficult to derive testable propositions from most theoretical discussions of personality.

On the other side, theorists pay little attention to empirical findings, except those appearing to support their positions. Yet they can hardly be criticized until a substantial body of replicated empirical findings has been developed. There are few well-established experimental facts in the amorphous literature reporting research using diverse procedures, procedures that all too often are modified in some potentially significant fashion from one study to the next. It would also be very difficult to identify instances in which a theory had been changed or a concept modified in the light of any empirical work.

One apparent exception to the assertion that concepts have not been derived from empirical data might appear to be the work using factor analysis. This statistical technique analyzes the correlations among a group of variables with the objective of identifying a smaller number of variables that will account for the observed relationships. Thurstone's Primary Mental Abilities and other classifications stemmed from factor analyses of various kinds of intelligence tests. Yet the major breakthrough made by Guilford (1967) in his model for the Structure-of-Intellect came not from identifying factors recurring in several studies, but from conceptually analyzing the kinds of tasks utilized to measure ability, from seeing that each involved a kind of content on which the subject performed a type of operation to obtain a specified category of product. Guilford is now engaged in testing his model by finding instruments that measure each of the many combinations of these three parameters (see Chapter 11).

Factor analyses of personality tests have yielded a multitude of factors. While some recurring factors seem reasonably well established, there has been little theoretical work based on them (for one exception, see Cattell and Scheier, 1961). These empirically based variables have not been fully capitalized upon and developed, even by the empirical researchers themselves, perhaps because those who like to make such quantitative analyses have little interest in substantive concepts. The neglect of these variables by theorists may also have a temperamental basis: many of those who work on personality at a conceptual level do not understand or trust quantitative analyses and prefer to rely on data from personal observation.

This inspection of the roots of personality measurement suggests some of the areas we shall explore later. Personality measurement has at its disposal many techniques from psychometric analysis and statistics, and much methodological sophistication. Hundreds of personality tests have been developed, a large number of them yielding dependable scores. But no important concept is measured completely by any one test or procedure, no test is congruent or fully coordinated with its target construct. Much remains to be done on the conceptual and operational levels, and especially on the interdependence of the two.

Implicit in the preceding discussion is a basic strategy advocated and developed in the following chapters. To advance the science of personology, intensive effort must be devoted to each major construct, to delineating it explicitly and systematically, and to creating measuring procedures conforming to the blueprints derived from such a conceptualization. Once we have created, tested, and refined these measuring procedures, we can begin to carry out empirical studies of the theoretical propositions involving that construct. At that later time, we can also initiate investigations of the interactions between that construct and other constructs. While it may seem conceptually naïve, given the apparent complexity of personality phenomena and the intricate ways in which constructs interact, to adopt the strategy of attacking each construct by itself, it seems methodologically fruitless to set forth into the morass of interacting concepts with observational tools of unknown efficacy and appropriateness.

Summary

Systematic efforts to measure personality variables began four or five decades ago. Clinical methods such as the Rorschach Inkblot Test developed simultaneously with inventories asking the subjects to answer questions about themselves. Intensive and multiple observations of subjects performing varied tasks were introduced in the 1930s. Comprehensive assessment, in which such observations were integrated with data from other sources, appeared to hold considerable promise, but simple and economical methods have been shown to have as much utility. These approaches by no means exhaust the diversity of methods that have been employed to study personality.

In spite of the range of techniques that have been created, the measurement of single constructs remains in an unsatisfactory state. Conceptualization and empirical research have been too remote from each other to interact for their mutual gain.

CHAPTER TWO

Orientations and Themes

Setting the Stage

PERSONALITY

Like most common and general terms, *personality* has many meanings. It can refer to an aesthetic object: a character in a novel or a salient figure in history. When applied to someone we know, it may be that which makes interactions with the other person a source of gratification or frustration; or it may refer to those features of the other person that make it possible for him to be of instrumental value to us in pursuing our long-range goals. Especially in a period some years back, it was used as a label for a global trait referring to a person's attractiveness or stimulus value. In applied work with people, it may identify the locus for those characteristics of a person that cause distress to himself and others. Personnel workers use it to refer to nonintellective attributes that play roles in job selection, classification, and performance.

More privately and personally, each of us thinks of his personality as "that which I am," "that which makes me a distinct and unique individual." This emphasis on individuality is a key feature of the personality domain. Ultimately, we would like to be able to explain and understand this individuality. For the present, however, our goal must be the more modest one of comparing individuals with respect to one attribute or a limited number of attributes. Like all scientific activity, the scientific study of personality must abstract from the fascinating complexity of personality one attribute after another, and subject each aspect to intensive study.

16

Tho torm *personality* can also be used to refer to general human tendencies, such as the disposition to defend oneself when verbally attacked and the disposition to suppress or repress unpleasant experiences. People are rather similar in many ways. These common patterns of reaction are increasingly being studied in experiments. Yet even these common attributes are much stronger in some people than in others, and part of understanding these dispositions is understanding the differences in their strength.

In most sciences, the objects studied are examined as members of a class: the physicist may observe a small sample from the infinite class of one elementary particle; the physiologist may study neural activity in a class of cells; the astronomer may focus on stars of a certain type. Typically, such scientists make an observation of the single member of the class solely to pool that observation with many others to obtain a dependable average value. They know that the several observations will differ from one another, but correctly anticipate that, with careful procedural techniques, the differences will be small, both in absolute terms and relative to the effect being studied. When these scientists are looking for covariation, for relationships between attributes, they once again are likely to observe several instances of Y at each value of X: they plot a trend of means rather than a trend of values for individual objects.

In contrast, much of personality work is concerned with measuring well the attribute as it occurs in the individual subject. A person coming to a mental hygiene clinic may be assessed for capacity to profit from a potential treatment. A job applicant's skill must be measured and compared to the level required for the job. The attributes of individuals must also be assessed in basic research: to determine whether the conservatism of sons is related to the conservatism of fathers, that attribute must be assessed dependably in each member of the pair. We know that fathers vary on conservatism, and sons also; we study the covariation of the attribute over the pairs, taking for granted the fact that the correspondence between father and son will also vary from pair to pair. These examples indicate that the science of personality depends on reliable measurement of the individual person, apart from his class membership, whereas most science seeks to measure the mean for a class of objects. This point (originally called to my attention by Ralph Heine, the editor of this series) underlies many of the special difficulties encountered in personality measurement.

BASIC RESEARCH AND OTHER SETTINGS FOR MEASUREMENT

This volume concentrates on personality measurement for the purposes of basic research, i.e., on measuring in connection with experimental testing of theoretical propositions or with other investigations intended by the researcher to contribute to the understanding of personality. The objective is to determine how such measurement can be improved so as to further the development of personology, the science of personality. This restriction has been imposed partly to limit the area to be covered by this small volume. More fundamentally, however, many underlying problems are common to both basic and applied work, although no attempt will be made here to point out the relevance to the latter.

Applied measurement often has the advantage of a more tangible criterion: frequently the objective is to determine whether the person falls in the class of those likely to succeed in a training program or on a job, or of those likely to benefit from a type of treatment. (For a creative technical treatise on such formal problems, see Cronbach and Gleser, *Psychological Tests and Personnel Decisions* [Second Edition, 1965].) To be sure, the problem of measuring the criterion is rarely a simple one. Even when the criterion refers to an attribute with clear social significance for an institution or for the individuals involved, careful analysis and measurement work are obligatory. But at the least, the range of possibilities is much smaller in such instances than in theoretical work, the investigator does have something to get hold of, and he can usually evaluate the quality of his measuring procedures relatively quickly and definitively.

Insofar as applied work is theoretically oriented, it becomes similar to basic research. On the other hand, measurement directed toward the economical assessment of an explicit criterion variable or toward the prediction of such a variable can be developed on a largely empirical basis. Once the investigator has access to large groups of those who meet the criterion and those who do not, he needs time, patience, and ingenuity to identify the measuring operations that most clearly differentiate the groups. A substantial degree of success has been obtained in such empirical or actuarial work. To date, actuarial methods have been shown to equal or exceed the best predictions by human judges bringing to bear all their knowledge and experience. (See pages 172–75.) In such comparisons, the actuarial method takes advantage of all the regularities that can be extracted from available data on similar cases and operates with findings made dependable by the large frequencies on which they are based. On the other side, the expert human judge attempts to place each case in a smaller subgroup for which he recalls that certain regularities hold. Perhaps his handicap is his inability to recall from memory all relevant data on each of the various subgroups.

A very significant kind of measurement is the assessment of the individual patient. Such testing can be done for two purposes: the diagnostician may simply be gathering information from which to formulate a personality sketch of the patient, as a basis for decisions during psychotherapeutic treatment; he may also aim at classifying the patient (dull normal, probably brain-injured, sociopathic, or whatever) so that the optimal treatment program can be scheduled for him. In principle, this latter type of objective is of the same general sort as the applied work considered earlier. The special consideration in such measurement is the serious cost of making a wrong decision and misclassifying the patient, a cost that may be a thousandfold higher than that of making an error in measuring a subject in basic research.

The Orientation of this Book

The remaining sections of this chapter indicate the basic approach of this book. They will examine the two fundamental strategies in psychological research. Then my underlying axiomatic values will be made explicit. Finally, major theses about personality measurement will be introduced. Each of these themes that run throughout the book will usually be developed more fully at a later point.

"THE TWO DISCIPLINES OF SCIENTIFIC PSYCHOLOGY"

In this classic paper, Cronbach (1957) distinguishes between experimental psychology and correlational psychology. In its basic form, the experimental approach studies the effect of an independent variable, a condition or a treatment usually manipulated by the experimenter. Some subjects are exposed to the condition, others are not, or the two groups may be exposed to different strengths of the condition. (For examples, the experimenter may manipulate the physical setting, the instructions, rewards or punishments, etc.) The fundamental requirement of this approach is that every other condition that might affect the variable being studied, the dependent variable expected to covary with the independent condition, is intended to be equal for the two groups.

Correlational psychology seeks to study individuals as they are: Does dominance vary with activity level? Does happiness vary with socioeconomic status? In such studies, the aim is to estimate the extent of each of the two variables, these being considered to be stable attributes of the subjects, so that measurements next week or three months later would agree closely with those made today. The correlational psychologist must design his measuring conditions so that they do not influence the data he obtains: activity level should not be determined in the late morning for some subjects and right after a heavy dinner for others; happiness should not be measured just after a national tragedy, such as the assassination of a beloved president. In particular, the investigator must minimize the influence of the act of measuring: applicants for a job cannot be expected to report candidly their dispositions to be lazy or to get into arguments with superiors.

Thus the correlational psychologist seeks to estimate, at one point in time, the more or less enduring attributes of a person: How much of X and how much of Y does he possess, in general? In contrast, the experimenter wants to determine some attribute of the person's behavior after he is exposed to a specified condition. In their measurement operations, both scientists measure some aspect of the subject's behavior at a point in time, but one interprets the manifested strength as an enduring characteristic of the person, while the other ascribes its relative strength to the preceding condition he has introduced.

The two approaches can be illustrated by a single study conducted by Alfred Collins and me. We were exploring the conceptualization and measurement of impulsivity, a construct that we defined as degree of inadequacy in performance of instrumental acts that are well within the capacities of the subject. We identified several forms of inadequacy, including omission of a required act, commission of an inadequate act, and inaccuracy. Our measures were a cancellation test (in which the subject drew a line through each occurrence of any of four letters, in long strings of letters), making an x that crossed within each of many small circles, counting randomly placed dots in a square, and successive subtraction of 7s from 300. The tests were given without pressure of time limits.

The subjects took the tests as part of a psychology course. One group of forty-four served as controls, taking the tests under standard conditions without any explanation or additional motivation. The other group of twenty-four was told that each subject would be paid a flat fee of $2 for taking these and other tests, plus a bonus that would depend upon the quality of his performance.

We planned the research to answer two questions, the first experimental and the second correlational: Does motivation (in this case, the monetary reward) lead to better performance, i.e., to less impulsivity? To what extent are these tests measuring the same variable?

The results can be seen in Table 2.1. Looking at the first column of data, we see that, on the average, the experimental group had smaller error scores on three out of the four tests. The differences do not, however, reach statistical significance. (It is probably worth noting that the strongest effect was for the test that came first, the cancellation test. Instructions often lose their effectiveness as an experiment or testing session goes on.)

Now consider the correlations among the tests. For the control group, they are clearly not positive: even though the tests could be shown to be reliable, they were not measuring the same variable in that group. On the other hand, the tests have positive correlations with each other in the experimental group. While the experimental condition of pay and monetary incentive did not significantly affect the mean scores, it did create circumstances under which the tests covaried and to some extent were measuring the same variable.

Since this small study involved both experimental and correlational approaches to the same data, it does not illustrate either approach in its purest

Table 2.1. *Mean scores and intercorrelations for four tests of impulsivity under two conditions*

	Group	Mean error score	X in O	Dot Counting	Subtraction
				Correlations	
Cancellation	Experimental	8.04	.55	.40	.43
	Control	11.43	−.12	−.07	−.23
X in O	Experimental	21.61		.32	.24
	Control	20.13		.12	.02
Dot counting	Experimental	14.04			.29
	Control	14.21			−.43
Subtraction	Experimental	.71			
	Control	1.04			

form. In these results, however, the experimenter finds that motivation and incentive affect the performances of the subjects on the four tests so that they covary, even though they do not greatly affect the mean level of performance. The correlational psychologist interprets the correlational patterns as indicating that these several tests do assess the same variable to some extent, provided that the motivations of subjects are made positive. Presumably, under the control conditions, subjects applied themselves to each task as their fancy struck them, probably with some trying harder on one task and others trying harder on another. Thus the correlational psychologist finds that, to measure impulsivity with these tests, he must standardize motivational level in some way.

As a quite different example of the two approaches, there is the work on novelty done by Maddi and his associates (1962). They administered three conditions to their subjects: one group heard a dull, monotonous recording; another spent the same time doing whatever the individual subjects wished (this group might be seen as a control group); the third heard a highly novel recording with many surprises and unusual features. Their independent variable was, then, the conditions varying from very low novelty of stimulation to very high. Their dependent variable was the desire for novelty inferred from stories the subjects composed for pictures. It was assumed that measurements of this desire would be dependent on the preceding conditions. (They determined the effectiveness of the experimental conditions by having subjects indicate on a checklist how they felt about the condition they had experienced. Following explicit rules, judges scored each story on the degree of desire for novelty shown in it. These independent scorings were then compared to make sure that the scores were reasonably objective and not too much influenced by the individual perceptions of any single rater.) They found that desire for novelty was higher in the group exposed to the monotonous condition, but that there was no significant difference between the free-activity and novelty groups.

A correlational study on the tendency to like novel experiences has been reported by Pearson (in press). She studied the relationship of this tendency to age, education, socioeconomic status, and a large number of other personality variables, testing many predictions based on her conceptualization of the tendency. Most of her predictions were confirmed. The study has too many detailed findings to be summarized readily.

Actually, she studied four forms of this tendency and found that, as predicted, the several forms had different patterns of relationships with other variables. The forms were based on source and type of experience. Thus liking unusual or new cognitive processes was correlated with age and with Murray's needs for Understanding, Achievement, and Nurturance. Liking active physical participation in thrilling activities was related to needs for Play and Autonomy, and to low need for Harm avoidance. (These two forms, it should be noted, were uncorrelated with each other.) Thus the analysis of tendency to like novel experiences into more specific forms proved theoretically and empirically fruitful.

Maddi's group also studied another aspect of novelty, the tendency to produce novelty in stories. On this variable, the group exposed to monotony scored lower than the other groups: they desired more novelty but, after experiencing monotony, did not have novel imagery that might satisfy that need. These findings also demonstrate the value of analyzing broad global concepts, such as preference for novelty, into carefully defined subconcepts. We shall have much more to say later about the necessity for such detailed identification and conceptualization of concepts.

The crucial difference between the experimental and the correlational approaches is in the type of question asked. The experimenter is asking: Do people generally tend to react in a particular way to the manipulated condition? The correlator asks: Do people whose behavior shows a lot of one tendency also have a lot of another tendency? Experimenters like Maddi generalize in three ways: from the sample of observed subjects to the population of people from whom the sample was drawn (in this case, from these male undergraduates at least to male students in similar colleges); from the particular condition to a class of conditions subsumed under the concept of the independent variable (e.g., from this monotonous condition to other conditions experienced as monotonous); and finally, from the measured aspect of the subject's behavior under the experimental condition to the concept of the dependent variable (in this instance, from the desire for novelty attributed by the subject to the characters in his stories to this desire as a momentary disposition of the subject).

The correlator also generalizes from his sample to some population of people. In addition, he generalizes from each of two samples of behavior to his concepts of the two variables whose relationship he is studying. For example, Pearson generalized from her subjects' expressed interest in particular imagined experiences as suggested by brief statements to her concept of each form of novelty-experiencing; she also generalized from subjects' answers to questionnaire items to each of several motives construed in Murray's need variables. She had to assume that her measures indicated the typical strengths of these dispositions in each subject during some time interval like a few months, strengths that are assumed to be affected very little by the particular situation in which the subject happens to be.

Note the fundamental difference between these two approaches in the type of variables being measured. The correlator is estimating more enduring aspects whose influence the experimenter tries to control or eliminate. Maddi's study would have produced more clear-cut findings if the desire for novelty were always determined completely by the preceding conditions and did not vary from person to person within any one condition. Pearson had to assume that the testing conditions affected all her subjects about the same amount, i.e., that some subjects had not been greatly bored just before taking her test of novelty experience and that others had not been stimulated by very novel experiences.

The correlator is interested in traits, in the differing personalities of his subjects. In contrast, the experimenter is studying states generated by the immediate effects of conditions: Does this kind of prior experience make people behave in a given way? Maddi and his associates used the free-activity period as a control condition to make sure that the level of desire for novelty observed after monotony would not have been found anyway. As it turned out, this group was important: without it, they might have concluded that monotony increases the desire for novelty and that novel experiences decrease it; with it, they could show that only the first statement was supported and that experiencing great novelty did not affect scores on this variable. We can see, then, that the two approaches are suited for investigating quite different types of questions concerning different kinds of variables.

The active reader should be feeling uncomfortable at this point. Do these two approaches, which are admittedly oversimplified here, really cover all of psychological science? Where can we classify studies of sex differences, of brain injury, of reactions to a presidential assassination, and of anxiety before a parachute jump? All categorical schemes are arbitrary in the sense that the same phenomena can always be classified in many ways; the question is which scheme is most fruitful for a given purpose. Differences in sex or in physical condition of the brain involve enduring characteristics to be investigated by correlational methods. Conditions that have short-term effects fall in the domain of the experimenter. He need not produce the condition representing his independent variable—he can take it where he finds it. He is always asking, "What does X do to people?" while his correlational colleague is asking whether this disposition tends to covary in strength with that disposition, averaging out or otherwise controlling the effects of the particular conditions under which the dispositions are measured.

With respect to measurement, the two approaches involve the same concerns: Has the influence of random determinants been minimized so that there is very little error of measurement? Has the possibility of systematic bias been reduced to an acceptably small level? Is the right aspect of behavior being measured? The comprehensive question is simply this: Can we generalize from our observations to the constructs in which we are really interested?

SOME AXIOMATIC PROPOSITIONS

This book is based on certain value judgments, certain convictions that will be assumed to be valid. One is that *the nomothetic approach is necessary for basic research.* Nomothetic measurement simply means the measurement of the same property in all subjects. After the experimenter has imposed his conditions, does one group show more Y-ness than the other? It is obvious that the same attribute must be measured in all experimental and control subjects. Similarly, each of the variables studied by the correlator must be assessed in each of his subjects. It may be presence or absence of a characteristic, such as a phobia or brain damage. It may be a matter of frequency, such as the number of words a person can define or the number of things that make him anxious. Or it may be a question of intensity: Does stress increase his heart rate a little or a lot? Does he recover from stress rapidly or slowly?

The idiographic approach, the study and interpretation of the particular individual, is of great value as a source of ideas and as a reminder of the complexity of the individual personality. We are all interested in individuals, in this person and that. But science is concerned with the general. Personology, the science of personality, is interested in people in general, or in people of a particular kind. In basic research, the study of the individual cannot be an end in itself, but only a means to a larger objective.

This insistence on the nomothetic approach may seem to rule out phenomenological, existential, or humanistic orientations. It is not intended to do so. These orientations are concerned with significant aspects of human experience which have rarely been subjected to careful scientific inquiry. Our argument is with those who assert that an intuitive understanding of another personality contributes to the science of personology. It does not advance the science even to study an individual and find a law or generalization that whenever he experiences A, he acts in X fashion. Now if we also find that another person shows Y behavior after experiencing B, and a third shows Z after C, and if we can see some characteristic common to A, B, and C, and also to X, Y, and Z, then we may tentatively draw a generalization that holds for all three people. For instance, A, B, and C may be threats to self-esteem, and X, Y, and Z may be mechanisms for bolstering self-esteem. It is not necessary that the experience be exactly the same for all subjects: love is (fortunately) an almost universal experience, and yet (also fortunately) the specific object of that love is different for each of us. So we may study love or threats to self-esteem, and these variables may be quite specific in their manifestations in different people. They can, nevertheless, be studied nomothetically as instances of the class of threats or the class of loves. On the other hand, the study of T's love for S, or V's love for U, is not part of science if the study is confined just to one of these unique relationships.

For the sake of clarity, let us reexamine this topic and distinguish three issues. The first is the matter of approach, the distinction between the nomothetic and the idiographic. My own position is that the substance of a science is composed of generalizations over classes of people or objects. The content of the generalization may be common attributes or it may be common structures or patterns, such as abstract properties: we can state that the need for Achievement varies with the subject's recent experience in a specified way; we can also state that each person has at least one central basic theme or unresolved conflict that keeps reappearing in his experience and behavior, the content of the theme or conflict being shared by few people, or even none. Note that the latter statement does not refer to any particular content.

The second issue concerns the study of the single case. It is quite possible to demonstrate regularities in the behavior of a single person, as behavior theorists have done. Frequently, of course, it is desirable to establish such regularities on one case before studying others. The value of such work, however, remains quite limited until the study has been replicated on other cases. Certainly the findings cannot be absorbed into the body of the science until such replication has taken place. Especially in psychology, we cannot assume that the processes and covariations observed in just one person are typical or representative of many or all persons, no matter how plausible, *a priori,* such an assumption may seem. The demonstration that a particular phenomenon can occur, because it is manifested by one person, provides us with an idea but not with a generalization.

The third issue is the distinction between the way we get ideas and the way we test or prove them; that is, the distinction between the source of an idea and the evidence contributing to our confidence in the likelihood that the idea is valid. Reichenbach has identified these aspects as the context of discovery and the context of justification (confirmation might be a better term). Lorenz and other ethologists got many ideas about behavior from observing a single organism, such as one goose. Many of Freud's ideas came to him while he was trying to understand the behavior of a particular patient. Such naturalistic observations are very valuable to the alert and active thinker. The ideas and concepts, however, cannot be accepted into the body of a science until more systematic investigations of their applicability have been made.

It may be apparent to the reader now (or it may become apparent as he reads later chapters) that many of the aspects of human experience that are of great general interest, aspects toward which phenomenological, existential, or humanistic thinking are directed, are simply more difficult to study scientifically than many topics to which psychologists have addressed themselves. But difficulty is always relative. Two decades ago, scientists could study dreams only from reports when the night was over. Since we know now that dreaming usually occurs when subjects are in a physiological state detectable from recordings of brain activity and movements of eye muscles, it is possible to wake a subject during or immediately after a dream and obtain a more complete report than he can give the following morning. Current dream research is much more developed than earlier work. Improvements in methodology can thus contribute greatly to advances in scientific understanding. In personality research, there is much room for such improvements, especially for better measuring procedures for central theoretical concepts.

Another axiom is that *measurement operations must be public and communicable.* While the judgments of an exceptionally sensitive clinician may provide valuable data at an early stage of investigation, he must be able to communicate his skill to others. Otherwise, all we can know is that it is possible to make certain discriminations, a tantalizing but useless fact unless we can somehow reproduce the discriminations by another method. Science is built on the consensus of informed scientists. The insights of the talented genius, no matter how exceptional, do not contribute to the field until others understand them. The path-breaking findings of an innovative empirical study cannot be accepted into the corpus of science until others are convinced that they are replicable.

A third axiom is that *the phenomena of personality are complex.* Several determinants can produce the same action or feeling, and several may contribute to any one occurrence of a phenomenon. From the other side, the same personality variable can be manifested phenomenally in various ways.

While comparisons with other sciences are perhaps reassuring, they give little help. Other phenomena are also complex, multiply determined, and so on. The chief difference is that in more developed sciences, the factors that can affect a phenomenon are better known (a rather circular statement). There may be another difference: the potential contributions of the various factors may be more equal in the science of personality than in other sciences. Thus when the length of an object is measured, temperature and humidity may influence the observation, but only to a very small extent. But when we measure anxiety, our observation may be greatly affected by the physical setting, the subject's immediately prior experience, the experimenter and his attitude toward the subject, and the significance of the stimulus for the subject—each of these having a potentially large effect. The effects of temperature on the observed length of a physical object may be large relative to the discriminations in which the physicist is interested, while personologists must now be content with much less precise determinations, but the physicist can more readily control temperature and can determine rather precisely the function relating temperature to length for each type of object, while the personologist can rarely introduce well-standardized controls or calibrate the extent of intrusive effects.

In principle, in both experimental and correlational work, the crucial problem is to measure each variable separately, standardizing or controlling all possibly influential variables except the one being measured (see Fiske and Butler, 1963). In personology, the problem has many aspects. The effects of the total situation must be made the same for all subjects in each group studied, and the situation must be designed so that these effects do not systematically bias the resulting observations. In other words, the resulting measurements should be primarily a function of reactions to the stimuli, not to the situation. For this to be so, the stimuli must be sufficiently compelling to determine the responses. The stimuli must be clear and unequivocal, must have the same external meaning for all subjects, even though the personal meanings or interpretations of the stimuli are associated with the strength of the disposition in the several subjects. The task the subjects are to perform, whether it is solving problems or indicating how they see themselves, must be clear and within their capacity. That is, the subjects must be given an explicit set of criteria to use in selecting their responses to each item or stimulus. It will be obvious, with a moment's thought, that the phenomena on which personality measurements are based, the subjects' experiences and reactions in the testing situation, are a particular class of occurrences that cannot be taken as sampling in a representative fashion all the natural events in the subjects' lives outside the measurement situation. The implications of this point will be considered in later chapters.

It is therefore not only the natural phenomena of personology that are complex, but also the phenomena in the measurement situation themselves.

To measure personality well, we must understand the psychology of behavior while being measured, a class of behavior that is determined by many aspects of personality (see Sarason, 1954, and Chapter 10 of this volume).

SOME PERVASIVE THEMES AND THESES

The preceding axioms are propositions with which most personologists will in principle agree. There is probably less consensus on the statements made in this section. Some central themes of the subsequent exposition will be presented briefly here for emphasis and to help the reader follow the course of the later arguments.

1. There are no ultimate criteria. Three to four decades ago, measurement psychologists were more diffident than they are today. Tests were often viewed as better or worse approximations to some ultimate criteria that might or might not be visible at that time. Even when intelligence became somewhat arrogantly defined as that which the intelligence test tests, one intelligence test (the Stanford-Binet) was often taken as the criterion for other tests that were less time-consuming, were group-administered, etc. Personality tests never really had an available ultimate criterion against which they could be compared, although few personologists would publicly state that the emperor wore no clothes. Today it is more widely recognized that the targets of personality measurement are a group of loose abstractions, usually given a literary definition rather than a scientific one. Even such socially relevant variables as those associated with mental health are poorly defined, in spite of the agreement on the significance of certain indices such as self-reported distress or the fact of being a patient (Jahoda, 1958; Szasz, 1960; Smith, 1968a).

2. We lack consensus on the definitions of constructs. Science requires consensus among qualified scientists. Any science that has developed beyond the most primitive early stages has facts, concepts, and laws on which there is very general agreement. While these may be modified or interpreted somewhat differently as the field advances, there is always a contemporary set of established facts and theories. These are the fundamentals. At any point in time, there are also concepts and empirical findings that are only tentatively accepted, or accepted by some and rejected by others. But the existence of such content does not negate the fact that there is agreement on some fundamentals.

Personology, the science of personality, is still in the primitive stage of development: very few empirical findings have been clearly established by consistent replications so that we can predict with high confidence that under certain explicit conditions a given result will be obtained. But more pertinent to measurement is the lack of consensus on concepts.

On the one hand, each personality theorist has his own concepts, which may be similar to but are never identical with some proposed in another theory. At times several theorists with the same general orientation will use the same terms in their theorizing, but close examination invariably indicates some differences in the connotations if not in the denotations of those terms. On the other hand, many concepts are used by eclectic thinkers or by those who do not espouse a specific theory. Such concepts are often given a label from everyday language, such as dominance or aggression. Since everyone is familiar with the general meaning of such a word, the need for precise definition is not recognized.

So we find that many personologists are often satisfied with using the same label even though each of them gives it a somewhat different meaning. To communicate their meaning, they provide what Underwood (1957) calls a literary definition. Apparently most writers expect that the meaning they attach to a concept will become clear from their discussion of it and of its relationships with other concepts. While such expectation may be appropriate in literary essays, it is not sufficient in scientific treatises.

A major reason for this state of affairs is the substantial degree of overlap among meanings held by various writers. Just as a group of educated people, when asked to define "conservatism," would produce a set of definitions that had much in common, so a group of personologists would give definitions of "anxiety" that had many similar features. But partial agreement is not sufficient in science.

The basis for such partial agreement is often the breadth or generality of the meanings. Most personality concepts are used to cover a broad range of phenomena or observations. They are very large categories. With such inclusiveness, it is easy to see how there can be many points of agreement between two definitions, and still many points of disagreement. At the very least, the central emphases of two definitions will usually be found to differ.

There is a class of apparent exceptions to the assertion that there is little agreement on definitions. Some concepts refer to scores from particular operations, and at first glance they would seem to have explicit and even operational definitions; for example, movement as noted in Rorschach responses, manifest anxiety as measured by the Taylor scale, and leveling tendency as determined by the Squares Test. But in each of these cases, the concept is taken to include much more than the particular disposition assessed—the Taylor scale, for instance, was constructed to get at general drive. Thus, rather than being examples of good coordination between concepts and operations, they are instances in which a particular measure is the favorite procedure, if not the only one used for assessing a very broad concept whose full scope cannot be encompassed by a single set of operations.

The solution to this problem is obvious. Theorists must develop more explicit definitions of their personality concepts. (See Chapter 6 and Fiske,

1966a.) As soon as one attempts this, one finds that it is necessary to delineate subcategories of the phenomena. Hence it seems best to consider the terms in current usage today to be labels for general domains, rather than for precise variables. Within each such domain, many subconcepts must be specified. For example, adapting the approach of Louis Guttman, the theorist can identify a behavioral facet encompassing a set of elements distinguishing particular forms of behavior, each being one aspect of the general concept. In similar fashion, a situational facet can be constructed, an orientation encompassing the several distinct conditions under which the behaviors may appear.

Why is such conceptual analysis necessary? Its value can be argued on many bases, such as the fact that science often advances by making a sharp distinction to correct an earlier oversimplification. But such analysis is certainly essential to adequate measurement. We cannot measure well when we cannot specify clearly what we are trying to measure, where it occurs, and when.

Given the range of personal definitions for the commonly used concepts in personology, it is not surprising that there is no agreement on the measurement operations for assessing any particular concept. Measurers using questionnaires write their own items for each variable. Those using performance or production procedures (such as incomplete sentences) create their own stimuli. Even those employing experimental manipulations utilize particular instructions or conditions that are not shared by others. While there is pressure to specify one's procedures, to make them public so that in principle they can be replicated, the community of personologists does not attempt to get personologists to conform in using standard procedures, because there is no consensus on which procedures should be generally used. (An apparent exception, such as the use of identical stimuli in Rorschach testing, is not really different: people trained in various schools administer and score the standard blots in somewhat differing fashions.) Lacking such standardized, generally accepted measuring procedures, each personologist feels free to utilize the particular methods he believes best, or perhaps with which he is most comfortable.

With this degree of individuality in the methodology of experiments, it is not surprising that personology does not have empirical generalizations that are universally accepted. And until we have established empirical laws, it is not likely that we will have common concepts and any generally accepted theoretical propositions. What is likely is that there will continue to be a proliferation of unsystematic theorizing, with intuitively plausible but basically vague concepts, and with abstract assertions that cannot readily be subjected to definitive empirical testing.

3. Constructs are construed by people. In the light of the preceding con-

siderations, it seems rather apparent that theorizers make up constructs, that their "concepts" exist in their minds and in the minds of the people who share their thinking. As George Kelly so ably pointed out in his *Psychology of Personal Constructs* (1955), people in their everyday lives construe the world, and scientists do much the same thing, but following somewhat different rules. While personal and scientific constructs refer to the outside world and to properties of phenomena in it, the constructs exist in the people using them.

In this context, a construct is a proposed attribute. As such, it is not evaluated as true or false, but as useful or useless. Given the variety of constructs developed for a domain, such as the phenomena subsumed under dominance, which construct, which definition of the variable helps us most in understanding these and other phenomena? Or is there a better construct or set of constructs for this purpose? Science advances by refining constructs and by developing new ones where needed to further our understanding, and especially by utilizing empirical data for guidance in such literal reconstruing or reconstruction.

4. Personality phenomena are diverse. The content or domain of personality includes such observations as "I am in a bad mood," "He never completes the tasks he undertakes," "That patient perceives the world as conspiring against him," and also the explanations for them. It is obvious that the range of phenomena and experiences currently included under the rubric of personality is almost infinite. As a consequence, many kinds of constructs and a wide variety of measuring operations are needed to build a comprehensive science of personality. It is to be hoped that the domain may be broken down into more homogeneous subdomains, for each of which an adequate small theory and methodology can be formulated. But one cannot be too sanguine about this possibility: the subdomains are interrelated. Our manner of perceiving is a function of our values and interests. Our manner of performing is related to our motives and our fears. The way others see us is determined in part by the way we see ourselves, and conversely our pictures of ourselves are usually affected by the way others see us. Yet one thing is certain: the optimal methodology for one of these topics or subdomains will probably not be best for another domain. The measuring procedures must be developed to fit the particular type of variable and conceptual orientation at which they are aimed.

5. Several viewpoints are used for observing personality phenomena. It is not possible to divorce the observation from the observer. The observer determines what he will look at and influences how he sees it, i.e., what the recorded observation is. Personality phenomena may be observed in oneself. One's dreams and one's thoughts and feelings are not directly available to anyone else. On the other hand, one's actions can be observed

by oneself and also by others. Observations by others may be restricted to
particular selected or experimental conditions or they may be accumulated
unsystematically in casual daily interactions. Observations may be made
by laymen with varying degrees of personal involvement with the person
observed. Finally, the observers may be experts with presumably minimal
involvement with the subject.

As will be shown later (Chapter 5), these several classes of observations
must be considered as distinct. The same physical event in space and time,
such as an overt action of a subject, may be the object of several observations, but these observations cannot be considered interchangeable if the
observers have different viewpoints stemming from their different roles or
reasons for making the observations or from their different relationships
to the subject. Each observation is, in a sense, perfectly valid. It is invalid
only to the extent that the personologist, in utilizing it, interprets it as
representing something other than what it inherently is, given the person
making the observation and the conditions under which it was made.

6. Personality phenomena involve processes. What is observed is people
doing things and experiencing things. Strictly speaking, people are not intelligent, or aggressive. Such statements are unfortunate elliptical ways of
speaking. Certainly people are not intelligent when they are asleep or aggressive when they are walking alone. We call a person intelligent when
we believe he has the capacity to act intelligently because he has acted intelligently. Personality phenomena refer to aspects of ongoing activity in
persons, such activity being external and visible or internal and inferred.
Such internal activity may be studied as neural or physiological by some
scientists and as subjective or phenomenological by other scientists. With
respect to observed behavior, Carr and Kingsbury (1938) have noted that
we begin with adverbs (he acted intelligently), then use adjectives (he is
intelligent), and later discuss nouns (he has a lot of intelligence): what is
actually a quality of an action is made into an attribute of a person, and
then becomes reified. We talk as if intelligence existed. It does not. All
that exists is the potentiality of behaving intelligently.

Personologists, then, study processes. Processes are, of course, constructs;
they are ways we choose to interpret what we perceive to be going on. The
construct of process appears to be a fruitful one, which we can use in
considering not only general personality phenomena, but also the phenomena occurring during measurement.

Any formulation of such processes identifies several aspects and phases.
There is the living organism in which a variety of processes are occurring
at any moment. The person is in a situation whose features may be impinging on his experience in particular ways. Then a stimulus occurs. The
person receives the sensory input and interprets it. It usually has some

meaning for him. The experiencing of the stimulus may evoke some motive to alter his current experience. He may act to effect such a change. When the action is completed, he may evaluate its success according to its effectiveness in bringing about the change he sought. But others may also evaluate the success of his action: Did he cope well? Did he act intelligently?

Different types of personality variables are used to refer to different aspects or phases of this process. Perceptual dispositions refer to what the person perceives and how he perceives it. Interests and preferences consider the evaluations he makes of his perceptions. Motives are used to classify the kinds of changes he wishes to bring about in his experience. There are variables to describe how people act, move, and express themselves. The way a person evaluates his actions is closely related to his picture of himself. And evaluations of effectiveness are made by others in measuring intelligence.

7. Behavior is inherently variable. Once we accept the fact that the phenomena of interest to us are aspects of processes in living organisms, it seems rather to be expected that the behavior of a person varies over time. Any one aspect of a process may be influenced by preceding aspects, and by the preceding state of the person as well as by the external conditions. Consistency in behavior is found when one or several of the determinants of a response (one aspect of the process) play major roles, with other effects having little or no influence. Under certain conditions, there is no question what one will do or how one will do it. But such consistency is to a large extent dependent upon previous experience and practice. When a person has learned how to do something, and has done it often, he will do it in a highly predictable manner.

On the other hand, when a person has a new experience, he may react differently the second time it occurs than he did the first. Tests are usually new experiences and subjects do change responses from the first testing to a second, but less so from the second to the third.

Furthermore, in the absence of compelling stimuli or constraining conditions, behavior is relatively variable. One's thoughts and feelings as one drifts off to sleep tend to be different from one night to the next. And dream content varies during the night, as well as from night to night. While doodles have some individuality, they tend to be different from one day to the next.

A problem in measuring individual differences is how to obtain scores minimally affected by this temporal variability within each person's experience and behavior and still representing the variation from person to person. With familiar stimulus questions and constraining conditions, it is easy to obtain stable behavior from subjects, but hard to get variation among people. With unstructured situations and vague stimuli, it is easy to get variation among people but hard to get stable responses from each person. With ingenuity and with understanding of the problem, one can find stimuli and conditions that will generate stable responses that vary among people.

8. Subjects react to being measured. Most psychological measurement takes place in situations set up for that purpose. While a subject may not know exactly what the experimenter is trying to measure, he realizes that the experimenter wants to find out something about him. A test involves a long process that includes a shorter process for each stimulus to which the subject responds. A major factor in the larger test process is the subject's awareness of being tested. Obviously, unless we only want to know how the subject reacts to being evaluated, we have to devise measurement procedures that will minimize the potentially intrusive effects of this situational component. More broadly viewed, we want to generalize from observations in the measurement situation to potential observations in other situations, an aim that cannot be realized if the unique features of the measurement situation play a major role in determining the subject's experiences and responses while being tested.

9. Behaviors tend to be highly specific. In discussing personality phenomena as process, we noted the many classes of determinants that can affect responses and aspects of behavior. Since these change over time, behavior is relatively variable from one occasion to the next. (Consider your own behavior one hour ago and twenty-five hours ago.) But much more obvious are the changes in behavior with changes in the situation (e.g., in class and at the ball park) and changes in the immediately effective stimuli (e.g., just before you receive your grades and just after). The observation of any one aspect of behavior can potentially be affected by many factors in the immediate situation. It is therefore difficult to find pairs of characteristics that are very closely related to each other.

More narrowly, let us suppose that we have been able to develop constellations of stimuli and conditions such that the subject responds consistently over time to each. There may be a large number, hundreds or thousands, of such constellations or complexes. Certainly there are more than we can cope with effectively in trying to understand personality. A major problem in personology is to devise categories of such complexes, to reduce the discrete data to a smaller number of indices with which we can work conceptually and empirically. What is needed is a taxonomy of complexes. The problem is exceedingly difficult because we must find categories that can be applied to all people or to all who fall in some reasonably large class.

It is a matter of empirical fact that these complexes yield behavioral indices that have little covariation between them, even for subsets with one or more common components. For example, consider the average correlation between the items in a personality questionnaire. It is typically in the order of .05 (see Fiske, 1966*b*). That is, from the response to one question, predictions of the response to another question will be barely better than chance. Now the only change from one item to the next is in the stimulus, the question; the general conditions remain just the same. And even if we adjust for the limited stability of the responses, the correlations will be raised only a few points.

Somewhat higher correlations between specific responses may be obtained in other circumstance. Thus the correlations between items in an instrument testing intelligence may have a somewhat higher average. But unless the contents of the two items are much the same, the correlations tend to be small. Outside of testing, there is little reason to expect higher levels of association between specific single responses.

At a less molecular level, the picture is not much better. Scores from intelligence tests may have substantial intercorrelations. Scores from personality measures typically do not exceed .40. The highest obtained correlations are found when the testing procedure is essentially the same for the two instruments and the items have very similar content. But even when different investigators devise questionnaires that purportedly measure the same variable, the total scores tend to correlate about .35, and often considerably less.

In Chapter 11, we shall consider at greater length the implications of this state of affairs. For the present, the essential point is that most of the behavior of interest to the personologist, even under the relatively standardized conditions of measurement, does not show much regular covariation over people. Even aside from the presumed individual differences among people on a particular variable, conditions and stimuli have different meanings for different subjects, and it is difficult to find those components of measurement (conditions and items) that are interpreted in much the same way by most people. People and stimuli interact, and so do people and conditions. We shall repeatedly be confronted by this disagreeable fact as we pursue the goal of trying to measure personality adequately.

Summary

"Personality" has many meanings, both lay and technical. Such definitions commonly refer to the individuality of a person; hence personology studies both classes of people and particular individuals, unlike sciences that study only classes. Thus personology uses the experimental approach to compare groups that differ in some respect and the correlational approach to determine covariation of variables over individuals.

This volume, concerned with measurement in basic research rather than in applied work, takes as axiomatic the nomothetic approach, the obvious complexity of personality phenomena, and the requirement that measuring procedures be public and communicable. Running through the book are several themes and theses: the absence of ultimate criteria in personological measurement; the lack of consensus on definitions of constructs; the obvious but neglected fact that constructs are created by people; the great diversity of personality phenomena; the separate viewpoints from which such phenomena can be observed; the fact that personality phenomena involve processes rather than static attributes, and that behavior is inherently variable over time; the complicating fact that subjects react to being measured; and the relative specificity of behavior as a function of stimulus and situation.

CHAPTER THREE

Personality, Process, and Systematic Observations

The Content to be Observed and Measured

Measurements are worthless unless they are measures of the right object, and of the right attribute of that object. There is usually little difficulty in deciding what the objects are that we want to measure; the real trouble comes in deciding exactly what attribute we want to measure and in determining whether we are measuring only that attribute and no other. Here we shall first consider what personality is, using personality as the label for the large class of attributes we want to measure. Then we shall consider how we seek systematic observations pertinent to any particular attribute. Later (Chapter 6) we shall examine the matter of specifying the attribute at which we aim our measuring operations.

Other volumes in this series discuss the nature of personality in full detail. They also provide explicit or implicit definitions, and close examination will show that these definitions are not identical: each author's definition is a function of his particular approach to personality, or his interests, of what he is trying to understand. Rather than attempting to distill a common essence from these definitions, I too shall be individualistic and, for the purpose of this volume, give my own definition.

DEFINING PERSONALITY

As a first approximation to defining this central term, I offer this: personality is the way a person characteristically interacts with his environment—

external, somatic, and intrapsychic. It is the way he functions, given the range of environmental stimuli he typically encounters. More fully, personality is the set of consistent ways in which he interacts with the internal and external stimuli impinging upon him. To be even more complete, we must add a qualification: personality is the way a person characteristically *is observed* to interact with his environment. This implication that what is seen as personality depends in part upon the perspective of the observer will be developed in the next two chapters.

This definition distinguishes two major classes of stimuli with which a person interacts, those outside the psychic self and those within it. The intrapsychic world includes all of the subject's mentation, all the content of his mind and awareness: his thoughts, feelings, and so on. Outside of these are the stimuli that impinge on him from beyond his body. Somewhat arbitrarily, bodily sensations are grouped with these outside stimuli simply because a person interacts with bodily sensations in much the same way as he does with external stimuli, in contrast to his manner of interacting with feelings, images, and thoughts.

Although the distinction between these two large classes has some value, it is largely a matter of degree, of where the person locates the source of the stimuli. Basically, the person interacts with his perceptions and interpretations of what he sees, these of course being mental content. Whatever the mental content and its attributed source, the crucial matter for personality is how the person values this content, what meaning he gives it, what effect it has on him. Then there is the further question of what he does about the stimuli. Does he want to change the nature of his interaction with his environment so that the stimuli no longer impinge on him, so that they impinge more strongly, or so that some other stimuli are experienced? Does he act so as to produce these changes?

Thus personality is an abstraction referring to an individual's observed interactions with the environment. When we talk about the personality of a particular individual, we refer to the content of these interactions, their kinds and their qualities. In describing a certain personality, we reduce the infinite number of these interactions to a limited set of statements about their general nature. We classify the interactions and, for each class, state some kind of representative value (mean intensity, relative frequency, etc.). But to see what kinds of classes may be used for this purpose, we must look more closely at the general nature of such an interaction.

THE GENERAL PROCESS

Persons are living organisms. As such, they are always functioning. Sequences of internal activity are always occurring. Not only are neural and physiological processes going on continuously and simultaneously, but also psychological processes are going on without remission. It is easy to see this in our own waking experience. There is a noise; we notice it; we may wonder what it is, and then decide what made it. We may be annoyed by it because we feel we must do something about it; we act to stop the noise. If we succeed in stopping it, we then return to what we were doing, or perhaps we now start something else. Or a thought may come to us as we are walking down the hall; we may put this thought together with another one, decide that we must do something tomorrow, and then think about something else. Meanwhile we continue the other ongoing process of walking. Successive moments of experience are related to each other. Each of several short bits of psychological behavior is linked in some way to the one preceding it.

Processes also occur as we are waking up or falling asleep. And when a person is asleep, he is dreaming part of the time, each dream consisting of a sequence of actions or experiences. In between the periods of dreaming, there seems to be other mentation going on. While there is good reason for arguing from the empirical evidence that such mentation is continuously present between episodes of dreaming (Dement, 1965; Rechtschaffen, 1967), the reader need not agree with that viewpoint to follow the main argument that psychological processes are present during all waking and at least most sleeping periods.

The notion of process is a construct. It is an abstraction that is created to help us understand behavior, especially the phenomena relevant to personality. It is of course only one of a number of constructions. For example, some psychologists used to use as a basic concept the notion that a response (behavior) is a function of stimulus and situation. Later it was recognized as more satisfactory to state that a response is a function of stimulus, organism, and situation. In discussions of personality, the construct of process, with its emphasis on temporal sequence, seems even more useful.

Interactions are processes. Thus we can reword our definition of personality to bring in that term. Since the phenomena of the personality domain are processes, personality is the general nature of the processes observed or inferred to be occurring in the person, these processes being stimulated by one or another part of his environment. This definition requires us to determine what the general nature, the general characteristics of these processes are. From all that is observed about a person, the common features are abstracted. The mass of observational data is reduced to the typical or average features, or to other concise descriptive terms.

Not only for studying personality, but also for understanding the measurement of personality, it is helpful to formulate a general picture of a psychological process. Psychological functioning can be looked at as a series of units, each unit being a separate process. Such a process may run its course very rapidly, perhaps in a second, or it may last much longer—for minutes, hours, days. Obviously, processes must overlap in time, with several going on simultaneously.

A process has several aspects. First, at the initiation of the process, there is the present state of the organism. Is the subject asleep or awake, and if awake, how alert is he? Sometimes a particular process may occur only when the subject is in a state that permits it. If the subject is preoccupied with some internal psychological activity or with some preemptive external stimuli, he may not receive and attend to a stimulus that would otherwise trigger this particular process. A second aspect of the setting is the external situation. The setting in which a person is may abort some processes or even block their occurrence. Usually, the particular setting is associated with particular processes already under way, and these processes may prevent others from occurring: the child fully absorbed in his play or his book may not hear his mother call him.

A process itself has several stages or phases. It is initiated by a stimulus impinging on a person, a stimulus from outside or from within (e.g., a loud noise or a thought). This stimulus is registered. It is perceived and interpreted, it is cognized.

Then the person begins to work on the interpreted input. He determines its personal meaning for him. Very commonly, he evaluates it as good or bad. During this assessment, a feeling tone may develop; the reaction to the stimulus is likely to have emotional features. From all this processing, a desire or motive is likely to emerge: he may want more of the experience generated by the stimulus or he may want to terminate the experience. He may also want to obtain some other experience.

Such desire may lead to an intention or plan. He may then initiate action to execute the plan. This overt action can be analyzed in several ways. The behavioral act can be described in terms of its expressive aspects, its style, its coordination. More important is the evaluation of the adequacy of the act. Does it carry out his intention? Such an evaluation can be made by another person who decides whether our subject accomplished his purpose, had the effect he wanted, solved the problem, or whatever. The act can also be evaluated by the subject himself. If he finds he was not successful, he can start a new process leading toward action that is more adequate for his purpose.

A process need not run this full course. A man may look at a passing girl and momentarily enjoy the sight, before he shifts his attention to some other stimulus. Or he may look at her and, recognizing her as a friend, greet her as they pass. Or, according to some reports, he may decide at once that he wants to marry her, thus initiating a much longer process.

We shall leave the general discussion of process in this incomplete form. The preceding exposition has been discursive and not rigorously systematic. We have not indicated each phase precisely or shown how one identifies the end of each phase and the beginning of the next. While a more comprehensive development of the concept is needed, such a treatment belongs in a volume on personality. For the purposes of this volume, it is sufficient to propose and apply the general notion of process and to analyze process into phases that help us to understand personality phenomena and their measurement. We shall assume that, in most instances, a given phase has been preceded by specific prior phases. The several phases will be taken as these:

1. Attending to a stimulus.
2. Cognizing and interpreting it.
3. Determining its meaning or significance for the subject.
4. Reacting to that meaning with feeling (affect).
5. Wanting to modify the experience.
6. Acting to execute the want or plan.
7. Evaluating the success of the action.

IMPLICATIONS OF THE PROCESS CONCEPT

The concept of a general process has many values. One is its constant reminder that personality deals with aspects of transient phenomena—experiences and actions. Another is its utility as a framework for organizing the many kinds of variables of interest to personologists. One may study what a person attends to: Does he attend to color or to form? Then there are cognitive styles: Can a person cognize an object or judge it independently of the field in which it is perceived? Does he tend to categorize things in broad or narrow terms? The next phase of the process involves interests and values: What objects and experiences interest a person, what does he value highly? What emotions or feeling tones does he tend to have?

Motivation refers to the directions toward which a person tries to change his experienced interactions with his world. Classifications of motives are based on kinds of experiences sought and kinds avoided. In the next phase, action, several classical personality topics enter. Within temperament are such matters as the speed of reactions and actions. The quality of instrumental acts is considered in studies of expressive movements and style.

Finally, there are the evaluations of actions. The field of intelligence, abilities, and aptitudes enters here. Given a task and a consensus on its solution, the performance of a subject can be objectively evaluated. But note that much of the work on perceptual and cognitive style also involves evaluation of the presumed adequacy of these phases of the general process. Such work often assesses the accuracy of the subject's perceptual judgments or the adequacy of his cognitive discriminations (see Gardner *et al.*, 1959).

Evaluations of actions are also made by the actor, the subject. They contribute to his perception of himself, and especially to his feeling of competence.

Thus the variables we wish to measure refer to aspects of phases in processes. The critical consideration from the standpoint of this analysis is the need to establish that the processes are sufficiently similar among subjects to permit comparable observations to be made. If we wish to order subjects according to their interest in a particular class of objects, we must present the same objects to all subjects and we must establish that the objects have the same meaning for everyone (aside from any effects of the given interest variable on such meaning). In addition, we have to make sure that the subjects are in similar states and in similar settings when we observe their degree of interest in the class of objects.

More generally, when we measure a variable referring to one phase of the general process, we have to be confident that the preceding phases have occurred in each subject and that these phases have been essentially the same. Otherwise, differences in observations or scores may not be attributable to the variable being studied. To give an obvious example, when we evaluate an ability, we must assume that each subject's responses stemmed from an intention to give the correct answer to each stimulus problem set before him.

Implicit in this discussion is the idea that psychological measurement involves processes. To measure a person, we use his responses to stimuli. We may simply observe his responses to natural stimuli or we may provide a set of stimuli. A psychological test is a task given to a subject, the task of responding in a particular way to each stimulus, each question or item. There is one process for the test as a whole, in which the instructions given the subject are expected to generate a motive to carry out the task set for him. But within this larger process, there is a separate process initiated by each stimulus item, each such process beginning when a subject attends to the item and ending when he turns his attention to the next item. These processes in testing will be examined more closely later (see Chapter 10).

As suggested earlier, much of the content of each process is available only to the subject. These are part of his experiences. He is aware or potentially aware of most of them. While these experiences are not directly available to others, his actions are in the public domain; others can observe changes in his posture or locus in space (his overt movements), his gestures and facial expressions. (They can, of course, observe his facial expressions better than he can.) So while the subject can experience his actions, others can too. We can also group with actions the physiological and neural changes that can be observed with appropriate recording equipment. Again, while the person can be aware that his heart is beating faster, he is less likely to be aware that his skin conductance has changed, and is very unlikely to experience change in finger volume or in electroencephalographic activity. (That there may be internal states imperfectly correlated with such changes is not relevant to this discussion.) There are, then, some contents that are directly available only to the subject and others that are directly available only to others. The phenomena pertinent to personality are perceived by at least two kinds of observers.

Just as minute particles in physics can be studied by observing the track they leave in a bubble chamber, so phases of a psychological process can be studied indirectly in various ways. An observer can often infer the nature of a process in a subject from the subject's behavior, i.e., from his overt actions. We can also ask our subject to take a test that will, we assume, produce certain processes in him, processes that can in part be described from his responses. The various modes of observing personality, of measuring aspects of these processes, are analyzed in Chapter 5.

Let us turn now from this conceptual analysis of what is being measured to the operations of measurement itself. How do we select the phenomena to be observed and measured? What are the components in the total procedure of measurement?

Extracting Order from Chaos

"Of course, all our knowledge has its origins in singular statements—the particular observations of particular individuals. One of the big, perplexing questions in the philosophy of science is how we are able to go from such singular statements to the assertion of universal laws" (Carnap, 1966, pp. 4–5).

This short volume cannot deal with the whole of that big question. It is concerned only with the way we go from observations to indices relevant to concepts, and in the other direction, from concepts to subconstructs to measuring operations permitting us to make pertinent observations.

In this discussion, the approach will be formal and atheoretical; it is not restricted to any one substantive theory. The topic is how we go from the infinite variety of phenomena pertinent to personality to the selected observations used in basic research. The first step is the identification of an area in this vast domain, an area of particular relevance to some concept or theoretical problem. This basic step will be discussed in Chapter 6. Here we shall present a methodological analysis, assuming that we have identified some collection of responses relevant to the construct and a category of stimuli relevant to such responses.

The extraction of order from the chaotic mass of pertinent phenomena is done by coping in some fashion with the various extraneous influences on the behavior we wish to observe and measure. One strategy is to establish conditions that minimize the effects of these outside influences. With this approach, we do not observe the phenomena as they occur in nature, but instead we induce the phenomena under controlled conditions. In effect, we try to study rather pure instances of the phenomena, but we must recognize that the attempt to eliminate these unwanted influences may introduce other effects. At the least, it may have the consequence that the phenomena we are observing are different in some respect from those we originally set out to study. The other strategy is to have these extraneous influences cancel each other out. In principle, if we observe a particular reaction under all possible circumstances and then average our observations, we can arrive at an index that is largely free of any systematic bias. Such an approach has to assume that no one influence is present a disproportional amount of time, i.e., that it does not affect so many of the observations that it introduces a distortion in our average index.

Available to the personologist is an infinite number of potential observations. How can he identify the phenomena he can use effectively for measurement? As we have seen, what we are dealing with are processes, ongoing interactions between the subject and his environment. In these processes, the subject perceives and reacts to a stimulus from the external world, from his body, or from his experience or mentation (e.g., an idea or an association). These stimuli are quite diverse in form, pattern, intensity, and meaning. Since a difference between two stimuli in any one aspect can potentially be associated with a difference in reaction, the processes initiated by stimuli can be equally diverse.

Confining our attention to the consequences of a single stimulus, we see that it may be followed by one or more incipient processes, perhaps getting to the interpretation and feeling stage, perhaps going on to the stage of desires or intentions to modify the interaction. Suppose a person says to you, "Why did you do that?" His remark may irritate you if you feel he had no business asking. It may also make you realize that he may have perceived your earlier action differently from the way you had intended him to see it, and you may decide to try to clarify the misunderstanding. From this single stimulus, one or more overt acts may be manifested. You may reply with irritation, "And why not?" But you may also tell him why you did it. Thus the phenomena of interest to the student of personality have tremendous variety; also, in the natural state of things, a single stimulus can lead to several reactions or processes in a single subject. It is also apparent that the same stimulus frequently initiates discriminably different processes in different subjects: a picture of a new sports car may stimulate one fellow to consider buying one while another decides that his present car is superior and a third ignores the picture; an advertisement for a dress may lead one girl to consider buying it and another to wish she had the figure to wear it, while a young man may wonder how his girl friend would look in it.

How can we measure, given this complexity? Fortunately, some processes are somewhat simpler, and many processes pertinent to personology are of the simpler sort. For example, some stimuli have a preemptive impact on a subject (e.g., a picture related to his hobby or a picture of a concentration camp), and he will react to such a stimulus in a way that is consistent over time. Hence one possibility is to look for regularities in the responses of a subject and then determine the stimuli eliciting these regular responses. The next step is to compare persons with respect to such response and stimulus regularities.

A paradigm for response regularity is the startle response. Some decades ago, Landis and Hunt (1939) studied the patterning in responses to an unexpected gunshot a few feet away. They found a general pattern of muscular contractions producing a change in posture that might be interpreted as getting set for physical action. While this complex reaction is much the same from person to person, subjects may differ in the extent or intensity of the reaction.

Unfortunately, there do not seem to be many such preemptive stimuli. To be sure, there are disasters such as shipwrecks and floods, but these fortunately do not impinge on everyone. Also, their effects on people can usually be observed only in retrospect. Even more serious is the fact that such stimuli cannot be found for most of the important concepts in personality; when they do exist, it is rarely true that reactions to such stimuli can be taken as adequate and comprehensive indices for the given variable.

Let us look at the problem somewhat more systematically. Each observation involves a *subject* who is in a *state* and in a *setting* or immediate environment, and who makes a *response* to a *stimulus*. (For a similar analysis, see Cattell's data box [Cattell, 1966].) To say the same thing in terms of process, each observation evaluates the action resulting from a process initiated by a stimulus, the process occurring within a subject in a psychological state and affected more or less by preceding stimuli and by less potent stimuli in his immediate experience. This latter formulation describes the matter in general psychological terms. The former statement provides an analysis indicating the components that, being most pertinent to measuring, will be examined in the following sections. While these sections are written from the viewpoint of an experimenter trying to measure, later discussions will explore the processes occurring in subjects being measured.

The objective is to obtain from such observations useful indices for each subject. The general term "index" is used in this volume to refer to a score or other measurement value assigned to a particular subject; it indicates how much of the pertinent attribute or concept the subject is assumed to possess, on the basis of his observed reactions. It is the value that is utilized in subsequent statistical analyses of relationships, analyses determined by the experimental question initially posed by the investigator.

For an index to be useful, we must be able to say something about the circumstances under which it was obtained. For instance, we may want to say that this index is the average response of the subject to this stimulus in this setting, the average being computed from a number of observations made over several minutes or several weeks. In this instance, we generalize over the time period covered by the observations; we may extrapolate beyond it, to a year ago or five years hence, if our knowledge about the variable appears to permit such an inference.

But without considerable knowledge about the single stimulus and about the particular setting, we cannot confidently extrapolate to other stimuli and other settings. This brings out an important feature of psychological measurement: most of the indices from measuring procedures are averages or other composites based on sets of observations. Usually the single observation is not considered sufficiently dependable to enter into statistical analyses. Even more critical is the fact that we must determine both the extent to which the observation represents our abstract concept and the degree to which it is influenced by other factors before we can decide on its adequacy for our purposes. These are the concerns of reliability and validity, technical topics to be examined more fully later (Chapter 8).

Dependability (reliability) is a property of measurements that is assessed empirically by determining the extent to which measurements agree with each other. Thus we can determine the dependability of a procedure for measuring heights of persons by repeating the operations several times. If the observed values agree quite closely, we consider the procedure a good one and may in the future be content with applying it once to each subject. There are, of course, norms for assessing dependability. In measuring individual differences, we compare the variation among repeated observations of each subject with the variation among the composite indices of the group of subjects. If the variation within each subject is substantially less than that between subjects, we call the procedure and the resulting indices highly reliable. Variation is usually measured by variance (the average of the squared deviations of observations from their mean), and a standard procedure for estimating reliability uses the statistical technique of analysis of variance (see McNemar, 1962).

But consider how we measure height: the subject removes his shoes and stands erect against a straight edge. Shoes are removed for two reasons: first, since the heels of shoes vary in thickness, they would introduce a random source of error (unwanted variance from irrelevant factors) into our measurements; second, even if all shoe heels were the same height, we would probably want to measure people's heights without their shoes or subtract this universal heel height from our observations to eliminate the constant bias in the measurements we would otherwise obtain.

Still another aspect of measuring heights should be noted. The observations obtained under the standardized procedure of having subjects stand up straight and as tall as possible would not agree with observations obtained when subjects were just standing still under ordinary conditions. Since most subjects do not stand erect at all times, the measurements obtained under ordinary circumstances would tend to be lower than those in the standardized procedure. Furthermore, they would be more variable. The same subject may stand straighter in the morning than after a day's work. Hence measurements of height are taken under standardized conditions that are not representative of everyday conditions, and in fact standardized observations are systematically biased upward. On the other hand, standardized measurements of height are more dependable than those taken under nonstandardized conditions, since they are less affected by the subject's state of alertness or fatigue, his mood, etc. Finally, note that people know when their height is being measured formally; their awareness and cooperation are prerequisites for the standardized operations. Even if we tried to measure heights under more natural conditions, subject awareness would probably make most subjects stand up straighter than they ordinarily do, just as a person tends to modify his facial expression when he sees that someone is taking a picture of him.

Many aspects of measuring height have parallels in the measurement of personality. Awareness of being measured may lead the subject to straighten up psychologically, to respond in a socially desirable way that will bias the resulting measurements. More generally, measurement under natural conditions would permit the obtained indices to be affected by many irrelevant influences, such as mood and recent experiences. (See the section on ideal measurement in Chapter 7.) Hence we usually measure under standardized conditions, conditions that generate data that are likely to be systematically biased when compared to observations under natural conditions, but which have higher degrees of such important properties as dependability and freedom from extraneous influences.

But let us return to the problem of going from single observations to indices. We want our indices to be determined as completely as possible by one source of variance, the variable being assessed. Conversely, we want to minimize or even eliminate contributions from all other sources. From the preceding discussion, we can see the two strategies open to us. We can institute measurement conditions that keep out extraneous factors. For example, we measure intelligence by obtaining a sample of intellectual performance in the absence of distractions such as interesting TV programs. Alternatively, when we cannot manipulate the experimental conditions to eliminate such influences, we can try to obtain observations under varied conditions, so that we may reasonably hope that the extraneous influences affecting one observation will not affect several others. Thus we can measure vocabulary by using words drawn randomly from a complete list such as a dictionary, rather than taking the words from a single book on philosophy, engineering, or art.

THE SUBJECT AND HIS STATE

Whatever analyses of indices we may plan to perform, we obviously need one index or measurement for each subject, even though this aim requires us to maximize the dependability and sufficiency of our obtained value for any particular subject, and although this orientation may increase the difficulty of our task (as discussed in Chapter 2). Of course, we are not trying to measure "the subject," even though we may speak elliptically in such terms. In any measuring operation we are trying to measure an attribute of the functioning of the subject, an attribute of his experience or of his behaving. We are looking for an average or typical value of that attribute, a value representing well the distribution of values for that attribute over some large and usually unspecified population of instances of such experiencing or behaving.

Even when the external environment is precisely the same at different points in time, the living organism cannot be thought of as "the same." On the one hand, preceding experiences leave their effects, which may be large or small. On the other hand, the organism may be in different states at different times. The state of the subject is one component of observations that is frequently ignored. By "state" we mean the degree of his freshness or fatigue, his alertness or sleepiness, his mood as affected by recent experiences, etc. Such states change over time, but it is impractical to measure a subject at so many points in time that the effects of states will tend to balance out. Hence we try to set up conditions so that the subject's state will make little or no difference. For example, the task and the stimuli can be made so compelling that the subject will respond pretty much the same way regardless of his state. Thus for most variables, we seek indices that reflect the strength of the variable when it is not significantly affected by the transient conditions in subjects.

Another way of looking at it is to say that we are looking for stable behaviors, for response dispositions that are consistent from time to time under objectively identical conditions. When we observe high stability of responses, we can assume that the responses are determined by the various components in the total situation: the setting, instructions, and stimuli, all of which we have controlled. Conversely, we can assume that the responses are not affected by the state of the subject since we postulate, with good reason and with some evidence, that such states do change from time to time.

Studies of variability and stability of responses indicate that stable responses can be obtained when the setting is structured, when the stimulus is structured and meaningful for a person, and when he has a practiced way of coping with the task as he sees it. (For a more extended analysis, see "The Inherent Variability of Behavior," Fiske, 1961b.) Many instrumental acts are highly stable, such as the way a person writes, speaks, and walks. Also, in standardized testing, it is possible to find hundreds or thousands of test items to which a person will give the same response on repeated trials, items for assessing intelligence, interests, attitudes, and even some personality variables. But the acts or responses that are stable for one person are not necessarily stable for others. Some people's views of presidential candidates, for instance, are quite fixed while the views of others may undergo marked shifts (as many did in the months preceding the 1968 election). Such a person might vote or reply to an opinion poll interviewer differently one week then he did the last. (As will be shown in Chapter 9, a major source of stability in test responses is the distance between the subject's position on the variable measured by the test and the item's position, the amount of the variable required to answer it positively. On a test in arithmetic, a subject repeatedly will give correct answers to items that are very easy for him, which are far below his level of achievement, and will give wrong answers regularly to items requiring more knowledge than he has; but on an item near his level, he will sometimes get it right and sometimes not. This effect has been clearly demonstrated by Tyler (1968) in personality tests. Although no one seems to have done so, it should be possible to apply this principle fruitfully in test construction. The items could be selected to cover the full range of possible endorsement values so that most subjects would respond consistently over time to most items, producing more stable data than are typically obtained by standard tests.)

Another difficulty in attempting to maximize stability of responses is that stable responses tend to be associated with variables that are of limited theoretical interest (such as psychomotor attributes or stimuli which generate responses that are relatively consistent from person to person and therefore are unimportant as far as individual differences are concerned, as are items about common knowledge or items referring to strongly indoctrinated cultural perceptions). But this difficulty can be overcome. With ingenuity and effort we can reach the objective of controlling the effect of the subject's state on the observations; we can identify observations that involve responses that are stable over time, so that the index derived from the observations will be stable. Thus each subject will tend to be assigned the same index on different trials and will tend to maintain his relative standing in the group; variance within any person over time will be small compared to variance among persons.

THE SETTING, THE CONDITIONS FOR MEASUREMENT

The setting obviously can affect behavior: jokes are appropriate at parties but not at funerals; spontaneous remarks and accounts of medical experiences occur more frequently in small talk among friends than in job interviews. The setting also affects the responses to tests. Members of street gangs, persuaded to come into a university building to take tests for research purposes, may indicate opinions and values that differ from those they express in their usual environment. It is impossible to observe a subject under varied sets of conditions selected to sample systematically those in which he usually functions. Furthermore, most psychological measurement requires special conditions, one of which is that the subject knows that he is being tested. While he may or may not have much idea about the exact variables being measured, he usually has some general notion. (See Chapter 10.) The standard way of handling this matter is to seek to develop a setting that will have minimal effect on the measurements, i.e., a setting that will not bias the subjects' responses in any particular direction. Actually, it would do no harm if each subject's responses were biased the same amount by the given setting. Most psychological measurement yields indices that are relative, which indicate the subject's position in some group, rather than being in absolute terms of distance from a zero point, as in measurements of people's height. Unfortunately, individual differences appear in such biasing factors: some subjects react more strongly to the setting than others, and these differences in extent of bias are themselves difficult to assess accurately.

How can we tell whether the setting has affected the measurements? Frequently it is possible to demonstrate such an effect; e.g., we can change one aspect of the setting and see whether that affects the group's average response, or whether the new measurements correlate with the old ones as highly as do measurements from a complete repetition of the original conditions. This would be a straightforward experimental study manipulating the setting. In contrast, it is not possible to establish directly that the setting has no effect, just as it is impossible to establish rigorously the null hypothesis (e.g., that there is no difference between two groups on a variable).

Clearly it is possible only to develop relevant empirical evidence in favor of the conclusion that there is no difference. For example, if our variable is measured in a setting common to several other variables, we may determine that it does not correlate more positively with these other variables than it should. In addition, we can try to show that our measurements in this setting do show appropriate (expected) covariation with other measurements derived from different measurement procedures and different settings.

THE TASK SET FOR THE SUBJECTS

In the preceding paragraphs, the term "setting" is implicitly defined as referring to the general context in which the subject finds himself: the place with its physical characteristics and the other people present. A common setting aids in making observed behaviors comparable and comparisons meaningful. Another way to make behavior more systematic by enhancing comparisons between responses of subjects is to induce all subjects to undertake the same task. Persons working toward the same objective behave more similarly than persons pursuing individual goals. Such a shared goal could be subsumed under the general term "setting." In analyzing measurement, however, it is important to keep the two distinct, because they function in somewhat different ways: the general setting usually affects responses indirectly (and minimally in the ideal case), while the task set for all subjects is an essential factor intended to contribute to the determination of all responses of all subjects.

Comparability of measurements is maximized when all subjects are given a task they understand, a task with an objective they feel able to pursue. In effect, this means that they feel they have criteria for selecting their responses, criteria that enable them to feel confident that a particular response is the one most suitable for the task as they understand it. In measuring ability, we ask subjects to give the right answers, and they are usually quite willing to do their best in carrying out this task. (Comparability is perfect when all subjects give right answers to all items, but such evident agreement on the task and on its execution does not give us the individual differences among subjects' scores that we seek.) In contrast, subjects taking a personality questionnaire are asked to mark the answer that is correct for them. Not only are they often uncertain what that answer is, but also, underlying their testing behavior, there may be more or less unwillingness to provide such revelations about themselves. (See Fiske and Butler, 1963.)

Another significant difference between the tasks used for measuring ability and those used to measure personality is that subjects are familiar with having their intellectual performance evaluated. At the very least, they are well practiced in getting set to perform as well as they can. In contrast, the everyday experience of subjects includes few occasions in which they are asked candidly to describe themselves and their behavior systematically, although most college students have often thought about what they are like. As a consequence we would expect just what we find, that responses to intelligence tests are typically more stable than those to personality tests.

In making the setting and the task objectively similar for all subjects, we are making the simple and plausible assumption that they will have the same meanings for all subjects. This remains just that, an assumption, unless there is some internal evidence in the subjects' responses or other information (such as posttest inquiries) that supports our expectation. At the present stage of development, an approach built on this assumption and backed by more or less direct evidence is the only way we can proceed. (At some time in the future we may find we can devise methods for adapting the setting and the task to each individual so that their meanings are more subjectively comparable from subject to subject even though they may take different overt forms, but that degree of refinement is far beyond our current level of sophistication.)

THE STIMULI

In extracting methodological order from the chaos of uncontrolled observations of personality phenomena, the stimulus has received major attention, and quite appropriately so. On the one hand, the stimulus must be controlled so that comparable observations can be made on different subjects. On the other hand, by maximizing the contribution of the stimulus to the obtained variance of responses, we minimize the contributions of the setting and other sources whose effects we wish to reduce.

Ideally, we want to identify stimuli associated with invariant responses. We would prefer that an individual subject always give the same response to each stimulus every time he experiences it. Only a small proportion of the infinite number of stimuli in people's lives meet this requirement, and many of these elicit the same responses in many or in all subjects. Again, among those that elicit responses that are consistent for each subject but differ among subjects, many are of trivial interest to personology (e.g., the question: "What is your full name?"). Hence we have to settle for less than the ideal in our search for stimuli that elicit highly stable responses in most subjects.

But no one stimulus is sufficient for measuring most personality constructs. Theories of personality involve broad constructs that cannot be represented by reactions to a single stimulus. And even when we analyze a large, general construct into smaller ones covering smaller areas, we do not feel we can rely on a single stimulus until we have established its suitability empirically. Whatever our *a priori* expectations and deductions about it, we may find that our chosen stimulus simply is not sufficient because it is too specific or because responses to it are determined in part by some irrelevant variable. Hence we look for sets of stimuli to which an individual will give responses that are relatively stable and at the same time sufficiently distinct from those of most fellow subjects to be differentiating. An index of an individual's performance is obtained by combining several of his reactions into a single score, typically by counting those that are of the same kind (e.g., are correct or indicative of the attribute being measured), or by computing their mean. Such combining of responses assumes that they do fall into the same class; if they do not, we cannot interpret the resulting index in a sensible way. Test theory, statistical techniques for analyzing response data, and techniques for constructing tests are all directed at coping with this problem. While this vast topic will be considered in more detail later (Chapter 8), we can indicate some essential aspects here.

In constructing a test, we must solve the central problem of identifying good items (stimuli). Suppose we have written a number of items that seem reasonably good to us. Or perhaps we have combed through instruments developed by others and found suitable items, or items we can rewrite for our purposes. How can we select the best items? If a good measure of our target variable already exists, our problem is simple to solve: we identify those items that are closely related to that measure, which is called a criterion. For example, suppose we wish to measure masculinity, and we assert that masculinity as we conceive it is much stronger in men than in women, on the average. We can select our items by finding those that men and women tend to answer most differently. ("Do you like to read articles on the latest fashions for women?" "Do you like to watch ball games on TV?")

Unfortunately, for most of the attributes of personality in which we are interested, there is no adequate criterion available to us. Where can we find acceptable measures of social adjustment, creativity, and dominance? Lacking such criterion measures, we have to use bootstrap operations: we have to find, among our tentative list of items, those that satisfy certain general requirements for good items and those that can be claimed to be suitable on indirect bases. For example, we can require our items to be ones that subjects tend to answer the same way if they are tested at two separate times. We can also require that subjects do not object to any item as being so ambiguous that they cannot tell what it means. Other evidence for suitability can be obtained from examining the correlation of each item with the total score on our preliminary test. If we assume that most of our tentative items do measure our target trait of dominance, then the higher any one item correlates with the total score for all the items, the better it measures dominance. A variation of this procedure is to obtain the correlations between all the pairs of items and then select those items that have the highest average correlations with other items.

These latter operations are intended really to make our test a good measure of whatever it is that it measures. In standard terms, such a test is reliable or dependable: we can count on it to measure well. But note that these operations do not tell us whether our test is actually measuring the attribute in which we are interested. Even though the items appear to be appropriate, they may in fact be measuring something else. The validity of a test is the degree to which it does measure the attribute at which it is aimed. We shall have more to say about validity later (in Chapter 8). For now, we can briefly note that apparent adequacy or face validity is not considered sufficient. If we do have an adequate criterion, we can assess validity in terms of the correlation between our test and that criterion. In many instances we have to assess validity by using a complex array of data to answer two questions: Does our test correlate with other purported measures of the attribute and with measures of similar or related attributes as highly as we predict it should, on theoretical or logical grounds? Conversely, does it have little or no relationship with variables that we believe are distinct and independent of our attribute? For instance, we might predict that dominance should be related to activity or energy but not to intelligence. And certainly it should not be related to any disposition to mark the "yes" answers on questionnaires.

Let us close this sketchy introduction to reliability and validity, two central concepts in test theory, and return to the topic of the item as responded to by a subject. This topic is important because it is the basic unit on which psychological measurement is built and because the crucial consideration is the relationship between this unit and the concept to be measured. For the moment, however, we are looking at the problem of reducing the heterogeneity of personality phenomena by identifying similar stimuli. This topic has a long history: for example, in a classic paper Heinrich Klüver (1936) noted that stimuli can be called equivalent if they evoke the same response. In most personality tests, the items are certainly not equivalent stimuli for different subjects: a typical mean intercorrelation between items is only .05. Only in carefully structured tests does this mean value rise to better than .20. These mean correlations between items are typically ignored. The test constructor cites the reliability of his total test, which can be interpreted as the expected correlation between that test and a hypothetical equivalent test. But high test reliabilities, even .90 or better, do not solve the problem of heterogeneity: they merely indicate that, by taking enough items—perhaps a hundred or more—it is possible to derive a composite index that has good dependability.

Note that we are looking here at covariation among items in the same test, taken under standard instructions and in a common setting. It will be obvious that responses to any one such item will covary even less with responses to some stimulus outside the testing situation. The problem of finding test items that will covary to a substantial degree is exceedingly difficult, and the difficulty is increased by the fact that we want such items to provide a sound basis for estimating the strength of some attribute of each subject's reactions to many other stimuli pertinent to the particular construct.

THE RESPONSES

In the last few pages, we have been looking at various determinants of responses and considering how to control them or how to minimize their effects so that the data for personality measurement will be more orderly than the phenomena observed in the natural condition. In that setting, we observe an enormous variety of responses: rarely are any two responses, even of one subject, identical. Fortunately, at any one time we are usually interested only in one selected aspect of the subject's responses. For many variables, we can observe that one aspect and ignore the other attributes of his responses. Thus we may study aspects of his speech in response to a variety of stimuli and situations without concerning ourselves with the content of his messages. Or we may be interested in his messages without regard for their phrasing, intonation, etc.

In much measurement work, the problem of response complexity is solved in a simple way: the test provides the subject with two or more alternative responses among which he chooses on some basis indicated in the test instructions. The subject believes that the only feature of his response that is important is its quality, i.e., which alternative he marks. Usually his belief is correct, because the scoring is based on the location of the mark he makes, not on the graphological characteristics of his checkmark or circle, not on the pressure he applied in making the mark, and not even on the time he took to select his response.

The use of the multiple-choice test format relieves the scorer of the task of judging or rating the subjects' responses, a perennial problem in standardizing free-response tests, tests in which the subjects construct and record their responses. In general, the more unstructured the test, the greater the difficulty in classifying free responses so that one can say that these subjects gave equivalent responses while other subjects gave different responses, indicating, say, a lower strength of the response disposition. Thus scoring the responses to information items on an intelligence test is much easier than identifying, among stories made up for pictures in the Thematic Apperception Test, those with a similar dynamic theme.

But even in multiple-choice tests, there is an assumption that when two subjects make responses that are identical with respect to location— i.e., when they choose the same alternative—the responses mean the same thing to the two of them. This is frequently an erroneous assumption. For example, the alternatives may be chosen to indicate degrees of liking. A response such as "dislike" may have a wide range of meanings for a number of subjects, while "dislike moderately" may have a much smaller range (see Jones and Thurstone, 1955; this topic is developed in Chapter 10).

Here is but one instance of the difficult problem of determining when two responses are equivalent, either two made by one subject or two made by different subjects. In this context, equivalence means that the two responses, or more exactly the values of an attribute of the two responses, can be considered identical and treated as such in deriving some composite index from them. This is usually more difficult than the converse problem of classifying two responses as different. In other words, one can have more confidence in making the judgment of difference than in making the judgment of identity, the judgment that they fall into the same category in the classification scheme being applied to the responses. In multiple-choice tests, the decisions are made simple by providing a number of responses, from which the subject chooses one. Free-response tests provide much more difficulty, since different words may appropriately be judged equivalent while similar words may, in the context of the two subjects' other responses, have to be classified differently.

In classifying responses and even in classifying stimuli, we are faced with a dilemma: the narrower the class, and consequently the more classes we set up, the greater can be the uniformity or homogeneity within each one; but the broader the class, the greater its apparent theoretical significance. Theorists in personology have almost invariably used broad constructs in their search for theoretical understanding. But it is becoming recognized that such constructs cannot adequately be represented by a single index, and it is clear that indices based on more controlled procedures, using stimuli that covary strongly among themselves, have relatively low intercorrelations. As a consequence, it has not been possible to subject theoretical propositions to fully definitive experimental tests. This empirical diversity among indices from various methods is not consistent with the hypothetical theoretical unity. The resolution appears to lie in collaborative efforts by theorists and methodologists, or in work by people who understand the requirements of both theory and measurement, efforts aimed at identifying theoretically significant subconstructs that can be measured adequately so that theories can be empirically tested.

MEASUREMENT AS EXPERIMENTATION

In principle, the task of personology is the same as that of any other science: to find order in the complex phenomena around us. Whenever possible, scientists utilize experiments: they make their observations under conditions in which every extraneous potential influence is minimized or in some way controlled. Personologists must learn how to do this. They must learn how to measure the variables in personality without having their measurements confounded by irrelevant effects (see Fiske and Butler, 1963.) Their objective must be to devise conditions such that all subjects will experience psychological processes leading to responses of the same kind, the responses differing in degree according to the strength of the variable in each of the several subjects.

We can now see that the following tactics contribute to this objective:

1. Making sure that the setting in which the measurements are made has essentially the same meaning for all subjects.
2. Minimizing the extent to which the setting itself contributes variance to the responses.
3. Setting for the subjects a task that is clear and unambiguous, which all subjects can perform, which is acceptable to all of them, and which is inherently so interesting that they will not be distracted from it.
4. Selecting stimuli that have the same inherent meaning for all subjects, i.e., stimuli that, given the setting and the task, will be perceived and interpreted in the same qualitative way by all subjects. Additionally, of course, they must be stimuli to which subjects will respond differently, as a function of their differences on the variable being measured.
5. Devising a response format that will enable subjects to indicate their responses readily and to feel confident that these responses represent what they wish to express, but also one that will permit the personologist to feel confident that each response has a common meaning for all subjects selecting it—and for all subjects rejecting it in favor of some other response.

The reader with some knowledge of general psychology will recognize that the problems of analyzing behavior into units are not those of personology alone. For example, in the work associated with behavior theory and stemming from the contributions of Skinner, similar issues arise. Schoenfeld and Farmer (1970) develop the notion of a behavior stream, which is compatible with the notion of process discussed here. They also consider the questions of how broadly or narrowly a response class should be defined and how exclusions from that class should be defined. They recognize the arbitrary nature of response classifications: for any class of responses, there will always be some nonresponses, observations excluded from that class, which are more similar to responses in that class than are other excluded observations.

CAVEAT

The reader should be reminded that this entire section, like the rest of the book, presupposes a concern for measuring in a theoretical context, such as the testing of conceptual propositions in basic research. The approach was introduced as atheoretical to indicate that it was concerned with the general methodology of controlled measurements, rather than with that most essential part dealing with relationships between operations and concepts (a topic discussed in other chapters). It is pertinent to the empirical study of any theory attempting to explain how and why one personality differs from another.

Some investigators use other approaches. A common practice is to assume uncritically that a test or other procedure that someone has labeled with a trait name is a sufficient measure of that trait when administered in a standard manner. The deficiency in that approach is the failure to consider how much of the trait concept the test measures, and what other influences make contributions to the measurements obtained.

A quite different approach has been advocated and pursued by other investigators who prefer to let the responses speak for themselves, rather than to identify constructs and set out to measure them. Such an investigator starts with behavior that has been recorded in some standardized fashion, such as the responses to some set of inventory items. He then searches for clusters of items that covary among themselves and covary less or not at all with items in other clusters. He may start with a rather general, fairly comprehensive set of items, or he may limit his work to items that fall into some very broadly defined area. By some method such as cluster analysis or factor analysis, he arrives at groups of items that are correlated with hypothetical, abstract dimensions. For example, the personality factors now measured in the 16PF Test (Cattell and Stice, 1957) are refinements of clusters originally formed by analysis of a general pool of items.

Once he has such a set of factors (or dimensions), the investigator seeks to identify each factor by intensive examination of the content in its set of items as contrasted with the content of other items. He may later check his interpretation of the factor by empirical studies of its relationships with other variables. He is, then, letting the items speak for themselves. He is establishing factors or dimensions in terms of their relationships with each other. These become the concepts with which he proceeds to work. Such concepts may or may not be similar to ones that have been identified *a priori* by others. Ordinarily they do have some resemblance to factor concepts obtained by others, but not equivalence.

Unfortunately, the empiricist following this approach tends to work atheoretically, typically being unwilling to speculate and unable to match his factors exactly with contemporaneous constructs developed by others. (An exception is Cattell, whose earliest work was essentially empirical but who later worked on the integration of his findings into the general literature on, e.g., anxiety; see Cattell and Scheier, 1961.) On the other hand, the more theoretically oriented investigator may feel that the factors do not correspond with his concepts, and may therefore ignore these empirical findings and build his own tests, whose psychometric properties may be less satisfactory.

While this lack of interaction between the empirically oriented and the conceptually oriented is highly regrettable from the larger viewpoint of the whole field of personology, it has one source that must not be overlooked. The empiricist typically ignores the major limitation on his findings resulting from restricting his analyses to data from a single orientation or perspective, while the theorist is usually willing to consider observations from varied perspectives. Neither type of worker, it would appear, has fully recognized the significance of the fact that observations from different perspectives are so different in quality and so independent empirically that they should be treated as relevant to separate constructs or subconstructs. These perspectives are the topic of the following chapter.

Summary

Personality is the way a person interacts with his external environment and with his intrapsychic world. In a living person, these interactions or processes are continuously occurring. The general form of such a process can be described. When it starts, the person is in a particular organic and psychological state and in an external situation. The process is initiated when a stimulus impinges on him, and he perceives and interprets it. After determining its personal meaning for him and experiencing some affect, the person may wish to change things, to alter his experience. If he acts on that wish, his actions themselves can be studied and their success can be evaluated by himself or by others. Each kind of personality variable can be seen as related to one aspect of such a general process.

How do we go from the infinite variety of phenomena pertinent for personality to the selected observations used in basic research? Each observation involves a response by a subject who is in some state and in some environment, and who is reacting to a stimulus. To obtain an index for the subject, we average responses, usually over stimuli, but sometimes over trials. To obtain dependable and comparable indices, we standardize measurement conditions. We try to get the subject in a suitable state that will not affect his responses. We make the setting the same for all subjects, and hope it will not affect their responses differentially. We give the subjects a task they all understand, one they can and (we hope) will do. We provide them with stimuli to which all will give responses of the same kind, though of varying strengths or degrees. But all of the several stimuli must elicit the same type of responses so that we can average the several responses of each subject to obtain our index. To make the responses of the subjects comparable, we often provide a set of alternatives from which the subject may choose. Properly carried out, any procedure for measurement is a kind of experiment set up in such a way that extraneous and unwanted influences on the observations are eliminated, minimized, or otherwise controlled.

CHAPTER FOUR

The Observational Data
of Personology

The Natural History of Personality

The study of personality originates in people's thinking about their observations of behavior and their experience. A person may start by recalling what he has observed other people doing and what he has heard them tell him about their experiences—what they saw, how they felt, etc. He may also recall his own experiences—his perceptions, his actions, and his feelings. He may remember clinical material presented in books or by patients he has observed. He may be reminded of characters in novels or plays, or of historical figures.

In such thinking, the content utilized by one person is not identical with that utilized by another. Even when two people have observed a third person, their perceptions will differ somewhat. And they will not agree completely on their views of literary or historical figures. Further, if the two consider the behavior of one of them, the person being discussed will often be surprised at the other's perceptions of him. The point is that the naturalistic observations utilized in thinking about personality vary with the observer, and especially with the point of view from which the observations are made.

Although that statement is generally accepted, there are differences of opinion about its significance. Some people say that the differences among observations by several people are simply due to the presence of errors of measurement, and that within such observations there is a core of con-

sensus, there is common variance that can be utilized for scientific work.
An alternative view is that these differences among observations are fundamental. They are systematic rather than random. Hence observations from
different points of view should be treated as different data, not as approximations of identical data.

For present purposes, it is not necessary that we agree exactly on when
data are essentially the same and when they are different. Most psychologists would agree that the data from two sets of questionnaire items are
practically interchangeable if scores derived from the two sets correlate very
highly (.95, or at least above .90). On the other hand, most psychologists
would agree that judgments about likability are not interchangeable when
one set of judgments is made by the subjects themselves and another by
their peers. In this case, we would expect to find systematic differences in
the averages as well as rather low correlations.

The argument for separate consideration of data from each viewpoint is
made here on conceptual or *a priori* grounds. The proposal is supported by
empirical findings: it is generally true that the more dissimilar the viewpoints from which observations are made, the lower the relationship between them. If one prefers, one can decide on an empirical basis when one
will consider two sets of observations to be worth consideration as separate
identities with distinct conceptual status. The proposition being made here
is a conservative one: since a change in any aspect of the procedure by
which personality observations are made can produce a change in the observations, we must accept some specified differences in procedures as producing not only different phenomena but distinctive data. As a starting
point, we shall consider differences associated with perspectives or viewpoints, since these not only produce divergent data but also are more plaus-
ibly seen as independent procedures.

Perspectives

A perspective is a viewpoint from which personality phenomena can be
observed. Each perspective is distinguished by the position or role of the
observer (subject himself, peer, psychologist, etc.) in conjunction with the
particular phenomena or behavior being observed (reactions to test stimuli,
problem-solving, recollections of prior behavior, etc.). The use of any common term, like "perspective," is dangerous in science because the term
may have inappropriate connotations. I am using "perspective" to refer not
just to positions from which an object (such as a large box) may be viewed,
but also to the likelihood that the overall content of the perception may
vary with the viewpoint. Consider the top of a tall mountain. It may be seen

more or less completely from different positions in the surrounding valleys; it may be studied at greater distance from other peaks; it can be seen in full from an airplane flying over it; and it will look still different to a person who stands on it. Thus a change in perspective changes the actual content of the perception and may lead to a different interpretation. Recall the fable of the three blind men feeling various parts of an elephant and making diverse interpretations about his morphology.

ONE OR SEVERAL PERSPECTIVES?

In most other sciences, the problem of multiple perspectives does not exist. The scientists in each of those disciplines have arrived at an unspoken consensus that their data shall consist of observations made by publicly stated operations that are, both in principle and in practice, replicable by any qualified worker in the field. If two scientists working on the same phenomena produce different observational data, they inspect their methods and refine them until they reach acceptable levels of agreement. If two scientists working at different institutions study the same type of phenomena and obtain different data, they also critically examine their procedures to locate the source of disagreement. When two different measuring operations do not agree, each is studied to see what its defects may be. Alternatively, the conclusion may be that the two procedures are not measuring the same variable. But all such methodological refinement is within the same basic orientation: the collection of observations by operations in which the identity of the particular observer is irrelevant. That is, in most sciences, the observer is interchangeable with other observers because his observations are not accepted as data unless they agree with those of other observers. There is only one perspective, and within that viewpoint the observer's identity does not affect the observations.

In contrast, personology does not have any one accepted orientation or viewpoint. Recall from the first chapter the discussion of the inventory approach. Inventories and similar techniques are used in research on self-concepts and on feelings or affects. In this work, the perspective is that of the subject. Personology also relies heavily on the clinical approach, especially when unconscious conflicts and motives are being studied. Here the perspective is that of the expert who makes observations of the subject's present behavior during interviews and projective tests or in other settings. The systematic observations of assessment programs, also mentioned in Chapter 1, likewise require the perspective of experts.

There are still other perspectives, including observations of performance under favorable conditions when one is interested in determining capabilities, and psychophysiological observations. While a particular perspective may clearly be the most appropriate one or even the only relevant one for a given theoretical problem, there are circumstances in which several perspectives may be pertinent.

For example, in studying achievement, an investigator may obtain from a subject (S) a self-report on his achievement orientation and a report on his past achievements; he may determine whether S shows a preference for achievement-related material to which he is exposed in the experimental room, he may also observe S's capacity to stay with a problem until he solves it; he can ask friends of S whether he appears to be achievement-oriented; he can follow a well-known technique, originating with McClelland (McClelland *et al.,* 1953), and get S to make up stories about pictures like those of the Thematic Apperception Test, then have experts score the stories for achievement imagery (experts can also be used in other ways, such as clinical interviews); finally, he could devise methods for determining whether S's physiological processes changed in any way when he was exposed to achievement-arousing stimuli (e.g., do his pupils enlarge when he sees a picture of the Nobel medal or of someone winning a championship?).

These various perspectives may or may not yield similar observations (e.g., see Weinstein, 1969). If they do not, is one to be preferred, or does each refer to a distinct definition? Since the various perspectives on achievement produce rather independent data with limited or no interrelationships, the question has a more obvious answer: fantasy need for achievement and self-reported need for achievement must be considered as separate variables; in addition, actual achieving and the need for achievement are clearly worth separate conceptual status.

It should be recognized that the indices obtained from each perspective are, in principle, quite objective in that the procedures by which they were produced can be described and, in many cases, replicated. For example, an experimenter may administer a form of a personality inventory to a group, and three weeks later another experimenter may administer the same or a parallel form of the inventory to the same group. The correlations between the objective indices, the scores obtained on the two occasions, can be very high, even though both sets of indices are based on data produced by the subjects from their perspective. Hence there can be a high degree of scientific consensus that the derived indices are the measuring indices obtained for these subjects by administering this inventory under the given set of testing conditions. Indices obtained by procedures derived from other perspectives can also be shown to be objective with regard to the operations employed to obtain them and replicable to a high degree. If each member of a team of fifteen co-workers rates every other member on cooperativeness, we find that the mean ratings made by half the group will agree closely with the mean ratings made by the other half.

The peculiar feature of personology is not that such indices are obtained in some esoteric way that cannot be spelled out or replicated; it is that personological indices may appropriately be based on observations from several perspectives. In addition, the correlation between indices based on diverse perspectives will be limited and may be essentially zero. To use the examples of the preceding paragraph, the co-worker ratings on cooperativeness would correlate only moderately with inventory scores based on the subjects' self-descriptions; certainly the relationship would be distinctly lower than that between the two sets of ratings by co-workers or between the two forms of the inventory.

PERSPECTIVES AND THEORIES

Each investigator asks questions relevant to his own interests. What researchers and students often fail to realize is that these differences in interest lead to different theories and hypotheses (see Mehrabian, 1968), and also to dissimilar kinds of data. The use of broad general terms, such as common trait labels, leads one to think that everyone is talking about the same thing, when a moment's thought reveals that each is talking about it from a special point of view. Somehow the failure to find empirical evidence for congruence among individualistic concepts or even among individualistically constructed measurement operations has not forced personologists to recognize and understand the basic difficulty caused by differences in both the personal interests and the diverse perspectives of investigators.

This analysis of perspectives enables one to see the pertinence of any particular procedure and also its limited domain of relevance. But these perspectives correspond rather closely to various pictures of personality formulated by theorists. There is a picture or model, usually identified as "self theory," concerned with the way a subject sees his experience, himself, and his behavior. George Kelly (1955) has explored this approach systematically. Gordon Allport (1937) also emphasized this conception of personality, for which the corresponding perspective is, of course, the self-report.

Another model or perspective on personality is that of psychoanalysis and dynamic psychology. The clinically oriented personologist, using what S tells him, his observations of S, and S's responses to projective tests, constructs a picture of S which emphasizes inferred inner drives and conflicts. Thus Henry Murray (1959) uses self-reports as grist for the clinician's mill; he feels that only an expert can tell what S is really like, what he values, etc. David Rapaport (1959) also relied on expert judgment. His primary data were the observations of experts because he believed that only they know what to observe and how to construe or interpret it.

Personality is sometimes seen as adequacy of functioning. Thus Witkin *et al.* (1962) ask whether S can differentiate figure from field, as in the

Embedded Figures or Rod and Frame tests. Gardner *et al.* (1959) stress the adequacy of cognitive controls. This view of personality corresponds to the perspective of performance tests.

An abilities conception of personality has been proposed by Wallace (1966, 1967). He argues that, instead of trying to study a person as he typically is, we should determine his capacities; we should see how extreme are the responses he is capable of making. This approach clearly falls in the performance perspective.

Then there is the personality as seen by others, construed from the behavior or the natural products of the subject. Gordon Allport (1937) has utilized this viewpoint, as have also, at times, Rogers (1959) and Cattell (1946, Chapters 8 and 9). The personality they consider is differentiated from that formulated by dynamic clinicians because the latter invoke esoteric concepts while the former stay closer to the language and terminology of the layman.

Although there are workers who utilize other perspectives, such as psychophysiological processes, there do not seem to be distinctive theories of personality extensively worked out for them.

Many personality theorists cannot be fitted neatly into any of these approaches. Allport, Cattell, and many others have used two or more perspectives at one time or another. Maslow (1954) uses observations by experts and ratings of products, as does McClelland (1961) in his societal work on achievement. Newcomb (1959) uses ratings of others and self-reports. But very few attempt to integrate several of the perspectives from which personality phenomena can be seen.

A major implication can be drawn from this discussion. The constructs of many theorists are based on their preference for a particular perspective on personality and therefore must be measured by procedures appropriate to that perspective. Getzels (1953) identifies three views: behavioral definition, social stimulus value, and depth; each must be researched by its own set of techniques. Statements from George Kelly's theory (1955) cannot be tested by indices provided by peers or experts; they must be tested with self-report data. But self-reports cannot be directly used to test psychoanalytic propositions. There must be congruence between the orientation of the construct and the perspective involved in the measuring procedure. Some constructs can be approached from several perspectives; others can be directly studied only from one vantage point.

Summary

When several people look at one person, they do not agree exactly on what they see and they usually have somewhat differing views of his personality.

More generally, the phenomena of personality vary with the perspective used. While most sciences require that observations be made by replicable methods, so that the observer's identity is immaterial, personology has a number of domains, each associated with the viewpoint taken by the observer. There is the perspective of S looking at himself, the view of his peers and associates, the perspective of the expert clinician, the psychophysiological approach, and the perspective evaluating S's capabilities.

Theorists have emphasized phenomena observed from a variety of perspectives. Hence the empirical testing of a theory should utilize procedures congruent with the theorist's perspective.

CHAPTER FIVE

The Modes of
Measuring Personality

In the last chapter we saw that personality phenomena are observed pre-scientifically from several points of view, and that these perspectives have been utilized both in theorizing about personality and in studying personality phenomena empirically. While the utilization of a variety of perspectives is an important fact, even more important to the systematic analysis of measuring procedures is the fact that a number of modes are used in the collection of personality data. These modes correspond somewhat to the several perspectives; the differences will be discussed later.

In measuring personality, we use actions, a phase occurring toward the end of the psychological processes taking place in subjects. These actions furnish the data for measurement, the information from which indices are derived. The crucial fact is that this information comes in various forms or modes, as outlined in Table 5.1.

Before considering the separate modes in the table, let us see what the rows mean. Each mode of measuring personality has several aspects or components. First, there is a protocol or data record. For the purpose of measurement, responses are recorded. These responses may be made by S, by an observer (O), or by an instrument. Note that this record of responses is not necessarily a record of the behavior (actions or experiences) on which the responses themselves are based. In self-descriptions, S may base his responses on recollections of earlier behavior. More generally, S records his responses to test items but does not record the contents of the thinking that led to the responses. Examples of data records are the answer sheets for

68

multiple-choice tests, the stories written for TAT cards, responses to Rorschach cards as recorded by O, and the pneumograph tracings indicating heartbeats.

The data record is later analyzed by the experimenter (E) to produce an index for S. E may count the number of responses of a certain kind, such as the number of correct responses on a test of information, or E may average the ratings of several peers. This operation entails the coding or classifying of each response (e.g., as correct). Such classification is a fundamental part of all measurement. In other modes, E may combine several data records, as in averaging the ratings of several raters. Occasionally O produces this index himself; he may be an expert judge whose dependability or agreement with other experts has been established previously. Once in a while the indices are produced by a particular O who, although not an expert, plays a specific or unique role in relation to S—spouse, mother, supervisor, teacher. We see, then, that indices are produced in one of three ways: the first is objectively, mechanically, or clerically, there being no question about the accuracy of the quite overt procedure for obtaining the index from the data record; the second is by an expert with appropriate technical qualifications, and yet his agreement (interchangeability) with other experts must be demonstrated; the third is by a layman whose accuracy and objectivity cannot be established, since there is no one else with the same relationship to S.

In some instances, the procedure may have additional steps. For instance, S's responses to the Rorschach Inkblot Test may be recorded by O and later classified by O to yield scores in a number of categories, indicating the amount of the blot interpreted in each response, the determinant of the response, the type of content, and its frequency in Rorschach records. As a separate step, several of these scores may be combined by a set of statistical rules to obtain a single global index, as in the Klopfer Prognostic Rating Scale (Klopfer *et al.*, 1954, pp. 688–99). Several scores may also be combined judgmentally, as in Beck's method for his Q-sort statements (Beck, 1954). In similar fashion, scores from an MMPI profile may be combined clerically to yield an index or to assign to a type, or they may be the basis for judgmental inferences of trait strength.

We can see that the procedures used to obtain scores—i.e., the chains of events between the original behavior of S and the assignment of an index to him—are quite diverse. At each step, data composed of many bits of information are summarized in a value that contains less total information but which eventually leads to classifications or orderings of the subjects. These procedures may be mechanical, objective, or impersonal; or they may require human judgments or inferences. (See the discussions of these steps in Meehl, 1954, and Sawyer, 1966.)

Table 5.1. Modes of measuring personality

	Mode 1	Mode 2	Mode 3	Mode 4	Mode 5	Mode 6
Mode label	Self description (past)	Current experiencing	Capabilities	Prior behavior	Observation of behavior	Psychophysiology
Data producer	S	S	S	O	O	Instrument
Index producer	E	E	E	O or E	O or E	O or E
Is S aware he is being measured?	Yes	Yes	Yes	No	Yes	Yes
Task given to data producer — S	Report your picture of yourself	Report your immediate experience	Give the correct answer			
Task given to data producer — O				Extract an impression of S from these materials	Give your impression of S	Identify designated psychophysiological responses
Major subclasses	Rating of trait / Report on interests or values / Report on attitudes or usual feelings	Perception / Judgment / Preference / Production of interpretation or story	Content / Operation / Product (as in the structure of intellect)	Identify designated behaviors / Give your impression of S	O questions S / O records S's responses to projective tests / O observes Ss interacting	Breathing / Sweating / Muscle tension / Heart rate / Blood pressure

Typical methods	Questionnaires Self-ratings Biographical inventories Attitude scales	Tests of Perceived movement Category width Figure preference	Tests of Ability Achievement Cognitive style Knowledge of special interest area	Ratings by associates Ratings based on records	Interview Projective tests Situational tests	Pneumograph Psychogalvanometer Cardiograph
Similar familiar experiences	Writing an autobiography	Telling a salesman which item you prefer	College Board examinations Tryouts for activities	Letters of recommendation	Interview for college admission	Blood pressure and pulse rate in medical examination

KEY:
S Subject
O Observer, who may also make judgment or inference
E Experimenter, who processes data record clerically or mechanically

Each column in Table 5.1 portrays a mode. *A mode is a class of procedures for measuring personality.* The classification used here is not a simple one: it centers primarily on the data producer and the task given him; that is, on the kind of measuring operation used. But each class of procedure gets at a particular substantive content, as indicated in a general way in the label and in more specific terms in the several major subcategories identified in the table.

While the table is rather technical and the differences between the several modes are somewhat complicated, everyone has experienced the modes in his everyday living. Some of these methods of observation may have been applied rather crudely, some more precisely, so the following examples should not be taken as illustrating the best procedures in each instance. (See the last row of the table.)

In Mode 1, a subject describes his past behavior. Most of us have written autobiographies, perhaps for an English instructor who wished to get better acquainted with us. Perhaps you have had a pen pal in another country to whom you wrote about yourself in your first letter.

Illustrations of Mode 2 (Current Experiencing) are not so common, but you may have been interviewed in a market research study seeking to learn about people's preferences among alternative packagings for products. Again, in a clothing store, a salesman may ask you which of several suits is closest to what you are looking for, so that he can show you others that may be even closer to what you most prefer.

All college students are familiar with the measurement of capabilities (Mode 3). Everyone has taken some kind of scholastic aptitude test. College Board achievement tests are also used to estimate how well you can perform in academic subjects. In extracurricular activities, there are tryouts for athletic teams, orchestras, and theatrical productions, the purpose being to select those students with the greatest capabilities in the given field.

Mode 4 (Prior Behavior) can be illustrated by letters of recommendation in which someone who has been in a position to judge you writes about his impression of you on the basis of his past observations. Transcripts of high school grades are another form of this mode.

Some students may have had no experience with Mode 5 (Observations of Behavior). Probably the closest approximations are interviews for college admission. Interviews for jobs are less clearly in this mode, since such interviews may be used primarily to obtain factual data and not so much to make a judgment about personality from the subject's behavior in the interview. Some students may have had interviews with psychiatrists, psychologists, or other professional people who were seeking to find out about their personal problems and to judge the desirability of counseling or psychotherapy. These interviews are typical of this mode.

Most students have not had experience with psychophysiological measurement for purposes of measuring aspects of personality (Mode 6). But everyone is familiar with the technique for measuring blood pressure by wrapping a cuff around the upper arm, and everyone has had a doctor or nurse record his pulse rate as part of a medical examination. These were base-line or resting measurements. They were not intended to determine your reaction to having a pretty nurse hold your wrist. In personality measurement, such base-line measurements are made before the presentation of any stimuli, for comparison with later reactions to stimulation.

These various examples bring out the important fact that there is a wide variety of procedures for observing personality, and the additional fact that different ways or modes are suited for different purposes. Table 5.1 is a formal classification of methods used in everyday life as well as in psychological research.

More technical examples of procedures used in each of the first five modes are given in Figure 5.1. (Many of these illustrations have been constructed for this purpose and have not been tested for their adequacy as items for measuring personality.) Under Mode 1 are two questions that might be related to sociability and to impulsiveness, respectively. Among the adjectives, the first and third reflect degrees of assertiveness, while the second and fourth reflect degrees of submissiveness. Under Mode 2, the first item indicates preference for familiar vs. novel similes (Pearson and Maddi, 1966). The next example can be scored for social meanings as opposed to meanings referring to physical properties or objects.

No illustrations seem necessary for aptitude and achievement tests. Hence the examples given for Mode 3 are measures of cognitive styles. The first assesses the ability to ignore the familiar patterns of words and locate the required sequence when it is split up among common words. The second example involves embedded figures. It is a measure of field independence (see Witkin *et al.,* 1962), the ability to perceive or judge accurately in the presence of distracting stimulation.

The rating scales in the example for Mode 4 might be used by an observer who had studied various products of a subject or by a person asked to provide information to be used in evaluating a subject's suitability for a job. Under Mode 5 are two kinds of projective techniques. The first is called "Sentence Completion," the protocols being scored for any of several personality variables. The second is part of a standard test that is generally administered individually, with oral instructions.

The Prior Behavior Mode (Mode 4)

The first basis for identifying and differentiating the modes is the context in which S is acting and responding. One mode involves the naturalistic situation. In this mode, we use the products of S's previous actions taking

Mode 1

Questionnaire:

    Do you like to go to parties?   Yes ? No

    Do you tend to make decisions on the spur of the moment?   Yes ? No

Adjective Checklist (check those adjectives that describe you):

    Forceful

    Obedient

    Dominating

    Meek

Mode 2

Which expression do you like better?

    Busy as a bee

    Busy as an ant

Give a phrase or brief sentence illustrating the meaning of each of the following words:

    friction

    club

    poker

Mode 3

As quickly as you can, indicate where the sequence *the* occurs in each sentence:

    He tried for all he was worth and yet he failed.

    No matter what men think, truth ever triumphs.

Is the first figure part of the second?

	Yes	No
	Yes	No
A	Yes	No

Mode 4

Rate the subject on each trait:

	Low	Below average	Above average	High
Dependable	___	___	___	___
Creative	___	___	___	___
Friendly	___	___	___	___

Mode 5

Complete each sentence with the first thought that comes to your mind:

    I am

    When Tom failed the test, he

  Draw a picture of a person.

Figure 5.1. Sample procedures for five modes

place under circumstances over which we have no control. For example, we can study people by examining their letters (Allport, 1965) or other personal documents (Allport, 1942). We can also examine S's literary or other artistic productions. We can obtain biographical information on his achievements, in school or out. This subclass of information relies on tangible records.

The procedures for obtaining data from such records are basically very simple in design. E asks one or more raters or judges (Os) to examine the material independently and to make a rating or judgment on each variable being studied. The important aspects are that E must define each variable and must indicate the kinds of evidence or clues he wants the judges to use. Usually there is a training period at the end of which E determines the reliability of each O, the extent to which he agrees with other Os or with E himself. If the reliability is satisfactory, O turns to the main body of material; if it is too low, he undergoes further training. When the judging task continues over days or weeks, it is desirable to check the reliability of each O occasionally to make sure that his frame of reference has not changed gradually over time. (For a careful application of such procedures to judgments of recorded psychotherapeutic interviews, see Butler, Rice, and Wagstaff, 1962; Rice, 1965.)

Note that no standardized instruments are used in such work. One reason is that, among the experiments employing such judgments, the variables and the materials vary greatly. Another reason is that such a procedure is not often used in a large-scale project, since these judgments are quite time-consuming and therefore expensive.

A second major subclass within this mode utilizes the impressions about S that have been stored in the minds of those who have observed his prior behavior. E can ask S's peers, his subordinates, or his superiors to be the Os making judgments or inferences about him. Ratings of enlisted men by officers were used in the Army during World War I. Peer ratings were often used during World War II. Efficiency ratings have been used for years in business and in the civil service. In research on children, parent ratings of their children's behavior are sometimes used—although in this instance, the interest may be in the parents' perceptions rather than in their ratings as objective reports. (For a discussion of rating scales, their properties, and their limitations, see Chapter 11 of Guilford, 1954.)

The identifying feature of this Prior Behavior Mode is that S is not aware that he is being assessed. More precisely, the information used in this mode was obtained under conditions entirely different from those in which the information is processed to obtain an index for S. To be sure, S may have realized that others would obviously see his products or his actions, and that they might pass judgment on them, as we all make informal evaluations about other people from time to time. Everyone knows that his superior has to evaluate him and his work. But S does not know that a psychologist may at some future time use these observations to assess his psychological characteristics.

In the other modes, the psychologist provides stimuli to which S reacts. These stimuli are usually the same for all Ss being measured and compared

at a particular time. Each S is aware that he is being assessed. These two
features are absent in Mode 4.

The Capabilities Mode (Mode 3)

In this mode, we ask S to perform, to do as well as he can on the tasks he
is asked to undertake. This is the standard approach used in testing ability
or academic achievement. Intelligence should be included within a broad
definition of personality since intellectual capacities and special abilities
influence personality. Achievement or acquired competence is pertinent to
personality insofar as it provides an indirect measure of some variable.
To illustrate, accumulated knowledge about the content of some area such
as music may be used to indicate strength of interest in that area. More
directly relevant to personality are capacities for coping with behavioral
data from other people, a kind of content included by Guilford (1967) in
his Structure-of-Intellect.

The measurement of capabilities is used in the assessment of cognitive
controls, a growing field of personality. For example, field independence is
measured by ability to judge the vertical when one's only strong cue is a
tilted rectangular frame (in this Rod and Frame Test, S's chair may also
be tilted), or when S must judge when his chair is upright when it is initially
tipped to one side in a small room that is also tilted (the Body Adjustment
Test); it is also measured by ability to determine whether a complex figure
contains within it a designated simple figure (the Embedded Figures Test;
see Witkin *et al.*, 1962). Another well-known test is the Stroop, which
assesses the extent to which the subject's performance is impaired when he
tries to name colors when these are the colors of inks used to print the
names of other colors: thus "red" may be printed in yellow, "blue" in
green, and so on.

The Current Experiencing Mode (Mode 2)

Another mode utilizing S's report of his immediate experience during the
testing is one in which there is no correct answer, as there is in the Capabilities Mode. E may present S with two designs and ask him which he
prefers, as in the Welsh Figure Preference Test. Or he may present a short
abstract motion picture sequence and ask S to report the direction of the
apparent movement; in this test the colors move in one direction and the
forms in the opposite, so that S's immediate experience indicates which
aspect of the stimuli is the stronger determinant of his perceptions. (Use
of this method, developed by E. H. Hess, was reported by Sinclair, 1956.)
Certain cognitive-style tests fall within this mode: e.g., measures of S's

categorizing tendencies, and of his estimates of the size of some category (such as the lengths of whales). Again, in the Terman-Miles test of masculinity-femininity, silhouette inkblots are presented along with alternative interpretations that are made with different frequencies by men and women. The alternatives S chooses indicate the similarity of his perceptions to those of men and to those of women.

The Self Description Mode (Mode 1)

A very common mode involves simply asking S to describe himself in one way or another. He may be asked to rate himself on instruments similar to those used for rating others in the Prior Behavior Mode. He can check those adjectives on a checklist which he feels describe him. He can complete a questionnaire such as the California Psychological Inventory (Gough, 1968), the Minnesota Multiphasic Personality Inventory (Dahlstrom and Welsh, 1960), or any one of hundreds of other similar instruments. Another format is the Q-sort, in which S sorts fifty to one hundred statements into perhaps ten piles according to the extent to which they describe him (Stephenson, 1953; Wittenborn, 1961; Block, 1961).

Roughly similar instruments are used to measure interests and values. Examples are the Strong Vocational Interest Blank (D. P. Campbell, 1968) and the Allport-Vernon-Lindzey Study of Values, mentioned in Chapter 1.

Finally, S's attitudes may be measured by his willingness to endorse or agree with statements reflecting designated attitudes. Many such attitude scales have been published, dealing with attitudes toward almost every conceivable subject (see Shaw and Wright, 1967). Such scales are used primarily in social psychology, although their relevance to personality is receiving increased recognition.

All three of these latter modes (Modes 1, 2, and 3) can be applied in a group situation. S is given instructions, is presented with the stimuli, and records his responses. That record is used later to obtain an index for S. Note that the presence of the examiner is not essential to the measuring process, since the examiner does not observe S for the purpose of producing information about him. The examiner is present simply to make sure that S is participating appropriately and cooperatively, that he is performing adequately for the purpose of measurement.

The Observation of Behavior Mode (Mode 5)

In this mode, the observer (O) is the data producer. He observes S and records his observations. This mode has so many forms that it may well need further differentiation. For example, although most observation of behavior is done with S's knowledge that he is being observed, there are a few exceptions. Children may be observed on a playground. When the children do not know they are being observed, this mode resembles the ratings based on prior behavior, except that the sample of behavior used in this mode is limited in time and place. A variation of this kind of observation is the situation test, in which adults are set a more or less realistic problem to solve under the eyes of observers. They may be asked to discuss a problem, as in the Leaderless Group Discussion (Bass, 1954), or to work on some physical task, as in several used by the Office of Strategic Services during World War II (see the *Assessment of Men* by the OSS Assessment Staff, 1948). S may work alone or in a group. In either case, he is aware that one or more Os are present, although they do not interact with him.

A very common form of this mode is the interview. Here there is direct interaction between S and O, the interviewer. O sets for S the task of answering O's questions and then provides such questions as the stimuli to which S is to respond. O's later questions often depend on S's answers to earlier ones, so that the questions may not be precisely the same for each S. But in some structured interviews (e.g., the Psychiatric Status Schedule, Spitzer *et al.,* 1966), O's behavior and questions are highly standardized, so that the procedure resembles the Self Description Mode (Mode 1) with the difference that here it is O that records the responses, rather than S.

In an interview, O may observe and record not only S's overt, intentional, goal-directed responses, but also his other responses—his gestures, his way of responding, and so on. Ordinarily O's record of all these responses is not complete: O observes and summarizes in some fashion, either making his summary available as a record to be processed by a psychologist or by processing his observations in his own mind and determining the index to be assigned to S. Note also that the O may be different for different Ss. If so, then the total stimulus situation varies in accordance with S's reactions to O's unique appearance, manner, and voice. The interview is used for a variety of purposes, such as opinion surveys, personnel selection, and clinical diagnoses.

In another common variety of this mode, O may ask S to respond to a stimulus by telling a story (as in the Thematic Apperception Test). O later analyzes the story, or typically the set of stories, and makes judgments about them. Another projective technique is the classical Rorschach (see W. G. Klopfer, 1968). O presents S with ten inkblots, one at a time, and asks S some question such as "What might this be?" This is a kind of structured interview or experiment, in which O uses a variety of information besides the verbal responses themselves: the time S takes to give his response, whether or not he turns the cards, and so on. Other techniques require S to draw persons or objects, or to complete sentences (see Murstein, 1965). Most of these projective techniques were originally developed for studying clinical patients. They are becoming more frequently used in basic and applied research.

The Psychophysiology Mode (Mode 6)

The last mode involves asking S to do something and recording his physiological processes while he is carrying out that instruction. To determine S's interest in particular types of stimuli, O may photograph his pupillary response (the pupil dilates with interest; see Hess, 1968). To study the anxiety produced by stimuli, O may record S's breathing, heart rate, muscle tension, or sweating. A complication in such work is the fact that the characteristic pattern of reaction to anxiety or to other affects unfortunately varies from person to person. Additionally, there are technical problems associated with differences in base-line values and with the application of the recording devices to the subject. This mode requires extensive training and experience on the part of O (see Averill and Opton, 1968).

Perceptions of the Measuring Process

In each of these six modes, a task is given to O or S. This task is rarely like any that O or S encounters in the ordinary course of his life. The closest similarity is in the preparation of letters of recommendation or other evaluative procedures. Most of the tasks are quite atypical. This feature raises a basic question: How can the psychologist generalize from responses made in coping with these extraordinary tasks to typical, enduring characteristics of S? This problem will lurk in the background throughout much of this book. For the present, one recommendation can be made: usually the ideal task is one that is so innocuous and unthreatening that reactions to the task per se have little or no influence upon S's responding to the stimuli as presented. (Even if the attribute requires that the stimuli be stressful, the procedure should be designed so that the fact that S is coping with the stimuli for purposes of measurement will contribute little variance to the observations.)

The task given to S or O, as indicated in Table 5.1, is presented in specific instructions as to what he is to do. By themselves, these instructions do not tell S or O what is being measured or why measurement is taking place. The table assumes that the purposes of E are essentially those implied in the instructions, an assumption that is not always true. In psychological measurement, it has become rather standard practice not to tell S what the research is all about, what specific variables are being measured, and what E expects to find. This custom stems from concern that the responses of S (or of O, for that matter) might be affected by such knowledge. For example, it has been observed by Orne (1962) that many Ss want to be good Ss, other things being equal, and want the experiment to come out right; that is, they want it to come out as E expects. If nothing else, such results mean to them that their time has been well spent in furthering science.

This practice of not telling the subjects the whole story has had one regrettable consequence. Now that the practice is almost universally known or suspected, Ss will often try to figure out what the experiment is about, and may allow their guesses to affect their responses. To minimize such effects, it is certainly wise to tell Ss as much as possible before the testing or experimenting, to promise to tell them more later, and to carry out that promise. While it is impossible to explain technical concepts and theoretical hypotheses to laymen in a few minutes, it is possible to indicate briefly the general purpose of the research and the general nature of the variables in everyday language that Ss can understand.

Not spelled out in the table are the instances in which E's purposes are concealed from S or O, and the instances when E actually misleads the data producer. Thus a standard, individually administered intelligence test, such as the Wechsler Adult Intelligence Scale, provides data from which E can derive indices of intellectual capabilities, and also provides the examiner with an opportunity to observe the functioning of S, and from this behavior to make judgments about work habits and personality attributes. While such measurement of intelligence is Mode 3, the judgments about personality traits are Mode 5 (Observation of Behavior). A subject taking the Rorschach test is asked to tell what each blot looks like to him; he is not told that, in addition to the content of his responses, his manner of responding and his selection of parts of blots to interpret will be used as bases for inferences about him, and he is not told that these inferences will include estimates of the level and quality of his intellectual functioning and judgments about his fantasy life as well as ratings on general traits of personality. In this case, the estimates of capabilities are made without telling S to give the correct answer (as in Mode 3). An even more complicated example would be a study of Ss by means of their perceptions of others. Here the Ss would be led to believe that they were Os observing and reporting on other people, when the real interest of E was in what their observations revealed about the observers themselves. If the Os were peers reporting their perceptions of other people's prior behavior, the Os would think they were performing a task identified here as Mode 4, whereas E would actually be observing them according to Mode 5.

To summarize: the classification of ways of observing is based on E's perceptions and purposes, regardless of what S and O believe. Observations reported by Ss or Os while performing tasks identified in Table 5.1 with one mode may be used not only to derive indices fairly directly from those tasks, but also to make expert judgments about other variables, often using what appear to be secondary or minor aspects of the observed behaviors. Mode 5, then, can capitalize on observations overtly falling under any of the other modes. These more devious and intricate procedures do not affect the basic theme of the table: observations of personality phenomena are made from several perspectives, and both the particular observations and the ultimate indices derived from each are distinctive and more or less independent of those derived from the other perspectives.

The Modes and Their Differentiation

From the discussion and from careful inspection of Table 5.1, we can see that each mode differs in at least one important aspect from each of the other modes, but no one basis of classification can be used to differentiate the several modes. This particular classification is clearly not a neat, logically elegant, aesthetically satisfying one. It was constructed to point up the major differences among the personality phenomena we observe and the ways we observe them. It is a *post hoc* categorization of the many methods now used for measuring personality. Perhaps a more systematic classification with some theoretical foundations will be invented in the future.

Why is this differentiation of modes important? It is rather obvious that people in general react differently to different tasks and stimuli. In a given condition, Ss are set to give a certain kind of response, among the infinite variety of behaviors of which they are capable. To measure individual differences, a task is specified in the instructions. Ss make responses of an appropriate kind and do not make any of the many other possible kinds. Within the class of appropriate responses, differences among individuals are then looked for. Furthermore, the stimuli presented to Ss usually vary in accordance with the modes, a factor contributing also to the specificity of the responses and of the indices derived from the responses. Thus different modes produce different kinds of information, from which are derived indices that are not interchangeable. No statistical tranformation changes one set of indices into another, as a physicist might transform readings on a centigrade thermometer to correspond with readings from a Fahrenheit thermometer.

Some of the modes can also be distinguished by the phase of the general process used. Recall from Chapter 3 the view of the phenomena of personality as processes. At an early phase, S perceives and evaluates the meaning of the stimulus for himself. Mode 2 seeks to obtain information on S's current experiencing, what he perceives, whether he likes it, and so on. Concurrent with that are S's physiological reactions to the stimulus, as determined by Mode 6. S's behavior as he interacts with his environment, as he copes or adapts, is observed in Mode 5 (Observation of Behavior). Mode 3 (Capabilities) considers the quality of S's performance when S is attempting to cope with specific tasks set by E, i.e., when S is trying to do as well as possible. A more general approach is involved in Mode 4 (Prior Behavior). Here the materials examined are of two kinds: either (a) the concrete, tangible products left from S's prior performance for one purpose or another or (b) the residual memories held by his associates, memories of S's prior behavior. In formal terms, Mode 1 (Self Description) is parallel to Mode 4; the difference is that Mode 1 uses S's own memories of his prior behavior and experience, rather than the memories of others. In practice, however, Mode 1 is more likely than Mode 4 to be affected by reactions to the measuring situation itself; quite understandably, an observer is more involved, more likely to be biased, and more likely to slant his reports when the person being considered is himself rather than another.

Not only can modes be differentiated by types of information used; they also differ in the actual measuring process resulting in indices. In the first three, where S produces the data record, S is given some objective in the instructions, a criterion to use in selecting his response, and usually he records his response by marking one of several possible alternatives provided by E for each stimulus item. These alternatives have, of course, been keyed or classified by E, with one of them identified as indicating more of the disposition or capacity than the others. After S has produced his data, E simply counts the number of such keyed alternatives selected by S.

In the mode using existing records or impressions of S (Mode 4), O determines what parts of the products are relevant and into what category each such segment falls. The production of the index may use a relatively objective procedure, so that any two Os arrive at very similar indices, or it may use the personal judgment or inference of one or more Os.

All the modes use the behavior of S in one form or another. All but Mode 4 utilize a measuring situation (laboratory or testing room) in which S knows that he is being measured—a total context not representative of much of S's experience in daily life. The first three rely on data produced by S in response to a task and a set of stimuli. The next three rely on data produced by another person from his observations of S's behavior or responses. The various subclasses for the modes begin to show the marked qualitative differences among them, and the indicated methods or procedures or tests further show the dissimilarities.

There is another aspect to the production of measurement data that is in part a function of mode. This aspect is the mental operation used by S or O in determining the response, the datum he will record. The operation seems fairly clear in Mode 3: when Capabilities are being assessed, S selects that response which he believes is correct. Again in Mode 2, S reports on his Current Experiencing according to the criterion furnished in the instructions; e.g., Which of these two figures do you prefer? But in the other modes there is often a mental operation in which various bits of information are summarized in a single response, just as a set of scores can be reduced to a single measure of central tendency, such as the mean. The question is: How is this reduction done?

To illustrate, a supervisor may be asked to rate S on how well S gets along with his co-workers. The supervisor will use his recollections of S's Prior Behavior (Mode 4). He will recall various times when he observed S with fellow workers. He may roughly average his several impressions of the smoothness of S's interpersonal relationships on these many occasions; but he may, instead, recall the one or two instances in which S's associates seemed to find him irritating, provocative, or otherwise objectionable, and give S a low rating primarily on the basis of these particular instances, which were not typical but seemed quite significant to him.

An expert O in Mode 5 also has alternative ways of determining his judgment. Suppose, in studying the protocol from a projective test, O finds one clear expression of aggression—one man beating up another. He will be likely to attribute to that S more aggression than to another S who gives no such response. But how much more aggression is indicated by two such responses as compared to just one? Or by two less aggressive responses (one man threatening another, or criticizing the other) as compared to a single, more aggressive response? In reducing several bits of relevant information to a single datum or rating, O may emphasize the number of positive bits, that number as compared to the frequency of negative instances, or the extremity of the positive instances—how intense, strong, prolonged was the action in each case? Os emphasizing different bases for judging the presence or the strength of an attribute are likely to produce different data. A similar consideration is involved in the processes by which S responds to a questionnaire item in Mode 1, together with additional considerations discussed in Chapter 10.

The one mode remaining to be considered, Mode 6, does not encounter these problems in the production of its data record, since the graphic recordings of psychophysiological processes are made by instruments rather than by people. This mode has technical difficulties of its own, however, with respect to the comparability of instruments made by different companies or technicians and to the equivalence of different techniques (for applying electrodes, as just one example).

Yet the recordings of Mode 6 have to be reduced to data. The electro-encephalographic record of activity in a particular part of the brain may be analyzed by a clerk or by a computer that has been given explicit rules for scoring the record. In some instances it may not be possible to define the scoring so objectively, and human judgment may be required. Suppose E wishes to determine whether S is in a particular psychophysiological state that is identified by a complex wave form. O must search the record and mark each occurrence of that pattern. Then O has to judge whether the rate of such patterns (the frequency during a unit of time) is high enough to conclude that S is in that state.

We can see, then, that in some modes the production of the data record involves processes that may be rather uniform among the several persons producing the responses in that record. In other modes there is a variety of ways in which the recollections or other bits of information may be reduced to a single datum, response, or rating. While little is known about these processes, since few empirical studies have been made of them, we can confidently predict that whenever the task of producing data permits O or S great freedom in the way he arrives at his data, the quality of the measurements and particularly their comparability will be impaired.

A major implication of these modes will be developed later. It will be argued that each mode measures a given variable in a distinctive way, yielding measures rather independent of those from other modes. Therefore constructs should be linked to modes. A general construct might have subconstructs for two or more modes, each such subconstruct having its own theoretical links to other constructs within that same mode or possibly in other modes. Since behavior is largely determined by setting and by stimuli, we must construe and measure it within such specifications.

Contexts

A major classification of ways of measuring personality is the context in which the measuring is done. This classification is completely independent of mode distinctions; in principle, each mode could be used in each of the three chief contexts. These can be identified by the purpose of the measurement. All personality measurement is for one or more of three purposes: (*a*) for the benefit of an institution (as in industrial personnel work), (*b*) for the benefit of the subject (as in clinical diagnosis and vocational counseling), and (*c*) for research purposes. The purpose of the measuring may influence the data producer—the S in the first three modes and the O in the others whenever that O is making judgments or inferences. The extent of such influence varies. In our culture, its effects are probably greatest in Mode 1, Self Description, and least in Mode 3, ability testing in which Ss almost always want to do as well as possible.

Closely related to the purpose of measurement is another aspect of context: Does S or an inferring O perceive his participation to be voluntary or coerced? Such a perception may also influence the data produced or the index derived from them. Lovell (1967) has sketched out three examiner-client contracts, concluding that the only acceptable one is, roughly, "You don't try to fool us and we won't try to fool you," a contract that is applicable only when S can feel unthreatened. Such a contract applies primarily to Modes 1 and 2 (Self Description and report of Current Experiencing). A comparable analysis could also be developed for the understanding between an O data producer and the psychologist he is serving.

Subject and Observer Variables

In all modes except Mode 4 (Prior Behavior), S is aware of the fact that he is being measured. Such awareness means that S's perception of and reaction to the various aspects of the measuring procedure must be considered as potentially affecting the observations. S may react to the context, to the physical aspects of the situation including the examiner and his behavior, to the task as a whole and its instructions, to the stimuli in the task, to his operations on the stimuli, and even to his own responses. The total situation may be stressful for S and may generate anxiety or other affective reactions.

One aspect of such reactions is their central tendency over the subjects. The strength or the typical quality need not impair the observations; e.g., the particular situation might motivate all Ss to try a little harder to carry out the assigned task. A weak common reaction might well not affect the utility of the obtained indices; e.g., it might merely raise all scores a point or two, a result that can be ignored in the usual case where we are interested only in the relative positions of the several subjects rather than in their absolute positions on the measuring scale. On the other hand, a strong effect could distort the scores, contaminating them by effects from a separate variable of personality.

Much more critical is the question of differential reaction, of the variation in reactions over Ss. If some Ss react strongly and some little, if some react with one feeling and others with another, the data are very likely to be distorted and contaminated. I.e., it is the interaction between S and procedure that is the greater methodological danger, not the effect common to all Ss. Unfortunately, not enough research has been carried out on the subject variables affecting personality measurements and little is known about them (but see Chapter 10).

In Modes 4 and 5 (observations of past and present behavior) there are observer variables in addition to the subject variables (We are assuming that the scoring in Mode 6 is so routine that none enter there.) When O observes another person, his involvement with S, his liking for S, his feeling of similarity to or difference from S may affect his observations and data, as can more general aspects of O's personality. Some empirical work has been done on such observer variables, but more is needed.

Subject and observer variables have not been considered in the discussion of each mode because they, like context, are pertinent to more than one perspective.

Modes, Perspectives, and Other Classifications

The classification by modes is only one of many that have been proposed. D. T. Campbell (1957) proposes three dichotomies for tests: objective (when there is a right answer) vs. voluntary (when S is told any answer is acceptable); direct (when the purpose is known to the subject) vs. indirect (when it is hidden); free response vs. structured (as in multiple choice). Some analyses are based on types of variables. For instance, McClelland (1951, pp. 579–87) identifies a class involving the self-schema which requires direct self-report (Mode 1), needs as inferred by judges from fantasy (Mode 5), schemata involving perceptions and values (Mode 1 or Mode 2) and traits or responses in actual situations (which could be measured by Mode 5). Another classification (Leary, 1957) identifies five levels: public —behavior as rated by others (Mode 4 or 5); conscious—as rated by self (Mode 1); private—rated from projective tests (Mode 5); unexpressed unconscious; and values (Mode 2?). Similar to the categorization developed here is one proposed by Cook and Selltiz (1964) of methods for measuring attitudes, a concern of social psychology. Perhaps the concept of modes can profitably be extended to measurement in other parts of psychology.

The orientation developed here differs from the usual, much simpler approach. An investigator typically selects a concept for study and then seeks a procedure for estimating that general concept. If he tries to use two quite different procedures, he will be plagued by disagreements between measurements obtained by different modes (and even by disagreements if both utilize the same mode; see Chapter 11). Instead, the conceptualizer should consider how the general construct will appear from a variety of perspectives, and should analyze and delineate a subconstruct for each relevant perspective. Each perspective is entitled to be given theoretical significance in its own right, at least in the present state of personology. For example, Krause (1961) examines six types of evidence for transitory anxiety: introspective report and response to stress (both appear to fall in Mode 2), clinical intuition and molar signs (Mode 5), physiological signs (Mode 6), and task-performance changes (Mode 3). Although he proposes to resolve the problem of this diversity by use of a synthetic criterion indicator, an alternative strategy would be to develop a conceptualization of transitory anxiety as estimated from each of these kinds of methods; e.g., experienced and reported anxiety is sufficiently important to merit theoretical analysis and experimental study in its own right, and so is anxiety as it affects task performance.

While the classification of modes resembles that of perspectives, discussed earlier, they do not correspond precisely on a one-to-one basis. Recall that perspectives apply to the theoretical-conceptual work, and many theorists do not limit themselves to data from a single mode. Perspectives emphasize the observer, who is only one component in the categorization of modes of collecting data. More generally, perspectives are more difficult to pin down than modes, since modes can be explicitly defined: one can point to a particular procedure and another person can replicate it, keeping all essential features the same.

The proposed classification of modes seems quite useful, although some further differentiations may prove desirable. One might attempt a formal classification of perspectives currently used by theorists. Because such an analysis seems more difficult, I have not given formal labels to particular perspectives in the preceding discussion. I believe that theorizing should deal with a specific class of observations, such as a particular mode, and hence that the perspective of the theorist and his observational mode should be a single unit.

One correspondence between current perspectives and modes is between personality viewed as the way a person perceives himself and the Self Description mode. There is another close fit between personality construed as capabilities and Mode 3, measuring how well S can perform. Modes 4 and 5 are less congruent with the perspectives involving perceptions and judgments of others. These modes have been differentiated in terms of observing S's actual behavior at a point in time vs. observing his products or recalling his prior behavior. But more important to the conceptualization of personality is the difference between judgments or inferences made by laymen, such as peers and significant others, and those made by experts versed in dynamic theory. The training of the observer is important not only to the quality of the observations, but also with respect to the variables being judged: a layman cannot make judgments about esoteric variables such as psychosexual type or strength of an unconscious conflict.

The lack of exact congruence between perspectives and modes can be taken to be a major obstacle to progress in personology as a science. Any given theory should be aimed at understanding a specified body of phenomena, i.e., phenomena observed in a particular way. To gather systematic observations about those phenomena, one or a very few modes of producing data and deriving indices have to be used. Scientific theory-testing requires congruence between concepts and operations, each concept having a coordinating or operational definition. If theoretical statements and the definitions of their terms do not indicate the operations coordinated with them, it is not possible to subject the propositions to testing in convincing experimentation.

Let us examine more closely the two terms "perspective" and "mode." A perspective was defined earlier as a viewpoint from which personality phenomena can be observed, each perspective being distinguished by the position or role of the observer in conjunction with the particular phenomena being observed. A mode was defined as a class of procedures for measuring personality. Modes are differentiated by the kind of O (including S as O for this purpose), by the task given O, and by the method by which indices are obtained from the observations, among other characteristics.

It is clear that "perspective" is a less precise term than "mode." "Perspective" is used in this book in connection with theoretical approaches to personality, to emphasize the point that theorists contemplate personality from various viewpoints. We have also noted that phenomena seen from any one viewpoint may not be identical with those seen from other viewpoints, and that even when the same natural event is seen from two perspectives, it is usually perceived and construed somewhat differently.

"Mode" is used here in discussions of measuring operations, and especially when links between operations and constructs are considered. Each mode is defined and specified fairly closely, while perspectives are left in rather general terms. In part because of these differences in usage and specification, the two terms are not seen as strictly identical. I hope that eventually the term "perspective" may be dropped as no longer necessary or useful.

Method Variance

Over a decade ago Campbell and I (1959) brought together evidence on the pervasiveness of method variance in psychological measurements. Generally speaking, we argued that convergence of measures of the same trait obtained by different methods and discrimination between measures of different traits were basic prerequisites for assertions about the validity of tests. These properties could be demonstrated in a multitrait-multimethod matrix of intercorrelations. We did not explicitly define either "trait" or "method," since we assumed that they were common and well-known terms.

But science often progresses by questioning assumptions. Just what is a trait? As a target for measurement, "trait" refers to a classification of phenomena seen from a specified perspective. (See the preceding chapter.) While one may want to use a label for a general trait or sector of personality, *the more important traits are the several forms of such global terms,* each associated with a specified perspective. E.g., one may wish to identify a global trait of dominance, the label referring to an area of personological interest. Within that area, there can be subconstructs or traits linked to perspectives: dominance as S sees it in himself, dominance as seen in past performances, dominance as observed by others, dominance as capacity manifested in a testing situation. Each such subconstruct should be construed in the milieu of the perspective being employed, i.e., from the explicit or implicit viewpoint of the theorist.

And what is method? What is meant by independence of methods? No definitive classification of methods has been worked out. This chapter proposes that the primary categorization for method is the mode by which the information is gathered. The subclassification within each mode may have to be somewhat specific to that mode—certainly the relative contribution to specificity of the various components can be expected to vary with the mode. To continue the classification of methods within each mode, the major components are the context in which the information is gathered, the specific task given to the data producer (S or O), and the specific stimuli used. As a first, *a priori* approximation, two procedures differing in any one of these components should be presumed to involve separate (if not independent) methods until empirical evidence to the contrary has been established.

Summary

Whatever the context for measuring personality, the procedures fall into six classes of observations: Self Description (as in inventories), reports of Current Experiencing (as in indicating preference for one stimulus over another), Capabilities (as in determining how many correct responses S can give on an intelligence test), judgments based on S's Prior Behavior (as in peer ratings), Observation of Behavior (as in projective testing), and Psychophysiological observations (of heart rate, muscle tension, etc.). The scheme provides a basis for specifying what we mean by the term "method." The classification is complex since it involves several aspects of the total procedure (who produces the data record, who produces the indices, what task is given the data producer, and whether S is aware he is being measured).

In each class or mode there is a data record which is analyzed to obtain an index, the actual operations taking various forms. The way that the subject or observer producing the data record perceives the measuring process may impair the adequacy of the ultimate indices. In addition, the mental operations of S or O require careful consideration and, if possible, standardization.

CHAPTER SIX

The Specification
of Constructs

Why should a book on personality measurement be concerned with constructs and their definitions? Constructs and their interrelationships form the body of a science. Empirical findings or "facts" are important only insofar as they have relevance for constructs and propositions about them. And of course, even an empirical finding that index X is related to index Y already involves concepts of X and Y at a low level of abstraction. There is little point in measuring something or in relating one set of measurements to other data unless the measurements are pertinent in some way to a construct. A basic consideration in planning to measure is the coordination between the measurement procedure and the construct at which the procedure is aimed.

Much has been written about the necessity for precise terminology in science and especially in psychology (e.g., *The Language of Psychology,* Mandler and Kessen, 1959). This requirement is particularly important in personology, where it is all too easy to label a trait or other variable with a word from everyday langauge. When this is done, both the writer and the reader are likely to accept the term without question, each having some acquaintance with it and many associations with it, and finding it easy to recall illustrations from his personal experience or the observations of others. A theorist may feel he is communicating well when he uses the common term, and the reader may feel he understands the theorist's writings, even though a cursory analysis of the word indicates that its meaning is rather vague and to some extent ambiguous or that it has several alternative meanings. In addition, the reader's personal associations and connotations for the term may be unlike those of the theorist.

When setting out to measure a variable, the researcher should first look around for an available measure that meets his requirements. By this tactic he may save himself the laborious task of developing his own meaure; but much more important is the desirability of a set of common measuring procedures, so that a body of knowledge can be built up about each procedure and about relationships between its indices and other sets of measurements, and so that studies can more readily be replicated. For example, an investigator wishing to study repression may select the frequently used measure of Repression-Sensitization developed by Byrne (1964). (See Fiske and Pearson, 1970.) But if no suitable procedure is found in the literature, the researcher must develop a procedure of his own, as Rotter (1966) did for his concept of the locus of control of reinforcement perceived as internal as opposed to external. His test was rapidly accepted by others in their research. Whichever course an investigator follows after searching the literature, he must have a clear picture of the target, the construct at which the measuring procedure is aimed.

Such conceptual pictures are rarely if ever available. If the reader questions that statement, he should select any personality variable and look for a comprehensive delineation of it, one that indicates with some clarity how one should go about measuring it. For instance, what is anxiety? Is it fear, dread, low self-confidence, tension, sweating palms, performance below capacity, or what? The problem is like that surrounding such terms as truth, freedom, and democracy: we all would claim to know what they mean, and yet when these enter into discussions, we find that we differ from our associates not only on the central meaning of each abstraction, but also on what should be included in the total definition. With so little consensus on meaning, we would expect little agreement on how to assess, say, democratization as an attribute of countries, and limited agreement on judgments of this attribute.

Given this state of affairs, the researcher must formulate his own conceptualization of his target variable. While published discussions may provide some useful material for him, he will have to do most of the work himself. He will find that published theories of personality were not written with a view toward facilitating the measurement of their concepts. Devising appropriate methods for systematic observation is the first step toward basic research to test theoretical propositions.

An explicit conceptualization of the kind outlined below has several functions. First, it provides a clear and systematic picture of the concept to be studied and understood. Second, it sets up a target at which to aim measuring procedures. With such a target, one can see what aspects of the concept are being measured by each procedure separately, and (if several procedures are available) what aspects are not measured by any of the set. Third, it facilitates the development of relatively pure measures of specific aspects of the concept and the determination of the degree of covariation between them, a substantial advantage over attempting to measure the whole concept in one procedure with the individual stimuli or items having typically very low intercorrelations.

Guidelines for Conceptualizing a Variable

Laymen and theorists arrive at their general concepts from their observations. Either in the wealth of their casual daily experiences or in their observations under limited conditions, they perceive some theme, some characteristic common to a cluster of observations. Giving the characteristic a name, such as the need for novelty, they find the name useful because it seems to apply to other, subsequent observations. This classifying, this extracting of observations with a common feature, is a first step toward theory.

Consider Figure 6.1. At the top there is a set of observations marked O_1. These designate the observations from which a theorist, T1, has derived his concept, the concept marked C_{T1}, the subscript indicating that it is his concept rather than a general one. Similarly, there are observations for Theorist 2 and for Theorist 3 (those marked O_2 and O_3, respectively), and the concepts that each has developed from his observations (C_{T2} and C_{T3}). Each theorist gives his concept a label. They may all use the same label (e.g., "need for novelty") or they may use similar labels: one person may refer to the "need for variety" (Maddi and Andrews, 1966), another may use the term "sensation-seeking" (Zuckerman and Link, 1968), and the third, "novelty-seeking" (Pearson, 1970). Since they seem to be talking about similar things, we decide that these concepts fall in the same domain, novelty-seeking, and so we link each concept to C, our general concept.

Look back for a moment to the top of the figure. Each O represents a natural event. The rays diverging from each C_T indicate the sector of these observations on which each T (theorist) bases his personal form of C, i.e., those observations that he would consider illustrations of it. The figure has been drawn to suggest that each of our theorist-observers might have been exposed to objectively the same natural events and that the same event (such as $O_{1,2}$ or $O_{2,3}$) might be included in the personal constructs of two or more observers.

But the representation of the original observations has been greatly oversimplified in Figure 6.1. To keep the figure clear, we have omitted the mass of natural events that are not included in any theorist's private concept of C. More basic is the absence of any indication that all observations made by a

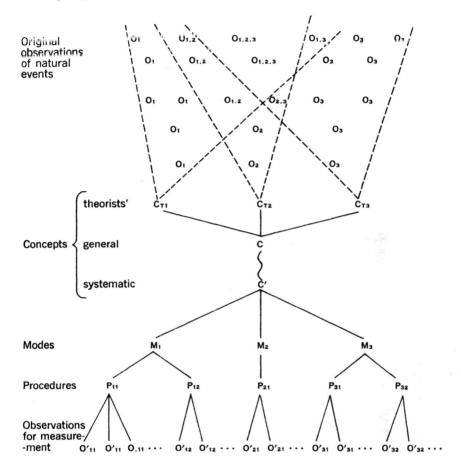

Figure 6.1. Links between concepts and observations

theorist are his private observations; in keeping with the general orientation of this book, each observation should be considered to some extent specific to the observer. The same natural event is perceived and construed somewhat individualistically, although there will usually be some consensus on the main overt features.

Suppose a researcher has selected a general concept, C, as his target. His first step is to decide what is the basic aspect, the core of his construct, C'. His construct is given a separate identification because he may well not include within his construct everything that might be subsumed under the looser, more general concept, C. Next, he selects the modes that appear appropriate for observing instances of C'. This is a critical step, since each mode requires its own subconstruct, and his further conceptualizing is done with respect to these particular forms of C'. Later, he decides what procedures he will use to collect systematic observations within each of these modes. For example, in Figure 6.1, P_{11} and P_{12} may be the procedures for M_1.

Just as the conceptualizer's construct is distinguished by a prime (C'), so the systematic observations made under particular measuring conditions are marked by primes to differentiate them from the original observations at the top of the figure. These systematic observations are also identified by subscripts indicating the procedures used to obtain them, the first subscript identifying the mode and the second the specific procedure under that mode.

A conceptualization of a variable can appropriately be called a working definition. Not only is the definition put to work in guiding the operationalizing of the construct for measurement purposes, but also that phrase helps to remind us that the definition will be modified in the light of empirical findings. The aim of science is to reach a set of constructs that provide maximum help in understanding the phenomena of interest; as empirical work proceeds, constructs must be refined or even altered to maximize their coordination with measurement observations.

In summary, we are arguing that a measurer must himself be something of a conceptualizer (unless he can get someone else to do that job appropriately for him). He must work toward the construction of a scientific language to replace the common language that has been used too long in personology, and which, as Mandler and Kessen (1959) show, has defects associated with reification, vagueness, and ambiguity.

WHAT IS A VARIABLE?

Within the orientation of this book, a variable is a quality of a stage in processes: it is one aspect of what takes place in some part of a process. Thus, associated with the perceptual phase of the general process outlined earlier, there may be a disposition to attend to color, and a disposition to attend to form. Other illustrations from later phases are a disposition to want to experience a sense of achievement, a disposition to move rapidly, a capacity to perceive hidden figures readily. These dispositions can be thought of as ways of reacting; "reacting" is used broadly to include perceiving, cognizing, and other internal functioning during a process.

So a variable is a quality in which the behaviors of people are believed to differ. But in what ways can they differ in it, and how should they be indexed with respect to the quality? The two major ways are strength or intensity and relative frequency. It is probably best to think of all qualities or variables as present to some degree in the behavior of everyone. Thus we can study the speed with which a person performs an action, such as writing, or the pressure he applies to the pen. For other kinds of variables, the appropriate sort of index is relative frequency. When a person perceives a set of colored objects, how frequently does he attend or react primarily to their color? In a standard set of situations, how often does he act so as to obtain a sense of achievement? It will be obvious that a variable is a hypothetical notion (see Chapter 2) whose degree is inferred from observations of one kind or another, i.e., from observations of some trace or product of a phase in a process.

Implicit in this discussion is the idea that we would like to determine the subject's typical reaction. In practice, we work from a limited set of observations under restricted conditions. Wallace (1966, 1967) has proposed that personology should be more concerned with response potentialities, with the strength of dispositions under maximally facilitative conditions. This view was adopted from the method for measuring intelligence and achievement, in which we do not attempt to determine how well the person usually performs, but rather how well he can perform under optimally favorable conditions. (It is the strategy used to get dependable indices of the heights of people—having them stand up as straight as possible.)

This new direction of thinking may prove fruitful and certainly should be pursued empirically. It does not, however, seem sufficient at this time. Before it can be useful, we must determine what kinds of relationships exist between such maximally facilitated responses and responses in a situation with less demand or pull from the stimuli and other conditions. While maximum responsiveness or potentiality may be easier to measure than more typical functioning, it seems unwise at this stage of the science of personality to limit our work to the most readily obtained observations, because they are likely to divert our efforts to rather restricted kinds of studies and theories. One could study the capacity to accept direction from others, but this work would not contribute much to the understanding of submissiveness in the authoritarian personality (see Adorno *et al.,* 1950).

There is another limitation to measurements of maximum responsiveness. While Ss are willing to try to do their best on an intelligence test, they may not be willing to reveal their capacities for producing socially disapproved responses. How would you react if asked to show how hostile and cruel a story you can make up? Or as sexual a story as possible? As Wallace himself notes, restricted dispositions manifested under such instructions may stem from limited capacity or from S's inhibition: he may be unwilling to reveal his private fantasies.

Wallace also advocates the development of a concept of response performance to further our understanding of personality. The roots of his position in learning and behavior theory are evident in his emphasis on studying reinforcement conditions as one class of factors controlling response performance. Of more relevance for our interest in general personality mea-

surement are his other two sets of situational factors: the situation-specific
hypotheses of the individual—his expectancies in the situation—and the
formal properties of situations. The orientations of Wallace and of this volume are quite similar in their emphasis on the necessity of considering variables as reactions or responses to particular situations as they are perceived
and interpreted by the subject. In this respect, response capacity is response
performance under rather atypical conditions.

THE SETTING FOR A WORKING DEFINITION

Let us consider in more detail the steps in conceptualizing a variable. Before the researcher becomes involved in the substantive content of his conceptualization or working definition of a variable, he should explicate the
setting. The first decision for him to make concerns the type to which the
variable belongs. Are the phenomena of interest perceptual, cognitive, inter-
pretive, affective, conative, instrumental or coping, effective, or what? I.e.,
to what phase of the general process do they refer?

Closely related to that decision is the matter of indicating the preceding
phases and conditions that must be controlled if one is to obtain data permitting comparisons between individuals. As we have seen earlier, the study
of differences in any one kind of variable, associated with any one stage of
the general process, requires that the preceding phases of the process must
have been essentially similar in the subjects being measured: quality of performance cannot be compared between individuals who see the general
setting very differently or who interpret the stimuli idiosyncratically; the
strengths of a motive cannot be compared when subjects are measured in
different states or have had distinctly different prior experiences with the
stimuli.

More generally, the researcher must consider his objective in developing
the conceptualization. A researcher may have a special, applied purpose,
such as to explicate a kind of motive particularly relevant to success in a
type of work. Or he may be seeking to pinpoint a capacity for profiting from
a particular form of verbal psychotherapy. In the subsequent discussion,
however, we shall assume that the researcher's goal is to delineate a concept that seems to have importance in general personality functioning. I.e.,
we shall assume that the researcher is engaged in basic research not limited
to a single context.

What is basic research as contrasted to applied research? The criterion is
the intention of the researcher: in basic research, he is seeking to advance
our understanding of a class of phenomena. Such understanding is achieved
through the development of theory, which is composed of constructs and
their interrelationships. While the constructs, to be useful in a general
theory, must apply to a wide range of pertinent objects or events, they must

be precise, communicable, and linked with particular operations that index them. The interrelationships may, in the early stages of a science, be stated in general terms, such as covariation, although the long-range ideal is to specify the exact function relating one construct to another. Thus, to test a small theory, a theoretical physicist may ask his experimental colleague to assess the prediction that there will be a change in X with different levels of Y under specified conditions; the observed results may lead to the theorist's discarding or modifying his theory, or to his pursuing further tests of predictive statements derived from it.

The point is that a variable should be a construct with a theoretical context. Such an assertion would not be necessary in a more advanced science, but it must be emphasized in personology, where one term is often used by a number of theorists to refer to somewhat different sets of phenomena. Impulsiveness or impulsivity has somewhat similar meanings for psychoanalytically oriented writers such as H. A. Murray and N. Sanford, but those meanings differ from that of George Kelly. In practice, the personality researcher has three choices. First, he can explicate and extend the concept of a particular theory (or, better, of a particular theorist). This is the alternative most likely to contribute to the field because it can build on what has already been worked out conceptually and perhaps also on relevant empirical work. Second, he can formulate his own construct as part of a total program of theorizing and experimenting. With this choice, he is committing himself to sufficient work to demonstrate the frutitfulness of his construct and its advantages over similar concepts. His contribution will depend upon the extent to which others, convinced by his demonstration, take up and extend his work. Finally, he may attempt to delineate an eclectic conceptualization for some common variable with the hope that he can capture enough of the consensual essence of that variable for his formulation to be of use to the work of others as well as to his own work. Others may recognize the value of his analysis, accept his particular conceptualization, and build on it. But they may merely misappropriate for research on their own private forms of the variable any measuring procedures he develops to operationalize his eclectic concept, continuing the common but harmful practice of linking a concept with a test just because both have the same vague label.

Whichever strategy he chooses, the researcher will want to consider the range to which the concept applies: all human beings, people socialized in the western European culture, or some smaller subcultural group. We trust he will not consider his concept restricted to college undergraduates taking psychology courses, the most common type of subjects in personality research! In most instances, he will limit the applicable population to those exposed to a common general socialization process. Occasionally he may wish to apply the concept to two groups separately but simultaneously—men and women, for example. The manifestations of a variable and its relationships with other variables may vary with sex, socioeconomic class, and national culture.

THE CORE OF THE CONSTRUCT

The next task for the conceptualizing researcher is to describe the unique quality to which his construct refers. He may wish to begin with a general account in lay language or literary terms. But he must then identify explicitly the core or essence of his construct. Illustrations can be drawn from work done in the author's research program. The core of dominance can be identified as acting overtly so as to change the views or actions of another. These are the effects of dominating actions. This core can be considered to be the common theme present in dominating a conversation so that others cannot talk, in persuading others, in telling peers what to believe or do, and in executing the role of leader. (This conceptualization was operationalized in some of the instruments used by Butt and Fiske, 1968.) To take another example, the core of affiliation can be stated as sharing experiences with another. The sharing may be as casual as remarks to a seatmate on a plane or as intimate as disclosing disturbing private experiences to a loved one. The core of impulsiveness may be taken as performing an instrumental act ineffectively when effective performance of the act is within the subject's capacity (see pages 20–21). This essence includes omissions and commissions in perceptual, cognitive, and psychomotor performance. In this specification for impulsiveness, the notion of lack of sufficient control is implicit but the idea of "acting on impulse" is not indicated (as some might prefer in their specification of the essence for this variable).

The core must be stated in such a way that it fits all manifestations that the conceptualizer wishes to subsume under the variable. This requirement may seem too restrictive. For example, the researcher may be interested in Rogers' concept of openness to experience (1959). An analysis of that variable (Pearson, 1968, 1969) reveals that it refers to a process with several phases. A person who is completely open to an important emotional experience attends to the relevant stimuli, recognizes and interprets them without distortion, reacts to them, and explores fully his personal reactions. While a single complex sentence (like the preceding one) can be formulated to cover the total picture of openness to experience, it is better to consider the construct of openness to experience as a general label for a class of closely interrelated subconstructs, one for each phase. In such an instance, the conceptualizer identifies as the core of each subconstruct the special quality involved in each phase.

Another illustration is intelligence. One could define intelligence as the capacity to carry specified cognitive processes through to a correct outcome, or to solve problems. It is, however, much more fruitful to consider intelligence as a general concept subsuming many specific subconstructs, each referring to performing a particular operation on a narrow class of stimuli to attain a given type of product, as systematically analyzed by Guilford (1967). (See Chapter 11.)

At this point, it is helpful to the conceptualizer and to those reading his formulation for him to state explicitly what he does not include within his concept. Thus, in delineating dominance, he might wish to exclude leading, which is influencing others when S has the support of a role position recognized by himself and the others. Again, openness to experience may (as above) be restricted to significant experiences on the grounds that many ephemeral experiences are of limited theoretical interest and that there may be a very limited range of individual differences in openness to such trivial events.

It is also desirable to make explicit the differences between the construct as construed by the conceptualizer and as construed by others. Dominance has been given a variety of emphases: it has been seen as being considered a leader by one's peers, as a constitutional drive to master others, as originating in aggression, and as being essentially instrumental. This aspect of conceptualizing, like some others, has the function of sharpening thinking and communication by indicating what connotations or associations likely to occur to the reader or the conceptualizer should be put aside. It is especially important in personology, where the terms and the phenomena of interest are so much a part of our general experience.

Another desirable consideration is differentiation between the given concept and similar, possibly overlapping ones. Thus dominance is similar to aggressiveness, as when a salesman tries to influence a customer's buying behavior, but it is somewhat different from aggression when that term is defined as wanting or trying to hurt another. It is also distinct from assertiveness, which is aimed at avoiding being influenced by others, although dominance and assertiveness overlap if assertiveness is aimed at influencing others. Again, dominance is separate from but may be facilitated by high energy output and activity. (See Butt and Fiske, 1968.)

The preceding paragraphs have considered the construct positively, and this is the natural way in which constructs are born. We see striking instances of some behavior, we begin to think about them, and then we assign a label to the class. In many sciences, it is sufficient to identify the positive pole of the variable, since the opposite pole is automatically given as zero. For variables in such sciences, absolute measurement is possible: the length of this object is twenty-three standard units and it is twice as long as that object. But consider the fundamental variable of time: it has no starting point. On the other hand, the difference between two points in time can be of any size down to zero or simultaneity. In psychology, and especially in personology, most measurement is relative: the index obtained for one person has little value by itself, but has meaning when stated in relative terms, that is, in terms of S's position within the group of Ss. Thus much psychological measurement is implicitly in terms of standard scores. Each person is assigned an index that can be transformed into units of deviation, upward or downward, from some reference point, such as a group mean. Such standard scores provide a common scale for all variables—such as time scores and performance scores. A product-moment correlation between two sets of indices is the average cross-product of the pairs of standard scores, one pair for each subject, regardless of the content units (e.g., seconds or number correct) used in each of the indices.

Such relative measuring may present no problem so long as it is quite clear that the same quality is being assessed in each subject, and that all subjects have that quality to some extent. But some particular characteristics of personality variables make it necessary to consider explicitly the low end of each scale. Take dominance as an example. High dominance is influencing others a great deal. What is the low end? If this opposite pole is construed as being influenced, as submissiveness, we have introduced another variable, a new quality. And this new quality may not be exactly the opposite of dominance because submissiveness has its own unique features. As the low end of dominance, one might consider self-sufficiency, a "live and let live" attitude, almost a withdrawal from interactions with others. But here again, a separate quality is being added to the original core of dominance. The limited number of empirical studies with pairs of opposites like those discussed above shows that they do not have perfect negative correlations of −1.00 with each other. (See Stricker *et al.,* in press; Tupes and Kaplan, 1961.)

These examples bring out the fact that the absence of one variable is often associated with the presence of another variable. The implication for measurement is that, if the indices for several persons are to be comparable, they must all reflect positive degrees of the variable, with systematic influences from competing variables minimized or ruled out. In measuring intelligence, we should be concerned if some subjects give no correct answers: they may not have understood the task and may have been doing something other than what the experimenter intended them to do. Thus the ideal test of intelligence is one for which each subject gives some correct answers. If the items have been ordered in terms of difficulty, the subjects with low scores should give correct answers to the easiest items, those that almost everyone answers correctly. Furthermore, when the subject gives a wrong answer, there should ideally be some evidence that he was attempting to solve the problem rationally If the problem is to multiply 12 times 13, the experimenter should be suspicious of such answers as −1, 25, or 1213.

Similarly in measuring personality, every subject should receive a score indicating some positive extent of the variable being measured. Those with low scores should respond in the keyed direction on the items most frequently answered that way. Again, ideally, each response should reflect some degree of the measured variable (even though the keying may require a large degree if the response is to contribute to the total score, with responses reflecting small degrees not being counted in the total score).

For example, suppose we had formulated a construct of social perceptiveness which we defined as the capacity to recognize the emotional states of others. To measure the subconstruct of ability to recognize sadness, we might photograph persons who were experiencing various degrees of sadness and ask subjects to rate each picture. The optimal procedure would be to have each subject rate the pictures on a scale with many points. (In this hypothetical example, we must assume we have a criterion; perhaps the task could be to estimate the degree of sadness reported by the person in the picture.) Then we could assign a score for each response by measuring the distance between the response and the criterion point for that picture. We would expect most subjects to rate the saddest pictures as sadder than the least sad. If we found one or more subjects whose responses seemed to be the opposite, with very sad pictures being rated as not at all sad, then we should conclude that we did not measure ability to recognize sadness in these subjects. They may have misunderstood the directions, they may have decided not to cooperate, or something else may have gone wrong.

MODES TO BE USED

A crucial part of conceptualizing a variable is deciding how it can be observed. If we wish to study a mood variable, such as elation, we might describe it in terms of the feeling experience and its concomitant manifestations in facial expression and gesture. Such a formulation would immediately suggest the general perspectives from which to observe the variable. The major one would be subjective report. Also available would be judgments by others, either laymen or experts. Note that the observations from these perspectives would be based on different phenomena: the subject himself would base his report primarily on his inner experiences; outside observers might use spontaneous speech or joyful vocalizations, and might also use any physical gestures that occurred, as well as the facial expressions. (The expert observers in this instance might use exactly the same cues as the laymen, possibly with different emphases; in other cases, such as in judging sadness or hostility, they might use more subtle, postural cues not noted by the laymen.) Note that, in principle, every observational feature available to the outside judge is also available to the subject in this example: the subject could note his vocalizations and gestures and could even note his facial expression if he stopped to think about it. But from his perspective, these would be less significant than his internal feeling tone.

Progressing further toward measuring, the conceptualizer identifies the modes of observation he wishes to include. Each such mode should be construed as a separate subconstruct. Each mode utilizes more or less distinctive phenomena by which to identify the variable, to describe it, and to measure it. If, in the case of elation, we correlated subjective reports with the judgments of experts, we would not find perfect agreement. And here we might decide to ignore the judgments of others and rely entirely on self-report. But suppose our construct were concern for the feelings of associates. We could use self-reports as one mode; we could devise a standardized procedure for observing current manifestations (e.g., by determining how much interest subjects had in stories about people's feelings); associates could rate subjects on the amount of concern they felt the subjects showed in general, or for the associates' own feelings; experts could make appraisals from interviews or projective tests; and, in principle, one might use recordings of physiological reactions, e.g., when associates were describing their feelings. Not only would these modes use somewhat different phenomena; they would also be getting at somewhat different subconstructs. The physiological indices might vary with the reactivity or lability of the subjects. The subject's concern as experienced by his actual associates might be attenuated by the subject's lack of spontaneity and expressiveness. The indices from different modes might be considered distinct. *A priori* analysis indicates that different phenomena are used. Even more telling is the fact that measurements from different modes never agree perfectly, even after allowing for the undependability of unreliability of each set of measurements. The incontrovertible evidence for lack of complete congruence between modes must be accepted. While one may hope ultimately to be able to differentiate the unique contribution of each mode from some hypothetical real, "true" variability, the wisest strategy for some time to come is to treat each mode as a construct in its own right.

It is especially desirable to include in the total conceptualization of a variable some prediction about the expected degree of relationship between indices from different modes. Thus one might predict close agreement between self-report and observers for moderate to high degrees of elation, while indices of defensiveness from self-report, peers, and experts might have no interrelationships.

FACETS AND ELEMENTS

Suppose our conceptualizer has done everything recommended above. He has identified the core of the construct and noted its similarities and differences when compared with other concepts. He has selected the modes to be used in observing it, each being a subconstruct. Is that sufficient? No. He still has a wide range of somewhat heterogeneous behaviors that he is subsuming under each subconstruct. He is now in the position of a botanist who decides to study trees or a geologist who starts to study black rocks. Further analysis and classification of the pertinent observations are needed for several reasons. First, such analysis leads to a more precise specification of the content of his subconstruct, of what is relevant and what is not, a product that helps him to clarify his own thinking and to communicate more clearly with others. Second, creating classifications of content helps him to determine what part of the subconstruct he is measuring with any procedure he has available or develops. Third, he can design his total measuring operation so that he obtains subscores for particular portions of his subconstruct. Then, when testing a proposition involving it, he can determine whether the proposition holds for all forms of the subconstruct or only for certain subclasses. He can also determine whether the several subscores are closely related to each other or are sufficiently separate to suggest that the subconstruct should be split into two or more new and distinctive constructs.

A useful framework for systematic analyses of a subconstruct can be adapted from Louis Guttman's concepts of facets with elements subsumed by each facet. Guttman (1965) has applied these concepts to ability and achievement while Foa (1965) has used them in analyzing interpersonal relations. Facets are ways of looking at a set of complex observations or data; elements are particular forms within a facet. (The facet-element approach has been extended to the concept of mapping sentences for test items and data analysis; see Guttman, 1970.)

Each facet is a way of classifying the relevant observations. For the behaviors grouped under a subconstruct, we can have several bases for classification. One would usually be behavioral: What are the particular behaviors or types of behavior observed? Another important one is situational: In what objective classes of situations do these behaviors appear (many other people present, one other present, one present in a particular role, etc.)? Other facets are useful for particular types of constructs. For a motivational construct, it is often appropriate to ask what other motives it serves, these motives being the elements of a motivational facet. For constructs dealing with styles of perceiving and cognizing, a pertinent facet may be sensory modality of input, and each element of this facet would be a specific modality—visual, auditory, etc.

Suppose we consider dominance as observed by the self-report mode. A major facet is the behavioral one, the forms of dominance. One may dominate by persuading others to one's viewpoint; one may also dominate by directing the actions of others. Another form of dominating behavior is social initiation: if one takes the initiative in conversation, and especially if one interrupts others, one is controlling their actions by not allowing them to speak. Furthermore, leading might be included as another manifestation —a leader influences at least the actions of the led in a situation in which such influence is expected by the leader and the led. Note that dominance might be construed to exclude initiating (if that is seen as primarily stem- ming from impulsiveness) or leading (since the social conditions are struc- tured rather than unstructured, as in the other forms). The scope of the content of a construct must, of course, be explicated in any formulation of it.

Empirical work (Butt and Fiske, 1968) has provided some support for an *a priori* ordering of these elements in the behavioral facet of dominance, based on the directness of the control. Initiating is clearly separated from leading, in self-report data, with persuading and directing falling in between; the data failed, however, to associate persuading more closely with initiating, and directing more closely with leading, as we had predicted.

Another major facet is the situational. Dominance may be expected to vary with the situation and with the other people present. Consummative situations, in which the purpose of association is simply to enjoy the situa- tion, can be differentiated from instrumental situations, in which the object is to get something done. The social setting may also vary in regard to the social distance between S and the others (from strangers through acquaint- ances to close friends and spouse) and also with respect to the number of others present.

People may dominate for a variety of reasons. Dominance is often in the service of some other motive (as Murray *et al.* [1938, pp. 151–152] show). Many such reasons have been suggested in the published discussions of dominance, discussions from the perspective of Mode 5 (Observation of Behavior). It seems very likely that different interpretations of the reasons for dominant behaviors would be obtained from Mode 1 (Self Description) or even Mode 4 (as in observations by associates rather than expert clinical psychologists).

Butt and Fiske (1968) have devised a set of instruments operationalizing these various facets of dominance for the self-report mode. Empirical trials of these experimental procedures have been fairly successful. The chief finding has been the feasibility of obtaining moderately reliable scores for various elements identified *a priori*. The intercorrelations indicate that subjects can differentiate such elements in their self-reports. Intercorrelations with self-report measures for other variables tend to conform with *a priori* expectations The general conclusion of this research is that a single variable can be meaningfully analyzed into psychologically significant components that are empirically separate to some degree. This finding is not surprising in view of the universal finding that self-report measures of the same variable, when developed in different ways by different people, invariably have an appreciable degree of specificity or uniqueness—in other words, no two such measures can ever be seen as completely interchangeable.

We have already noted that the facets to be posited for a given construct should be determined by the nature of the construct. Generally it is necessary to have one facet for the manifestations and one for the background or setting. Usually there should be a stimulus facet. These latter (setting and stimulus) are combined in the S-R Inventory of Anxiousness (Endler, Hunt, and Rosenstein, 1962), in which S reports how much of each of fourteen modes of response he would experience in each of eleven situations, such as being on a ledge high on a mountain or taking an important examination. A similar inventory has been constructed for hostility (Endler and Hunt, 1968).

For some constructs, especially perceptual or cognitive, the stimulus facet can be clearly specified by qualitatively different kinds of stimuli. For example, field independence as assessed by capacity to see embedded figures needs a facet for the kind of figure—letter, number, or abstract symbol. Consider also the content categories in the Structure-of-Intellect model developed by Guilford (1967). In other kinds of constructs, the major facet divides a total process into phases, as for openness to experience, discussed above. Of course, one may choose to consider this construct as the general term for a set of constructs, one for each phase—an alternative that might be viewed as more consistent with the fact that most personality concepts refer to one stage in a general process.

In selecting the most pertinent facets and elements, the objective is to maximize the internal consistency of each subscore and the discrimination between subscores for different elements. I.e., within the domain of a construct as approached from a perspective, the goal is to identify components such that each can be measured with a high degree of psychometric adequacy (each is a relatively pure measure) and such that, taken together, the whole domain is covered. While this goal could be approximated very closely with a large number of lengthy procedures, a reasonable approximation can be obtained by devising procedures measuring essential elements in each of the major facets, such procedures having adequate psychometric qualities and having the advantage of permitting the researcher to learn more about his construct from their differential patterns of correlation with outside variables. (For examples of analyses oriented toward measurement in a different domain, see *Taxonomy of Educational Objectives, Handbook I: Cognitive Domain,* Bloom, 1956, and *Handbook II: Affective Domain,* Krathwohl *et al.,* 1964. See also the analysis of creativity by Jackson and Messick, 1965, and the strategy for studying normality advocated by Scott, 1968 [pages 1001–2].)

CONDITIONS

Implicit in the statement of the situational facet is the fact that the construct can be observed in some situations and not in others; e.g., dominating acts occur primarily when a person is with other people. But in addition, some situations are more conducive than others to manifestations of a concept. Especially for conceptualizing motives, it is very desirable to consider what conditions are maximally facilitative, what conditions elicit the concept-relevant responses in most people or elicit them in strongest form. Obviously these conditions are often the ones that should be utilized in measuring operations, provided that they are still within the range of common, every-day settings. As suggested earlier, the use of extreme instructions may be necessary for measuring response capability (see Wallace's views, discussed above), but capacity to create a very hostile story for a picture in the Thematic Apperception Test (TAT) does not necessarily indicate that the subject is typically hostile in his daily interactions.

It is also desirable to include in a conceptualization any relevant specifications concerning the state of the organism. For example, playfulness and preference for variety in stimulation are manifested when people are relaxed and in a pleasant mood, not when fatigued or depressed. Related to organic and psychic states is the question of the presumed stability of the pertinent response phenomena. Observations of mood variables are expected to differ from day to day, while success in problem-solving should be highly consistent.

NECESSARY AND DESIRABLE CHARACTERISTICS
OF CONCEPTUALIZATIONS

There is general agreement among methodologists on many points in the preceding recommendations. A conceptualization of a variable should make quite explicit what is included in the construct and what is excluded. It should also make quite clear the conditions required for manifestations of the variable. While there also seems to be agreement on the importance of indicating how the variable may be observed, some would not accept the view that each mode should be seen as a separate subconstruct; such people would prefer to see modes as yielding more or less distorted or biased pictures of the real thing. The argument in a preceding section for setting up subconstructs is in part advocating a psychological tactic: such an approach emphasizes the obvious obtained discrepancies between measures from different modes, and postpones for the present the question whether a psychologically meaningful way can be developed for combining such separate indices into a single comprehensive score for each person on the general concept. At this stage of personality measurement, it is essential to confront and cope with the universal finding that each mode produces its distinctive set of indices, which at best covary only modestly with those from any other perspective.

Again, some methodologists would not accept the recommendation to analyze the concept into facets and elements. They would hold that a concept may be used simply to refer to a somewhat heterogeneous collection of responses, and may do so quite usefully and fruitfully. The argument of this volume is that broad, general definitions indicating the approximate territory covered by a concept do not provide sufficient guidelines for test construction and evaluation (to say nothing of sufficient precision and communicability for the development of theory). Only with explicit specification of components can one determine whether one's instruments cover the intended domain and whether the domain is covered uniformly. Furthermore, when a researcher defines a concept as a heterogeneous collection, he has no basis for determining whether the internal consistency of his test for that concept is appropriate. If the need for achievement includes not only accomplishing but also manipulating, organizing, aspiring, competing, and persevering (Murray, 1938), how much correlation should we expect among the items covering the whole domain? On the other hand, items referring to manipulating should intercorrelate very substantially, and so should items referring to persevering and to each of the other behavioral elements.

OTHER ORIENTATIONS

The preceding guidelines for conceptualizing a variable were presented in terms of quantifiable variables, variables involving continua or dimensions onto which persons can be placed, according to whether they possess more or less of the attribute. Of course, the viewpoint argues that for each concept there need be several such continua: a conceptual one for each mode and, empirically, one for each score obtained from a measuring procedure. The guidelines are stated in terms of quantifiable variables because they are the kind that are being increasingly emphasized in personology.

Many of these guidelines can also be applied to another type, qualitative variables. A number of qualitative or categorical variables are of significance to personology. These include such demographic variables as sex. There are also typologies: introvert-extrovert (Jung); oral, anal, or genital character type (Freud); defenders and sensitizers in perceptual experimentation, etc.

Eventually, all such types will probably be seen as the extreme poles of a continuum along which people vary. To date, there has been no clear empirical evidence for pure types, evidence placing some persons wholly in a type and everyone else wholly outside it. (For a judicious examination of the topic, see Dahlstrom, 1971.)

Categorical variables seem simpler than continuous, quantifiable ones. It seems easy to decide whether or not a person makes a certain type of response, whether or not he likes baseball, etc. But close inspection shows that such classes or types are generally obtained by dichotomizing a continuum, by arbitrarily dividing it into two parts when finer divisions could be made. Categorical variables are frequently used in unstructured situations, e.g., when a child is asked to name his favorite hero, or when an adult has made up a story for a TAT picture and its major theme is classified. Such responses are methodologically difficult to handle. From one positive, observed response, we can tell something about the disposition into which we categorize it, but we cannot tell anything about any other category except that, at the time he responded, the dispositions associated with other categories were relatively weaker in strength. Thus, when we utilize such response data, we can place most confidence in the index for the category the subject uses most frequently, and successively less confidence in the indices with decreasing frequencies, each such index being relative to the strength of the other indices.

We are, then, essentially considering the placement of each subject on each of a series of common dimensions, continua that we consider one at a time in basic measurement work. This is the nomothetic approach, as contrasted with the idiographic, in which one seeks to depict and understand each person separately, with emphasis on his individual, probably unique personality. These terms were introduced into American personology in the thirties by Gordon Allport (1937).

It is difficult if not impossible to consider measurement without regard to substantive theory. My own theoretical position has influenced much of this volume. People writing from other positions would certainly discuss measurement with altered emphases. For example, a person espousing social learning theory would place more stress on the contributions of situations to behavior in and out of the testing setting. He would also examine the reinforcements that S had obtained in each situation, and the resulting expectations held by S about what would follow his behavior. (See Rotter, 1954, 1960). Again, in another volume of this series, Carson (1969) discusses the person's predominant styles or profile of styles in interacting with important others and with various classes of others. This Sullivanian orientation might lead to a different set of emphases in considering personality measurement. I believe, however, that the general strategy outlined in this chapter and the whole approach to measurement presented in this book are pertinent to research work from most theoretical positions commonly held today. While particular applications might require minor modifications, the basic general principles still apply.

In the preceding sections, we have talked about responses and manifestations of concepts. What about latent variables, what about unconscious needs? In principle, there seems to be no reason why they should not be conceptualized in much the same way as overt variables. The chief difference would lie in the kinds of phenomena considered relevant to such latent characteristics. The principal perspective for studying them is, of course, that of the expert making inferences from interviews, projective tests, dreams, and free associations.

THE EMPIRICAL ALTERNATIVE

Let me remind the reader once again that there is an alternative approach to measurement and concept formulation, the empirical one. One can start, as many have done, with the responses to a wide range of stimuli and, by factor analysis or other techniques, determine which stimuli covary and thus establish clusters of items that seem to be measuring the same variable. By inspecting the set of items assigned to a factor, and by finding out the correlates of total scores for that factor, one arrives at an interpretation or label for it. This is essentially what Cattell did to obtain his sixteen basic personality factors, now measurable by his 16 PF Test (Cattell and Stice, 1957). Similarly, one can take the items found to be associated with an attribute, such as introversion, dominance, or social desirability, and factor them to obtain subfactors. That would seem to lead to elements that might well be similar to those set up *a priori* in the approach described earlier in this section.

So the empirical approach starts with data and induces or infers concepts, which presumably are modified in the light of subsequent empirical work. The other approach starts with concepts and propositions about their relationships, and then develops measuring procedures to use in testing hypotheses derived from the propositions. The observations and especially the obtained relationships between measurements indicate the adequacy of the conceptual system: almost invariably the empirical work forces some modifications and revisions. In this progressive oscillation or cycling between the empirical and the conceptual, it would appear that it should not make any difference on which side one starts. In principle, this is true. In practice, of course, one's starting point depends upon one's interests and preferred ways of working—it depends on the personality of the investigator. The real problem is that most students of personality stay in one domain or the other, rarely shifting entirely to the opposite type of work. Thus the empiricist seldom uses his empirical factors as the basis for intensive and extensive theorizing; little theory has been built on the findings of factor analyses. The personality theorist continues to expatiate on his views, some times citing published findings congruent with them but spending little time himself on the collection and analysis of pertinent empirical data.

The two approaches are similar in other respects. While the empiricist almost invariably starts with some implicit or explicit concepts—of the domain of personality, for example, or the domain of the trait to be analyzed factorially—he usually limits his observations to one mode. Much of the early work of Cattell (1946) and of Guilford (1959, Chapter 8) was restricted to questionnaires, the self-report mode. Few such people have worked with several modes and integrated them as Cattell (1957) has done. Similarly, theorists start with their unsystematic observations (recall Figure 6.1), but they also tend to restrict themselves to one or two perspectives in both their conceptual and their empirical work.

A major thesis of this volume is that, contrary to the present state of the field, conceptual work and empirical work in personology should be closely coordinated and both should be recognized as utilizing a set of modes for observing the phenomena of personality. For the present, the coordination will probably have to occur within the minds of individual researchers. In the future, when theorists and experimenters learn to communicate accurately with each other, we can have a collaborative division of labor like that between theoretical and experimental physicists.

From Construing to Measuring

A GLANCE AHEAD: PROCESSES IN MEASURING

The rest of this volume focuses primarily on measurement. Most procedures for measuring personality involve the behavior of the subject being measured, i.e., they require responses by the subject as their original data. Such behavior can be viewed as one particular form of the general process notion developed earlier (Chapter 3). The reader will recall the argument that each type of personality variable is associated with one phase of that general process: perceptual, cognitive, valuing variables are associated with early phases, motives with a middle phase, characteristics of actions and evaluations of actions with later phases.

For the conceptual study of any characteristic of one phase in this general process, it is necessary only to postulate that the preceding phases have occurred. But for measurement, for purposes of comparing individuals with respect to any one type of attribute, it is necessary that the preceding phases have been highly similar for all subjects. The assessment of capacity or effectiveness provides a clear example. In such a case, all Ss must be alert and responsive; in addition, the external conditions must not generate such disruptive processes as feelings of inadequacy and ineffectiveness, especially not with different Intensities in different Ss. The stimulus item must be perceived and cognized the same way by all Ss, except for differences associated with differences among Ss in the capacity being assessed. All Ss must have the same intention of making a response that solves the problem posed in the test. Finally, comparable levels of carefulness must be evident (unless carefulness is construed as part of the effectiveness being assessed).

Thus the measurement of capacity or effectiveness, which is generally considered to be reasonably successful, involves the total formal process delineated above. In contrast, the measurement of a personality attribute typically involves some smaller number of phases. Yet it is commonly considered to be less adequate. Although many reasons have been offered for this inadequacy (e.g., Fiske, 1963b), a major one that is most pertinent here is the problem of eliciting overt and objective responses indicative of content and functioning which are largely internal and not observable in everyday life. For example, a test may require S to indicate which of two stimuli interests him more, whereas he would simply look a little longer at one of them if he encountered them outside the testing room. Or we try to determine what desire or motive is generated in S by a stimulus he has cognized, interpreted, and reacted to, when he might, in everyday life, have experienced that motive briefly but not initiated any overt action to implement that inclination.

Also pertinent is the fact that our success in measuring effectiveness is limited to capacities for such intellectual functioning as recalling and reasoning. We are less successful in assessing capacities in interpersonal relationships, effectiveness in particular roles (teacher, parent, spouse, etc.), and ability to cope with psychological stress or trauma.

In psychological measurement, each stimulus item has a specific process following it. These several specific processes have many common antecedent conditions associated with the testing situation itself and with the instructions from the experimenter (E), instructions that S has accepted. So, in addition to the shorter processes associated with particular items, we can see the total testing operation as a longer process within which these item processes occur. This more comprehensive process is initiated by the stimuli provided in the instructions, which gives S a set to follow a specified procedure. Each time S selects his answer and makes an overt, recorded response, he is executing an act determined by his general intention to comply with E's specifications. The general test-oriented process ends when S has answered the last item or when he hands in his test booklet.

As an illustration, consider a test in which the items are simple ambiguous sketches or figures (Cattell and Warburton, 1967, Test T 172, pages 505–6).

S is instructed to decide rapidly what each picture is, to choose between two alternative interpretations, one involving human influences and the other natural physical influences. We can assume that S looks at the picture and at the alternatives and sees which way of cognizing the picture feels better to him. Thus S goes through a guided cognizing process. When he has completed that, he makes a mark next to the selected cognition, carrying out his intention of going through the test-relevant process initiated by his perception of the instructions and his acceptance of them.

In some instances, S may look at the picture and interpret it, cognizing spontaneously without regard to the testing process. He then attends to the requirement of marking one response by reading the alternatives and seeing which comes closer to his original interpretation. If neither is very similar, he may then have to consider the two proposed cognitions to see which feels better to him.

Note that a cognizing process takes place with each item. It may be spontaneous or it may be a decision between the stated response alternatives. This process occurs within the larger test process, in which S is oriented toward successive cognitions as part of the task of marking one alternative for each picture. The important point is the identification of the two discrete kinds of processes, one involving interaction with each item and one involving coping with the task set by the instructions for the test. The two are quite distinct. An uncooperative subject may glance at each item and mark no responses, or only those that represent his spontaneous cognitions, thus experiencing the item processes but not carrying out the general test process. Alternatively, S might pretend to carry out the test process by marking responses randomly, without looking at and cognizing the stimuli.

One must recognize that measurement is possible only for a limited range of the total array of psychological states in which a person can be, and that the measurement situation also severely restricts the values that can be taken for the role and set components. In other words, the necessity of maximizing the comparability of conditions among subjects, i.e., of standardizing the test administration, and the fact that in most instances of personality measurement the subject cannot help knowing he is being measured—these two considerations taken together reduce the theoretically unlimited range of potential behavior to a particular subgroup of responses from which adequate indices can be obtained in the measurement process.

Psychologists must continually remind themselves that S is always responding to the testing situation and to the test materials themselves. E can never be certain that components of the testing conditions are not disturbing his measurement operations, are not contributing unwanted variance to his scores. There are probably ways around this obstacle, however. Just as a set of conditions and procedures has been devised to provide the optimal assessment of human capacities, so it may be possible to create a testing method with an explicit rationale such that personality variables can be measured effectively if not optimally.

THREE TEST DESIGNS

Suppose that the examiner has carefully and analytically thought out his conceptualization of the target attribute, following the "Guidelines" in this chapter, and has determined the essence of his concept. For dominance, this might be controlling or influencing another person; for impulsiveness, it might be executing instrumental acts ineffectively. Does E, the examiner, elicit in the test situation the process delineated in his conceptualization? The answer is frequently no. But the same answer often holds in the measuring of ability.

In measuring capacity, E often provides S with a problem and sees whether S can solve it. E.g., he may assess reasoning by asking S in what way two things are similar. But often E sets a different kind of task: he may ask S to define a word. In this instance, S is not directly demonstrating his capacity at that moment; rather he is showing that his capacity is such that he has previously acquired the meaning of the word. So E is testing for the products associated with the postulated capacity, and is using the process of recall rather than the process of learning the meaning of the word. Again, E can measure capacity by obtaining life data: Did S complete high school, college, or doctoral training? What level of vocational achievement has he reached? (To be sure, a collection of such indicators can be used with confidence only as positive evidence for capacity: low observed values may indicate either low ability or lack of opportunity. Unless capacity is narrowly defined, underestimations of ability may be made when these common correlates are the only data used.)

So, even in measuring intelligence, E may not elicit in the testing situation the exact process in which he is interested. Instead, he reasons that if he provides a task and stimuli, and if S manifests a specific type of response, E can safely infer that a certain process took place just before the response, a process that could not have occurred unless a different but related kind of process had occurred in S frequently in the past. Thus E infers from the observed response to the process leading to it, and from that to earlier processes indicative of the ability; finally, E generalizes over time back to the present and concludes that S still has the capacity E wishes to measure.

Among personality tests, the same kinds of design are used. In a few instances, the construct-relevant process is elicited in the testing room by using *simulated stimuli*. A test of figure preference may present a pair of figures, one simple in structure and the other complex, and S indicates which he likes better. In a color-form motion-picture test in which the forms move in one direction while the colors move in the opposite direction, S reports the direction of the apparent movement and unwittingly indicates whether he attends more to color or to form. Responsiveness to color is assessed from Rorschach responses. Field independence is measured by ability to detect a figure embedded in a larger pattern. Note that this cognitive style, like many others, is really a capacity; the score is the number of correct responses. (See the examples for Modes 2 and 3 in Figure 5.1.)

Some investigators (e.g., Spielberger and Lushene, 1971) have stressed the concept of state in contrast to the concept of trait, with its semipermanence. In the simulated stimuli design, S is actually in the process (state) to which the construct refers: he functions more or less intelligently, he experiences more liking for one stimulus than for another, or he perceives in a particular way. A moment's thought reveals the limitations to the applicability of this design. E.g., practical considerations prevent psychologists from eliciting high levels of affective intensity in most measurement situations. Again, dispositions involving long temporal periods cannot feasibly be elicited.

This simulated stimuli design is so named because the stimuli may not be strictly and fully representative of any category of stimuli. Typically, the stimuli are developed specifically for testing purposes and they may bear little resemblance to natural stimuli. They are used, however, to simulate natural stimuli for the purpose of eliciting the construct-relevant process in the testing room.

A very common design utilizes an *a priori related process,* a process that E postulates to covary with his construct. As in the earlier example of word knowledge as a measure of intelligence, the rationale is that a particular related process will occur in S in the testing room if he has had certain experiences in the past or if the strength of the target variable is high for him. An exhibitionistic person will presumably say on a test that he would rather be an entertainer than a clerk or a forest ranger. A dominating person will be likely to say that he has often got other people to do as he wishes. The *a priori* process may deal with reports of relevant products of the disposition: if a person says he owns a large collection of classical records, it is likely that he enjoys classical music. The same inference can be made from knowledge of famous composers or from ability to recognize excerpts from great music. (The potentialities of this design are well demonstrated by A. B. Sweney in Chapter 9 of Cattell and Warburton, 1967.)

Any item in a test with this design may not be a valid indicator for a group of subjects and especially not for a particular person. A child in a musical family may have unwillingly acquired considerable knowledge of music and composers in spite of his active dislike for music. Hence such items, devised on *a priori* grounds, must be subjected to empirical evaluation, by item-test correlational analysis at the very least.

A third type of design is based on an *empirically related process.* In this type, E may actually have no interest in what occurs within S when he encounters the stimulus. E simply determines whether S makes those responses that have been found empirically to be associated with a criterion classification of subjects. For example, the clinical scales of the Minnesota Multiphasic Personality Inventory were developed from comparisons of the responses of diagnosed clinical groups with those of apparently normal persons. Again, vocational interests are determined from the Strong Vocational Interest Blank by keys identifying responses made more often by those settled in each vocation than by people not in that vocation.

Note that the rationale for this design does involve a process notion. E assumes that when some of his test subjects give responses like those of his criterion group, these observed responses stem from processes that have some similarities to those that went on in his criterion group. To make this assumption plausible, E collects both the criterion data and the subsequent decision data under comparable conditions; in other words, he standardizes the testing conditions so that the processes in both groups are initiated by the same general and specific stimuli, objectively viewed.

There are relatively few personality tests based on the simulated stimuli design, a design in which the construct-relevant process occurs in the testing room. The design is used for measuring cognitive and perceptual variables, and for some variables pertaining to the way a person works and expresses himself. It can be used to assess interests and values only when such attributes can be represented by stimuli that can be brought into the testing room. Similarly, it cannot ordinarily be utilized for measuring the strength of a motive as manifested in action.

An intriguing type of design is employed in the S-R Inventory of Anxiousness (Endler, Hunt, and Rosenstein, 1962), mentioned earlier. In this inventory, S is asked to imagine that he is in a particular situation (such as on a ledge high on a mountain) and then is asked to indicate the degree to which he would experience each of a number of response modes (e.g., "Heart beats faster"). Like all personality tests, and perhaps more than most, this test requires S's cooperation. While it is, strictly speaking, a test using an *a priori* related process, it does simulate natural stimuli more or less well. Psychometric studies of this instrument and of others asking the subject to imagine some situation suggest that the design has considerable promise. This particular inventory is described because it illustrates well the dual processes involved in the great majority of personality tests. The cooperative subject can presumably place himself, in his mind's eye, in the situation portrayed, even though he has never experienced it in his life. He can introspect to determine his implicit reactions to that situation. But then he is required to complete the test task that has been set for him: for each response mode, he must choose one of the ordered alternatives printed in the booklet. No matter how representative his current feelings may be of his natural reactions, he can still readily manipulate (minimize or maximize) the reported strength of his reactions.

In the empirically related process design, E ignores both the process evoked by the stimulus and the process involved in response selection, as required by the task given to S. The method uses averages of stimuli and of many individuals to achieve its moderate successes. When presented with a test using the *a priori* related process design, S is quite aware of the test task, although he may have little idea what attribute the test is intended to measure. Typically he is not asked to maximize anything, although when a questionnaire format is used he is asked to maximize the accuracy of his reporting, a criterion that is difficult for him to apply at the moment or even in any subsequent review of his responses. In contrast, the simulated stimuli design usually poses an easily understood task: "What is the right answer?" "What did you see?" or "Which do you like better?" Furthermore, in selecting his response, S can rather readily accept and apply the criterion specified for him. He can feel at ease about doing what E wishes, both because the task is straightforward and because he feels no hesitation about making his perceptions and preferences known to E.

The trichotomy outlined above is based on the relationship presumed to hold between those processes and responses that E identifies in his conceptualization of his construct and those that occur in the test situation. It is relatively independent of other classifications. For example, it is possible to think up an application of each of these designs for most of the modes of observation presented in Chapter 5 (see Table 5.1, pages 70–71). Certain designs do, however, tend to occur more frequently with certain modes. Mode 1 (Self Description based on past experience) typically uses the *a priori* related process or the empirically related process design. Reports of Current Experiencing (Mode 2) are usually in response to simulated stimuli. Capabilities (Mode 3) are almost always measured with simulated stimuli. Prior Behavior (Mode 4) does not use any of these designs, since the indices are derived from impressions based on responses to natural stimuli, rather than stimuli provided for purposes of measurement. Observations of Behavior (Mode 5) and of Psychophysiological responses (Mode 6) typically involve simulated stimuli or an *a priori* related process.

Summary

We cannot measure a variable well if we cannot describe it. The target for measurement should be explicitly conceptualized, to clarify our own thinking and to enable us to communicate accurately with fellow scientists. A variable is an aspect of what occurs during a stage in a process. A construct is the label and interpretation someone gives that aspect. A conceptualization is, of course, developed for a purpose: in basic research, a construct is usually construed in the context of a particular theory. The steps toward a working conceptualization of a construct may be outlined as follows:

1. The setting for the construct
   (a) Theoretical context
   (b) Type of variable
   (c) Kind of index

2. Delineation
   (a) Core or essence
   (b) Differentiation from similar and overlapping constructs
   (c) Specification of low end

3. Analysis and planning for measurement
   (a) Modes to be used
   (b) Facets and their elements (for each mode)
   (c) Relevant conditions and states
   (d) Appropriate test designs

The conceptualization centers on the unique quality of the construct, on its core or essence. It must specify not only the high end of the continuum, but also the low end; it must indicate what similar content is excluded from the formulation. It must state the modes to be used in observing it, each mode being best taken as a distinct subconstruct. Each such subconstruct can then be analyzed into facets. The behavioral facet would have an element for each form of behavior to be included within the subconstruct; the elements in a situational facet might be the several kinds of relevant situations. The conceptualizer also considers the conditions and states facilitating the appearance and observation of a construct.

Variables and subvariables may, of course, be identified purely by empirical procedures such as factor analysis. Such empirical approaches, however, have not appeared to be as theoretically fruitful as the *a priori* formulation of constructs.

In measuring a construct, we elicit a total test process within which separate processes occur for each stimulus item. These shorter processes may be of the kind specified for the construct; e.g., the subject may be indicating the degree of liking he experiences for the stimuli (figures, pictures, or whatever), but for practical or technical reasons the test uses *simulated stimuli* rather than stimuli from everyday life. Or the test design may utilize an *a priori related* process, as when the subject reports whether he usually likes complex rather than simple figures. Finally, the test may involve a process known to be *empirically related* to that identified with the construct.

PART TWO

Measuring

Introduction

Up to this point, we have considered what we measure and how we should specify that target. In Part Two, we examine the technique of measuring. As implied earlier, each final index is obtained from a set of measurements, usually one measurement for the response to each stimulus. While the ultimate concern of personality measurement is with generalizing from observational data to unobserved phenomena identified with the construct, it is necessary also to evaluate the degree of confidence with which one can generalize from data derived by the measuring operation to hypothetical data that might be obtained at other times or with other stimuli or even with other orientations and settings.

Although we try to design tests so that responses to them will be stable over time, some variability does occur. To understand its sources, we can consider what behavior and what aspects of behavior outside the testing situation are stable. Regularities in the settings and the stimuli encountered by a person are associated with regularities in his behavior, especially for instrumental acts, which are practiced ways of coping.

Also to be considered is the critical and obvious fact that subjects react to tests and to being tested. A variety of motives may be aroused in a subject who is taking a test, many of them potential impediments to the experimenter's goal of obtaining adequate measurements. Subjects may try to present themselves in a favorable light. They may also select answers on other irrelevant bases, such as a preference for answering yes. In responding to a single item, subjects may interpret both single words and the item as a whole idiosyncratically.

Test scores, like other behavior, are determined by many influences. The particular effects associated with any one test make its scores relatively specific, so that its correlations with other measures of the same concept tend to be low. To measure a given concept, personology needs tests that can be considered interchangeable with other tests, i.e., tests that show highly similar patterns of relationships with important variables indexing other concepts. The limited evidence available suggests that few personality tests meet this criterion.

CHAPTER SEVEN

Some Fundamentals
of Measurement

Ideal Measurement

In any human endeavor, it is wise to know exactly what we are trying to do. If we have an explicit goal, we can more readily tell when we are off the track, when our efforts have been diverted. A goal can also provide a norm by which to evaluate our progress and the adequacy of each step along the way. Equally important, the setting of a goal may help us to widen our outlook by calling to our attention possibilities that might otherwise be overlooked.

A FANTASY

Let us engage in a bit of fantasy. Suppose we had unlimited resources of money, time, and technical assistance. How would we go about measuring personality? We would be seeking to determine the typical experiences and reactions of each subject. More exactly, for each concept of interest to us, we would want to determine S's average (mean or modal) reaction. We might also want to determine the range or variation of these reactions. (We are simplifying things here and assuming that our concept refers to a single, identifiable reaction.) Since reactions are a function of the situation, to a greater or lesser degree, we want a value for our subject for every relevant situation.

Given our tremendous resources, we might try to obtain a videotape record of S's behavior over an extended period—perhaps several weeks. We might also want simultaneous records from two or more angles, to be

122

sure we had a complete picture. Then this vast array of material could be searched for instances of the concept-designated reaction. By prodigious effort, we could obtain frequencies of each such reaction of interest to us, and could also determine the average strength, intensity, and duration of each type of reaction.

The advantages of such data are obvious. They would have been obtained under natural conditions rather than in the laboratory or testing room, and there would have been a variety of situational contexts and specific stimuli present, rather than a single context and one or a few kinds of stimuli. Thus, in principle, we would have been observing the behavior referred to in our conceptualization of the construct, the description being of natural, *in vivo* behavior.

But would it be possible to obtain such a protocol without the subject's knowing that it was being done? (We assume that we have been completely ethical and obtained S's permission to do this at some time, but without telling him when.) It might be possible at some date in the future (1984?), with further advances in technology. At this time, it does seem impossible.

But would S's awareness of being recorded make any difference? We could not definitively answer that question without a controlled experiment, comparing the reactions of subjects when they were aware and when they were not. Some evidence suggests that subjects may become so accustomed to continual surveillance that they almost ignore or forget it (see Soskin and John, 1963). Reactions to being observed and measured are probably most pronounced at first and diminish as the observation continues with no apparent undesirable consequences for the subject. TV cameras have been placed in homes recently and seem to produce videotapes revealing little concern with the camera, but such methods are still in the exploratory stage.

Would our protocol be long enough? Would we have enough instances to enable us to arrive at a dependable index, one that would allow us to predict S's reactions confidently in the next few weeks or months? For most concepts, three weeks would be ample, but not for reactions to such strong stress as loss of loved ones. More generally, how could we be sure that the period provided a representative sample of the conditions and contexts in which S usually lived? That is a minor question that could be resolved. More important is another consideration. We measure in order to compare people. Suppose we have these elaborate extended protocols for several subjects. We are confronted with the obvious, that their environments are quite different.

Let us not be defeated easily. Let us hire and train a group of analysts who will study the protocols and devise ways to classify all the situations in which each subject was taped. With sufficient effort, we could rate each situation as to type and intensity of the press to which S was exposed. ("Press" is a technical term [Murray *et al.*, 1938] for the labeled forces impinging on a person.) We could then make statistical adjustments for differences between the arrays of contexts for our subjects. Again, we could do the same thing for the particular focal stimuli preceding the reactions for each construct. And of course we would have several judges work independently to decide when the relevant reactions occurred. With adequate training, it might be possible to obtain high degrees of agreement among the judges (high interjudge reliability).

We would, of course, be limited to the subject's overt behavior, to his physical movements and his speech and other vocalizations. Even in this imaginary research, we would not know directly anything about S's feelings and inner experience. So, even with unlimited resources, we could not directly measure everything with which personology is concerned. Moreover, current evidence suggests that a tremendous investment would not be warranted until we had solved the problems associated with the subject's awareness of being observed and until we have more confidence in the feasibility of controlling for differences in experienced environments and stimulation. We are forced to conclude that the theoretically ideal measurement of personality not only is unfeasible and impractical, but also involves several serious methodological difficulties. Similar difficulties occur in the less than ideal measurement of personality practiced today, as we shall see later.

REALITY

Are there more realistic alternatives? We can look for records of S's past behavior, and personologists often do just that (see Allport, 1942, 1965). While such records (e.g., artistic creations) are very satisfactory for getting at some variables, they cannot help us much in studying many others, and such records are not available for many people. We can ask other people about S's behavior, but each such person is acquainted with only a segment. Furthermore, such reporters may not give us completely accurate reports because their personalities may distort their perceptions. Also, when a person reports on another person, he becomes in effect a subject who is aware of and may react to the fact that he is reporting. This approach is identified in Chapter 5 as Mode 4.

We can ask experts to observe and rate the subject (Mode 5). It is difficult to do this without S's knowing such observing is taking place, and his knowledge may affect his behavior. Also, it is expensive to provide the expert with more than a limited amount of material or opportunity to observe.

We can turn to the subject himself for reports on his past behavior (Mode 1), with the possible biases associated with his subjective perceptions of it and his desire to make a good impression or avoid creating a bad impression. We can also ask the subject to take part in more or less realistic situational tests, such as a leaderless group discussion (Bass, 1954) with other subjects (Mode 5), or give him a task for which there is a right answer (Mode 3). Finally, we can ask him to report on his immediate experience when we present standard stimuli (Mode 2). A promising form of the latter approach is to ask the subject to imagine that he is in a particular situation and to report what he would feel (see the S-R Inventory of Anxiousness, Endler *et al.*, 1962, and the Individual Reactions Inventory, Pearson, 1968, 1969). This technique may be effective because it seems relatively harmless to Ss; its applicability, however, may be limited to a few types of variables.

These various approaches have been listed in roughly increasing order of dependence on the subject (assuming that the first, ideal approach is done without his knowledge). Higher and higher degrees of cooperation are required, and more and more willingness to be candid and not deceive the experimenter. Also running through these approaches is an increasing degree of departure from the natural, everyday situation. But note that S's behavior provides the phenomena used in every mode, and this behavior is equally real in each: the sole question is the extent to which the indices derived from it reflect the target construct in which we are interested. With increasing degrees of departure from the natural situation, we depend increasingly on S's cooperation, and we are likely to introduce influences associated with the contrived situation used for measuring. Hence, even though S's behavior is equally real in natural and laboratory settings, the potential systematic contributions of extraneous factors are much larger in the testing situation and may reduce the extent to which the obtained measurements are determined by the target construct.

Thus the personologist has a range of possible strategies. He can try to stay as close as possible to the natural observations from which his general concepts were originally extracted (see Figure 6.1, page 93), developing complex procedures for classifying the phenomena into his conceptual framework and for categorizing and assessing the contributions of naturally occurring stimuli, settings, and states of the subjects, so that the raw data can be adjusted to provide indices for the several subjects which can be meaningfully compared. Alternatively, he can set up standardized procedures for obtaining more systematic observations, these procedures utilizing particular settings, subject states, and stimuli to elicit behavior related to the essential substance of his target construct in a designated way. At this time, strategies of the latter type seem more promising. It seems to me that progress in improving personality measurement is likely to come from gaining insight into the limitations of systematic, standardized measuring procedures and from ingenuity and creativity in devising new techniques that will reduce or remove the undesirable effects of such limitations. This personal conviction stems from recognition of the power of experimentation, in which E systematically eliminates or controls potentially important influences, as opposed to the serious limitations of field studies, where E must depend on the limited range of naturally occurring sets of conditions and on statistical controls. For example, an E who has devised a new measuring technique can test the degree to which it functions as its target construct is believed to function. He can test his understanding of the construct by making predictions about his measuring procedure and determining the extent to which the predictions are empirically confirmed. (See the discussion of construct validity in the next chapter.)

Whatever general strategy the personologist adopts, he must be able to evaluate the adequacy of his method. No one method, no one type of measuring procedure can be fully evaluated by itself. While a single method may be shown to be a reasonably satisfactory approach to a construct, the determination that a method is the best one, or the best for a given purpose, can be made only by demonstrating its superiority over other methods. And although a personologist may decide to limit his work to a construct as observed in a single mode, his colleagues will ultimately want to know how findings from that mode relate and compare to findings from other modes.

Among the various modes for observations, there is only one by which the subject can be studied without his being aware that he is under scrutiny, that he is being tested, assessed, or evaluated: Mode 4 utilizes judgments of other people based on phenomena occurring before the act of measurement. The phenomena may be products of the subject (essays, artistic creations, diaries, letters, etc.) or they may be the behaviors of the subject which these people have observed for one reason or another. The observers may be friends, peers in school or work, supervisors, teachers, etc.

Potential limitations of this mode are associated with two factors. The materials available are necessarily restricted, the products by their existence or nonexistence and the behaviors by the type of relationship between the observer and the subject, and therefore such material has varying degrees of adequacy for the purpose at hand. The second factor is the psychology of the observer. If he is a layman providing ratings or other descriptions of the subject, not only will his individual perceptions of the subject be a function of his personality, but also his responses describing the subject will be influenced to some degree by the fact that he knows he is producing measurement data and often knows its purpose. Thus everyone realizes that a letter of recommendation is very likely to present the candidate in a favorable light, rather than portraying him dispassionately and objectively. (The recipient has the difficult task of deciding how much bias is present in the letter, and sometimes must even estimate the direction of such bias.)

The observations of professional people are also susceptible to bias and idiosyncrasy Experts may have positive or negative personal reactions toward subjects which must be guarded against. Furthermore, the judgments of any observer can be described analytically by such parameters as average level (e.g., degree of favorableness), differentiation between variables, stereotypy, etc. (see Cronbach, 1955). Perhaps we should calibrate observers as we calibrate other recording devices.

The possibilities for "nonreactive research in the social sciences" have been intensively examined by Webb, Campbell, Schwartz, and Sechrest (1966) in their book on *Unobtrusive Measures*. They consider the potential value of using physical traces, archives, and undetected observation. Their proposals are much more feasible for studying differences between groups or effects of particular conditions than for measuring individual differences. The serious student should, however, study this important volume as a possible source of inspiration on new techniques for assessment.

MEASURING IN A TESTING SITUATION

Many of the potential difficulties stemming from the psychology of observers are similar to those associated with the psychology of the subject being measured in a testing situation, a topic to be examined later (Chapter 10). At this point, consider measurement in a testing situation. Most of the modes (1, 2, 3, 5, and 6) utilize phenomena in a situation created for the purpose of measurement. We shall discuss such measurement in general terms, the issues applying to a greater or lesser extent to each of these modes.

Strictly speaking, when we measure in a testing situation, we are restricting ourselves to studying behavior in that particular kind of setting. The ultimate objective must be to demonstrate that our findings are not limited or biased by this restriction. The advantages of this strategy, as compared to observation based on natural settings, are several. First, the situation is exactly the same for all subjects. That is, it is identical in its objective, physical features, a fact that does not guarantee that it is psychologically identical for all subjects. Unless the construct being assessed involves reactions to being evaluated, the situation must be designed to have minimal influence on the responses of the subjects. The personologist can, to some extent, determine the adequacy of this aspect of the design by some post-test exploration of subjects' perceptions of and reactions to the situation. Second, the stimuli can be controlled and the responses available to the subject can be restricted so that they all involve the quality relevant to the dimension being measured. (These matters were examined in more detail in Chapter 3.)

But the use of a standardized testing procedure does not solve all prob-

lems It may not be possible to introduce all relevant stimuli, for practical
or ethical reasons: for example, consider the stimuli pertinent to measuring
reactions to extreme danger or other traumatic stress, and those for sexual
responsiveness. That issue is related to the broader question whether, in
our measurement operations, we can ever elicit all reactions relevant to our
construct, be they feelings or actions.

The most serious matter is the extent to which the indices obtained in a
testing situation serve our purpose by capturing the essence of the construct
being measured. From the indices obtained under the conditions for measurement, can we generalize to what ideally we would like to have? E.g.,
can we safely infer that our indices, combined in some appropriate way,
closely approximate the values we would have obtained by appropriate
methods based on comprehensive and exhaustive observation of the subject
in his everyday life, all within a particular perspective? This is the matter
of validity, the crucial aspect of all measurement, the objective toward
which all other concerns are directed. The other central concept in psychometric theory, reliability, deals with means to that end, with the degree to
which one can generalize from the indices obtained under specified procedures to indices that might be obtained under procedures differing in one
or more respects. (See Chapter 8.)

If we adopt a measurement strategy relying on responses in a testing situation, we should not feel that we have settled on a poor substitute for the
real thing. Consider the parallel case of measuring intelligence. There are
two options. We can get judgments about a subject's intelligence either by
examining the products of his intellectual behavior in everyday life or from
people who know his work. The alternative is to measure performance
under the optimally facilitating and standardized conditions of a testing
room. Psychology has chosen the latter alternative. The voluminous literature on mental tests has come to fruition in an analysis of intellectual functions identifying three facets: the content (with such elements as verbal and
symbolic), the operation (evaluation, cognition, etc.), and the product (units,
relations, etc.). This is Guilford's creative structuring of *The Nature of
Human Intelligence* (1967), a construction built on the findings of systematic testing in controlled conditions. The use of facet theory in designing
and constructing ability tests is advocated by Humphreys (1962).

But note that tested intelligence is optimal performance, not typical performance. An ability as tested is usually superior to the ability as reflected
in everyday performance, when S is functioning on less structured tasks and
is subjected to distractions, conflicting motivations, etc. Following the example of intelligence, we might approach personality as response capability,
the view of Wallace considered earlier (Chapter 6). But rather than following that aspect of the example by facilitating the manifestation of the most
extreme response of which the subject is capable, we can adopt another

aspect, the procedure of eliciting S's cooperation in performing the task set for him, as is done in measuring cognitive styles and controls. The task itself can be designed to focus the subject's attention on the construct-relevant part of the general process—perceiving, cognizing, valuing, intending, executing, etc.

IDEAL TESTING

At this point, we shall consider the circumstances under which ideal testing would occur, an ideal that in principle is quite within the range of possibility. (This extends the description of our objective as sketched toward the close of Chapter 3.)

Subjects are present in the testing room in a state that permits the construct-relevant process to occur: they are alert, well rested, and free of tension. They are there of their own free will rather than under compulsion. They are given instructions about the total situation and about the task, information that is completely acceptable to them; they experience no conflict that might generate defensiveness or some other competing or conflicting disposition. They then approach the test stimuli with a motive to produce responses of a specific kind, responses meeting the criteria indicated in the instructions. (At this point, the reader may wish to review the discussion of "Contexts" [pages 84–85] and the notion of "test contracts" between examiner and subject.)

At any one time, different people are experiencing different moods. When E is not measuring mood, he must make certain that mood does not bias S's responses. If the testing situation is sufficiently pleasant and if the task and items are sufficiently interesting, the effects of prior mood can be minimized. Furthermore, E can well afford to take a few minutes to try to generate in S a temporary mood appropriate to the procedure he is using.

While the stimuli themselves may be unfamiliar, even in this ideal measurement, their meanings are readily grasped. Taken by itself, each stimulus has the same meaning for each S (except for effects associated with differences between Ss in the strength of the target construct). From the point of view of E, the stimuli may be identical with those encountered in life, may be similar to such stimuli, or may be symbolic of them. It does not matter as long as E can be confident, on some objective basis, that they will elicit the processes and reactions in which E is interested.

Still ideally, S interprets and reacts to the stimuli as he does to any stimuli. He may feel motivated to act in one way or another. But here the testing context intrudes. S must conclude the test process by selecting and recording an appropriate response as previously instructed. If S has the opportunity to evaluate his responses, he will feel satisfied that they meet E's criteria, which he has previously accepted.

Thus, even in ideal testing, the construct-relevant process generated by each stimulus item occurs within the larger framework. In a sense, this condition is quite realistic in form. the flow of personal experience involves shorter processes occurring within the duration of longer processes. One always has reasons for being in particular conditions, reasons that have some potential effects on the processes elicited by the focal stimuli that occur within that context.

The crucial matter is the extent to which the larger, task-reactive process is subordinated so that its effects can be minimized. Roughly and phenomenologically speaking, how often during a test does S think of the fact that it is just a test? (Of course, S may not even be aware of influences from the testing conditions; see Kroger, 1967; Eaton and Fiske, in press.) In ideal testing, S becomes highly involved in the task and in the stimuli; his experience and responses are determined by the immediate stimuli and the task orientation rather than by processes (such as defensive strategies) aroused in him by the assessment setting itself. In other words, in ideal personality testing, E and S are working together, as they do in ability testing, with both of them aware of the ways in which the situation departs from everyday life. (See "The Experimental Conditions for Measuring Individual Differences," Fiske and Butler, 1963.)

THE ISOLATED CONSTRUCT AND INTERACTIONS AMONG CONSTRUCTS

Many personologists concerned with human dynamics are dissatisfied with measuring one construct at a time, the strategy advocated above. In everyday life, just as manifested intelligence is affected by motivation, so manifestations of one motive are affected and even blocked by other motives. How can we learn how to understand the naturally occurring phenomena of everyday life by measuring constructs in the aseptic, restricted conditions of the testing room? Two types of answers can be given to that question.

First, it may be that we cannot attain a complete understanding of naturally occurring phenomena until we can dependably measure their several aspects and qualities as they occur naturally, something that is difficult to do. We have had only limited success in this approach. Yet we may be able to achieve some partial understanding by recognizing the nature of the problem and by seeking ingenious ways of indirectly observing and measuring the phenomena. Recall that, in physics, invisible particles can be detected and identified by the tracks they leave in a cloud chamber. We now get a past experience of S as recorded in his mind (using Mode 1) and past behavior as observed by others (Mode 4). Perhaps new methodological insights will enable us to use these modes even more effectively than we do now.

Second, a promising strategy is to undertake the easier task of learning how to measure important constructs one at a time in the testing situation.

As we learn more about such constructs in such pure and simplified form and as we learn more about how to obtain dependable, replicable indices, we can devise experimental procedures for studying interactions between constructs, two at a time, and even three at a time. For example, we can work on competing perceptual tendencies, such as the dispositions to follow the movement of color rather than of form, as Thurstone (1953) and E. Hess (see Sinclair, 1956) did. Or we can determine the relative strength of two motives, comparing such observations with indices for each motive measured alone. In science, it is often better to tackle a problem first in simplified form and then study it in its full complexity.

The Single Datum

THE MEASUREMENT DECISION

Measurement is the assignment of numbers to objects according to certain rules. The rules specify the conditions under which such assignments are made. These conditions include the characteristics of the measuring situation and, in psychology, the task set for the subject, the stimuli, the response format, etc. They also specify the procedure for coding each response by a number and the way in which these numbers are treated to arrive at a composite index. The purpose is to assign one number to each object, i.e., to each person measured. In this section, we shall be concerned with the rules for coding each response. More exactly, we code each response in terms of some aspect that is significant for the construct being measured.

In measuring, we have a series of categories, and in principle we ask for each, "Does this response fit into this class?" We usually impose the rule that there can be only one positive decision, all the others being negative: the response can fit into only one class. Additionally, it *must* fit into one of the classes, although that rule may be softened by having a class of omissions or some other catch-all category that may later be ignored.

Thus in scoring a response to a Rorschach inkblot, we decide whether the response is to the whole blot, some major part, a small detail, etc. But such a response has several other features. We can also classify it according to the aspect of the stimulus that determined it—the form, the color, or the texture of the stimulus. Still other classifications are by content and by frequency (popular, original, or in between). Although such multiple classification of a single response is not common in psychological measurement, Rorschach scoring does remind us that any one classification pertains to only one of the several aspects of a response.

The same scheme applies to quantitative classifications. In measuring a person's height, we decide to employ a scale with specific values, perhaps inches if we do not need more refined steps. In principle, we have about a

hundred values and ask which one would most appropriately be assigned
to the subject. The measurement decision is an easy one. Even if his height
as projected onto our measuring scale falls exactly halfway between two of
the inch marks, we can have the convention of assigning the higher of the
two values. (In passing, note that we do not measure a person's height directly, as we might the height of a square bookcase; instead, we extend
orthogonal, ninety-degree projections from the soles of his feet and from
the top of his head to a parallel straight edge. There is some degree of in-
directness even in much physical measurement.)

The basic decision is really which category is more appropriate than any
other. In any classification scheme utilizing qualities, rather than quantities
on a continuum, there will always be particular instances in which the
object seems to fit into more than one category, and some rule or procedure
must be invoked to make the decision; similarly, in measuring by successive
ordered categories, there will be responses that fall so exactly between two
steps that their assignment must be done arbitrarily.

Classifications can be guided by standard cases or examples (rather than
abstractly defined categories), as in classifying the content of Rorschach
responses. Early scales for handwriting quality provided examples to guide
the judges. In some of the earliest personality ratings (about the time
of World War I), marker points on a scale were illustrated by the name of
a specific person as rated by some criterion judge. Obviously there is a
dilemma here. On the one hand, the scale may be identified on the basis of
someone's prior judgments, which themselves are fallible. On the other
hand, verbal definitions of scale points are likely to be abstract, imprecise,
and open to subjective interpretation by the rater. The most fruitful resolution is to find verbal descriptions on the meaning of which a high degree of
consensus can be demonstrated.

THE RESPONSE ATTRIBUTE RECORDED

The single basic datum in observation and measurement can take various
forms. One form records whether the total response is made. Thus a rat
running a maze may or may not enter the first blind alley. This indicant
is rarely used in personality measurement except in modified form: Among
a subject's free responses, does he give one of a particular kind, such as a
response to an inkblot as a whole? Very common is the datum based on the
response's being X or not X; e.g., on a multiple-choice test, the keyed
response to the item or a nonkeyed response. Strictly speaking, this decision
refers to the location of the response mark in one precoded spot or another
on the answer sheet. The X or not-X datum is really a special dichotomous
case of the multistep classification of the response in terms of strength or

intensity: the nonkeyed category includes all strengths below some criterion, the keyed all above. The subject may provide the datum by his choice of the position of the mark he makes on the precoded, ordered scale presented to him (as on a rating scale), or a scorer may do the coding (if the subject rates by marking a point on a continuous line or if he responds by choosing words to write out).

In other parts of psychology, such as learning, temporal characteristics of the response are used as data. In operant conditioning, the rate of the response (frequency per unit of time) is the central datum. Also available are its duration and its latency. Temporal data are rare in personality measurement, although time for first response is often recorded in the Rorschach examination and latency is used in free-association tests to identify personally significant associations. The neglect of temporal indicants is associated with the use of group testing, in which only total time can feasibly be recorded, and with the use of instructional sets that are often designed to avoid disturbing the subject by motivating him to respond under pressure of time.

The preceding discussion has not considered the stimulus. In the majority of measuring procedures, the datum from the response to one stimulus is treated as interchangeable with that from any other. An exception is the method used for the Thurstone attitude scales, in which the datum for each "agree" response is the scale value of the statement as determined previously from independent judgments ("disagree" responses are ignored).

One purpose of this examination has been to stress the fact that the typical datum for measurement is only one aspect of the response, even when the subject is responding to test items. For example, we could note not only the location of S's mark but its graphological characteristics as indices for the speed, physical effort, and psychomotor control involved. A more important purpose has been to remind ourselves of the many possibilities that can be used in innovative test design, depending upon the nature of the construct being assessed.

POTENTIAL INDICES

Consider some of the indices that might be used in measuring dominance or some specified form of it. In doing so, it will be necessary to go beyond the consideration of the specific response associated with a given stimulus to consider more comprehensive indices. The conceptualization of dominance (D) will be assumed to include all processes in which S contemplates changing his interactions so as to control the views or actions of another person, whether or not he subsequently acts to produce this effect. Such a process involving dominance can occur at any time: when the person is with other people; when he is alone and planning some action; when he is asleep and dreaming; even in the mental content that seems to occur be tween dreams. (This concept of dominance is broader than our earlier one.)

Hence the index of D may be defined in a variety of ways:

1. The number of times (frequency) during a year or other stated time interval when S experiences a D process.
2. The total amount of time per time interval that S is experiencing a D process in any of its phases (such as planning to engage in D behavior or actually initiating D behavior).

These definitions are obviously too heterogeneous for most purposes. One could go to variables restricted to latent (L) content in fantasy, usually (but not necessarily) when no other person is present or being interacted with.

L1. The frequency of D processes when no action can result.
L2. The corresponding total duration of all D processes.

Looking at the behavioral or manifest (M) side, we could define variables in terms of the occurrences of the process in situations where action could be undertaken—usually when other people are present, when the situation would permit S to execute acts involving the D process.

M1. The number of times per time interval that the process occurs in such a situation.
M2. The total amount of time the process is going on per time interval in such a situation.

These seem very close to what we would like to measure. They could be approached by the use of simulated stimuli. But we may want to get closer to observable material.

M3. The number of times per time interval that the process occurs and leads to an action (any action, from a gesture to a long-term plan).
M4. The total amount of time S is acting as determined by the D process.

To be an individual difference variable, each of these definitions must assume that the conditions for all subjects are comparable: both the opportunities (the likelihood of accomplishing the intended effects) and the instigations (the demand values of the stimuli) must be essentially equal or equated. Hence we may prefer the following:

M5. The number of times S experiences the D process during the occurrence of a set of common stimuli, each impinging on S separately.

M6. The scale value (in terms of demand value for D) of the weakest stimulus (among the standard set) that will elicit the process.

M7. As in M5, the number of times S experiences the D process, but also acts on the basis of the motive.

M8. As in M6, the scale value of the weakest stimulus eliciting the process, but with the process continuing into the action phase.

Alternatively, the definition may restrict the range of demand values of stimuli considered:

M9. For stimuli that universally evoke the D process, the strength of actions resulting. (Strength might be assessed temporally or in terms of energy or effort expended on such actions.)

Which of these operational indices should be chosen? The decision has to be made in part on the basis of practical considerations examined earlier, but in part for other reasons. Which are most congruent with the perspective being used? Which come closest to the flavor of the conceptualization of dominance that is being followed? Which are most congruent with the connotations of the theoretical propositions to be tested? The decision may not be easy to make, but it must be made deliberately. Even when the design of a measuring procedure is determined largely by practical considerations, as it unfortunately is in many cases, the test designer should identify for himself the nature of the operational index utilized. When a test is found to have inadequate reliability or validity (by methods considered in the next chapter), a possible reason is the use of an unsuitable index.

Summary

While it might seem that we should aspire to a hypothetically ideal measuring operation in which S's actions would be completely recorded for days on end, it is doubtful that we would find such a protocol satisfactory for methodological and practical reasons. In addition to the ethical aspect of recording with his permission but without his knowledge, there would be tremendous difficulties in judging the behaviors and in assessing the environmental forces present for each relevant behavior. In reality, we have alternatives ranging from the mode in which S's previous behavior and products are used without his prior knowledge that they would be so employed to modes requiring S's active collaboration.

By measuring in a situation designed for the purpose, we can control many of the conditions and components that vary all too freely in the naturalistic situation. We cannot, however, employ all possible conditions and all possible stimuli. An optimal approach is to design the testing conditions to maximize the determination of responses by the levels of the construct in the subjects, minimizing the contributions, common and differential, from the obvious fact that S is being tested. At the least, we should fully develop and try out this approach, which is methodologically similar to that used in other natural sciences.

In measuring, we select an attribute of the response and classify the response accordingly. We map the response into a set of categories, which are commonly ordered on a scale. This step, taken in conjunction with that of summing over many opportunities for responding, can lead to any one of a variety of indices.

CHAPTER EIGHT

Indices: Their Models
and Their Evaluation

The individual datum is the unit on which we build to obtain an index, each datum being too specific or too undependable for us to use in studies of the relationships associated with a construct. A dictionary definition of "index" is "a number derived from a series of observations and used as an indicator of a condition; as, an index of intelligence." English and English (1958, page 258) note that "the term is almost synonymous with variable but is used where it is admitted that quantification is incomplete or imperfect." This connotation is quite appropriate for most measurement in psychology, especially in personality. The term frequently refers to a score, but "score" has the undesirably narrow connotation of being based on a test. So "index" is used here to refer to a number derived from a series of observations and viewed as representing, to some extent, the degree of a construct (or subconstruct) attributed to a person. Sometimes it will be used collectively to refer to a set of such numbers, one for each of several subjects.

The primary concern of this chapter will be how we go from the units or data to the index, and how we evaluate the quality and adequacy of an index. The combining of data into an index is a step that, like many other aspects of measurement, is done so routinely that we take it for granted and do not consider its implications. We rarely ask ourselves whether we are prepared to make the assumptions required by our combining operation.

Strictly speaking, we begin ordering persons when we classify them in terms of their response to any one stimulus or item: those giving the keyed response are considered to show more of the attribute than those giving any

137

other response. But at that level, it is usually not necessary for us to have in mind a picture of the scale on which we ultimately wish to place each person. At the index level, we must have such a picture or model to make clear how we are measuring or scaling the subjects.

Measurement Scales

The classical exposition of scales, written by Stevens (1958, 1968), distinguishes four types. (See Figure 8.1.) The *nominal* or *categorical* scale is composed of qualities or classes with no order. Examples are sex, marital status, and eye color. Each person is assigned to one class. The *ordinal* scale involves ordering of persons with no assumptions about the distance between them. Thus the contestants in a foot race can be assigned places —first, second, third, etc.—by observing the order in which they cross the finish line. In ratings by a peer, each subject in a group can be ranked on the specified attribute.

Categorical Scale

Redheads	*Blonds*	*Brunettes*
Joe	John	Jane
Tom	Jim	Jean
	Mary	Bill
		Fred
		Dorothy

Ordinal Scale

Rank on examination

1	Jean
2	Joe
3	Fred
4	Mary
5	
6	
.	
.	
.	
.	

Interval Scale

Scores on final examination

40	Jean
37	Joe
36	Fred
34	Mary
33	Tom, John, Jim
32	Bill
.	
.	
.	
.	

Ratio Scale

Heights (in inches)

72	Bill
70	Fred
68	Jean
67	Joe, Tom
65	Mary, Jane, John
65	Jim, Dorothy
.	
.	
.	

Figure 8.1. Examples of types of scales

If we have information about the distances between persons, we can have an *interval* scale. Thus we could record the time interval between the winner of the race and the next person, and between every other successive pair. A better example is the measurement of temperature, by a clinical thermometer, a hollow column on which degrees are equal distances apart and within which a liquid expands or contracts. Intelligence tests with time limits use items as units. The subject's score is the number of correct answers produced. But a zero score does not mean that the person has no intelligence. In much psychological measurement, we use equal-interval scales with an arbitrary zero point rather than a meaningful absolute zero.

Finally, there are scales with absolute zeros. Runners in a race can be timed. Temperature can now be measured in degrees from absolute zero. Reaction time can be measured from presentation of stimulus. Such scales are called *ratio* scales, because we can say meaningfully that one runner is twice as fast as another, that one reaction was three times as fast as another, etc. (In addition to these four basic scales, there are special cases that fall between them, usually involving partial ordering. Each of these other types is based on information that is more than that necessary for one type but not sufficiently complete to permit classification into the next higher type. See Coombs, 1952, Chapter 1.)

Each scale requires more information than the one below it. The ordinal requires not only classes, but also an ordering of the classes; the interval requires the measurement of the distance between classes; and the ratio requires that the observations be categorized into classes designated in terms of distance from a fixed, meaningful reference point of zero. With each such increment of information, more refined statistical analyses become possible. Ranking permits the determination of covariation between orders. Equal intervals make it possible to measure variation (variance or standard deviation). Ratio scales are rare in psychology and little psychological theory requires such scales. The coefficient of variation and the geometric mean are examples of statistics requiring a ratio scale.

Measurement is the assignment of numbers according to rules. The rules are determined in part by the kind of scale we intend to use. Measurement is sometimes called the mapping of observations, and the kind of map obtained depends upon the type of scale used. We select the type of scale on the basis of our evaluation of what the measuring procedure will yield. Thus we can ask raters to order persons on friendliness and they can do it with some feeling of confidence, but they may have much less confidence about judging whether the distance between the persons ranked first and second is 1.5 or 1.8 times the distance between the second and third persons. Hence even though we may be convinced that persons can be described by indices on an equal-interval scale, we may choose to place them only on an ordinal scale, at least for each observer. We could, of course, take the rank indices for each of several observers and, by the use of an appropriate scaling technique (see Guilford, 1954, Chapter 8), place our subjects on an equal-interval scale on the basis of the total set of data. In going from data to indices on a scale, we make assumptions. We must be sure that the measuring operations permit such assumptions. Frequently we cannot be absolutely sure; we can only make a careful judgment. In selecting and using a measurement scale, as in other uses of models, the decision about the appropriateness of the model is a complex one based on prior findings about and with the model and also on the degree to which the results from the particular application are congruent with the model.

Thus it is the nature of the data that determines what types of scales can be applied to it. If we judge that a given type of scale can be used, we can also use any of the preceding types, since they make less demands of the data. But ordinarily we use the most rigorous type of scale possible, so that we can extract as much information as possible from our observations. Moreover, we can also apply more powerful statistics in our analyses of the data: the Pearson r utilizes information about the distances between subjects, rather than treating adjacent ranks as equal distances apart (as in rank correlation coefficients), and can be used with more assurance in more complex statistical techniques.

In measuring intelligence and personality, the equal-interval scale is the measurement model most commonly used (usually without explicit demonstration of its fit to the data). Not only is it applied to indices for subjects as the data for statistical tests; it also is involved in most of the psychometric models for going from units (responses) to indices (scores for subjects). While measurement models for scales are concerned with the mathematical and statistical properties of the scales used for indices, psychometric models consider jointly the substance of the construct, the nature of the items, and the meaning to be ascribed to the indices. Whereas these types of scales apply to all measurement, regardless of content, the psychometric models examine the structure of measuring procedures in terms of stimulus characteristics and index forms. ("Psychometrics" is a loose term meaning measurement in psychology, although some people use it to refer to mental testing, or just to the testing of intelligence.)

Psychometric Models

MODELS WITH UNDIFFERENTIATED STIMULI

Going back to our fantasy in Chapter 7 about complete observation of an individual for a period of time, we could simply count the number of times he manifested a behavior identified with our construct. This would be using a frequency model based on the rationale that the more frequently a person manifests relevant behaviors, the more he has of that attribute and therefore the higher the index we will assign to him. Similarly in an unstructured testing situation, as in the Rorschach examination, we could count the number of responses made (an index of productivity) or the number of responses with human content.

Let us call this *Model A*. One of its characteristics is that there is a standard period of observation, determined either by a time interval or by a fixed sequence of experimental operations, as when S looks at each Rorschach card as long as he wants before being handed the next one. Another characteristic is that the same observational protocol can be used to measure any of a large number of variables, since the stimuli either are not controlled by E or are not selected for pertinence to a single variable. To arrive at an index, E simply counts the number of occurrences of relevant behaviors, i.e., those determined to be included within his construct. (See Table 8.1.)

Table 8.1. Psychometric models and their indices

| | Conditions for observations | Typical index | |
		Dichotomous scale (e.g., 0–1)	Multistep scale
Model A	Unselected stimuli	Frequency of 1s	Total or average
Model B	Stimuli are selected as pertinent to construct, but not otherwise differentiated	Frequency of 1s per set of stimuli	Mean response strength
Model C	Stimuli are pertinent and are ordered	Frequency of 1s per set of stimuli	Mean response strength
Model D	Stimuli are pertinent and scaled	Assignment of median scale value for endorsed items	Scale value for point of maximum response
Model E	Any of above	For which variable does S have the highest score?	

But any such frequency index must be relative to a base. Continuous observations would be for a limited time period, so that our index should be rate—i.e., frequency—per day or hour. The total set of S's Rorschach responses has a base of ten cards; the index for responses with human content can be relative to that base or a percentage of total responses. When such bases as the ten Rorschach cards are constant for all subjects, the indices are typically stated in terms of simple frequency. But for many purposes, such as comparing scores on different tests, it is desirable to use the mean, i.e., to divide by the number of items or stimuli and get a *relative frequency* measure.

We saw earlier that naturalistic observation has the limitation that different subjects may have experienced different stimuli, so that counts of responses may not be strictly comparable. To avoid this problem, much measurement involves the presentation to the subject of stimuli having relevance to the specific construct being assessed. Hence when measuring one variable at a time with such specific stimuli, we have a special case that can be identified as a *specific relative frequency model* (see Fiske, 1963a) or, more generally, as *Model B*.

In Model B, the stimuli are selected to be appropriate for a specific construct. All scored responses are treated as alike and interchangeable, regardless of any differences between them in form, intensity, latency, etc. Thus in a maladjustment inventory of the early type, in which each item referred to a neurotic symptom, two people could receive a score of, say, 5 by answering positively two independent sets of five items, i.e., by having no positive response ("symptom") in common. The two would be considered to have the same degree of neurotic tendency in spite of the completely different symptom pictures. In this example, it is really the items that are treated as interchangeable. Strictly speaking (and in thinking about measurement it is desirable to be quite precise), the responses here are identical: the subjects marked "yes" five times. But is neurotic tendency best measured as the number of symptoms displayed?

In free-response methods, such as the Rorschach, quite idiosyncratic responses may all be scored as Original. The unit in each such case is a particular type of response to a stimulus, the stimulus being any one designated as appropriate for eliciting responses scored for the construct. For all kinds of frequency models, the scale is taken by fiat to be equal-interval: each positive response is taken as worth one step on the measurement scale. (This is the routine practice, but if we do not wish to assume that the differences between adjacent steps are equal, we can assign ranks to the frequencies, whatever the intervals between them. In such ordinal data, the distances between people with adjacent ranks are treated as equal rank differences, regardless of the differences in their frequency scores. For example, if the first three subjects have frequency scores of 12, 6, and 5, we can either treat the intervals as having a ratio of 6 to 1, or as being equal in that the three subjects are ranked 1, 2, and 3.)

THE CUMULATIVE HOMOGENEITY MODEL

The weakness of the frequency models lies in their criterion for classification of responses as positive. While this categorizing may not be a problem when one is determining the rate at which a pigeon pecks a disk in a Skinnerian conditioning experiment, it may be a real limitation in personality measurement, as in measuring neurotic tendency. What strength of a tendency makes it neurotic or maladaptive? One can determine vocational interests by counting the number of S's responses that are the same as the modal response of some reference group in a vocation, and not be troubled by the dissimilarities among the various objects chosen as liked, because there is a unifying concept of similarity to the reference group. But when a less global construct is being measured, it seems reasonable to seek evidence that the several responses are homogeneous, are manifestations of the same construct.

One way to obtain such evidence is by ordering the stimuli, or the standards to which the person is compared. That is, the stimuli are seen by E as having different values. E can order them on some basis regardless of the temporal order of their presentation to S. To illustrate from another field, consider the measuring of hardness in mineralogy. The basic operation is simply to determine what will scratch what. One can set up ten standard types of mineral in order of hardness, so that each will scratch every mineral below it. Then one can measure the hardness of any new mineral by determining how many of the standards it will scratch. This would be an ordinal scale. In weighing, we also have standard reference points, weights of one pound, of two pounds, etc. Again we can determine whether our object to be measured is heavier than each of our standard reference points. We then assign a number according to some rule: we may arbitrarily assign 7 to all objects heavier than our seven-pound standard but lighter than our eight-pound standard. With length, the rule may be to assign the number for the calibrated point closest to the object's length. In each of these cases, there is an ordered set of standards against which to compare the object being measured.

These three physical examples correspond to the *cumulative homogeneity model* in psychometrics (Loevinger, 1948; Fiske, 1963a), which we shall label as *Model C*. The clearest psychological examples are in ability and achievement. In arithmetic, one can establish a series of problems such that most subjects will give correct answers to the first and several more, but finally reach a point beyond which they cannot give correct answers. In high jumping, the bar is started at a height that everyone can clear; it is then gradually raised, with the athletes failing to clear it at one height or the next until all have failed. So in psychological measurement of a conceptually pure dimension, we can seek stimuli such that each S will give positive answers to the first few, and will continue to give positive answers to subsequent stimuli up to some point, after which he will give negative answers to all later stimuli.

For example, consider some items from a questionnaire given to some high school boys, asking them to indicate what kinds of things they would be likely to tell a casual acquaintance, a particular person selected by each S. This Self-Disclosure instrument was derived from the work of Jourard and Lasakow (1958). Some data are given in Table 8.2. These items were selected, from among the total of forty, to represent topics that vary in the extent to which these boys were willing to disclose their feelings. The data agree well with what we would expect: some topics are clearly more intimate and private than others. Hence these stimuli provide a graded set of standards for measuring self-disclosure.

Table 8.2. Frequencies of positive responses to self-disclosure items

I would tell this casual acquaintance about	*Number answering positively (out of 39)*
My favorite reading matter	38
Whether or not I believe in God	35
Whether I consider my family to be upper, middle, or lower class	29
All my present sources of income, and the amount	25
To whom I owe money at present, or from whom I have borrowed money in the past, and how much	20
Aspects of my personality that I dislike or worry about	16
Which parent I prefer at the moment	10
My most shameful thoughts	5

Data provided through the courtesy of Gerald Goodman.

The boys differed very widely in the number of items they would be willing to disclose to the particular casual acquaintance. Three boys gave positive responses to all forty items, but one boy gave positive responses to just three. Analyses of the full set of data yield some of the most favorable evaluative indices we have found. It is clear that this instrument measures a highly homogeneous dimension: subjects differ widely in their reported willingness to disclose things about themselves; topics vary greatly in their perceived intimacy; and these degrees of perceived intimacy apparently have much the same order for each subject.

In psychology, there are few or no scales that are completely homogeneous and consistently so over time and over repeated samples. One could construct such a scale for trivial variables like height by asking "Are you taller than five feet?" "Are you taller than five-two?" etc. Such questions would be largely redundant, and it is easier (and less annoying to a subject) simply to ask him how tall he is. The point is that psychological measurement cannot find stimuli that are psychologically identical in quality but differ in degree and which also are answered completely consistently by subjects at different points in time. We can, however, find stimuli that come fairly close to that ideal. A major thesis of this volume is that we should try to maximize this approximation: we should try to measure narrowly defined variables that can be measured by stimuli that are highly homogeneous.

The word "homogeneous" in the name for this model requires a further bit of explanation. The empirical demonstration that the items in a scale fit this model, that those who pass (answer positively) any item also pass all items before it, does not guarantee that the items are measuring the same conceptual dimension. As a simple and extreme example, consider a scale with three items: I have one head; I am a man; I am over seven feet tall. All those answering yes to the second item will be found to have answered yes to the first (provided the subjects are normal and are answering honestly). Similarly, the few who answer yes to the third item are more likely to be men and to have answered yes to the second item. But clearly the scale is not measuring any one thing.

In devising a scale, however, if one has a carefully defined concept in mind, if one has many items that cover the possible range of endorsement values from near .00 to near 1.00, and if one finds a pattern closely approximating the ideal of the cumulative homogeneity model, one can conclude that the scale is technically homogeneous and that the content of the items is homogeneous. These conditions are most likely to be found when the construct is narrow rather than when it is broad, like adjustment. In the sense used here, homogeneity includes two aspects: a stepwise increase in the amount of the attribute that S must possess in order to give positive answers to each of the ordered items, and high correlations among items, as high as their differing endorsement values will permit.

Although we shall return to a more extended discussion of these aspects and of this model at a later point, one further comment is necessary here. Because scales tend to have limited homogeneity, it is customary to score them in terms of number of positive responses, the same procedure as with frequency scales. The rationale is that we want to use all available information. If a person has one or more negative responses among his string of positive ones, or if he has one or more positives among his string of negatives (as almost everyone does), it seems wiser to include such items in arriving at his index. Another consideration is the difficulty in determining exactly where his string of positives ends and his negatives begin. The "out-of-line" responses, those not consistent with responses on items just above or below a particular item, are most likely to occur at just that point, for reasons to be brought out later.

OTHER MODELS

A somewhat related but less common psychometric model is the *differential homogeneity* one, *Model D* (see Loevinger, 1948). Like the cumulative homogeneity model, it uses an interval scale. The classic example is the Thurstone type of attitude scale. In this technique, a series of statements expressing attitudes on the topic (war, religion, etc.) are rated by judges in terms of the strength and direction of attitude, e.g., on a scale from very favorable attitude to very unfavorable. Those items on whose scale position the judges agree closely are used in the instrument, each such item being assigned the average judgment as its scale point. The subject indicates those statements with which he agrees, i.e., those he feels come close to his position. For his several positive responses, the corresponding scale points are examined and the median point is assigned to S as his score. The median is used rather than the mean, so that any response that is clearly unlike S's others will not be given undue weight (the subject may have misunderstood the wording or been careless, or the response might involve an error of measurement for some other reason). A more contemporary example is the work of Loevinger (1966) in assessing milestones of ego development. Another is the developmental hierarchy formed by the six types of moral thought identified by Kohlberg (1963). It is postulated that each person attains some one type, having previously attained each preceding type. The position of a subject is determined by presenting him with a moral dilemma and exploring his reasoning about his resolution of the dilemma. The scoring involves thirty aspects of morality, each aspect or dimension having six levels corresponding to the six types.

Another psychometric model is the typology, a nominal scale (Model E). This topic was also discussed in Chapter 6. Typologies are relatively rare in personality theory today, since most theorists agree that it is not sound or realistic to consider all people as falling into two or more clear-cut, mutually exclusive types. People are not purely X or purely Y, but rather each person has some X and some Y in him. Moreover, research studies have failed to find empirically any pure, mutually exclusive, and exhaustive typologies. It is instructive in this connection to consider Jung's theory. The formerly popular typology of introvert vs. extravert was a gross oversimplification of his sixteen-category system. But attempts to classify persons into his types have not succeeded (see Stricker and Ross, 1964); instead, each basis for classification seems to be a continuum, and more unimodal than bimodal. In Rorschach scoring, subjects are sometimes classified as extratensive or introversive, with a middle group being labeled ambiequal. This typology is obtained by comparing the relative size of two composite scores, the weighted sum of all color responses and the sum of human movement responses. Hence the classification is ipsative, being based on relative strength of the two dispositions within the subject.

All of the examples discussed above have a common feature: the basic scoring is dichotomous. Each observation or each response to a stimulus is judged as within the designated class of keyed responses or outside it. In Models A, B, and C, the procedure involves counting the number of keyed responses, assigning each an implicit weight of 1. In Model D, the Thurstone type of attitude scale identifies S's median positive response and assigns him the numerical scale value of that item. In judgmental methods using Model D, responses are assigned to one of the several ordered classes, each response thus being counted as 1 for one class and 0 for all other classes. S's class assignment is then made by certain decision rules.

Items can also be scored on a multistep scale. We can rate S on each of a number of such scales and then combine these ratings. Or he can respond to a Likert-type attitude scale with several alternatives for degrees of agreement and several for disagreement, each being assigned a score from, say, 1 to 5 (for a scale with five alternatives). The same models can be applied to such scores. See the last column of Table 8.1.

To use Model A, a score is assigned to each occurrence, and these are added to obtain an index. An observation may be made at fixed intervals, such as once every five seconds or once a minute, a scale score being assigned to each observation. If the variable may not be manifested at all at any one observation point, E may wish to assign a score of 0 to such non-occurrence.

If E is using Model B and has a fixed set of relevant stimuli, he can derive an index by obtaining the mean scale score for each response. For example, E can time the latency of each response, i.e., the interval between presentation of stimulus and response, and average these times. His average may be either the mean, the median, or the mode. But these are not the only possibilities. If he wanted to give more weight to larger scores, he could obtain the geometric mean; or he could square each score, find the mean of these squares, and take the square root of that value to obtain an index back in the range of the original response scores. (In one interesting test, the Desire for Certainty Test [Brim and Hoff, 1957], S makes a judgment in response to each item and also rates his degree of certainty in that judgment. These two numbers are then multiplied to obtain the score for the item.)

For Model C, the score can be the total or mean of the item scores. Such a score does not, of itself, make use of the ordering of the items. Alternatively, E could determine how many of S's responses exceeded a given scale point. Such a procedure does not use all the information available in the multistep scaling of the items and amounts in practice to scoring each response as above or below the dichotomous cutting point on the scale.

Scale scores for items could be used in Model D by determining the point at which S's responses have their highest values. E could use that point at which the scale value is highest, but to obtain a more reliable index, E would probably want to take the average of several adjacent scale points, as in the "running average" used in economic analysis.

Typologies (Model E) can be considered to be multivariable approaches, with S being assigned to one type by identifying his strongest disposition. From this orientation, Model E is a procedure different from the other models. In effect, E obtains several scores for each S, using some one of the other models, and then identifies S's highest score. So Model E can, in principle, be based on simultaneous application of another model to several discrete variables.

We see, then, that among the first four models, the basic differences concern the stimuli: Are they identified or not? Are they controlled by E? Are they scaled by E? The models are not identified by the scoring of items: the basic scoring can be either presence or absence of a keyed response, or scoring on ordered steps.

It is worth noting that a large number of procedures can be used for going from items to indices; simple counting and averaging are not the only ways. (Recall the potential indices listed toward the end of the last chapter.) Indexing can also be based on the most extreme level reached by S in his responses. And we have limited our discussion here to explicit and objective procedures. A judge may, in arriving at his final indices or ratings, utilize other, more complex methods. While he may not be able to tell us exactly how he reached his judgments, it is possible to study his judging processes by seeing how well various mathematical models fit his set of reported judgments.

THE MEASUREMENT SCALES AND
THE PSYCHOMETRIC MODELS

What are the connections between the various psychometric models and the measurement scales considered earlier? The measurement scales are pertinent at two levels, the scoring of each response to yield an item score and the combining of item scores to obtain an index. When items are scored dichotomously (e.g., as 0 or 1, or as 1 or 2), we are using only an ordinal scale: we have just two ordered categories. But when such item scores are added to obtain a total score or composite index, we are assuming that the interval between 0 and 1 for one item is equal to that for every other item. When multistep scoring is used for an item, we are assuming equal intervals between each pair of adjacent steps. Once again, when such item scores are combined, we make the additional assumption that the intervals between the steps for one item are equal to those for every other item. From items scored in these ways, we obtain composite indices using equal interval scales. (If we choose merely to use the order of such indices, we are converting these scores into an ordinal scale.)

In the special case of Model D, the items have scale values that are used as the scores for positive responses to these items. These scale values and therefore the scores are considered to be on an equal-interval scale. Hence the score assigned to a subject on the basis of his positive responses is also on an equal-interval scale.

Note that in none of these instances is there a meaningful zero point. In some cases, the item score may have a meaningful zero point. For example, the item score may be the time taken to respond. When the item score has a meaningful (rather than an arbitrary) zero point, the composite score based on several item scores also has a meaningful zero point. Only in these instances can the indices for subjects be considered to be on a ratio scale. Thus for most measurement in psychology and especially in personology, the indices are on an equal-interval scale at best. More generally, the scoring of the items will ordinarily determine the most powerful measurement scale that can be used for the composite scores or indices.

A CRITIQUE OF THE PSYCHOMETRIC MODELS

Each of these models has its advantages and disadvantages, and therefore its areas of most appropriate application. Model B (and especially the relative frequency form) is useful when the relevant construct is broad and known to be heterogeneous and one wants just a single comprehensive score. It is particularly suited for constructs that may be manifested in two or more mutually exclusive ways. Thus the variable "inaccuracy in appraising one's capacity" may take the form of overestimation *or* underestimation, the variable "lack of realistic anticipation" may appear as excessive optimism *or* pessimism, etc. While these could be distinguished in measuring behavioral adequacy (see Cartwright, Kirtner, and Fiske, 1963), one might lump all manifestations of the particular kind of inadequacy into a single instrument.

The cumulative homogeneity scale (Model C) is appropriate when the target is construed as a unidimensional subconstruct, such as an element for one facet as seen by a given mode, as in the guidelines for conceptualization presented in Chapter 6. As will be shown later, it is possible to determine not only how well an instrument built on this model differentiates people, but also how consistently the stimuli are differentiated by subjects and how much of the variance in the data is unwanted variance due to person-item interaction, instability of response, random errors, and other intruding factors.

The differential homogeneity model (Model D) is more suited for dimensions that have a particular kind of order, such that a person is equally different from two others at the same distance from himself but in different directions. The paradigm is the bipolar attitude scale from very pro to very anti. While growth stages closely approximate this model, a person is typically more similar to another at a stage below him than he is to someone at a stage he has not reached, since he has experienced the earlier stages but not the ones ahead of him. The typological model (E) seems best used as a very first approximation. In earliest work on a variable, one may want to sharpen the contrast by studying extreme groups. Alternatively, it may be of value is assessing particular kinds of pathology. More generally, it may be appropriate where the conceptual framework being investigated does not require that all subjects be classified confidently on each construct.

PSYCHOMETRIC MODELS AND QUALITIES OF RESPONSES

The discussion of psychometric models has been in quite abstract terms. Given numbers that are scores for items, by what rationales can they be combined to obtain an index for each subject? The presentation could be abstract because the models can be used with a wide variety of variables. Recall from Chapter 6 that one way a variable may be defined is in terms of responses with a specified feature, such as responses with a given content. For such variables, we often score in terms of frequency. But a variable may also be defined in terms of other qualities, such as strength or intensity. Sociability may be measured in terms of strength of desire to be with others, anxiety under stress may be assessed in terms of intensity. Other qualities of responses may also be employed. Speed of response is used in word associations, delayed responses often indicating conflict areas. Duration of response may indicate importance or preoccupation with its content. Whichever quality is most appropriate for the variable, it can be scored for each response and the responses combined by an appropriate model.

The reader may find it helpful to return to the last section of the preceding chapter to see how different qualities can be used in measuring dominance. While frequency and duration are used in various indices, other aspects are also suggested. The reader may be able to think of still other indices that could be developed for just this one concept.

Generalizability for a Single Test

Pause a moment to consider the substantive implications of combining data from items into a single index. Aside from the nominal scale, the measurement scales all assume the same quality is the referent of the index for each subject; the ordinal scale involves simply more or less of the quality, the interval and ratio scales assume that each unit on the scale represents the same quantity of the quality. Among the psychometric models, typologics usually refer to different qualities, but the two homogeneity models (Models C and D) assume that the same quality is present throughout the scale, (an assumption which may not hold for the developmental examples of Model D on page 146). When one obtains an index from a frequency model (Model A or B), one again assumes that the same quality is reflected in each datum (and in addition usually assumes that each datum represents the same quantum or amount). When such a model is used, it is typically recognized that the response units are somewhat specific, although they do have a common feature. Thus in counting responses to the Rorschach, we lump together complex, integrative whole responses and casual interpretations of common sections and responses to small details, regardless of content, determinant, or originality. The common feature in all is that S perceived something in the blot and decided to verbalize his percept to the examiner. As another example, consider a neurotic inventory with each item referring to a different symptom. Each positive response increases the subject's neuroticism score by one unit, regardless of the seriousness or intensity of the symptom. As measured by such an inventory, neuroticism is the number of symptoms reported, the common quality being that each is taken as partial evidence for neurosis or mild psychopathology. Hence frequency models often are used in assessing global, admittedly heterogeneous variables without regard for recognized distinctiveness among the manifestations so grouped together.

One basic reason for combining units into indices is just this lack of qualitative equivalence among units. We could try to capture the entire content of a variable into a single item and have Ss rate the amount they possess. But we are afraid to rely too heavily on any one response and so we seek replicative measurements. Since we do not want to insult or irritate the subject by simply asking him to respond again to the same item, we write a number of items, and necessarily more specific ones. But each such narrow item refers to only part of the variable (e.g., one aspect of one element in the behavioral facet) and is clearly not precisely equivalent in its quality to any other item. Empirical evidence demonstrates such lack of interchangeability: two items rarely order subjects in exactly the same way.

INTERNAL CONSISTENCY

Implicitly recognizing these considerations, we obtain our indices and then determine how justified we are in treating them as dependable representations of whatever they measure. We could evaluate the index by examining the intercorrelations among the several items. It is more convenient, however, to obtain a single descriptive statistic. The usual coefficient of internal consistency, the kind of reliability being considered here, estimates the correlation we would expect to obtain if we correlated our indices with another set of indices obtained on a comparable set of items, a parallel test. Without going into the technical specification of such a parallel test, we can phrase the relevant question as: How much difference did it make that we used this particular set of items rather than some other set obtained by the same procedures? Stated another way, how confidently can we generalize over items from our set to other items of the same kind? Implicitly, we are talking about sampling of items, but as Loevinger (1965) has pointed out, in test construction we never explicitly draw a sample from a specified population of items. Instead, we put together a group of items that appear satisfactory, try them out, and eliminate the unfit, the ones with poor psychometric properties.

STABILITY

Another feature of our obtained indices is their date: the Ss were tested at a particular point in time. Was there any unusual effect operating at that moment? Messick (1965) has shown that a national tragedy like the assassination of President John Kennedy will affect test scores. More commonly, the question is whether individuals are differentially affected by recent experiences so that their relative positions in a group change over time. We assess stability over time simply by readministering the test after an interval of sufficient length so that subjects will not be likely to recall their previous responses. From the degree of agreement between the two sets of indices, we decide how confidently we can generalize from indices obtained at a particular time to other points weeks or months earlier or later. Time is an important aspect of measurement and will be examined more closely in Chapter 9.

GENERALIZATION OVER PRODUCERS

In Table 5.1, "Modes of Measuring Personality" (pages 70–71), the second and third rows refer to the producers of the data and of the indices. For the first three modes, in which the subject produces the data, there is no need to consider the representativeness of the data producer. There is only one subject, and the only possible question is the consistency of his responses over time (his stability of response). Similarly, when the indices are produced by machines or clerks, the indices are presumably not affected by the producer (assuming that occasional checks are made to guard against machine malfunction, carelessness, or misunderstood instructions for scoring). But whenever the data or the indices are produced by an observer, and especially in Modes 4 and 5, we must ask whether other observers would produce very similar indices. In effect, we want to generalize over all pertinent observers, usually over all qualified experts or over all cooperative laymen. Whenever judgments or inferences about people are involved, we can be certain that two judges will not always agree perfectly with each other. In such instances, we want to determine the interjudge reliability.

(A graduate student sometimes has to develop new rating procedures for his dissertation research. Especially for such original judgment methods, he must show that others can reproduce his judgments to a reasonable degree, i.e., that he can communicate to others what he is doing. When he uses two additional judges, one can predict quite confidently that these judges will not agree with each other as well as they agree with the student. Being more highly motivated, the student himself makes the ratings more carefully than the others; in addition, he usually does not communicate [orally or on paper] everything about the way he rates.)

INDICES OF HOMOGENEITY

At this point, we shall have to consider some material that is more technical than most of the preceding content. For many years of psychometric thought and practice, the term "reliability" has most commonly been used to refer to internal consistency, the extent to which the various units (items or other component scores) agree with each other. The standard coefficient has been derived by a number of workers (see Tryon, 1957), its most general form being Cronbach's alpha,

$$\alpha = \left(\frac{n}{n-1}\right)\left(1 - \frac{\Sigma V_i}{V_t}\right)$$

where V_i is the variance of part i of a test (these variances being summed in this equation), V_t is the variance of the total scores, and n is the number of parts. It is desirable that the parts be items because the formula then gives unique results; if the parts are larger, up to halves, the formula will give slightly different results when the parts are established in different ways. In the particular and common case in which this formula is applied to items that are scored dichotomously (correct vs. incorrect or keyed-unkeyed), it is identical with the classical Kuder-Richardson Formula 20, or K-R 20, as it is often labeled.

In interpreting values obtained by this formula, we usually look carefully at the variance of the person scores, V_t. Not only do we want our test to spread out subjects so that they are differentiated as much as possible, but it is also known that the obtained reliability is a function of this variance, as the formula shows. For the same test and population, a sample of persons with high variance of total scores can be expected to yield a larger reliability coefficient than a sample with small variance.

More recently, there has been increasing interest in considering other indices for evaluating how well the parts of a test are measuring the same thing in the several subjects. Cronbach and his associates have been intensively examining the whole topic of such generalizability, with attention to coefficients appropriate for particular purposes, such as when each subject is observed under different conditions. In a classic paper (Cronbach, Rajaratnam, and Gleser, 1963), these workers approach the whole problem from a broader perspective than the usual one; additionally, they urge that the evaluation of reliability or generalizability should consider other values as well as the conventional index of internal consistency.

About the same time, I was reaching a similar conclusion (Fiske, 1963a). While the work of Cronbach and his associates utilized variance estimates, I elected to stay with simple statistics describing the obtained data. In other words, instead of being concerned primarily with estimating values for other conditions, I held that the experimenter should evaluate the data from a particular study in its own right: How well did this particular instrument do in measuring what it measured when applied to these particular subjects under specifiable conditions at this point in time? Thus the approach described below is directed toward assessing the quality of the measurement operations in a given application, for either basic or applied purposes. It is not directed toward an evaluation of the instrument itself, regardless of the conditions under which it was used, and not even toward evaluating the instrument when used in the general class of conditions represented by those for this particular application. To be sure, if the measuring operation works well in the immediate case, it is more likely to be useful in future applications, but it should be reevaluated in each such application. Anyone who has tried to replicate psychometric findings, even with carefully randomized subject sampling from an identified population, has encountered both the usual variation from sample to sample and the occasional salient finding peculiar to the particular sample.

My interest in this problem stemmed from the conviction that much personality measurement was deficient for two reasons: the items in the typical test were not measuring the same thing and the items did not have the same meaning for different subjects. It therefore seemed important to have indices not only of the homogeneity of items in the usual sense but also of the homogeneity of persons as they responded to the items. I therefore selected the cumulative homogeneity model (Model C) as the appropriate psychometric model. The ideal was taken to be the pure measurement of one quality at a time, one quality for each set of items. This set should have diverse endorsement values. The endorsement value of an item is the proportion of subjects endorsing it, i.e., answering it by marking the response alternative which is keyed. In the ideal, these values are evenly spread out (have a rectangular distribution) over practically all of the total possible range. Thus the items would serve as standards, like the minerals or weights mentioned earlier.

If all the items were measuring exactly the same quality in every subject, the arrays of responses would be maximally consistent for every subject and for every item. By shifting the rows (the data for subjects) and also the columns (the data for items), we could rearrange the data matrix containing all the responses of the subjects so that the subjects were ordered by their total scores and the items were ordered by frequency of endorsement, from high to low for both sets. Then all positive responses would be together in one half, the upper left triangle, and all the negative responses would be in the other half, the lower right. Each person would show a series of positive responses to more frequently endorsed items and then a series of negative

Table 8.3. An ideal data matrix and its homogeneity indices

| | Items | | | | | | | | Subject | Subject |
Subjects	1	2	3	4	5	6	7	8	scores	means
A	1	1	1	1	1	1	1	1	8	1.00
B	1	1	1	1	1	1	1	1	8	1.00
C	1	1	1	1	1	1	1	0	7	.88
D	1	1	1	1	1	1	1	0	7	.88
E	1	1	1	1	1	1	0	0	6	.75
F	1	1	1	1	1	1	0	0	6	.75
G	1	1	1	1	1	0	0	0	5	.62
H	1	1	1	1	1	0	0	0	5	.62
I	1	1	1	1	0	0	0	0	4	.50
J	1	1	1	1	0	0	0	0	4	.50
K	1	1	1	0	0	0	0	0	3	.38
L	1	1	1	0	0	0	0	0	3	.38
M	1	1	0	0	0	0	0	0	2	.25
N	1	1	0	0	0	0	0	0	2	.25
O	1	0	0	0	0	0	0	0	1	.12
P	1	0	0	0	0	0	0	0	1	.12
Item totals	16	14	12	10	8	6	4	2		
Item means	1.00	.88	.75	.62	.50	.38	.25	.12		.56

Variance of		Amount	Proportion of total variance	Homogeneity coefficients
Person means,	s^2_{Mp}	.082	.33	
Item means,	s^2_{MI}	.082	.33	$r_{tt} = .86$ $r_{ii} = .43$
Remainder,	s^2_e	.082	.33	$r_{gg} = .93$ $r_{pp} = .47$
Total,	s^2_t	.246		

responses. Each item would be answered positively by subjects scoring above some point and negatively by subjects with lower scores. An example of this ideal data matrix is presented in Table 8.3. (In this contrived illustration, the number of items and the number of Ss are small for convenience.)

Such an ideal may seem curious: it portrays a highly redundant set of observations. Its merit lies in the inferences that can be drawn from it and also in its maximum differentiation between subjects. In this ideal case, the largest possible number of discriminations would be made, with the smallest possible number of tied scores.

The matrix for actual data is never as neat as that in Table 8.3. Instead, the row for a typical subject may look like this:

                          1 0 1 1 0 1 0 0
or like this:

                          1 1 0 0 1 0 1 0

The columns will have a similar appearance: mostly 1s toward the top (but with a sprinkling of 0s) and mostly 0s toward the bottom, with an occasional 1.

I came to my conception of the ideal test, as represented in matrices like that in Table 8.3, from my concern with assessing the agreement among subjects in their interpretation of items. If the subjects do agree, they should show similar patterns of response; the rows should resemble each other as closely as the subjects' scores permit. Thus two subjects with scores of 6 and 5 should ideally have identical patterns of response, except that the first should have a 1 for the sixth item, where the second has an 0. Consider the classical rationale for items: if the items are measuring the same thing in all subjects, then the items should correlate well with each other and should make the same differentiations among the subjects. The conception outlined here applies the same kind of rationale to subjects: if subjects perceive and interpret items in the same way, they should produce rows of responses that correlate well with each other and should make similar differentiations among the items.

The value of this approach will become clearer in the following discussion of the indices that can be computed from such a data matrix. These indices show not only whether subjects are spread out and differentiated, but also whether items have diverse proportions of keyed responses they elicit and are distinguished from each other by the subjects. In addition, the indices indicate the extent to which the total set of responses contains variance due to person-item interaction, to responses—by individual subjects to particular items—which are not consistent with the rest of the responses for that subject or to that item. It is very sobering to see that, in the typical test in standard use today, a major part of the total variance in the responses is associated with this interaction. Compared to measurement in the natural sciences, measurement of personality is extremely crude. As indicated in the earlier chapters, this crudity is associated not only with the measuring procedures themselves, but also with the inadequate delineation of the constructs at which the procedures are aimed and with the tenuous coordination between the constructs and the procedures.

Computing the Homogeneity Indices

For purposes of presenting the computation and interpretation of the indices in this approach, we shall stick with items scored dichotomously, one answer being plus and assigned a unit score of 1, the other being given zero. The method is, however, quite general and can be used with multistep scoring of items. Many details of the method and computations will be omitted here to save space. They are available elsewhere (Fiske, 1963a, 1966b). For these computations, it is not necessary to write out the actual data matrix or to rearrange it by ordering subjects and items by means. (In the actual test booklet presented to subjects, the items need not be ordered by endorsement values, as they are in our example.) Such a visual picture of the data is often of value, however, in indicating particular subjects or particular items that are markedly out of line.

VARIANCES

Starting with the data matrix for N subjects responding to n items (e.g., with sixteen subjects and eight items in Table 8.3), we obtain the total variance. The simplest way is to multiply the proportion of plus responses by the proportion of minus responses ($.56 \times .44 = .246$ in this case). We then compute the subjects' mean scores, each such mean being simply the subject's total score divided by n, and the variance of these means around the grand mean (around .56, the proportion of plus responses). For these contrived data, this variance is .082. The item means are also calculated, by dividing the number of plus responses for each item by N, and the variance of these means around the grand mean is obtained. This variance is .082, identical with the variance of person means, as we would predict from inspection of the data. By subtracting these two variances from the total variance, we obtain the remainder variance, which again is .082 for this idealized matrix. This latter value can also be computed directly but more laboriously by finding the variance of the observed values in the matrix as discrepancies from the expected values. For any one person and any one item, the expected value is the grand mean plus the deviation of the person's mean from the grand mean plus the deviation of the item's mean from the grand mean. We can compute each expected value, subtract it from the observed value, and square the discrepancy. The remainder variance is the mean of these squared discrepancies.

The ideal is taken here to be the maximal discrimination of subjects and the maximal discrimination of items, i.e., a rectangular distribution for each. See the distributions in Table 8.3. (The distributions are flat across all possible values except zero, this exception stemming from the ideal of having each subject answer at least one item in the keyed direction, to indicate that he is responding to the items in the same fashion as every other subject.) To see why a rectangular distribution, a distribution that is flat from one end to the other, yields the maximum number of discriminations, consider a test with nine items, yielding ten possible scores from 0 to 9. If each of ten Ss obtained a different score, they will be discriminated as well as possible: except for the first and the last Ss, each person will have a score that is higher than that of some other Ss and lower than the rest. Now contrast that with a distribution of scores in which four Ss score 7 and the other six score 8. Here we have many ties, and any pair of subjects is at most separated by only one score point. In some practical situation where E is using a cutting score of 7, he might be satisfied with such a distribution, although he might feel uneasy about the dependability of his classification—some Ss might obtain scores of 8 through error of measurement when they should have scored 7. But for basic research, we ordinarily wish to discriminate each S as well as possible from every other S, and hence a rectangular distribution is desirable. A somewhat similar rationale can be offered for setting a rectangular distribution of item endorsements as the ideal. Intuitively, such a distribution can also be viewed as analogous to a set of standards, as in calibrations of a ruler with inches marked off.

With these rectangular distributions of person means and of item means in the ideal case, the variance of person means ($s_{\mathrm{M}p}^2$), the variance of item means ($s_{\mathrm{M}i}^2$), and the remainder variance (s_e^2) are all the same, having the value of .082, and thus each is one-third of the total variance (.246). Since total means and therefore total variances differ from test to test, it is useful for comparative purposes to determine the proportion of the total variance taken up by each of these three components. While each proportion is .33 in the ideal case, in almost every empirical case, the remainder variance will constitute by far the largest proportion, between .6 and .8 for typical tests (see Table 1 in Fiske, 1966b); the proportions for the other components will generally be well below .33.

Like the conventional correlation coefficient and other abstract numbers, these homogeneity indices cannot be interpreted readily without some experience with them and without some grasp of their formal properties. The investigator with such preparation will find them quite useful. The proportion of total variance taken up by what is left over, i.e., the remainder variance, is the best single index of the quality of measurement in terms of the proposed ideal. When it is relatively low, the experimenter knows that most of the variance is associated with persons, with items, or with both, and little is associated with person-item interaction. A person and an item interact when the response of the person is determined by factors other than the person's mean on the items and the item's general tendency to elicit plus responses. Such interactions, leading to idiosyncratic responses, may be due to any of a variety of influences: carelessness, misreading the item, interpreting the item very subjectively or personally, etc. These are obviously influences the experimenter wants to minimize.

There is another component in the remainder variance when the items are scored dichotomously. This is artifactual variance due to such scoring. Even in the ideal data matrix, the actual observations of 1 or 0 will not correspond exactly with the values expected on the basis of the appropriate item and person means. The expected values are mostly fractions (e.g., if the total mean is .5, the person mean is .8, and the item mean is .4, the expected value is .7). In each such instance, there is an unavoidable discrepancy because the subject is not allowed to give such fractional answers. This artifactual variance, the mean of these squared discrepancies between the expected values and the observed values, amounts to .083 or one-third of the total variance in the ideal case. In any actual data, this artifactual component will take different values (which can be computed from the discrepancies between the expected values and 0 or 1, whichever is nearer). It will, however, always be a large contribution to the remainder variance. The extent of this artifact decreases as the number of steps for scoring each item is increased, but it is still sizable in the usual range of scoring steps.

If the subjects are discriminated well, if their means are spread out fairly evenly over the possible range, the proportion of variance associated with subjects ($s_{M_p}^2$) will approach .33. Differentiation among subjects is generally accepted as a goal in psychological measurement.

Less accepted is the goal of having items that are spread out over the possible range. Some classical psychometric theory takes as a goal the dependability of classifying subjects as above or below some cutting score; for such an aim, it can be shown that all items should have about the same endorsement value, the specific value being a function of the cutting score to be used. (See Gulliksen, 1950.) But for studies testing theoretical propositions, we usually want to measure each person as precisely as possible. We want to optimize the dependability of subject placements at all points on the scale, a goal that seems best pursued by having items spread out so that, for most pairs of subjects with adjacent scores, the difference between their scores will be produced by their different responses to an item near their scale positions. Referring back to the example of weighing objects, we need a seven-pound standard to discriminate between two objects weighing six and a half and seven and a half pounds respectively; standards weighing six and eight pounds will fail to discriminate these objects.

HOMOGENEITY COEFFICIENTS

These variances of persons and of items, taken absolutely or proportionally, have considerable utility. Alongside them, much the same picture can be obtained in terms of homogeneity coefficients. One coefficient is the conventional index of the internal consistency of the total test, r_{tt}. This coefficient was identified earlier in this chapter as alpha. As mentioned above, this is the estimate of the correlation that would be obtained between this test and a hypothetical one prepared in the same way but with different items. For the example in Table 8.3, r_{tt} is .86.

But this coefficient is a function of the total number of items. If we had several items with the pattern of responses for Item 1, and the same number of items with the pattern for Item 2, etc., the coefficient would approach 1.00. Given even a bare minimum of internal consistency, it is theoretically possible to lengthen a test many times and thus raise r_{tt} to any desired value.

A better index of the quality of the items composing a test is r_{ii}, the average intercorrelation between the items, a coefficient that is not affected by the number of items in the test. Hence we can directly compare the values of r_{ii} for different tests, regardless of their length. This coefficient can be obtained by actually computing all the intercorrelations between items and obtaining their mean. Fortunately, it can be obtained more readily by application of the classical Spearman-Brown formula to r_{tt}. (More formally, it is an intraclass correlation and can be computed as such, as Cronbach and his associates [1963] show.) For the data in Table 8.3, r_{ii} is .43.

Suppose we exchange items for persons. Using the same formulas, we get the dual of r_{tt}, namely r_{gg}. This coefficient estimates the correlation between the items' endorsement values for this group of subjects and the values for the same items for a similarly obtained second group of people (r_{gg} stands for the correlation between groups just as r_{tt} stands for the correlation between tests). The value for our example is .93. This coefficient has limited value because it varies with N, the number of subjects. With larger samples, it increases, just as r_{tt} increases with additional items. But for a fixed number of items, the actual intersample r (rather than the estimate, r_{gg}) can be useful for comparing the stability of item indices across samples (e.g., Goldberg, 1968a).

What is valuable is r_{pp} (the dual of r_{ii}), the average correlation between pairs of persons. In the ideal case, the correlation between each pair of persons is the maximum possible. Consider Subjects E and F in Table 8.3.

They have identical arrays of responses and therefore intercorrelate 1.00. But now consider F and G, whose rows look like this.

$$
\begin{array}{llllllllll}
\text{F} & 1 & 1 & 1 & 1 & 1 & 1 & 0 & 0 \\
\text{G} & 1 & 1 & 1 & 1 & 1 & 0 & 0 & 0
\end{array}
$$

These two persons correlate only .75, not 1.00. Similarly, F correlates with J only .58, and with P only .22. The correlations decrease as the distributions of responses become more dissimilar, even though the correspondences between the rows is in each case as similar as allowed by the total scores of the subjects. (The reasons for this decrease are rather technical: they are related to the use of dichotomous scoring. As the difference between the means increases, the standard scores for the two possible raw scores [1 and 0] become increasingly different, so that the cross-products are increasingly lower than when the standard scores for each person are identical, as in the case of identical rows of raw scores.) As a result of this effect, r_{pp}, the average correlation between persons, is approximately .50 (which is of course the same as that for r_{ii}) in the ideal case with a rectangular distribution of person scores. The value of r_{pp} is .47 for the small contrived data matrix in Table 8.3.

This coefficient, r_{pp}, is useful because it indicates the degree of correspondence between the answer patterns for the several subjects. For the model advocated here, the correspondence should be maximal: all subjects should answer each item the same way, except for differences associated with their total score. Substantively, such correspondence means that the items have the same meaning for all subjects, any difference in responses being due to differences in the amounts the subjects possess of the quality being measured. Just as r_{ii} tells us the extent to which the items are measuring the same quality in the several subjects, so r_{pp} tells us the extent to which the subjects are being measured on the same quality by the various items. To illustrate by an extreme example, suppose some subjects are answering in accordance with the examiner's instructions but some are answering in terms of the social desirability of the item, some on the basis of item length or complexity, and some on the basis of how they feel the average person would answer the item. For each of these subgroups, the items might have very different means, and even if the correlations between individuals within each group were quite high, the more numerous correlations between individuals from different groups would be low, so that the average correlation, r_{pp}, would be greatly reduced.

These homogeneity coefficients tend to vary with their corresponding variances. A mathematical basis for this covarying can be seen in the fact that the variance of person scores enters into one formula for computing r_{tt} (and therefore r_{ii}), while the variance of item scores can also be used to obtain r_{gg} and r_{pp}. A related consideration is the general principle that, if two variables are related to each other, the observed correlation between them will vary with the variances of the variables in the sample used. Simi larly, over tests, r_{ii} varies with the spread of person scores. If s_{Mp}^2 is large, r_{ii} will tend to be large. And if the items are spread out so that s_{Mi}^2 is large, r_{pp} will tend to be large. Thus the variances and the homogeneity coefficients give us much the same evaluations of a data matrix. When we are interested in the differentiations between subjects and between items, the variances (in absolute or proportional form) will be more helpful in interpreting what is going on. When we are concerned with the consistencies among items and the homogeneousness of the subjects, the experimenter will find the coefficients more useful.

OTHER COMMENTS ON THE HOMOGENEITY INDICES

The approach presented above argues that no one index fully indicates the adequacy of a test. The proportion of remainder variance is a useful general index and must be low in a fully adequate instrument. But for most tests, it will indicate more or less adequacy without showing the source of any inadequacy. In both the model and the ideal, there are two sources of inadequacy: failure to differentiate and spread out the subjects and failure to spread out the items. The first can be seen in low values of person variance and low values of r_{ii} (and consequently of r_{tt}, the standard coefficient). The second is shown by low values of item variance and low r_{pp}.

A test may be deficient in either respect or in both. Inadequacy of one sort can occur when the test is quite adequate in the other respect. For example, the Hy scale of the MMPI has low values for r_{ii} but high values for r_{pp} while some other scales have higher values for r_{ii} than for r_{pp} (again, see the table in Fiske, 1966*b*).

The reader should also recognize that this set of homogeneity indices can be useful for evaluating tests against other norms. For example, the preceding exposition has taken as the norm or ideal a data matrix with rectangular distributions for persons and items. But one might believe that a normal distribution of person scores was the goal to be approximated. If so, he would probably find that the best distribution of item means would be not rectangular but U-shaped. (This and other ideals have not been fully explored.) In actual practice, distributions of person scores tend to be unimodal rather than rectangular. Even with such distributions, it is possible to improve greatly over the usually obtained values for the several homogeneity indices. Most tests have relatively low indices of consistency among items and among people: values for r_{ii} and r_{pp} are typically below .10, although for carefully structured tests they can reach .30 or more.

As noted earlier, some classical psychometric theory argues for minimizing the variance of item means (particularly when the goal is to classify subjects into two groups) An argument against that recommendation stems from the finding that stability of response is associated with person-item distance when persons and items are located on a common scale (see the paper by Tyler [1968] and the discussion of it in Chapter 9). If items are spread out, the typical subject will have many items at a considerable distance from his scale point, thus minimizing the number of responses he is likely to change on retesting.

Finally, this section has been written in terms of items and tests. It must not be forgotten that these matters of generalizability apply equally to other procedures in which a series of responses is obtained from each subject or observer and some composite score is derived from these data (e.g., ratings or judgments about products). For the approach developed here at length, the chief restriction is that each subject must have responded to each of a fixed series of stimuli.

Generalizability beyond the Single Test: Approaches to Validation

In the preceding pages, the topic has been the evaluation of response data from a given test, without regard to any other data about the subjects tested. The basic question has been the extent to which the several items are measuring the same quality in the individual subjects. It was assumed that we wished to maximize this consistency, regardless of the relationship between the obtained indices and other data. We considered generalizability over time, over items, and over data and index producers. But our evaluation based on the homogeneity indices or other statistics applies only to the given instrument, with its specific format, instructions, type of item, etc. Sometimes this is all we can do: we can say only that this instrument in this application measured well or poorly whatever it is that it measures. But what does it measure? This is the question of validity. Several ways of answering it have been developed by psychologists, but each answers a slightly different question, each sets its own standards for appraising a measuring procedure. We will present these in order of generally increasing rigorousness, from agreement with general impression of the variable being measured through agreement with other measures of the variable and with more trusted measures or "criteria" to congruence with the total conceptualization of the target construct.

We may, on occasion, be forced to rely solely on expert judgment to determine what a test measures. We examine the test format and instructions and decide that, assuming the subjects respond as we want them to, we are measuring their knowledge of American history, their self-confidence, or their disposition to categorize things broadly. If other qualified people reach the same decision independently, we may consider that our test has *content validity*. This approach to validation is also called face validity. When the procedure is misused, critics call it faith validity.

Bitter experience has taught psychologists that it is unwise to rely on face validity. Especially in the personality domain, tests do not always measure just what we think they should. Furthermore, it is common to find that one man's content is not the same as another's: your test of anxiety may have face validity and so may mine, but the two tests may correlate only .50 at best, and more likely .35 or less.

The principal method for determining the validity of a test is to obtain its correlations with three types of measures: measures of the same construct, of related ones, and of presumably unrelated ones. Consider first the correlations with measures of the same construct. In personality research, such correlations are typically low. Occasionally the correlation will be fairly high, when the two tests have the same format. But the correlation will never be maximal: it will never reach the limit set by the internal consistencies of the two tests (the precise limit being the geometric mean of those reliabilities). To some extent, scores from each test are determined in part by something specific to that test.

CONVERGENT AND DISCRIMINANT VALIDATION

Suppose we have two instruments, each measuring two or more traits. A minimal and basic requirement for the validity of these tests is some correlation between them: if the two tests measure the same traits, the two scores for each trait should be positively related. This convergent validation is a modest requirement, and yet one that is often not met. Donald Campbell and I (1959) have presented instances of this negative finding. Note that such lack of relationship may stem from the invalidity of one test, of the other test, or of both; one cannot conclude which without further data. (We assume here that we have *a priori* reasons for expecting that the two tests do measure exactly the same traits, and not just the same general concepts by different modes.)

The other basic requirement that Campbell and I proposed was that the correlation between the two scores for Trait A (one from each test) should exceed the correlations between Trait A as measured by one test and Trait B as measured by the other. If dominance as measured by self-report correlates more highly with energy as rated by peers than it does with peer-rated dominance, something is wrong with one of the three indices. An index does not have discriminant validation unless it correlates more highly with indices from a separate instrument measuring the same quality than it does with such indices measuring other qualities. These essential requirements are really quite lenient. Psychologists should not rest content with barely satisfying these specifications.

If these two basic requirements are met, one can go on to see whether other desirable patterns are also found. For example, one could hope that dominance from self-report would have a higher correlation with peer-rated dominance than with self-reported energy. Typically, this will not be the case: variables that are presumed to be positively related to each other will correlate more highly with each other in the matrix for a single test or method than they will with the variables of the same name as measured by other methods. The same method will contribute more common variance to two traits than one trait will contribute to two different methods of measuring it. Even·when variables are presumed to have no relationship with each other, the obtained correlations will usually be positive when the indices for the variables are obtained from a common instrument or method. Such correlations have been attributed to method factors, i.e., to things specific to the method (see Cartwright, Kirtner, and Fiske, 1963).

The Campbell-Fiske analysis involved the multimethod matrix referred to above, i.e., the correlations between indices from different methods. It forced psychologists to recognize the major contributions of measuring procedures to scores. But that paper did not define method; rather it assumed that it was clear when two indices used the same method and when the methods were different. It has been said that science progresses by re-examining and testing its assumptions, often finding that they are not valid. Rather than assuming that the notion of method is clear and obvious, let us examine it. There is a hint in the paper being discussed. The section on "the test as a trait-method unit" proposes that there is method variance associated with the use of any one method, variance that may contribute to the obtained variance for any index based on that method. But rather than view such variance as confounding or contaminating, let us be realistic and accept it as a fact of life. There is no measurement without the use of some "method." Coming at the matter another way, we always measure from a perspective; all measurements are obtained by some means of observation, and that means is an essential aspect of the resulting measurements.

Recall the discussion of perspectives and modes in Chapters 4 and 5. All measurement of personality uses one mode or another. None is free of mode variance. The differences between modes are both fundamental and, typically, large. Hence it seems wisest to approach measurement in terms of classes of measuring operations, one class for each mode, and to postpone until later the question of the degree of agreement between modes. For each construct, our goal thus becomes that of measuring as well as possible each of the subconstructs, one for each mode of observations of phenomena relevant to the general contruct.

Within each mode, however, measurement can be done in a number of ways. First, it can be done under different conditions. Second, different tasks can be given to the data producer. Finally, different stimuli can be provided, stimuli with different content. Thus the loose and undefined notion of method should be replaced by more precise terms. The many methods or ways to measure personality can be classified on at least four bases, with their probable order of discreteness being first modes, and then conditions, tasks, and stimuli. Typically, the degree of correlation between two measuring procedures will depend upon the number and kind of classifications they have in common: procedures from different modes will correlate least, procedures from the same mode but under dissimilar conditions will correlate a little better, and procedures sharing the same mode, conditions, and task will correlate still better, but yet at a disturbingly unsatisfactory level as long as the content is dissimilar. (Some empirical findings on relationships between tests using the same and different modes will be considered in Chapter 11.)

More exactly, the correlations between separate procedures should be predictable from the conceptualization of the construct. Very commonly, it will become apparent that, for the subconstruct for a given mode, there is really only one appropriate set of conditions and only one suitable task. (See Chapter 6.) For example, to measure interest in a class of objects as experienced by the subject when he sees them, one can use only Mode 2, report of immediate experience. If such interest is inferred by judges studying facial expression, a different mode (Mode 4) is employed. If the indices are based on pupillary or other physiological changes, the observations involve Mode 6. These two latter modes are more indirect and less congruent with the conceptualization.

CRITERION-RELATED VALIDITY

Suppose we have devised a test for measuring degree of psychopathology. This is an undesirably broad construct but convenient as an example. It also can be a central one for some research problems, as operationalized in the Health-Sickness Rating Scale of the long-term Menninger study of psychotherapy (Luborsky, 1962). If we have just built our test, we might give it to a group of patients with presumably varied degrees of pathology, and then get clinicians, psychologists, or psychiatrists who know them well to rate them on degree of psychopathology. This technique would tell us something about the criterion-related validity of our test, the clinicians' ratings being the criterion we want to approximate as closely as possible. *Criterion-related validity* is the extent to which a test is a valid measure of (correlates highly with) a given criterion. It has two forms. If the ratings were made at about the same time that the test was taken, we would consider the findings relevant to the *concurrent validity* of our test. If the ratings were made some time later, the applicable term would be *predictive validity*. In general, predictive validity will be lower than concurrent, since not all subjects change in exactly the same way over time. For example, our patients may have had some kind of therapy between the testing and the rating. Since some would benefit more from this than others, the predictive coefficients would be lowered by this varying factor. It can be seen that these approaches are concerned with the practical validity (Campbell, 1960) of the instrument: Does the test have practical value for predicting later indices of pathology? Is this test of practical value as an economical substitute for clinicians' contemporaneous ratings?

Our test of pathology may not correlate very highly with the ratings. In addition to considering how we might improve our test, we must also look at the criterion. Suppose we found that our test correlated better with ratings by some clinicians than with those of others. If, *before* seeing the correlations, we had judged the first group of clinicians to be more skillful, we would feel more confident about our test. Also, if we found that clinicians did not agree well with each other in rating pathology, we might again feel better about our test. Consider the history of intelligence tests. Originally, Binet used teachers' judgments as a criterion for selecting items and refining his test. But later, when test construction was further advanced, the tests were considered to be better measures of intelligence than were teachers' ratings. (Now we are again wondering how adequate the standard tests are. As Guilford [1967, pages 471–72] points out, these tests emphasize some aspects of intelligence to the gross neglect of others.) The analogy is, of course, not a close one unless our test were to become well known and unless there developed a consensus among qualified persons that it was the best single procedure for assessing pathology.

The important point is that any criterion is itself a measure. Applied psychologists began to recognize the problem about three decades ago. For example, during World War II, tests were developed to predict aptitude for being a bombardier. These tests were correlated with accuracy on practice bombing runs, a criterion with high face validity, and of course a more practical one and a purer measure of aptitude than accuracy under the varied conditions of actual combat. To the dismay of the psychologists, the correlations were essentially zero. Further investigation revealed, however, that the criterion was quite unstable: accuracy of bombing on one day had almost no correlation with accuracy on another day, with a different pilot, different wind conditions, etc. An undependable criterion measure cannot be predicted. (See also "Validity for What?", Jenkins, 1946.)

CONSTRUCT VALIDITY

In the early work on measuring individual differences, psychologists had less confidence in their tests and more faith in criteria. Especially with the many efforts to measure things that had practical importance or social value, they concentrated on their tests and took their criteria for granted. Gradually it became evident that criterion measures often lacked sufficient internal consistency, stability, or interjudge agreement to provide adequate norms or ideals to be approximated. In applied psychology, it was learned that apparently obvious criteria were themselves fallible and had to be refined or taken as incomplete. For example, the amount of life insurance sold by a salesman was not exactly the quantity to be maximized: it had to be qualified for the potentialities of the territory in which the salesman worked, for the number of policies that lapsed in such a short time that it cost the company money to write the policies, and so on. Thus it was rare to find a single criterion that comprehended the total picture of a man's performance on his job.

In other work, there was no adequate criterion. In much basic research, the constructs of interest cannot be defined or designated by pointing to experiences of subjects, manifested behaviors, or objective records. The problem was brought to a head in the early fifties when a committee from the American Psychological Association and two educational associations was preparing *Technical Recommendations for Psychological Tests and Diagnostic Techniques* (1954). It became evident that content validity and criterion-related validity did not cover testing in personality research and in clinical diagnosis. How can these concepts be utilized definitively in assessing the adequacy of tests for anxiety, ego strength, or latent hostility? The idea of construct validity was developed to meet this problem.

Construct validity was explicated by Cronbach and Meehl (1955), two of the committee that had prepared the *Technical Recommendations*. The essence of the notion is really quite simple, although it is sometimes misunderstood and is frequently invoked in inadequate or incomplete empirical work. Construct validity refers to the simultaneous validating of the test and of the construct. The construct must be taken as part of a nomological net, a set of interrelated theoretical propositions, a small theory. From these propositions, the experimenter can derive a set of testable hypotheses that can be examined in empirical data gathered under an appropriate design. Thus anxiety proneness might be predicted to be related to palmar sweating under psychological stress and to peer ratings of tenseness, but to be independent of intelligence and value orientations. The experimenter's test of anxiety proneness could be administered to a group of subjects along with a series of measures for these other variables. If an empirical study of sufficient scope produced a pattern of relationships between the measure of anxiety and the other measures which fitted precisely the pattern predicted *a priori,* the experimenter would have substantial evidence favoring the judgment that his test had some validity and would also have evidence supporting his conceptual work.

But suppose that the findings did not correspond at all with the predicted pattern. The experimenter would then have to choose among several interpretations: his test might be completely invalid, his theoretical propositions about anxiety might be wrong, his empirical hypotheses might be incorrectly derived, or his construct of anxiety proneness might have no scientific value. The difficulty might reside solely in the test, solely in the conceptual framework, or partly in each. Fortunately, such completely negative results are not typical; more common is a pattern of findings that partially confirm and partially disconfirm the predictions. In such instances, the experimenter must modify or redesign his test, must modify or rewrite his definition of the construct or his propositions involving it, or both.

Thus construct validity is concerned simultaneously with the validity of the test and with the validity of the construct. In this context, the validity of a test or other measure is the degree to which it can confidently be taken as congruent with the construct as specified, the degree of fit between the measuring operation and the conceptualization. The validity of a construct is its theoretical utility, its value for understanding and explaining the phenomena being studied.

The notion of construct validity is a case in which methodology is ahead of empirical research and much current theory. Since the introduction of the term, many studies have been published with titles like "The Construct Validity of . . ." Most of these are disappointing. They report the correlation of one test with one or two measures to which it should be related, according to someone's assertion. It is difficult to think of a paper that could be considered a model of research on construct validation. For example, considerable research has been done on Rogers' theory, and especially on the conditions for successful counseling (Rogers, 1959). Many of these studies involved the creation of an instrument to measure one of the conditions, its application to a number of clients, and the computation of the relationship between the measure and success of therapy. Such an obtained value is just one of the several that must be studied to evaluate the validity of the instrument and the validity of the construct.

A more satisfactory investigation was carried out by Pearson (1969). She set out to test the presumed relationship between two of Rogers' concepts, openness to experience and organismic valuing. She found it necessary to construct new measures of these variables. But when seeking conceptual guidance for the specifications, she found Rogers' discussions insufficient. He had developed his theory on the basis of his experience in counseling and had arrived at expositions that helped him to understand therapeutic work. So Pearson worked out conceptualizations of these variables which extended Rogers' conceptualizations and which provided a basis for developing measuring procedures.

This illustration shows us that construct validation must be programmatic. It must include a series of steps and studies. It requires an explicit delineation of the construct, together with a conceptual network around it, spelling out its assumed relationships to a variety of other variables. There is very little theorizing in personality which has generated not only conceptualizations of all central constructs and specifications for their measurement but also sets of propositions of the form: "Construct A is highly related to Construct B," "Construct A has a low negative correlation with Construct C," etc. And such propositions rarely make explicit the conditions under which they are presumed to hold.

Construct validation also requires the development of procedures for measuring both the construct of central interest and each of the other constructs in the theoretical network. It requires demonstration of the psychometric adequacy of each procedure in terms of its internal characteristics and its correlation with other measures of the same construct, a small research program in itself. We know where we want to go, but we need the vehicles to take us there.

By this point, the thoughtful reader will probably have an uneasy feeling that this discussion of construct validity has a familiar ring, and he will be correct. What is new about construct validity is the term itself and the explicit conceptualization of this methodological concept. Previous discussions of test validity considered the matter in too narrow a context: most psychometricians were so preoccupied with the tests themselves and their psychometric properties that they neglected the target constructs at which the tests were aimed. This neglect stemmed from their concern with practical applications in some instances and from their particular value orientation in others. But the difficulties were not solely their responsibility. Most theorists, especially in the area of personality, have shown little interest in or understanding of measurement problems; they have discussed their concepts in a loose literary fashion, without explicit formal definitions or indications of appropriate and feasible ways to operationalize them.

The notion of construct validity refers essentially to the basic course of science. Scientific progress requires interaction between theory and experiment. A scientist has an idea—a concept and some thoughts about what it is and what it is related to. He tries out his idea, he sees whether it holds up in empirical work. Almost invariably, his empirical findings indicate that his idea must be modified in some way. Having revised his idea, he again gathers empirical evidence. The whole interactive process may take place in the activity of one scientist or may involve a group of workers, some who are specialists in theory and some specializing in experimentation.

It should be noted that disagreement between theoretical statements and empirical findings may be resolved in two ways. It may be decided that the theoretical propositions must be changed. But it may also be concluded that the empirical procedures were not appropriate: the experimentation may have faulty design, the data may be contaminated by irrelevant factors, or the data may not even be relevant to the theoretical statements.

(Three kinds of validity information—content, criterion-related, and construct—have been formally described in a manual on *Standards for Educational and Psychological Tests and Manuals* [American Psychological Association *et al.*, 1966], prepared by a joint committee of the APA, the American Educational Research Association, and the National Council on Measurement in Education. This formulation is a current standard treatment of these topics, of reliability, and of other issues pertaining to the evaluation of published tests. It was developed from the *Technical Recommendations,* mentioned earlier.)

THE UNITY OF GENERALIZABILITY

In the literature on measurement, reliability and validity are usually treated separately. While it is generally recognized that reliability is crucial because it sets a limit to validity, the fundamental complementarity of the two topics has almost been lost in the discussions. Both refer to aspects of generalizability. The goal of measurement is to obtain indices that can be used to represent specific constructs. On the one hand, the indices must not be contaminated by systematic effects from other variables or by assorted random influences. On the other hand, the construct taken as corresponding to the index must be restricted to what the index represents: vocabulary scores are relevant for a specific part of intelligence, not the complex totality of intellectual functioning. Indices of the need for achievement derived from stories made up about four pictures represent achievement fantasy, desire to achieve as observed at one point in time and under particular conditions; they are not an adequate representation of subjects' manifested efforts to achieve over the course of several years, and certainly not of the subjects' total disposition to achieve, combining both their desires or intentions, their efforts, and their actual achievements in all areas. No one measure should be expected to represent such a heterogeneous collection of subconstructs.

For measurement data to be of high quality and utility, we must have evidence that we can generalize from it in several ways. Most fundamental is generalizing from our index to the subconstruct (validity). But to have confidence in such generalization, we must also have good grounds for generalizing from the moment the indices were obtained to other points in time, from the particular index producers to others, from the particular conditions of measurement to other appropriate conditions, and from the given set of stimuli to other sets. These are forms of generalization that are usually grouped under reliability, although the generalizing from particular conditions to other conditions might be classified as an aspect of validity. Reliability and validity are really on a continuum of generalizability: reliability refers to generalizing about the test as a test; validity refers to generalizing beyond the test to a concrete criterion or to a construct.

In each of those generalizations subsumed under reliability, the range of hypothetical specifications included is determined by the conceptualization of the construct. We do not want our measure of current mood to correspond exactly with measures taken next month. We do not expect an index of facility with numbers to correlate perfectly with indices of verbal facility. The scope of the subconstruct specifies the scope of the generalizability to be sought for the measuring procedure aimed at it.

The Role of Expert Judgment in Personality Measurement

In all modes of observing personality phenomena, the data record is produced by a human being. In all but Mode 6 (Psychophysiology), the recorded responses are more or less under the conscious control of S or O, and are generally the products of intentional acts by that person. Such use of persons as instruments is unavoidable if we define our target constructs as phenomena observed from a specified perspective. But ordinarily we use the observations of these persons as data from which we derive indices by standard mechanical processing. An alternative is to have S or O produce the index himself. For example, the most direct way to determine how S sees himself is to ask him to rate himself on the concepts of interest to us (rather than taking his answers to a lot of questions and combining them). Similarly, to determine how his peers see him, we can obtain ratings from them. In these instances, a layman is producing the final indices, but a layman with an explicit perspective. Another common procedure is to have experts produce the final indices.

Expert judgment, a form of measurement using Mode 5, has played a major role in the personality field. It has been, and to a large extent still is, the major perspective used in clinical diagnosis. It is still employed in basic research, though to a smaller extent than in years past. How adequate and how necessary is it in personality measurement?

It is necessary in psychotherapy because the therapist must diagnose the immediate state of his patient from time to time during a therapy hour without the intrusive effects of measuring procedures. Human judgment must also be used when preliminary work is being done in a previously unexplored area.

As the tone of those statements indicates, however, it is my conviction that it should not be used in measurement whenever satisfactory alternatives are available. I hold this position for many reasons. First, the degree of agreement between expert judges usually leaves much to be desired. The individual judge always contributes some idiosyncratic component to the indices he produces. (As one of many examples, see the differences among highly experienced clinicians in Alexander, French, and Pollock, 1968.) Thus generalizability over human judges is always less than optimal. Second, judges differ in their skill, in their adequacy as measuring instruments. (Again, see Alexander *et al.,* 1968.) If it were possible to calibrate human judges, to find those judges who could make dependable and valid appraisals for specified constructs, one might place more reliance on measurement by this means. Third, human judgment is a more expensive procedure than many other methods of collecting and indexing data. Fourth, the human judge may not be able to tell us how he arrived at his judgments.

The crucial question is, of course, whether the human judge can contribute something unique to measurement, whether he can produce indices that are more valid than any that can be produced by other means. Those clinicians who must use their judgment many times a day in assessing patients usually believe that their judgments are more accurate than other potential indices. Other students of personology working in different settings question that view. Because of the complex nature of construct validation, it has not been possible to determine whether expert judgment is superior to alternative methods in clinical practice. The only pertinent empirical tests have involved criterion-related validity.

The issue was brought to a head in Meehl's classic monograph, *Clinical vs. Statistical Prediction: A Theoretical Analysis and a Review of the Evidence* (1954). In the many studies he examined. Meehl failed to find one in which clinicians were superior to quantitative, objective methods of arriving at predictions. These objective methods may be standard tests scored clerically or they may be ad hoc tests with scoring weights determined from prior statistical analyses. The subsequent literature has failed to change this conclusion. (One possible exception has been vigorously disputed: see Meehl, 1965, and Goldberg, 1968*b*.)

The case in favor of clinical judgment has been ably presented by Holt. Holding that most published comparisons have involved a naïve clinical method, he urges the study of a sophisticated clinical approach. In this method, qualitative data are used as well as objective scores. Actuarial techniques, quantification, and statistics are used wherever appropriate, "but the clinician himself is retained as one of the prime instruments, with an effort to make him as reliable and valid a data-processor as possible; and he makes the final organization of the data to yield a set of predictions tailored to each individual case" (Holt, 1958, p. 4). He is, then, proposing the search for "the optimal combination of actuarially controlled methods and sensitive clinical judgment for any particular predictive enterprise" (page 12).

In his monograph, Meehl pointed out that judgment can enter both in the production of data and in the combination of data to yield a prediction or an index. More recently, Sawyer (1966) has extended and clarified the analysis, noting some of the semantic confusions. Applying his framework to forty-five studies, he finds an apparent superiority for mechanical modes of both collection and combination of data, and believes that the clinician is more likely to contribute through observation than through integration. A strong case can be made for the value of the expert as an observer or data producer, especially for subtle and technical constructs. The delineation of modes for observing and measuring personality in Chapter 5 is, of course, another formal analysis of the matter. Since its orientation is toward basic research, it does not include the empirical derivation of statistical procedures for predicting a fixed criterion.

The psychology of the human judge is a fascinating topic that cannot be examined in any detail here. The reader can readily think of many reasons why people are likely to develop more confidence in their judgment than objective circumstances warrant. A person whose work and livelihood depends upon his judgment must have such confidence to keep going. Unfortunately, people tend to remember the instances when their judgment was correct and forget or explain away the times they were wrong. Similarly, a person sees corroboration where it does not actually exist. A demonstration of the dangers in personal validations exemplifies the problem. Forer (1949) gave a test to a class and later handed each student a personality sketch allegedly based on that test. This sketch, containing thirteen statements from an astrology book, was identical for all Ss. The consensus of the class was that the test was very effective and that the personality sketch revealed basic characteristics of their personality. More significant are studies by Chapman and Chapman (1967, 1969) in which naïve judges studied a set of projective protocols (e.g., drawings of persons) together with contrived symptom statements randomly paired with them. The judges tended to agree with each other in their reports of correlations between attributes of the drawings and the symptoms, correlations that were illusory because there were in fact no such relationships in the material. More disturbing yet, the erroneously reported correlates were strikingly similar to the reports of practicing psychodiagnosticians concerning the relationships between symptoms and characteristics of such drawings. Human judgment, unsupported by empirical evidence, is a risky basis for measurement indices, even though the expert may be valuable and often unique as a source of observational data.

Human judgment has its place, primarily where alternative methods of collecting data and producing indices are not feasible or available. Human judgment has its deficiencies, just as other measuring procedures do. And like these others, it too must be assessed to determine its generalizability over judges, times, conditions, and subjects, as well as its validity for each construct to which it is applied.

Summary

In scoring items or observations, and especially in deriving an index from a series of units or discrete bits of data, we utilize a measurement scale: nominal, ordinal, interval, or ratio. We also employ a psychometric model: we may simply count frequencies, we may view stimuli and subjects as located on a homogeneous scale from less to more or on a scale homogeneous in some other way, or we may classify subjects into types.

When we combine units into indices, we need to know the extent to which all these units are measuring the same thing so that we can generalize over units; we also want to generalize over points in time and over data producers. For analyzing the homogeneity of a matrix of responses to several items by several subjects, one can determine the proportions of the total variance associated with persons and with items, and the proportion associated with all other influences, including person-item interaction and idiosyncrasy. Alternatively, one can determine the extent to which the items intercorrelate over people and the extent to which the subjects intercorrelate over the items. These two sets of indices supplement each other.

To find out how confidently we can generalize beyond a given test and its resulting indices, we can study its intercorrelations with measures of similar and of different variables. Logically, two measures of the same construct should correlate, and correlate more highly than they do with measures of different constructs. The ultimate test of both an instrument and its construct is carried out by seeing whether the test correlates with diverse other variables in the pattern predicted from *a priori* propositions, such correlations being expected to be high in some instances and low or zero in others. For some purposes, the validity of a test may be judged by close examination of its contents, but this approach is risky in personality measurement. At times our concern may be with the capacity of the test to predict a criterion as measured now or at a future date. Through all these assessments of a test, from its internal consistency to its construct validity, there runs the same question: How confidently can we generalize from one observation to another observation, from test to test, etc.? The full appraisal of a test involves several kinds of studies, all related to generalizability.

People are often used to provide data and indices about subjects. Such methods have advantages but also disadvantages. In the published literature, there is no compelling empirical evidence that the expert judge can predict a criterion better than indices derived objectively by actuarial methods.

CHAPTER NINE

Behaving and Changing

The Stability of Behavior from a Short-Term View

Personality was defined earlier as the way a person functions, the way he interacts with his environment (page 37). It includes the way a person receives stimuli, deals with them, and acts so as to change the input he receives. The person may move so as to receive the stimuli more intensely or he may do something to eliminate stimuli that are themselves unpleasant or which evoke unpleasant associations for him. Thus personology studies living people who are experiencing, feeling, thinking, and doing.

At a more molecular level, this living and experiencing and doing can be described as processes that began, continued, and terminated, or which were aborted for some reason, or which were interrupted and sidetracked, only to be resumed later (see Chapter 3). A person may feel a bit uncomfortable and shift his position in his chair. A young man may wonder why he feels uneasy about something a friend says to him, until he is distracted from that effort by seeing another friend he wants to speak to. A college senior may start to consider what he will do next year, find the problem difficult and frustrating, and start thinking about his date for that evening.

THE STREAM OF EXPERIENCING

Think of a person falling asleep. Each of us is familiar with this experience and has heard other people discuss it. All sorts of things go through our minds: we recall and review what we were just doing and what happened earlier in the day. We may think about what we are going to do tomorrow. We may think about pleasant or unpleasant times in the past or about what may happen next month or next year. Actually, we do not usually think

about these things as we think about a math problem; we do not think systematically and purposefully, seeking a solution. Rather, we let these mental or hypnagogic images come to mind and disappear; the contents often
change abruptly, for no obvious reason.

But from time to time we attend to a noise from the street, or to the tick-
ling of a corner of our blanket. Or we may simply turn over, hardly aware
of any reason for doing so, though some somesthetic stimulus may trigger
the action.

In somewhat similar fashion, we may wake up, not knowing what stimulus, somatic or external, disturbed us. As we lie half awake, we may hear
someone's alarm clock and ignore it. Later, our own clock buzzes, and we
shut it off. Sooner or later, the external environment impinges on us sufficiently so that we get out of bed and begin our familiar routine for pulling
ourselves together to prepare for the day ahead.

During these periods, the contents of our minds at any moment seem
quite random. Certainly they vary from moment to moment, with little or
no repetition. And much the same can be said for dreams. The systematic
collection of dreams, by waking a person after his electroencephalogram
indicates that he has been dreaming, yields reports with no repetition within
any one dream, and little or none between one dream and the next. (See
Fiske, 1961b.) Similar experiences occur when a person is in sensory isolation. An experimental subject may be instructed to lie without moving in
a soundproof room in the dark for several hours. Except for those subjects
who are upset by this experience and keep thinking about getting out of it,
subjects report quite varied mental content (Fiske, 1961a.)

The point is that mental content under all these conditions shows almost
infinite variety, not only from person to person but also from time to time
in the same person. The regularities that do occur are largely those generated by successive reappearances of external stimuli. The stability of behavior, the repetition of particular thoughts or responses, is associated with
the stability of the environment, the recurrence of specific stimuli and situations, and their impact on behavior. We develop and practice certain
ways of doing things, like turning off the alarm clock, signing our name, or
saying hello, repeating each act as the external situation calls for it.

One form of situationally determined consistency is associated with role.
A salesman learns to greet each potential customer in a pleasant manner
and to express a positive, interested attitude of helpfulness. But away from
work, his behavior toward his friends may have a consistently blunt tone.
At home, he may display regularly a cool and reserved attitude toward his
children.

It is extremely difficult, if not impossible, for personology to study the
stream of experiencing as it occurs in one person (though novelists have

attempted to present such material). Like other sciences, the science of personality studies regularities and consistencies, at least as a first step. So what we seek to measure are the ways a person usually behaves, the regularities in his perceptions, feelings, and actions. To measure individual differences between people, we present the same stimuli to each of them and observe their responses. But these stimuli must be familiar ones, or ones that subjects can fit into their usual ways of perceiving and interpreting stimuli, so that we can observe learned and consistent reactions. If we present very strange stimuli, the person's responses may be different from one presentation to the next, as they often are to inkblots and other stimuli used in projective techniques. To be sure, the manner in which a person responds to strange stimuli may be more or less consistent from time to time, but the content is quite likely to vary.

The reader may feel that we have presented the extreme case to argue for variability of experience and behavior from moment to moment, and he will be right. Things are often clearer and more simple under extreme conditions. Furthermore, everyday behavior is also highly variable from one minute to the next. Systematic, continuous observations provide evidence for this statement. (See Barker, 1963; Barker and Wright, 1951.) The consistencies during a day in a person's life are not so much in the content as in the ways he does things. A person repeats himself verbatim only rarely —unless he has had an unusual accident or caught a very large fish. But he speaks with the same phrasing and he walks and gestures in the same style. And he persistently seeks the same satisfactions and avoids the same disturbing experiences.

Between the extreme variability of experiences and behavior when the environment has little or no impact and the marked consistency of signatures and other stylistic, instrumental acts, there is a wide range of behavior that varies in stability according to the particular circumstances and the kinds of stimuli that occur. Some situations and stimuli permit spontaneous responses, others impose constraints. At play, one is more free and variable, while at work (especially when the boss is present), one is more stable and consistent.

Some indirect evidence on the contribution of situations to behavior has been provided by Endler and Hunt (1968). They have devised questionnaires in which a person is asked to report how he would feel in each of about a dozen situations. For example, in their Inventory of Anxiousness, the situations include going to meet a new date and entering a competitive contest before spectators. The subject reports the extent to which his heart beats faster, he gets an "uneasy feeling," and a number of other modes of response. Analyzing the variance of the responses, Endler and Hunt find that situations contribute 4 percent for men and 8 percent for women.

These amounts may seem trivial, but the total scores of the subjects themselves contribute only 4 or 5 percent. Modes of response contribute about 25 percent: some modes are much more common or intense than others. The rest of the variance is contributed by combinations or interactions of these components and by residual variance not specifically identified (this latter source contributing about 35 percent). Rather similar contributions were found for their Inventory of Hostility, except that subjects contributed 15 to 19 percent and modes of response only 15 percent. Situations alone or in interaction contributed more than a fifth of the variance. While subjects alone or in interaction contributed more, it was often not much more.

This evidence is only indirect because subjects were reporting on what they had experienced or what they imagined they might experience. We must also keep in mind that the size of these values is affected by the content: all the situations were included because they do elicit the reaction to some extent. If more extreme or more everyday situations had been included, the contribution of situational variance would undoubtedly have been larger.

STATE VS. TRAIT

The Inventory of Anxiousness measures the state of anxiety in each of several situations. Each response indicates how the subject feels under particular conditions, not how anxious he feels most of the time. Ordinarily, however, personologists measure traits: Does the subject generally feel tense and anxious? Is he typically friendly? Such trait measurements are a generalization or average over most situations, or over most appropriate situations. (A person usually feels friendly only when he is with other people.)

In recent years, psychologists have become interested in measuring the states of people at particular moments. (See Cattell and Scheier, 1961; Spielberger and Lushene, 1971.) They are seeking to assess the state of the subject at a particular moment. Obviously, their interest is not in just any moment. It is not important whether a person at some arbitrary point in time feels optimistic or pessimistic. The measurement of states is significant when we know what the preceding situation has been; e.g., how does a person react to frustration? Such measurement is used in experimental studies when the conditions have been controlled or manipulated by the experimenter.

CONSISTENCY OF BEHAVIOR OVER REPEATED OBSERVATIONS

Behavior shows stability under three kinds of conditions. One kind includes those situations in which a person has to cope with stimuli and has a way of doing so which he has practiced repeatedly in the past. The clearest examples are instrumental acts, acts that serve a purpose. In signing your name, you produce the same response every time. There is a marked consistency among the many signatures that you have written. In fact, a stranger will give you money when you sign a traveler's check because he knows that it is practically impossible for someone else to reproduce your signature when he writes at normal speed. You have signed your name countless times; a forger would have to practice a long time before he could sign your name your way at reasonable speed. Again, we can recognize people at a distance by the way they walk. We recognize voices over the telephone by the way they say hello. Such acts are not only done individualistically and characteristically by each person, they are also done very consistently from time to time.

People are also consistent in what they seek. Some people regularly seek attention when they are with others. Some people pursue the affection of almost everyone they meet. Others seek to be admired. These needs are highly stable and persistent; they direct the person's behavior whenever a suitable opportunity is offered. Since these are all ways of coping with life, they can be considered to be part of a broader class that includes the instrumental acts discussed above. When conditions elicit coping behaviors, goal-oriented responses of one kind or another, the observed responses tend to be stable over time.

Another kind of consistency occurs when no ulterior goals are being pursued. Suppose a person is asked to give a response to each of forty-five inkblots, as in the Holtzman Technique (Holtzman *et al.*, 1961). What kind of consistency will be found among the forty-five sequential responses? For any one quality of these responses, the consistencies or regularities are found in subjects whose responses do *not* have that quality. For subjects giving responses with that quality, such responses occur irregularly or occasionally and not in succession. For example; we do not find repetitions of the same content: subjects do not like to keep repeating themselves. Similarly, we do not find long strings of responses involving the color of the blots. But we do find that some subjects give many reactions to the color, and others give few or none. Statistically, when we analyze the sequences of such responses, we find some subjects are highly consistent in *not* responding to the color, in *not* responding to the shading, or in giving responses that do not have human content. In other words, subjects who respond some of the time in a given way can be considered less consistent in this respect than those who never respond that way. To take another example, a person who perceives animals in these blots may give such responses perhaps 30 percent of the time, so that, on the average, one response will be an animal, the next two will not, and the next one will be. In contrast, a person who gives only one or two animal responses will rarely change from an animal response to a nonanimal response.

This relationship between the strength of the disposition and its variability is to be expected on mathematical grounds when the disposition is scored with two categories, such as animal vs. nonanimal content. The most variability will be found when both categories occur 50 percent of the time. As the nonanimal response occurs more frequently, the variability becomes less (the stability of that response becomes greater), and when all responses are nonanimal, the person is completely consistent in this respect. Similarly, as the disposition to give animal responses increases from 50 percent toward 100 percent, stability increases.

But exactly what do we mean here by consistency? Two meanings of the term are relevant to what has been said up to this point. In some earlier parts of the chapter, we were implicitly talking about the relative frequency of a particular act, or of an act with a particular quality: when such a given class of acts is observed in a great majority of the available opportunities, we consider that the subject is being consistent. The same holds true for the discussion of inkblot responses with a particular characteristic. We have said that the greater the frequency of nonanimal responses (for relative frequencies above 50 percent), the more consistent the nonanimal response becomes. What is added here is the intuitive notion that with such increases, the frequency of one such response following another becomes greater and greater. It is really this impression of consistency as frequency of successive pairs of the designated response which is being considered when we say that the nonanimal responses are more consistent that the animal responses. Statistically, the variance of the two is the same, since the variance refers to the single distribution of animal and nonanimal responses. Psychologically, the person giving mostly (say, 85 percent) animal responses will seem to an observer (and to himself) to be more consistent in this respect than will the person giving 15 percent of such responses.

(The preceding analysis assumes that each of the successive trials is independent of the earlier ones, an assumption that generally holds true. Note, however, that if one subject gave forty-two animal responses followed by three nonanimal, and another gave twenty-five animal followed by twenty nonanimal, we would consider the two to be about equally consistent, regardless of the difference in their relative frequencies.)

Relative frequencies over 50 percent are found with practiced ways of coping, and hence the stronger the coping response, the more stable it is. At the other end, the weaker the positive disposition to give animal responses and the larger the disposition not to give animal responses, the more stable are the responses in this respect. (In this analysis, we ignore all other characteristics of the response: its use of color, its human content, etc.)

When the responses are scored on a continuous or multistep scale, a similar model often applies. For example, the variation among shots at a target is greater for the novice than for the expert, who clusters his shots in and around the bull's-eye. In reaction time, low means tend to go with low variances. In these examples, stability of response is low variance and it tends to be related to mean responses that are closer to some limit—the bull's-eye or the instantaneous reaction. Thus once again the more adequate the coping response, the more stable it is.

In other instances, there is also a relationship between mean or level of responses and their variation. On a multistep rating scale that is bipolar and has a neutral point in the middle, the variation over successive trials tends to increase as the mean moves away from the middle but then becomes smaller again as the mean approaches the end of the scale.

It is important to recognize that in these cases of continuously scored variables, the relationship between mean and variance is not mathematically necessary. If a skillful subject had a gun with a defective sight and was given no knowledge about his performance, he would cluster his shots consistently about some spot on the target other than the bull's-eye. Similarly, it is in principle possible for one subject to take exactly one second for each of his reactions and another subject to take exactly two seconds. The mathematical factor affects only the limits: with a mean of zero on a scale from 0 to 10, the variance has to be 0; with a mean of 1, the variance cannot exceed 9 (but may still be any smaller value down to 0); with a mean of 2, the variance can be any value between 0 and 16. Although, given the mean for these conditions, there is a statistical expectation for the variance that increases with the mean up to the middle of the scale, the critical factor appears to be psychological: it is the capacity to avoid wild shots and to keep shots close to the bull's-eye which gives the expert his low mean (distance from center of bull's-eye) and low variance; it is the capacity to avoid long reaction times and to keep each one relatively short which produces the low mean and accompanying low variance in those data. I.e., the relationship between mean and variance (or stability) is best interpreted as due to common factors influencing both, not to one of these values determining the other.

THE STABILITY OF MEASUREMENTS

Much of the preceding discussion has considered the stability of general behavior. (For a more complete account, see Fiske, 1961*b*.) But what about the stability of measurements? We take it for granted that we usually wish to maximize such stability. If our measurements of a personality trait vary from time to time as a function of the subject's mood, physiological state, or time of day, the data for any one time will be poor approximations of the typical or average strength of the disposition.

The stability of the observations of Prior Behavior (Mode 4) will obviously depend on a wide variety of factors that are beyond our control except insofar as we can select the samples of behavior that are examined. The stability of Indices based on Mode 5 techniques (Observations of Behavior) depend on the extent and variety among the observations from which the observer makes his inferences. Strictly speaking, we cannot assess the stability of such indices because the observer cannot sensibly repeat his observations on the same subject. His previous contact with that subject does not allow the two sets of observations to be considered interchangeable. In Mode 6, the stability depends upon the nature of the psychological situation in which the psychophysiological observations are made. There are also a number of technical considerations (involving the way the index is derived, the use of base lines, etc.) which are pertinent. Psychophysiological measurement requires intensive training and experience. It cannot be adequately examined in this short volume.

To understand about stability of responses in the first three modes, we must go back to something left implicit in the earlier, more general discussion. When a person has to cope with a situation, and can cope with it, his behavior tends to be consistent over time. When a person is in an unfamiliar situation or when he has no way of coping with a situation, his behavior may be less consistent. Consider a hungry rat placed in a maze for the first time. He runs around exploring it, and if he finds a food box, he eats. Placed in the same maze the next day, he explores less, tending to move in the direction of the food box. With successive trials, his behavior becomes more and more stable. He enters each blind alley less and less. Eventually, he runs rather consistently by one route to the food.

A person placed in a strange testing situation and given an unfamiliar test confronts a sort of maze. To be sure, he knows that he is expected to give some answers but he does not know how he should select them. If asked to say what is true for him, he still has only a general goal, which may be difficult to reach for many items. The examiner, the test, and the situational demands are factors that are usually new to the subject. The one major exception is tests using Mode 3 (Capabilities), in which the subject is asked to give the correct answer; in this culture, children learn early about such demands. Similarly, subjects can become familiar with an examiner, as students do with their teacher. Finally, there is the test. As we shall see shortly, subjects become more consistent in their responses to a test with repeated testings.

For the sake of economy, however, we cannot test subjects five to ten times so as to obtain stable responses. One partial substitute is to provide sample items for the subjects to try—a procedure that is standard for tests of ability, especially those that are timed. Curiously, no one has ever tried giving subjects time to look over personality tests before they take them, a procedure that might well lead to more stable answers as well as to greater cooperation by the subjects. (Such a study is now being conducted by R. Tracy.) To maximize the stability of responses (i.e., the stability that would be found if the test were repeated), we should design the testing situation so that its meaning for the subject is clear and so that he can accept and cope with its demands. Similarly, the stimuli and the responding process itself should have clear meanings and implications for him. For example, tests using Mode 1 should use language that is familiar to the particular group of subjects, preferably the phrases they naturally use in describing themselves and others. (This recommendation does not necessarily mean that the test should be couched in the current jargon of a group. Many fad words and phrases are really quite ambiguous or equivocal, and may change their meanings over the course of a few months.)

Mode 2 procedures (Current Experiencing) should tap the subjects' established ways of perceiving things. The Capabilities mode (Mode 3) causes fewer problems. Presented with a set of questions and asked to give correct answers, all but the most uncooperative subjects will ordinarily do so to the best of their ability. As a result, the stability of tests of capabilities is higher than that of any other type. Ninety to ninety-five percent of the responses of such tests are unchanged on repetition. Tests of interests and values tend to be almost as stable. On the standard questionnaires, 70 to 75 percent of the responses will be repeated. On inkblots, roughly half of the responses may be repeated. But responses to incomplete sentences are changed the great majority of times. (For the possible effects of such changes on interpretations, see Fiske and Van Buskirk, 1959.)

These figures apply to separate responses. As one would expect, the stability of scores derived from these responses varies in the same way over types of tests. Examination of these different kinds of instruments suggests that the stability of both test responses and scores follows the generalization given earlier: when a person has to cope with a situation and can cope with it adequately, his behavior is likely to be stable. The less structured projective techniques provide little guidance as to how a subject should cope with them, and hence responses to such procedures are less stable. This ordering of procedures also illustrates another general principle indicated earlier: the more the subject's behavior is determined by the situation and the stimuli, by the outside environment rather than by what is going on within him, the more stable it will be.

Before leaving the topic of stability in scores and responses, we should consider two points. Stability is a kind of reliability (see Chapter 8). It is computed by determining the relative agreement between the two measurements of the person's position in his group. Such correlations vary somewhat with the range or variation within that group, so that they tend to be smaller with more homogeneous groups. Consider, for example, measuring the heights of several subjects who have, on the basis of many repeated measurements, been determined to be sixty-six and one-quarter inches tall. If we measure each of them today and again tomorrow, we will obtain a coefficient indicating little or no stability in their heights, simply because all the variation on both days will come from errors of measurement, from their standing straighter one day or the other, from carelessness, etc.

The second point is that behavior is less stable than we ordinarily think it is. We perceive others and ourselves as being quite consistent. We do this for at least two reasons. First, we expect people to behave as they generally have in the past, and we ignore small variations from our expectations. Second, it is much easier to think of other people as having fixed dispositions, rather than as varying somewhat from time to time. We tend to think of most people as expressing the same mood from day to day, the few exceptions being those whose mood changes are very obvious and inconvenient to us, those we call moody.

FACTORS AFFECTING THE STABILITY OF TEST RESPONSES

In addition to the factors considered above, a number of others are associated with the stability of responses and scores (see Fiske, 1957, 1961*b;* Goldberg and Jones, 1969). A major one is a function of the subject and the item taken together. Consider a test of auditory acuity. A subject always hears sounds that are clearly above his threshold and fails to hear sounds that are well below it. Sounds closer to his threshold are heard sometimes; those right at it are heard about half the time.

Consider Figure 9.1. Suppose that the line represents degrees of loudness, the numbers being tones with increasing loudness from the first to

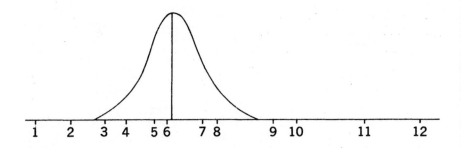

Figure 9.1. A general model of a subject's threshold

the twelfth. A subject's auditory acuity is assumed to vary from moment to moment, the curve above the line representing the frequency with which his threshold is at each point on the line. Our subject always hears tones numbered 9, 10, 11, and 12, and never hears those numbered 1 and 2. He rarely hears number 3, sometimes hears number 4, and he hears numbers 5 and 6 about half the time. He usually hears number 7. He hears number 8 every time except on those occasions when his threshold is temporarily above that point.

The same diagram might also represent ability to recall a series of digits, with the ability fluctuating according to the indicated distribution: subject can always repeat two digits correctly, almost always get four digits right, but misses on six about half the time. Once in a while, he gets eight right, but he never gets ten or more.

A similar model seems to hold for personality tests. The items of such a test can be scaled by technical methods. (Scaling means assigning numerical values or points on a continuum, values with certain properties.) This scaling of items can be done from the endorsement values, the values indicating how frequently they are answered in the keyed direction. The numbered points in Figure 9.1 can also be taken to represent twelve scaled items.

Subjects can also be scaled on the same abstract continuum. Rasch (1960) has devised a method for doing this so that the values for the items remain the same even when different subjects are used, and so that the values for persons are not affected by the items used. With both persons and items on the same scale, it is possible to compute the distance between them. If the vertical line in the center of the distribution in Figure 9.1 represents a subject's point, we can see that he is close to items 5 and 6, but far from 2 and 10, and even farther from 1, 11, and 12. In the earlier examples of hearing and memory, we noted that our subject was consistent in his response or performance when the stimulus was far above or below his point: e.g., he was consistently right in repeating short series of digits and consistently wrong when he attempted very long series. Tyler (1968) has shown that the same relationship to stability is found for responses to personality tests: a subject is more stable over time in his responses to items at some distance from his own scale point and less stable in responding to items near his point. Thus our subject would consistently endorse items 1 and 2, and consistently not endorse the top four items. He would endorse or not endorse items 3 through 8 depending upon where his point was at that moment. The model as applied to personality assumes that a subject's point varies around its mean, just as auditory acuity or ability to recall digits varies from time to time. Tyler's findings fitted this model.

Tyler also found that the converse was true: the responses to an item were more stable if its average distance to subjects was greater than the average distance for another item. The obvious implication is that a test with items well spread out will have more stable responses and more stable scores than a test with many items bunched together toward the middle of the scale. This study provides another argument (see Chapter 8) for dispersing items along a scale when one wishes to measure each person as stably as possible. (It is still true that, if one just wants to divide a group reliably into two halves, one should use items that are passed by about half the subjects.)

Another factor affecting response stability is familiarity with the test items. Such familiarity appears to be gained only by answering those specific items, and by looking at them in the same way each time. Schubert (1969) found that answering similar items and making an independent judgment about the items (instead of applying the item to oneself) did not produce an increase in stability.

These increases in stability with exposure and practice can be considered a kind of learning, even though the only reward for the subjects would seem to be that they can complete the instrument more easily and more rapidly on the later trials. Probably this learning comes simply from subjects' tendency to think about the item in the same way they have thought about it before. Note, of course, that the subjects do not necessarily give better responses to later trials. Those responses tend to have slightly higher internal consistency but no one has provided convincing evidence that responses to later trials are more valid.

On the other hand, there is evidence that subjects do learn from early trials, in the sense that they may get better scores on later ones. Many students in high school take a preliminary scholastic aptitude test and then a later one, tending to do better on the second test because they are familiar with the type of test and the type of item, and perhaps also because they function better the second time, being less anxious about the type of test as they become more familiar with it. There is also considerable evidence (Windle, 1954, 1955) that subjects obtain slightly higher scores on tests of adjustment when they take them for the second time. The reason for this mean gain is unclear. Perhaps subjects are less anxious when taking such a test for the second time (people do tend to be more anxious about the unknown and unfamiliar than about the familiar), and perhaps people give more defensive answers when they are less anxious. I.e., when, on the second trial, they encounter an item that is a little difficult to answer, subjects may tend to give themselves the benefit of the doubt and choose the socially more desirable alternative. If experience with a test contributes to test-wiseness, then the preceding interpretation is supported by Stricker's finding (1969) that measures of test-wiseness tend to be correlated with measures of the tendency to give socially desirable answers. He measured test-wiseness in a number of ways: ability to identify the variable an item was measuring, to estimate an item's frequency of endorsement, to estimate its social desirability rating by others, etc.

These findings suggest that tests should be designed so that very little adaptation is necessary. We can also draw the more remote implication that, once again, items should be easy for subjects to answer: the more difficult it is for a subject to select an alternative readily, the more likely it is that some unwanted influence will enter and swing the balance toward one alternative (usually a more favorable one). This latter point was made by Cronbach (1946, 1950) in his classic papers on response sets, systematic response dispositions other than the trait being measured. Such sets or styles will be discussed in the next chapter.

The Long-Term Stability of Personality Measurements

Up to this point, we have been considering the stability of behavior in the short run. From minute to minute the stimuli impinging on a person change, and his responses change. From hour to hour a person's state may change as psychological events affect his mood and as his physiological condition varies with time since last meal, time since he woke up, etc. From day to day his preoccupations differ.

Much of the work evaluating the stability of a psychological test uses intervals between testings of one to eight weeks. The period selected is intended to be long enough so that it will be unlikely that a subject will remember how he answered the items the previous time. Subjects usually want to appear consistent—consistency is considered a virtue by most people in this culture—and so would make the same responses again if they could remember their earlier ones. On the other hand, the interval should not be so long that significant events are likely to have occurred between the two testings, events that might appropriately lead to changes in responses. E.g., a freshman tested when he enters college is likely to have somewhat different attitudes toward college life, toward university administration, and toward national policy than he has later in the year after exposure to other students with different backgrounds and after courses in subjects he has never studied intensively before.

The stability of personality over a period of years is largely beyond the province of this volume. A few remarks about it may, however, help to provide some perspective on measurement of short-term stability and change. In general, the longer the period between observations, the greater the change. This tendency is of course stronger during the first two decades of a person's life, during his formative, developmental period. Another way of stating the matter is to say that behavior is determined by constitutional or innate factors established before birth and by experience. With increasing age, the experiential component increases its contribution, not only as the person's range of experience is expanded but also as certain experiences recur and the person develops more or less consistent ways of coping with them. I.e., he learns new things and he practices old habits.

The problem of long-term stability is the topic of *Stability and Change in Human Characteristics* (Bloom, 1964). In this thorough and intensive review of the literature, Bloom examines data on the stability of various types of characteristics. He indicates that the correlation between measures (e.g., at two points in time) can be interpreted in terms of the percentage of elements common to the two sets of measurements; another interpretation is that the square of the correlation is the percentage of variation in one set of measurements which is accounted for by the other set (e.g., the later set as determined by the earlier set). While the interpretation of correlation coefficients is a technical matter requiring some statistical sophistication, this latter kind of interpretation can be used safely in the present context.

Measures of Capabilities, Mode 3, are quite stable in adults. Even over a decade or two, observed correlations may be .80 to .90, and estimates of the relationships are even higher when allowance is made for the unreliability of the tests. In Mode 1 (Self Description), measures of interests over similar intervals may have coefficients between .65 and .75. Measures of other personality traits in that same mode may be as high but are likely to be lower, sometimes very much lower. In general, from the rather limited data available, it appears that personalities change more over time than many of us would expect. What with the great stability of physique, style, and expressive movements, and the natural tendency to expect consistency in the world around us, we probably tend to see most people as remaining much the same over the years, noting only the marked exceptions and explaining these by particular circumstances.

Observed stability during developmental years is of course lower. Perhaps the most remarkable aspect of the few longitudinal studies of children throughout their development is the fact that moderate stability has been found. While some personality theories (like the psychoanalytic one) would predict such stability in basic features of personality, these observations are somewhat surprising in view of the fact that they must involve different kinds of procedures at different age levels: different tests, different observers, and different conditions. It is difficult to assess the extent to which these factors lower the observed relationships; the stability of personality during the developmental years may be greater than the amount that has been reported.

The naturalistic observation of consistency in personality has yet another aspect. In people we know well, we can usually see one or a very few pervasive dispositions, tendencies that appear in a wide range of contexts. One person may continually seek reassurance and approval from others, pursuing them insatiably, in a variety of ways. Another may persistently compete with others. A third may regularly seek evidence of the superiority he would like to be convinced that he possesses. Yet another may routinely act so as to avoid blame or shame. These core strivings have been conceptualized in several ways. Murray *et al.* (1938) write about the unity-thema in the study of a personality. Allport (1961) sees cardinal dispositions to which most behavior can be related. Dynamic theorists use terms such as focal or nuclear conflict, often referring to a developmental problem that the subject has not completely worked out. Such central themes are likely to be rather individualistic if not unique in their specific content and in the sets of conditions in which they are most readily observed. Hence they are fairly easy to identify in case studies but difficult to study systematically. As a result, the research literature on this topic is almost nonexistent. The problem deserves the effort necessary to develop appropriate methodologies and to execute careful empirical studies.

The Study of Change

MEASURING EXPERIMENTAL EFFECTS

There are two major paradigms involving change, depending on whether the change is very rapid or very slow; whether it occurs in seconds or minutes, or only over days, weeks, or months. The first is found in many experimental studies in which an experimental group is exposed to one condition and a control group is exposed to a neutral condition, or two groups are exposed to contrasting conditions. In such studies, it is often assumed that before treatment the experimental group was comparable to the control group but was rapidly changed by the experimental treatment. For example, Kroger (1967) compared mean scores on scales of the Strong Vocational Interest Blank for two groups tested under different experimental conditions, each of which might change the subjects in a particular way. One group of ROTC cadets were asked by an officer to volunteer for a research study. The cadets were assembled in an ROTC classroom; the examiner was a military officer in uniform. They were told that the general purpose of the study was to determine "what makes a good military officer," but were assured that the results would not be seen by their superiors. The second group were asked by letter to volunteer for a study of "artistic creativity," and were told before the test that the general purpose was to determine "what makes people artistically creative." The two groups took the same test under different titles, each appropriate to the alleged purpose. (A subsequent study, however, found no effect from just test title alone.)

The rate of volunteering was 90 percent in the military context but only 55 percent in the artistic. Often such a difference can invalidate the findings. For this study contrasting two extreme groups, this uncontrolled variable might affect the influence of a single condition but not the conclusion that the conditions had different effects.

Note, however, that the selection conditions might have biased the results in the experimenter's favor. Suppose those subjects who accepted the request to participate in a study of artistic creativity were interested in art, whereas those who rejected the request of their military officer were not interested in the military. Kroger looked for some bias of this kind by comparing volunteers and nonvolunteers for the artistic condition and found no differences on several variables.

Kroger predicted that vocational scales most clearly related to the conditions (e.g., army officer and architect) would be influenced most, that scales somewhat related (e.g., purchasing agent and psychologist) would be influenced less, and that neutral scales (e.g., chemist and social worker) would not show differences. Most of his predictions were borne out.

To check on the effectiveness of his experimental manipulation, Kroger gave the subjects a written postexperimental inquiry. Subjects who seemed to accept the ostensible purpose of the testing without voicing any doubts showed stronger influence from the conditions of testing.

This study demonstrates the possible effects on test scores of the character of the situation in which people are tested. The effects were consistent and statistically significant, but they were not large in absolute terms: the largest effects for the total samples were differences of 9 score points, or about 20 percent. The conditions were intentionally subtle, in contrast to those of a later experiment in which subjects were asked to maximize their scores in one or the other of these directions and the differences were much larger (Kroger, 1968).

This latter study is perhaps more typical of studies of experimental conditions, since the responses were more largely determined by the conditions than in the earlier one, in which the subjects' normal interests contributed most of the variance in their test scores. Obviously, in designing studies of immediate effects, one seeks to use a plan in which such effects will have the greatest opportunity to operate.

In the study in which subjects were explicitly asked to play the role of military officer or creative artist, what was measured in each subject was his capacity to play the assigned role. This was a role he probably had never consciously tried to play before, and so perhaps indicated role-taking ability. But note that Kroger did not really measure this directly. Probably for economy and other reasons, he did not test each subject twice, once under standard, neutral conditions and once under the experimental instruction. Instead, he assumed that the mean scores for each group under neutral conditions would be very similar, so that the effect could be demonstrated by comparing the mean scores under the two experimental instructions.

Even though he was interested in immediate effects as determined from mean differences, his measurement problems were much the same as those in measuring individual differences among subjects on a more enduring trait. Did conditions other than the instruction to enact a role increase or reduce his scores? Would large monetary rewards have produced larger effects? Did the conditions affect different subjects differently? On the other hand, he did not have to be concerned about whether subjects interpreted the content of items individualistically and about possible differential reactions of subjects to the examiner. Once he had demonstrated his intended effect, he could ignore those possible biases that could only reduce the observed difference. He needed only to ask whether he unwittingly increased the effect by some factor irrelevant to his design. It is difficult to conceive what such a factor might be, in this particular instance.

While the measurement of experimental effects may often be somewhat easier than the measurement of enduring traits, both share the problem of generalizability. When measuring individual differences, the experimenter wants to feel confident that he can generalize from his testing situation to other situations and from the scores obtained with his measuring procedures to a subconstruct or construct. Similarly, the experimenter manipulating conditions wants to generalize from his specific manipulation to other effects (e.g., to other types of situational demands and to demands with different content) and to other situations (e.g., he might want to generalize to testing for purposes of selection, although it is well established that scores may be influenced by subjects' desire to obtain scores that are favorably viewed in a particular context). Also, the experimenter wants to generalize to his concept of the effect. In Kroger's work, this would involve generalizing to other types of subtle situational pressures and to pressures with different content. A single study of this kind offers no evidence of the possibility of such generalizability. It would have done so if Kroger had compared his two experimental groups with a comparable sample from the same population, a sample tested under standard instructions and neutral conditions. To some extent, the absence of differences on neutral scales serves that purpose.

The difficulties about generalizing from a single study are illustrated by an experiment by Eaton and Fiske (in press), who also sought to bias subjects' responses by subtle conditions. This study obtained much weaker effects. Was this due to the use of younger subjects, captive subjects (in intact school course sections), the same examiner for both conditions, a different test, a different design in which subjects were pretested under neutral conditions by a different examiner, or some combination of these factors, or some other factor? Only additional research can provide a clear-cut answer.

Eaton and I were interested in the hypothesis that score changes effected by such subtle biasing conditions are produced by changes in the responses of subjects to items that have scale points near their own. Recall, earlier in this chapter, the account of Tyler's work, which indicated that such items are more likely to be changed on retest, even under the repetition of the same standard conditions, and which noted that such items are those most likely to be affected by such irrelevant and unwanted subject dispositions as response sets. It was predicted here that these items would also be more likely to be influenced by external, situational pressures. Some evidence supporting this prediction was found.

THE MEASUREMENT OF THERAPEUTIC TREATMENTS

The measurement of the effects of psychotherapy or some substantial training experience provides another paradigm involving change, a paradigm with major social significance. Such change is much slower but more enduring (less reversible) than change effected by experimental manipulations. Consider first the behavior therapies. Perhaps the most rigorous empirical work on behavior change has been done on the treatment of phobias. A typical design involves the identification of subjects who report a specific phobia, the demonstration of their fear (e.g., by obtaining self-report or psychophysiological measures—Modes 2 or 6—of their experience when actually confronted with an appropriate stimulus such as a live snake), and a series of sessions in which the subjects are increasingly desensitized by exposures to such a stimulus or its representation (such as a stuffed snake), exposures gradually approaching the real thing, but carefully programmed not to generate substantial negative reaction. Considerable change may be observed after such treatment. The subject may report that his fear of snakes is greatly diminished or he may demonstrate to the experimenter in the laboratory that he will now actually touch a live snake.

The empirical work on such desensitization has yielded very promising results. (See Paul, 1969.) Subjects do show marked reductions of reactions to the feared object. While reports of such gains in outside situations may be treated with caution or skepticism, reports of current reactions in the laboratory room are somewhat more persuasive and demonstrated reductions in physiological effects are even more so. Such an approach has attracted many researchers because it involves a type of therapeutic treatment that can be standardized to some degree and which is open to objective examination.

The problem of measuring subjects' reactions to a feared object that can be presented to him in the laboratory is relatively simple. The major questions concern generalization. Does measured reaction to a particular snake serve as a good estimate of reaction to other snakes? Little has been done on this question, most investigators assuming that reaction to one snake or to snakes of one kind can be generalized, even though subjects might realize sooner or later that experimenters are likely to use only harmless snakes in such work. Does reaction in the laboratory permit generalization to the outside world? Actually, a person rarely encounters snakes in most parts of this country, so reports of reduced fear of snakes must be interpreted as less fear in situations where snakes might be seen. There is great likelihood that expectation effects will bias such reports. The subject knows that the experimenter expects him to report reduced fear. In addition, after having been treated in a series of sessions taking up a number of hours, a subject is more likely to feel that some change must have occurred. He does not want to feel that he has wasted his time, and he may have become persuaded by the experimenter's apparent confidence in his treatment procedure.

A major weakness in some interpretations of this work is their generalization from the subjects studied to patients with disabling phobias and to patients with other diagnoses. Certainly such generalization to patients is hardly warranted when the subjects are college students who have merely reported a particular fear when given an inventory of fears, but who have not sought treatment or been referred for treatment. Additionally, phobias are relatively uncommon; no generalization to other diagnoses can be made from observations of people with this particular symptom.

Measurement in research on other, older forms of individual psychotherapy shares some of these difficulties and faces some much greater obstacles. In these as in all other forms of treatment, the assessment of outcome is particularly perplexing. Some treatment is aimed at ameliorating conditions that are almost as specific as phobias, such as concern about forthcoming examinations or distress following a particular trauma— the death of a loved one, for example. Other treatment is aimed at reducing chronic distress or coping with recurring periods of depression. And intensive, prolonged treatment in psychoanalysis may seek even more profound alterations in psychological functioning. The qualitative nature of the problems brought to psychotherapy varies widely. Moreover, the treatment may become focused on functional inadequacies other than the presented complaints. Certainly the whole matter of assessing deficits and pathologies in the personality realm enters into the picture. Only in a rather small proportion of cases can the effectiveness of treatment be evaluated from observations of reactions to and success in coping with a rather specific situation, such as confrontation with a snake.

An additional objective is the measurement of psychological assets and strengths. In some instances, the objective of treatment may be primarily the reinforcement of these strengths rather than the reduction of the stresses, the latter often lying outside the capacities of the patient or therapist to alter. For example, the therapist may help the patient to adjust to a physical handicap or to a life situation that cannot be ameliorated. Given these various considerations, it should be apparent that the selection of appropriate concepts to be measured in research on therapeutic outcome poses almost insuperable obstacles. The progress of research in this area has been hampered further by the lack of consensus on measuring procedures. Each investigator selects his own assortment of instruments, occasionally using a standardized test, sometimes employing an instrument developed in an earlier study by others (but often with some significant modification), and typically creating new procedures. Most regrettably, such new procedures are rarely evaluated for psychometric adequacy or they utilize the judgment of particular judges at the institution supporting the research program, so that replication by others is essentially impossible.

Many other kinds of measurement are necessary in studies of therapeutic effectiveness (see Fiske *et al.*, 1970). Some are relatively straightforward, such as the demographic characteristics of patient and therapist. Others involve the description of the therapist's training, experience, and theoretical orientation. More difficult is the description of the treatment itself, since description in objective terms obviously requires measurements at the level of categorization, although ordered scales would also be employed here. Other significant variables in such studies are the expectations of therapist and patient, as well as the attractiveness of the particular patient to his therapist and the similarity between patient and therapist. Methods for assessing such variables are just beginning to be worked out.

It is clear that research on therapeutic effectiveness must entail measurement from several perspectives and use procedures involving a number of modes. For example, therapists' orientations and objectives can be learned by obtaining reports from the therapists themselves, by determining how they are perceived by the patients, and by having qualified observers observe, or even follow videotapes of, the actual behavior of the therapists during the treatment periods. Each of these perspectives would yield psychologically significant information. Even more important is the use of various perspectives in assessing outcome. Cartwright, Kirtner, and Fiske (1963) found distinct factors among widely varying measures of changes accompanying therapy. The clients or patients themselves produced two factors associated with different kinds of content in their self-reports (Mode 1). The therapists contributed an evaluation of change separate from these. A diagnostician making inferences from Thematic Apperception Test protocols added another perspective. Finally, a judge listening to very early and very late treatment interviews produced still another viewpoint. (These three are in Mode 5.) Even this large-scale investigation did not include all the important possibilities. No measures of changes in Capabilities (Mode 3) were employed. No effort was made to determine whether the clients' Immediate Experiencing (Mode 2) was modified by the treatment. Reports from people who were psychologically significant to the clients (Mode 4) were not tapped. And no attempt was made to measure psychophysiological processes (Mode 6).

Measuring Change

The measurement of change, such as from before to after treatment, may seem deceptively simple. Analysis reveals, however, that it is an exceedingly complex matter, a topic involving a number of technical issues. The following discussion is intended not to prepare the reader to conduct studies of change but rather to bring out some of the complexities so that he can exercise due caution in considering published reports of research on such changes and so that he will not undertake investigations himself without adequate preparation and assistance. (The reader intending to examine this problem intensively can begin with the discussion and the references in Fiske *et al.,* 1970.) At least three major aspects of the problem must be examined: the control of pretreatment differences, the effects of unreliability in the measuring procedures, and the selection of the index appropriate to the question being asked.

INITIAL LEVEL

Suppose a researcher wishes to determine the effectiveness of a program designed to increase carefulness in routine operations. As measures of successful training, he can use work samples of appropriate kinds, such as clerical tests in which S indicates whether two strings of digits are identical or not. In this instance, E has a criterion or norm, the perfect score, obtainable only when S is sufficiently careful to make no mistakes. In principle, E can evaluate his program by assessing error scores or departures from perfect performance.

More commonly, E would want to compare his program of active treat-

198 Measuring

ment with another program or with no treatment at all. The latter might
be used when E wanted to show that his program had some effect or produced more improvement than was obtained simply from repetition of the
test, from practice or familiarity with it. E must, however, consider
whether the motivations of a no-treatment group will be sufficiently different to vitiate the comparison. Ideally, E could assign subjects to an experimental and a comparison group by careful randomization, and then test
the significance of the difference between the experimental group measured after training and the control group measured just once, or between
the means of two treatment groups tested after the treatments. The question being attacked here is "Is Treatment A better than no treatment?"
or "Is Treatment A better than Treatment B?" Note that in these designs
there is no attempt to measure change in any subject, but only the presumed change as inferred from any difference between the groups. Implicit
is the assumption that the two groups had equivalent mean scores before
the training (the treatment), and therefore that the finding of a dependable difference on the tests is associated with the effects on the experimental group of the particular training being investigated.

Some researchers may not feel comfortable about such assumptions
or about dependence on the effectiveness of randomization. They may
therefore wish to add two other groups, both tested before treatment as
well as after, but one receiving the training of particular interest and the
other receiving another kind of training, or no training. These designs
permit the evaluation of effects from prior testing. All these designs have
been well studied and methods for analyzing their findings are available.
(See Campbell and Stanley, 1963.) All involve the study of differences
between groups treated in different ways. Such designs are ordinarily to
be preferred whenever the nature of the treatment and the testing makes
pretesting feasible. The designs using just one testing employ a simple and
direct outcome index, which may be evaluated as departure from ideal or
by comparison between groups. The other designs involve indices derived
from both posttreatment data and pretreatment data. Each of these two
kinds answers a particular sort of question.

INDICES OF CHANGE

Suppose a researcher wishes to study the effectiveness of his program as
a function of intelligence or age. He may not wish to classify his subjects
into several ordered groups according to intelligence, but rather to obtain
an index of gain from treatment which can be correlated with his measure
of intelligence. For such an investigation, the selection of a suitable index
is more complicated. A single posttreatment score will not be adequate,
since these values may be determined in large part by pretreatment dif-

ferences: e.g., the gains may be much the same in the more intelligent and the less intelligent subjects, and any observed relationship between post-treatment score and intelligence may be a function of the relationship between pretreatment score and intelligence. The problem then is to remove the effects of pretreatment level of performance on the measures of performance after treatment. More generally, how can the change or gain of each individual be measured?

A simple difference score, obtained by subtracting initial score from final score, is not adequate. A little algebra will show that such differences in random data can be expected to correlate $-.71$ with the initial scores and $+.71$ with the final scores, since each set of scores contributes 50 percent of the variance in the difference scores and the square of the correlation indicates that contribution. What is needed is an index that adjusts the final scores by statistically removing from them the contribution of the initial scores. Depending upon circumstances, analysis of covariance or indices of residual gain may be suitable.

EFFECTS OF UNRELIABILITY

The measurement of an individual's change over treatment is particularly sensitive to unreliability. A raw difference score is plagued by the unreliability of both of its components. In addition, the higher the correlation between the two, the less reliable the difference score. (At the extreme, if the correlation equals the average reliability of the two scores, the variation of the differences over the subjects must be attributed solely to unreliability, to measurement error.) All attempts to eliminate the effects of initial scores must take into account their reliability. In a particularly thoughtful and scholarly contribution to this problem, Tucker, Damarin, and Messick (1966) show that the true difference score can be expressed as the sum of the true independent gain score (independent of initial measure) and the true dependent change score (entirely dependent on initial measure), and provide equations for estimating these terms.

To bring out the importance of unreliability, consider what happens when an unreliable measure is applied twice to the same subjects. The subjects who have the lowest scores on the first test will show a clear tendency toward higher scores on the second. If a treatment has intervened, an experimenter is likely to note such changes and say that his treatment helps most those who are in greatest need of help. But such regression toward the mean is just what statistical theory predicts: such extreme scores are more likely to have had a sizable component of measurement error pushing them downward on the first testing. This effect and the caution that must be observed in interpreting such changes can be understood by also looking at the highest scores. With no intervening treatment, they will tend to be

lower on the second testing because the measurement errors raising the
initial scores tend not to operate on the second testing. (Psychometric theory typically assumes that the errors of measurement are independent from
trial to trial, an assumption that appears to be only partly true in practice.)
These effects of unreliability contribute to the likelihood that initial scores
will correlate negatively with raw difference scores and that final scores will
correlate positively.

SUBSTANTIVE CONSIDERATIONS

Most of this discussion has been in abstract quantitative terms. The substantive side is also important. If 100 is a perfect score on a test (e.g., of
carefulness), is a gain of twenty points from 30 to 50 equal psychologically
to a gain from 79 to 99? I.e., are these two gains at different ranges on the
scale of equal magnitude? Furthermore, is it more difficult for a reasonably
careful person to improve his performance to a nearly perfect score of 99
than for a careless person to obtain a score of 50? The investigator must
consider his measurements in terms of such substantive issues peculiar to
his construct and to his measuring procedure, as well as considering the
more abstract methodological issues.

A similar issue in measuring heart rate and other physiological indices
has been discussed by Lacey (1956). Since any induced excitation of an
autonomically innervated structure instantly initiates a series of changes
serving to nullify the disturbance, the recorded response is a function both
of the induced magnitude of autonomic activation and of the autonomic
changes restraining and limiting the effects of the initial disturbance. These
latter effects tend to make larger contributions when the initial level is already high; hence large gains may be associated with lower initial levels
and small effects with higher starting points.

As a final word on measuring change, a note of caution must be sounded
about self-reports of change. A patient who has asked for help and who has
spent considerable time and energy (as well as dollars) on treatment is
likely to believe that he has gained from the experience, whether or not
other observers perceive any gains. He may have to believe that his expenditure has not been in vain. Similarly a therapist must have some confidence
in the efficacy of his procedures and may be compelled to believe that
something has been accomplished for a patient after treating him for a long
time. In one study (Fiske, Cartwright, and Kirtner, 1964), the therapist's
rating of the success of the treatment correlated with length of treatment
even though length was not correlated with measures of change derived
from pre- and posttreatment ratings made by the therapist or with almost
any other measure of change.

In self-report measures to be used in measuring change, it is important to specify the period of time that S should consider. A good example is found in the work of Bradburn (see Bradburn, 1969; Bradburn and Caplovitz, 1965). Bradburn assessed current levels of positive and negative affect by a few questions qualified to refer to the past week only. Using a specified period is much better than saying, "How do you feel now?" or ". . . at this moment?" These phrases might lead to responses too susceptible to influence from momentary states. On the other hand, one should not expect questions such as "As a child, did you have many playmates?" to be answered differently after therapy. Hence standard questionnaires must be used with great caution. Yet such reporting *may* be different after treatment: the patient may now see his childhood differently and quite accurately give a different response. Subjects' answers about previous experience are always largely determined by their present perceptions and their present outlook, and may also be influenced by current mood. These observations should help us to see the role of the present in the subject's reports of his past.

Summary

When a person is free from the impact of outside stimulation, the contents of his experiencing are constantly changing. Regularities in experiencing and in responding tend to be associated with regularities in the stimulation received from the world around a person. Behavior becomes increasingly stable as the demands of the environment become more effective, especially when a person has the means to cope adequately with these demands. Practiced ways of coping, such as psychomotor patterns in speaking and writing, are highly stable. On the other hand, actions that are primarily expressive of immediate feelings and perceptions may be less stable over time.

In repeated testing, it appears as though the subject learns to adapt to taking the test with a pattern of responses that becomes increasingly stable, a trend reminding us that, in any first exposure to a test, the subject is confronted with an unfamiliar set of stimuli in a rather atypical situation. The influence of these characteristics should be minimized in designing a test and a testing situation. In tests of many kinds, subjects answer easily and consistently those items that are remote from their own position on the scale for the variable being measured (e.g., in ability testing, items that are very easy or much too difficult for them), but tend to give unstable responses to items near their point or threshold.

Personality measures are naturally more stable over time in adulthood than in a child's formative years. But throughout a person's life, there are often one or a few enduring themes that play a major role in his behavior and contribute to its stability.

Short-term change associated with a clear experimental condition is relatively easy to study, but questions about the coordination of measuring procedures and their target constructs raise problems of generalizability. Specific therapeutic treatments aimed at desensitization or relief from phobias appear to have clear value, and seem to provide good material for the study of therapeutic processes, since considerable standardization is possible. Yet problems are still present concerning generalization from the laboratory or treatment room to outside situations. Measurement in studies of the effectiveness of more common forms of psychotherapy faces more difficult problems in each of the several classes of variables involved in such research studies.

The complexities in measuring change are particularly great in studies of changes in individuals, as opposed to comparisons between mean group changes. Serious technical obstacles are involved, associated primarily with effects of unreliability in the measuring procedures, but also with differences in the pretreatment levels of the subjects. Substantive issues also enter. Researchers in this area must think through their experimental questions and their methodologies with greater care than usual.

CHAPTER TEN

A Human Being
Takes a Test

All of us have taken tests of one kind or another, and most of us have taken one or more personality tests. Perhaps this common experience has led psychologists to feel that they and everyone else knows what testing is like, from the subject's point of view, so there is no need to investigate this topic. Certainly little research has been done on the reactions of subjects to taking tests. Other reasons include the view that research and measurement should be objective in personology as well as in other parts of psychology and in other sciences, and if scientific procedures are objective, it is unnecessary to be concerned with how a given subject feels about being tested. Related to that reason is the view that the subject's feelings do not affect his scores.

The contrary view is that the psychology of the subject is crucial to understanding personality measurement. When we measure attributes of people by eliciting their responses to our tests, we are interacting with people who are conscious of what they are doing, and usually are more or less aware of what we are trying to do. Being aware, subjects react to tests and to being tested, and these reactions may impair the utility of our observations, whatever the purpose for which we are making them.

Just as personality is the way a person interacts with his environment, personality measurement is the way a person interacts with a testing situation, with the physical setting and its psychological implications, with the examiner giving the test, with the test as a whole, and with each piece of it, each item or stimulus. Such interactions occur in most of the modes de-

lineated in Chapter 5. These are especially important when S is describing
himself (Mode 1) and when he is reporting his current experiencing
(Mode 2). They are somewhat less important when S's capabilities are
being determined (Mode 3) because they have less effect on performance
scores. Such testing activity is designed to motivate Ss optimally, and most
Ss in our culture do try to perform as well as they can (but in some other
cultures it is not acceptable to surpass one's peers). They are pertinent in
Mode 5 because, even though an observer provides the final data and S's
behavior is not used directly, S is still aware that he is under observation.
They may also be significant when psychophysiological observations
(Mode 6) are being obtained, since S obviously knows that something is
being done to him to obtain data.

Although, by definition, S does not interact with the measuring in Mode 4,
we still must consider the circumstances in which the observed behavior took
place or the products were formed, and the way in which S reacted to them.
Additionally, the observers in this mode are themselves Ss in one sense:
they may react to their role with concern for the investigator's view of the
adequacy of their observations and for the possible consequences that their
observations may have for the subject.

This chapter will consider the reactions of subjects to tests and to taking
tests. It will discuss the psychology of the subject. While it will emphasize
the role of these reactions in personality measurement, and particularly in
measuring individual differences, the problem of subject reactions is not
limited to such work. It enters into measurement of group differences and
into studies of the effects of experimental manipulations. For example,
there is a considerable body of research on evaluation apprehension
(Rosenberg, 1969). Another reaction variable is suspicion of the deception
sometimes required by an experimental problem. This reaction can obviously affect empirical observations; it also correlates with some of the subject variables considered in this chapter, including a negative relationship
with acquiescence (Stricker, Messick, and Jackson, 1967).

The Layman's View of Testing

How does the layman see psychological testing? Testing is obviously much
less important to people than many things, like war, taxes, and elections.
While children and college students have considerable, if not excessive,
experience with tests, adults encounter tests much more rarely, the most
likely occasions being when entering military service, when applying for
a job, and when seeking help for psychological problems. It may have been
many years since older adults took a test.

To survey the views of laymen, a representative sample of 589 American adults was interviewed through the facilities of the National Opinion Research Center (Fiske, 1967). About two-thirds had taken some test since their schooldays. These people felt that tests were not so good as interviews for finding out whether a person is qualified for a job or for admission to school. They evaluated tests as good for finding out about aptitudes and skills, and about likes and dislikes, but somewhat less adequate for measuring how a person gets along with others and what his personal problems are; it is intriguing to find that these views of laymen correspond rather well with those of psychologists.

The respondents were instructed to imagine that they had been asked to take a test under specified conditions. To make the simulated situation more realistic, they were then asked to respond to a few items from the supposed test. When asked what the test was supposed to find out, they were once again rather accurate. The intelligence test was seen as such, incomplete sentences were seen as a personality test, etc. Among reactions to the simulated tests, interest and curiosity were commonly voiced, but indifference was also frequent. Only small portions of the sample reported negative reactions, and these were diverse: discomfort and anxiety were reported more often than tension, annoyance, boredom, or frustration, but each of these latter did occur in some subjects. Thus three general classes of reactions appeared: curiosity, interest, and positive feelings; anxiety, tension, and other unpleasant feelings; and critical or negative evaluations of the test and of testing.

Subjects were also asked to report how they had felt about the last test they had taken in real life. These reports were somewhat more negative, indicating that the simulation technique had not been fully effective. All in all, a wide range of feelings was reported, some rather positive but many negative in one way or another. Since diverse reactions can have diverse effects, it is important to minimize the influence of these reactions on responses to the test itself, so as to keep the circumstances of testing quite uniform for all the subjects.

One of the most important findings was that the patterns of reactions were much the same to all six simulated tests: an intelligence test, a preference inventory, an interests test, a standard personality inventory, and two projective tests (incomplete sentences and inkblots). The reactions also differed rather little between the two simulated contexts, taking the test for research purposes and taking it as part of applying for a job. It is evident that subjects react primarily to being tested; the particular situation and the type of test are secondary. To test a person is to try him, and a person on trial is threatened by the possibility of being found wanting. When we give a subject a test, we must recognize that he perceives the possibility of the test's indicating that he is inadequate in some way, that he does not meet the standards set by himself or others. This feeling is probably stronger when one is taking a new test with unfamiliar content. (See Chapter 9.) On later exposures to a test, he at least knows the kind of stimulus he will encounter, even though he may not know exactly how his responses will be interpreted and evaluated by the examiner.

The Psychology of the Subject Taking a Test

THREE KINDS OF STIMULI

The environment to which S reacts while taking a test can be seen as providing stimuli at three levels: the testing situation as a whole, the particular test, and the items of that test. In studying S's reactions to testing, it is necessary to keep all three in mind, even though it is difficult at times to separate their influences. For example, the way S sees the total situation will affect the way he perceives and responds to single items.

The importance of the total situation is rather obvious. Thus Davids (1955) reports more favorable means for several measures of adjustment for Ss being selected for a job than for Ss tested anonymously for research purposes. (In addition, the several diverse measures had higher intercorrelations under the anonymous conditions, perhaps because the variances were also larger.) A subject who is applying for a job that he wants very much can be expected to answer some questions differently from the way he would answer if he were seeking psychotherapeutic help. This part of the environmental impact is often neglected in planning for giving tests: E assumes, often correctly, that S knows why he is being tested. But often E may find it more comfortable for himself to pay minimal attention to the reason S is there, especially if he is there involuntarily (as when an instructor in introductory psychology announces, "Instead of a lecture today, you will take some tests"). If E gives any reasons for their taking the tests, the explanation is likely to be in very vague and general terms, such as "These are part of a research study I'm doing."

The general instructions or reasons why S is there and is being asked to take the tests set the tone for the whole session. They give S a set toward the tests themselves and toward the stimulus items in each test. As any general psychology textbook indicates, such sets can have major effects upon subsequent behavior.

In addition to what E says about the rationale for the testing, there are other situational influences. The physical aspects of the testing room and also E's appearance and behavior may make some difference, especially when E is testing S individually. These factors will be discussed later.

Within the testing situation, there is the test itself. Ordinarily, the printed or oral instructions for a test say something about what the test is all about, but only in very general terms. It is doubtful that such partial information fully satisfies S's curiosity about the instrument. The most crucial part of the instructions for a test are those that set the task for S, which tell him specifically what he is expected to do. These can, of course, have a tremendous effect upon S's responses. For example, a subject who is asked to indicate whether he likes or dislikes each of a series of activities or school subjects will usually give very different answers than those given when he is asked to create by his answers a very favorable picture of himself or is asked to answer the questions as he thinks a particular kind of person would answer them. Finally, there are the several items in the test. S's reactions to items have been discussed in earlier sections of this book and will continue to be a matter of central concern to us.

In planning for a testing session, we need to consider each of these three levels—what the situation, the test, and the items will mean to our subjects. We also have to consider how the three fit together and interact; e.g., is the test task as stated consistent with the way the subjects interpret the situation as a whole? Given the general setting and the specified task, is it reasonable to include items with a particular content? E can check the compatibility of these three sources of influence first by putting himself into the role of S and seeing how he could feel, and later by trying out the test and the instructions on a pilot group, carefully arranging that trial so as to obtain, after the testing, quite candid reports from the subjects about their perceptions, feelings, and interpretations.

As with many other topics in psychology, there are two ways of approaching S's reactions to taking a test and to testing. (See Chapter 2.) One is in terms of group effects, such as the comparison of simulated contexts in the survey described earlier in this chapter. Another example of this approach is the comparison of subtle situational pressures in the work of Kroger (1967, 1968) and Eaton and Fiske (in press). (See the section on "The Study of Change" in Chapter 9 above.) These studies show that even subtle pressures can affect test responses; stronger pressures, such as the strong desire to obtain a job, can be expected to have more marked effects, especially in highly motivated or in less ethical subjects. In comparing groups or experimental conditions, the researcher must take into account the general or average interpretation of the test and of the testing situation for the sample as a whole.

The second approach examines individual differences in reactions to tests, in Ss' interpretations of tests, and in the extent to which these influence responses. For example, Schachtel (1945) noted that testing situations have different meanings for different people, and that these meanings influence test performance. In particular, interpretations of a testing situation are influenced by the subject's attitudes toward authority and competition.

Somewhat later, Sarason (1954) observed that we cannot expect all subjects to deal with the same test task in the same way. Thus psychologists have been warned for many years that it is necessary to attend to what a test means to a subject.

These views were directed especially toward projective testing, in which rather ambiguous or unstructured tasks and stimuli are given S, part of the examiner's interest being in how S chooses to cope with the problem posed to him. In general, the more restricted and specific the task, the less the influence of S's interpretation. Yet even in testing capabilities, subjects handle the matter in various ways. In speeded tests of intelligence, some subjects emphasize speed and try to answer as many items as possible, while others emphasize carefulness and try to avoid giving wrong answers; the orientation of the subject depends upon which goal has more utility or payoff for him (see W. Edwards, 1961). Moreover, subjects solve problems in a variety of ways. When French (1965) made inquiries of Ss who had taken some tests, he found that several styles of problem-solving were used by subjects, some of which were similar to what are called "cognitive styles." Some subjects, for example, adopt a scanning approach while others focus on specific parts of the problem.

It may be desirable to review and distinguish two points that have been made in the preceding pages. One is that subjects almost always know that they are being tried or tested, and that regardless of what particular variable is being measured, they react to this awareness. Some subjects are more concerned about being tested than others, and these differences may have differential effects on how they go about taking a test, effects to be considered later in this chapter. The other point is that subjects usually have only a general idea about what a personality test is measuring. They often think that the test measures some aspect of how good their personality is, i.e., how well adjusted they are, and they are likely to be partially correct (since so many personality variables are evaluative, having good and bad extremes). Note that it is not important that subjects do not know precisely what variable a test measures. This partial ignorance does not contribute to the effectiveness of the measuring procedure. In fact, it may well impair the effectiveness: insofar as perceptions of what the test tests vary from one subject to another, there may be diversity in the way they approach and respond to the separate items. Here is another respect in which measures of ability and aptitude have an advantage over measures of personality. In the former, all subjects know that the test measures how well they can do something, and this common knowledge tends to make their tactics and strategies in coping with such a test more homogeneous than those of subjects taking a personality test.

THE MOTIVES OF SUBJECTS

While taking any test, a subject may be influenced by universal motives toward self-preservation, self-protection, and the maintenance of self-esteem. Subjects do not want to select an answer to a question which will raise doubts in their minds about the accuracy of their description and evaluation of themselves. And even if they choose a positive, favorable answer, their consideration of the rejected negative alternative may still raise such doubts.

Fortunately, people also want to feel competent and adequate. This need can be satisfied by making sure that subjects find the task within their capacity: they should not be asked to make discriminations they feel are too fine. Again, subjects want to be accepted. Other things being equal, they would prefer that E feel positively toward them; they would like to help E by being good subjects. (See Orne, 1962.)

Other general motives include a need for novel stimuli and a desire to avoid boredom. Within limits, curiosity works in E's favor. Any particular test is to some degree a new experience for S. But there is the associated apprehensiveness about the unknown: Will the test cause S to experience negative effect? Again, there is the desire to avoid monotony and boredom. The novelty value of any test diminishes rapidly as the test goes on and on. Also, a long series of tests will gradually become monotonous, even when the battery is arranged to maximize variety, simply because they are all tests.

The psychological principle of least effort must be considered. Unless the situation and the test materials arouse S to expend effort freely, he will tend to adopt a tactic for answering each item as quickly and easily as possible, thus completing the task with the minimum expenditure of energy. (The problems in minimizing the irrelevant and interfering motives of subjects are faced in all research with human subjects; for example, see Schultz, 1969.)

This sketch has presented relevant motivations in hierarchical order. The first ones are potentially very strong and can block any effects from the later ones. For example, S will continue taking a long and boring test because he does not want E to disapprove of him. This is especially true in regard to ability tests, in which the instruction to do as well as possible is accepted by S. This instruction is congruent with the stronger motives in the hierarchy.

In some personality tests using Mode 2 (Current Experiencing), S carries out a kind of performance task in the test situation: he cognizes, judges, indicates his immediate feelings or preferences, etc. While these procedures resemble ability tests, they usually do not urge S to show how competent he is. The motivating force is more cooperation than challenge. In other words, he has less personal need to follow the instructions. Going one step further, questionnaires (Mode 1) are still more unlike ability tests in these respects.

In testing for maximum capacity (Mode 3), the task instruction readily elicits an appropriate quality and degree of motivation that is consistent with natural reactions to being tested. In testing for typical performance, for what S ordinarily sees, feels, and does, there is no such single strong motive that E can evoke in S. Moreover, the familiar reactions to being evaluated are likely to emerge unless E is most skillful in designing and administering his procedure. Obviously, then, the more a test of personality appears phenomenologically to be a test of ability, the more adequately it can control potentially intrusive effects of motivation.

In planning the conduct of personality testing, we want to avoid arousing the prepotent needs, such as preservation of self-esteem. We seek to elicit not just cooperation but active involvement. We can facilitate this set by increasing S's interest in the test and its content. Here is an area in which personality tests have an advantage over tests of aptitude: personality tests can be more personal. Perhaps this personal involvement is part of the reason for the apparent success of tests asking S to "imagine that you are . . ." in some situation.

We can also increase S's attention and involvement by structuring the task so that he experiences minimal uncertainty about just what he is supposed to do and how he is to select his responses. In devising a test, an E who gives some thought to how S will experience it should create an instrument with better quality and effectiveness than one who ignores S's perception of the test. It is a wise expenditure of time and effort to try out a test under highly permissive, anonymous conditions, seeking to elicit S's maximum cooperation. Then, after the test, E can ask subjects how they felt about it, and in particular what they found objectionable or difficult. E might also give the test to a group of subjects with instructions to mark items they had difficulty in answering, those they found ambiguous, etc.

Following the survey described earlier, I have sought more detailed information about general reactions to tests, especially personality instruments. After taking a short personality test, the subjects were asked how they felt when they received the test and when they were taking it, and a number of other questions. In their free responses there were criticisms of testing and of particular tests and their format. Some subjects, for example, dislike having to choose between two broad responses, such as true and false, because neither applies, or because they want to indicate a more differentiated reply. Subjects also make explicit their concern with the potential effects of the test results on their lives, but go beyond that issue to express concern with the possibility that E or others may evaluate them unfavorably in the light of their responses.

Also present, but presumably less disturbing, is the idea that they simply are revealing themselves to someone else: taking a test has the potentiality of requiring an uncomfortable degree of self-disclosure. Furthermore, some subjects express concern about the self-revelation that may result from thinking about questions on a test. Such subjects do not want to find out about themselves. A clear example is this item: "Once in a while I feel hate toward members of my family whom I usually love." This question forces S either to reject the possibility immediately or to consider whether he has ever experienced such hatred. Recollections of these feelings can be unpleasant if not disturbing.

These data provide objective support for the naturalistic observation that subjects want to know more about tests than they are usually told. They want to know what the test is measuring and how it works. To be sure, they usually have a fairly good idea about the kind of thing being measured. Yet they seek more definite information. Here is an area in which the interests of E and S may be most antagonistic. It is undoubtedly not possible to design informative instructions for tests of some constructs in such a way that subjects will not be deceived and will not be threatened. Most personality concepts are evaluative: there is one end of the continuum that seems more desirable. It would be hard to describe such a variable to S in a way that would make him feel that any standing on the variable is perfectly acceptable. For some attributes, however, it is possible to be much more informative than instructions usually are. Some preliminary work suggests that more adequate data can be obtained for these variables when E is candid and obviously aware of S's desire for information.

Of particular interest are subjects' responses to the question "Under what conditions would you feel most relaxed and cooperative while taking such a [personality] test?" Among the variety of answers, the most frequent was when the test was anonymous or the results would not affect the subject. Some suggested being tested in a classroom or large group, although a few said they preferred to be alone. Other points mentioned were absence of time pressure, the soundness of the test, and an examiner whom they trusted. Also volunteered were such replies as conditions in which the test would be useful to someone, or in which the results or scores were subsequently explained to them, and times when S was in an appropriate mood.

Note that these free responses were made after the subjects had already answered many other questions. If these were listed and presented to subjects, it is very likely that most of them would be endorsed by most subjects. Certainly these points can be used to guide the design of optimal testing situations.

THE EXAMINER'S RELATIONSHIP TO THE SUBJECT

As we mentioned earlier (p. 85), Lovell (1967) has sketched three possible contracts or relationships that the examiner can establish with his subjects. The one he calls the strong personnel contract is quite authoritarian. It says in effect: "While we cannot explain what this is all about, be assured this testing is important and the information will be used in many important ways. Be conscientious! If you do try to create a favorable impression rather than answering honestly, we shall find out and it will reflect badly upon you." The weak personnel contract is much the same, but says that the examiner is interested in S's ability to create a favorable impression, since that is useful in life. The client contract is much more subject-oriented; greatly condensed, it would read: "We really want to know what you think and how you feel. We will treat your responses confidentially. They will be used for research or to help you. We would like you to agree to the proposition that you won't try to fool us and we won't try to fool you. If after careful consideration you can't make that agreement, please don't take this test." Lovell argues that this contract is the most ethical, is the one most likely to lead to valid measurement, and is the one that permits the broadest range of psychological services to be offered. He grants that it restricts the activities of the personnel psychologist.

Certainly this client contract is most compatible with the reports of subjects about the conditions under which they would feel most cooperative. Some psychologists would object, however, that it rules out some psychological experimentation where deception is necessary to the design. Also, is it fooling the subject when the examiner does not tell him what variable is being measured or lets the subject believe that the test is measuring one trait when actually it is measuring another? We shall go further into matters of privacy and confidentiality later in this chapter. For the present, it is sufficient to state that the examiner must appreciate S's feelings and concerns and must take precautions to avoid harming him in any way. It is of course to his own best interests to make clear to S that he is doing so.

Considerable research has been done on the effects of the examiner on test responses. Masling (1966) provides a good introduction to this work. For example, subjects drawing male figures are more likely to add a mustache if the examiner has one. As one might expect, these effects seem to be stronger on projective tests than on more structured tasks, such as measures of ability. Yet even here, maximum effort may not be made if subjects are not in rapport with the examiner. In measuring intelligence, Palmer (1970) has demonstrated the positive value of having the examiner spend enough time with a child to make certain that the child feels comfortable with the examiner, presumably minimizing suspicion and maximizing cooperation. Possibly facilitating the same objectives in personality research are the approaches that have been tried by Jourard (1969) and his students. They have shown that subjects give different and more open responses to experimenters who have spent a short time getting acquainted with and revealing themselves to the subjects. Conceivably, the examiner who gets subjects to trust him by revealing himself to them might minimize some of the unwanted effects of the testing situation on personality measurements and thereby improve the adequacy of such measurements.

The effects of experimenters on responses are not limited to self-report, projective techniques, and measures of capabilities (Modes 1, 5, and 3). Such psychophysiological responses as pupillary dilation may also be affected by the experimenter (Chapman, Chapman, and Brelje, 1969).

Dimensions of Test-Taking Behavior

RESPONSE SETS

Few papers have had as much impact on the testing field as one by Cronbach (1946), "Response Sets and Test Validity." He demonstrated that responses to a test typically show the systematic operation of one or more variables other than the one the examiner is trying to measure. Reliable individual differences are present in the number of "yes" responses marked, in the number of "?s" if that option is provided, in the number of items checked on checklists, etc. The more these dispositions contribute systematic variance to test scores, the less valid the scores are likely to be. To illustrate in another context, judgments of length are influenced by whether the object is in a horizontal or vertical position and by the apparent mass of the object. These systematic biases impair the usefulness of estimates of length. (Fortunately, we do not have to use human judgment for such measurement!) Similarly, some subjects show a disposition to give "yes" responses; if all the keyed responses in a test happen to be "yes," such subjects will receive scores biased upward.

Cronbach labeled these dispositions "response sets." Over the various items of an instrument, the subject seems to have a set toward giving a particular kind of response, a class of responses that is not necessarily related to the variable being measured. Other sets include evasiveness, tendency to omit responses to some items, tendency to use (or to avoid) extremes when the response alternatives have several ordered steps, and tendency to prefer certain steps on such a response scale.

Figure 10.1 lists a number of response sets and other systematic reactions to measuring procedures. These are classified by the mode of observation in which they are particularly prevalent. The same tendency may, however, appear in data produced within two or more modes. For example, carelessness may be evident in all modes; dispositions characterizing self-descriptive responses may also be found in data produced by observers in Modes 4 and 5. It will be obvious that this listing goes beyond tendencies associated with particular kinds of instruments to include tendencies found in data from observers as well as in self-report data. When one person rates another, he may show certain response sets or reactions to the judging task just as a person does in rating himself.

Mode 1 (self-descriptive reports)
    Social desirability: marking the more favorable response alternative.
    Acquiescence: agreeing with attitude statements; marking the "yes" alternatives.
    Extremity: marking the more extreme alternatives on a graded list, as in a multi-step rating scale.
    Evasiveness or cautiousness: unwillingness to commit oneself; marking the "?" or "can't say" alternatives.

Mode 2 (reports of current experiencing)
    Carelessness: making inconsistent judgments.
    Deviance: marking many unusual responses, those infrequently marked by others.
    Productivity: making many or long responses to a free-response test.

Mode 3 (tests of capabilities)
    Gambling: guessing when unsure of correct answer.
    Speed: attempting to answer as many items as possible in the time allowed.
    Accuracy: trying to avoid making any incorrect responses.

Modes 4 and 5 (observations of past and present behavior)
    Halo: allowing one's general impression of the subject to affect one's ratings of specific characteristics.
    Leniency: tendency to rate everyone as above average.
    Position set: tendency to mark an item, especially on a multistep rating scale, in the same general position as the mark for the preceding item.

Figure 10.1. Some response sets and other systematic reactions
to measuring procedures

The purpose of the list in Figure 10.1 is to point out that many kinds of systematic response tendencies may be detected in measurement data. While it gives the more common dispositions, it is not intended to be complete. For example, there are tendencies that are almost the exact opposites of those given in the figure. Under some circumstances, such as when seeking help for one's problems, one may tend to produce a socially undesirable picture of oneself. Or a subject may display a set toward negative responses rather than positive ones. There are also sets that are found particularly in

tests of aptitude or achievement, such as tendencies to select the first response alternative, or the longest one.

Note that response sets and other systematic reactions to aspects of the
measuring procedure may be found in every mode and kind of personality
measurement except physiological indices (Mode 6). Ratings of oneself or
of others are particularly likely to contain such biasing influences. In addition, they are found in other kinds of human judgments, such as psychophysics. They may even enter into the way a person reads a dial or other
objective recording device: without specific instructions, some people will
read to the nearest large mark on the calibrated scale, others to the smallest
unit, and a few may interpolate between these units.

Response sets do not enter when subjects have a clearly presented task
and can give a precise answer that they know is correct. Sets have maximum influence when the task is ambiguous, when the response alternatives
are vague or general, and when S is unable to give an exact answer that he
can verify. To oversimplify a little, they enter when S is in doubt about
what response to make. These sets indicate the way S copes with the uncertainty about the criteria for selecting his response. It is almost as if he had
developed certain rules: when in doubt, say "yes" or mark the "?"; in making judgments, be cautious and do not endorse extreme statements; when
given a task and a time limit, try to get as much done as possible, etc.

Since response sets are ways of coping with an uncertain task, a variety
of response sets may be found in the responses to a single test. For instance,
in the well-known and much-used Minnesota Multiphasic Personality Inventory (MMPI), one can find a set to omit responses (subjects are instructed to omit responses if they are uncertain), a set toward carelessness
(determined from responses infrequently endorsed by normal people), and
a set to lie (determined from items concerning socially desirable actions
that very few people can truthfully attribute to themselves). These sets are
assessed by three validating scales. An answer sheet with a high score on
any one of them should be discarded because of the high probability that
the content scores are not valid for that subject. Reliable acquiescence
scores (tendencies to mark "yes") can also be found.

For almost a quarter of a century since Cronbach's original papers (1946,
1950), psychologists have studied response sets. One particular focus has
been on social desirability, the tendency to give answers that will create a
good impression. While the disposition to lie (as measured by the L scale
of the MMPI) is usually not strong, the tendency to give oneself the benefit
of the doubt and mark the favorable alternative is very widespread. Psychologists have been concerned with such tendencies ever since personality
questionnaires were first created. It has been repeatedly demonstrated that
subjects can fake a good impression of themselves when instructed to do

so. But such a demonstration leaves open the question of how much faking or slanting of responses actually occurs in standard testing. Allen Edwards (1957) stirred up considerable controversy by his monograph on social desirability. He argued that much of the variance in questionnaires can be attributed to the influence of this variable rather than the variables the instruments were constructed to measure. He offered two lines of evidence. First, he built an empirically derived scale for measuring social desirability as a variable in its own right. He then reported very substantial correlations between this scale and many others, positive relationships for favorable traits and negative for unfavorable. He claimed that this scale measured social desirability and not the disposition to deny symptoms, even though thirty of his thirty-nine items, taken from the MMPI, are keyed "false."

He also provided evidence at the item level. He had subjects rate the social desirability of a positive response to each item on many scales. Then he correlated these ratings with the proportions of subjects endorsing that answer under standard testing conditions. The results were startling: many high correlations (even into the .80s) were obtained. From these data, he argued that the social desirability of the response is a major factor in S's decision to endorse it.

Several objections can be raised to his argument about the strong contribution of social desirability to item responses. A technical and minor point is that he overestimated the strength of the relationship between the ratings and the endorsements because he used proportions of endorsement covering most of the range from .00 to 1.00. A more appropriate procedure might be to utilize the values of the more frequently endorsed alternatives (e.g., an item with a distribution of .30 and .70 would be treated in terms of the response chosen by 70 percent of the subjects) and the ratings of social desirability for these alternatives. With the range of endorsement values being only .50 to 1.00, the correlations would be somewhat smaller.

A more important point is that the mean rating of social desirability for an item may not represent well its social desirability as perceived by a particular subject. When correlations are computed for each subject between his own ratings and his endorsements, the values are much lower than the ones for group averages reported by Edwards. Even with these lower but positive relationships for individuals, what is the direction of influence? Perhaps subjects tend to rate as desirable whatever characteristics they perceive in themselves, rather than to attribute to themselves those characteristics they deem to be socially desirable.

One final objection: Is it not true that those items rated as more desirable by people actually occur more frequently in the population than do items rated as less desirable? E.g., "sociable" would seem to apply to more people than "argumentative," and would certainly be rated as more socially desirable. These objections are directed at the extreme view of the influence of this response set. If these several objections have some validity, they do not mean that there is no tendency to select responses on the basis of their social desirability, but rather that such a tendency operates in a limited way on some responses of some subjects.

These last two points indicate the difficulties in determining cause and effect or direction of influence from correlational research. An observed correlation between Measure A and Measure B may result from A influencing B, from B influencing A, or from C influencing both A and B. Unfortunately the problem of response sets is very difficult to study effectively by experimental manipulations. Attempts to study acquiescence by writing reversed forms of items, for example, have been criticized on the grounds that the reversals were not adequate. Attempts to separate content from set have also failed to win general acceptance. (For a review of some recent literature on the problem, see Fiske and Pearson, 1970.)

AN OVERVIEW OF RESPONSE SETS

During the last decade there has been a great deal of research on response sets, and vigorous controversy about them. Some hold that such commonly used tests as the MMPI yield scores determined primarily by dispositions toward social desirability and toward acquiescence and not by the attributes by which the scores are labeled. Others maintain that response sets have relatively little influence. More careful definitions and more developed conceptualizations of response sets, and further research coordinated with such conceptual work, will undoubtedly indicate that the truth lies somewhere between these two extreme views. Rather than trying to review the massive body of literature on the topic, we can state a few propositions that now appear to have some validity and can make some suggestions about what a test constructor can do about potential response sets.

1. Response sets in some forms do exist. At the least, reliable individual differences can be demonstrated in the number of socially desirable responses and in the number of "yes" responses. If the constructs of social desirability and acquiescence are equated with these two measuring operations, respectively, these dispositions exist.

2. Operationally defined in this way, response sets show some consistency over similar instruments. While such consistency is perhaps not so high as the limited consistency found for substantive content scales, it is found when the two or more instruments present the subjects with similar formats and content, i.e., when the tasks of selecting responses have similar ambiguities and tend to elicit similar uncertainties and ways of coping.

3. On theoretical grounds, a clear case can be made for the view that re-

sponse sets lower the validity of some instruments for measuring personality. The larger the contribution to the systematic variance of a test made by response sets—i.e., by dispositions conceptually independent of the substantive target construct—the smaller the contribution of the target construct. That proposition is, of course, tautologous if such contributions are taken as proportions of the total amount of systematic variance.

It is possible that response sets are most apparent when a test has been poorly designed and has little validity even under favorable conditions that minimize the influence of such sets. Sets can operate most readily when subjects experience doubt or conflict about which response to give, conditions under which responses are less likely to provide dependable information. Thus sets may be seen as sometimes increasing the amount of systematic variance in test scores, replacing residual or error variance. Residual variance is variance not associated with any identified source; it is the variance produced by many small effects, such as the idiosyncratic interaction between a single subject and a given item. Such contributions of a response set may or may not affect the utility of the test, depending upon the relationship between the psychological variable underlying the response set and the target construct at which the test is aimed. Curiously, there is little direct empirical evidence that response sets reduce the validity of tests.

4. As I have just suggested, response sets are themselves psychological attributes. To understand and cope with them, we must see them as more than sterile, operationally defined variables, as ways in which subjects cope with the task of responding to items. Each such set is a complex, multifaceted variable. For example, factor analyses of ratings of items for social desirability yield many factors, many forms of social desirability. There are even differing viewpoints from which social desirability can be judged: one may emphasize conventionality, another self-esteem (N. Wiggins, 1966). All this work deals with group data, with features common to a number of persons if not the total sample. The contribution of personal, individualistic perceptions of social desirability has not been adequately determined. Once again, it is evident that much conceptual work is needed, that each response set requires the same careful delineation as that given to other personality attributes, as advocated in Chapter 6.

In particular, the extent of psychological overlap between the particular response-set attribute and target variables must be examined. For example, if acquiescence to authority is seen as part of authoritarianism, then more authoritarian subjects should tend to endorse direct statements of opinion presented on a test. If knowing what others deem desirable and striving to achieve it is part of sociability, defined as relating easily to others, then subjects high on that variable may tend to portray themselves in a favorable light.

If the essence of these propositions is granted, what can we do about response sets? Obviously, we must recognize the potential problem they pose. In planning any personality measurement, we must consider whether there is a possibility that subjects may have difficulty in carrying out their task as we intend them to, and if so, how they might overcome that difficulty. Once a preliminary form of the measuring procedure has been prepared, there is no substitute for a pretesting (as indicated earlier) to collect not only a sample of data to determine the psychometric adequacy of the procedure, but also information on the subjects' reactions to it, by posttest inquiry under conditions maximizing candor and cooperation.

Measuring operations should obviously be designed to reduce the likelihood that response sets will intrude. These sets are potential tendencies in subjects and appear when the situation evokes them. While S's state may increase the probability that a set may be elicited, the primary source is S's perception of and reaction to the testing situation. Thus the social-desirability set is more likely to emerge when S is applying for admission to a school he wishes to attend or for a vocational position he wants to hold, as contrasted to completing a test anonymously in a research study.

The more structured the context, the instructions, the content, and the response format, the less likely it is that response sets will appear. "Structure" is an abstract term. In this discussion, it refers to consensus among subjects as to meaning. Such consensus can be obtained by explicitness and concreteness. For ideal testing, as we have seen in Chapters 3 and 7, the total situation must have the same meaning for all subjects, the instructions must be clear and must be interpreted the same way by all subjects, and the content of the items must have the same objective meaning for all subjects, although of course the personal meaning may be exactly what the test is trying to find out and may be the basis for differential responses. Very central is the response format: subjects must agree on the objective meaning of each response alternative offered to them. In sum, we must make the items easy for the subjects to answer. Unless the content of the target construct makes it completely unavoidable, the content of the items should not be threatening, disturbing, highly personal, or emotionally loaded.

Although various methodologies have been proposed to control response sets, none appear to be fully adequate. One can call attention to such sets, for example, by having subjects give two responses to each item, one the ideal answer and the other the answer for themselves. Such a procedure probably changes the way in which sets can operate without eliminating their influence. One can use a forced-choice format, requiring subjects to choose between alternatives matched on social desirability. This approach has been criticized on the grounds that such matching uses ratings that are made by a different group of subjects, probably from varying viewpoints, and hence the social-desirability values may not be the same as those for the population of interest, to say nothing of being equal to those for each of the diverse individuals in that population. Another kind of control involves the independent measurement of the subjects' dispositions toward giving socially desirable answers and the adjustment of their content scores for the extent of this effect. More fully, one administers a test of social desirability itself (such as Edwards' scale), finds the correlation of this scale with the test in which one is interested, and then gives that test. From the correlation, one determines the contribution of social desirability to each test score and then subtracts that component. This approach makes a doubtful assumption about the adequacy of such estimation of response-set contribution from the score on just one of the several somewhat independent measures of the response set. It also assumes that the measure of the set and its correlation with the substantive test provide equally good estimates of the contribution of the set to the test score for all subjects.

One step can be recommended without hesitation. If the response format is yes-no, the test should be constructed so that about half the keyed responses are yes and half are no. Although this procedure does not prevent an acquiescence set from lowering the utility of the scores to some extent, it does prevent such a set from introducing any systematic bias into the observed scores.

OTHER SUBJECT VARIABLES

Response sets are but one type of subject variable, a subject variable being a characteristic on which subjects show differences and which affects test-taking behavior and responses. Another kind is test-wiseness, a concept mentioned in the preceding chapter. In a recent paper, Stricker (1969) studied several kinds of accuracy in perception of tests: ability to estimate the desirability of each item, ability to estimate the proportion of subjects endorsing an item, ability to recognize items measuring the same trait and to tell how each would be keyed. In addition, he measured role-playing ability, capacity to fake a very favorable impression or a very unfavorable impression. Each of these measures had good internal consistency. The first three had little or no correlation with each other or with the role-playing measures. Faking good was significantly related to faking bad on the same personality variable, but not necessarily on other variables.

The measures of test-wiseness were not related to measures of ability or of defensiveness. They were, however, related to some measures of social desirability. Probably as a consequence of the latter, the two estimation measures also correlated with questionnaire scores on Emotional Stability but not with more neutral variables such as General Activity or Sociability. The pattern for the role-playing variables was rather similar.

This study is rather typical of most research on this whole topic in several respects. It identified and measured reliably several subject variables, it found the relationships among them low or absent (contrary to expectation), and it found a somewhat consistent pattern of relationships to standard test responses, though the relationships were limited at best. Perhaps such a study is best seen as strengthening the conclusion that responses to a test are determined to varying extents by other variables related to the variable measured by the test and by subjects' perceptions of and reactions to the test.

Another class of subject variables includes demographic characteristics: age, sex, education, etc. For example, the observed correlates of dominance scales may be somewhat different for the two sexes (see Butt and Fiske, 1969). Such differences seem more likely to reflect true differences than to stem from differences in test-taking behavior. Yet it should be noted that, in taking tests, women generally are more conforming and cooperative than men.

Ambiguity in Questionnaire Items

Ambiguity in questionnaire items was one criticism of tests voiced by subjects in the investigation mentioned earlier. Subjects say they often are not sure what an item means. There is objective evidence to support their statements, obtained by asking subjects to paraphrase or restate an item in their own words. To take an item almost at random, consider restatements of "I usually feel that life is worthwhile." A plurality fall in a class represented by "I feel life is worth living." But a sizable proportion say things like "Almost always I feel life is enjoyable." A few say, "Do you experience satisfaction with your daily life?" Many individual interpretations are also given. We must recognize that a precise paraphrasing is difficult, even for a person with considerable verbal facility, and that it is therefore conceivable that subjects found much the same meaning in the original statement but were unable to put it in new words. Yet one can readily imagine a person agreeing to a statement that life is worthwhile or worth living, but not endorsing a statement saying that life is almost always enjoyable or even generally satisfying. Note also that the several paraphrasings change the qualifier "usually" contained in the original statement.

The above example is fairly typical. A plurality but usually not a majority give interpretations fairly close to the original wording. Each of two or three smaller groups give some modified, restricted, or distorted interpretation. An appreciable proportion give their own individualistic interpretations.

Test constructors tend to write items with qualifiers, knowing that no one feels the same way all the time, or does something at every opportunity. But unfortunately, qualifiers mean different degrees for different people. Phrases such as "like very much" or "like fairly well" seem to have more varying meanings to subjects than "like slightly" or "dislike slightly." "Average" or "OK" are worse than any of these (Jones and Thurstone, 1955). And how often is "sometimes"? For about a quarter of the population, it is 20 percent of the time or less, but for another quarter it is 40 percent or more. Toward the extremes, as for the phrase "almost never," there is less range of opinion (see Hakel, 1968; Simpson, 1944). These data make it clear that two subjects with identical views of themselves could honestly answer an item differently because the qualifer has different meanings for them. Conversely, two unlike subjects could give the same answer.

Items with unusually ambiguous words can often be identified by item analyses (e.g., by their low average correlation with other items presumed to measure the same variable) and then eliminated. Yet the range of meanings for such common terms indicates that verbal inventories can never attain high precision of measurement.

In contrast, the measurement of ability and aptitude utilizes items that are less ambiguous. Similarly, but perhaps to a lesser extent, the items used in tests of interests seem less ambiguous to subjects, at least in the context of indicating likes and dislikes. This lower level of ambiguity contributes to the higher quality of measurement in these two domains, along with the more structured tasks involved in these tests. Ordinarily there is no question in S's mind about the instruction to give the correct answer or to say whether he likes something, and he can follow it with little difficulty.

The Process in Responding to an Item

We have considered earlier the question of subject reactions to tests as a whole. But exactly what goes on when S is responding to an item? Not very much is known about that process, which is, of course, a form of the general process examined in Chapter 3 and other preceding chapters. For one thing, it is difficult to study. S cannot report his thoughts while responding without considerably distorting the process itself. Free reports immediately after answering are likely to be encumbered by rationalizations and by fresh additional associations.

One study of these processes used a questionnaire that S answered after each of ten items. From his replies, his process for each item was coded as based on "general impression of self," on "several relevant instances," or on one of several other bases. These first two seemed like processes that test constructors would deem appropriate, i.e., what they would want subjects to do. The others were not appropriate. They included reinterpreting or qualifying the item in some way to make it easier for S to answer it, or answering it on the basis of no experience or just one instance. Items eliciting higher frequencies of appropriate processes had higher item-test homogeneities in the experimental group and somewhat higher homogeneities in a group tested under standard conditions. Appropriateness of process was not, however, related to the response stability of items in any clear manner. (See Turner and Fiske, 1968.)

The same data were examined in terms of subjects. Some subjects appeared to use appropriate processes more than others, and such processes seem to be related to response stability for subjects. Continuing work on the same problem, Mrs. Ruth Kuncel and I developed an instrument in which subjects responded to ten items and then completed a questionnaire indicating which of the six bases had been involved in their process of responding. Psychometric analyses of the data from that instrument yielded quite favorable values. Yet inspection of the actual answer sheets raised questions in our minds. All too frequently a subject's responses were much too similar from one of the original test items to the next. We were forced to doubt that subjects could recapture with any accuracy the actual process of responding that they had experienced earlier, even with the item restated to refresh their memories. To study these processes more intensively, we have gone back to the original interview procedure first used by Thomas A. Tyler, but with modifications. Now the subject responds to several items orally, and then gets a signal to describe what went on in his mind as he responded to the last item.

The protocols indicate the elusiveness of the process. Very often the answer emerges as S reads the question, with hardly any mental content intervening. Sometimes the report is so brief that it is hard to tell exactly what happened, or even whether S interpreted the item in the usual way.

Here are a few replies, with omissions of references to the wording of the original question:

"It was actually a very quick response. I guess I just sort of believe that I do enjoy . . . and I really don't have to question that."

"My main thought was that, while this was not so much true in the past, now it is true more and more, so that I could pick the word 'usually' and say that now it is 'usually,' now I do so more of the time."

"Well, first of all, I wondered what a good deal of my time was and what . . . meant. And I really gave my answer very hesitantly."

"I thought of specific instances where I had . . ."

"Again, it was something recent. It was [one instance]."

" 'It was a stupid question' came through my mind."

These examples were selected primarily for simplicity and for ease of understanding without knowing the original test question. No examples are given of the occasional elaborated and complex associations. The quotations indicate the variety of processes that can occur, and some of the bases for selecting responses. It is remarkable that such diverse processes can yield data with even modest consistency, dependability, and utility.

The Rights of the Subject

In closing this chapter on the human being taking a test, let us consider what his rights are and what responsibilities we have to protect those rights. There has been considerable public discussion of these topics, and even Congressional hearings (e.g., see the *American Psychologist,* 20, no. 11 [1965]; 21, no. 5 [1966]; 22, no. 5 [1967]).

Much of the furor has focused on invasion of privacy, on questions deemed too personal, too prying. While psychologists must recognize these protests and attempt to interpret their work to the public, the objections seem greater outside the testing situation than within it. The typical subject objects to few items during or after a test, even when invited to mark objectionable items (Butcher and Tellegen, 1966). In the survey of lay opinion described at the beginning of this chapter, less than 2 percent of the respondents felt that tests are prying or invade privacy. Anonymous reactions to the MMPI, the test most criticized by public figures, are actually no more negative than those to tests explicitly constructed to avoid religious, sexual, and bodily content (Fiske, 1969).

Similarly, the layman may feel that psychologists treat replies as statements of fact. For example, when a child says yes to the question "Do your parents fight a lot?" a psychologist takes this not as the observation of an objective observer but rather as a report of the child's perception. Furthermore, the layman may expect psychologists to look at each response of each subject, not realizing that experienced psychologists are familiar with both common and unusual responses and don't look up the replies of particular subjects in order to gossip about them or peer voyeuristically at them. I have never heard of any breach of confidentiality in the processing and scoring of tests or in the analysis of data collected for research purposes. Although I have not seen the files of any ethics committee for a professional organization, I doubt that breaches of confidentiality occur more than very, very rarely in connection with clinical, counseling, or other service-oriented applications of tests.

Just because psychologists take such confidentiality for granted, they should not ignore such publicly expressed concern about privacy. Psychologists in the measuring field have neglected their public relations. They must try to explain to concerned persons how tests are built and used. They must also take these reactions into account in selecting the content of their instruments. Only in rare cases should it be essential to ask questions that seem even to antagonistic critics unduly personal and prying.

The cries of invasion of privacy stem from the conviction that a person has the right to determine for himself what information about himself will be made available to others. Certainly in research work, the psychologist must recognize and respect this view. Subjects should not be given personality tests against their will. While it is impossible to explain each test and what it measures, it is possible to assure research subjects that their responses will not be used in any way harmful to them.

Additionally, the psychologist should consider his own purposes. To obtain the cooperation required to produce useful data, he must communicate to his potential subjects his awareness of their concerns about unfamiliar tests, and he must reassure them that their responses will be treated confidentially. But from first to last, he must know and adhere to the Code of Ethics of his professional organization, the American Psychological Association (APA, 1968), and to his own code of personal ethics with its emphasis on respect for the rights of others as fellow human beings.

The Need for a Positive Approach

Almost invariably, a subject has some negative feelings and attitudes toward any test he is asked or compelled to take. These may well impair the quality of the measurements obtained. They are less likely to do so when the testing involves aptitudes and abilities because subjects want to do as well as they can and examiners want them to perform at their best (see Fiske and Butler, 1963). They are more serious handicaps to measuring personality because the purposes of the examiner and the subject are less congruent there: the examiner wants certain information from which he can derive an index, but the subject does not know exactly what the examiner seeks and what its implications may be for him.

Part of the difficulty is that psychologists are used to having captive subjects. Students must take achievement examinations and ability tests. Job applicants must take selection tests. Patients feel obliged to take clinical tests so that they can get help. Generalizing from these experiences, the psychologist conducting research tends to expect subjects to acquiesce to his expectation that they will take his tests for him.

In designing a test and the situation in which it will be given, the psychologist should do more than attempt to minimize the evocation and operation of potentially negative reactions. He should seek ways to elicit positive attitudes and active cooperation from his subjects. He can consider this a challenge to his psychological sophistication. He should actively pursue this positive approach for two reasons. On the one hand, it is to his personal advantage to do so, since it will improve the quality of his measurements. On the other, he has an obligation to treat his subjects with the respect due them as fellow men, the respect with which he would want to be treated if he were in their position.

Summary

While taking a test, a subject reacts not only to the several items or stimuli but also to the test as a whole, to the examiner, and to the total context of being tested. The layman perceives tests as having some value. As a subject, he has a general idea about what a test is trying to measure. A subject may be interested in the test he is taking, may feel anxiety or discomfort when being tested, or may react critically. These feelings stem from the subject's realization that he is being assessed or evaluated in some way not fully clear to him. He may be concerned about what he is revealing to others and also about what he has to face in himself when responding to the items.

A wide variety of motives may be elicited in a subject being tested, motives that can affect his responses unless the requirements of the task severely limit his possible responses. Hence tests should be designed so that subjects will feel relatively comfortable and unthreatened and so that all subjects will perceive and execute the test task in the same way (their responses yielding different scores only insofar as they vary on the target construct). The examiner should seek to elicit the subjects' willing cooperation.

When subjects take tests, and especially when they have any difficulty in answering an item, they may make responses determined by irrelevant factors. They may mark the more socially desirable alternative, so as to portray themselves in a good light; they may be inclined to mark "yes" rather than "no," or the reverse; they may, on many items, avoid choosing either of the definite alternatives if a noncommittal response is permitted. These intruding response sets can be controlled to some extent by careful design of tests and of testing situations. While it is clear that systematic variance attributable to these sets can be identified in many common instruments, there is an unresolved controversy over their significance: Do they fatally infect these instruments or are they a minor weakness? The debate is confounded by the loose conceptualization of these extraneous attributes of behavior. Response sets are but one type of subject variable affecting scores and relationships between them. Sex and other characteristics have important effects in research on many constructs.

The effectiveness of questionnaires is attenuated by variation in the meanings that subjects attribute to an item. Not only the specific content but also the qualifiers (phrases referring to relative frequency, for example) are interpreted diversely. In addition, items may elicit various processes in subjects. While some responses to questionnaires may have such appropriate bases as the subject's general perception of himself, others may be based on a private meaning given to the item by the subject, an interpretation clearly differing from that made by other subjects. Such undesirable processes in responding appear to reduce the quality of items, and may be more frequent in some subjects than in others. Close examination suggests that answering an item is often a more complex matter than one might expect it to be.

While psychologists are careful to protect the confidentiality of responses and scores, some laymen see testing as an invasion of the subject's right to privacy. Some of this concern seems to be based on a misunderstanding of tests and the ways they are used, a consequence of psychologists' neglect of their public relations. Yet under all circumstances, a psychologist measuring attributes of another person must adhere to the Code of Ethics and must respect the rights of his fellow human beings.

CHAPTER ELEVEN

The Specificity of Behaviors and of Measurements

Almost every human act is unique: a precise and complete physical description of it would yield measurements that differed, at least to some small degree, from the complete description of any other act, even one that was extremely similar. When a person says hello, the sound pattern is relatively idiosyncratic: it can be distinguished from the sound patterns for that greeting as spoken by other people. But two such sound patterns from the same person will typically differ in inflection, enthusiasm, or warmth, as well as in length, pitch, or loudness, these differences having some associations with the person greeted, the setting, and other conditions. In this chapter we shall consider such specificity—its sources and its effects on measurements. Involved in this discussion will be the reactions of subjects to tests (examined in the preceding chapter) and the stability-instability of behavior, which was the topic of Chapter 9. The problem of specificity has been raised not only toward the end of Chapter 2 but also, more or less directly, in almost every subsequent chapter.

In methodological terms, the problem as it is manifested in measurements can be formulated rather simply. (1) The correlations between pairs of items from a single test are very low. Mean correlations of .04 to .08 are typical; means above .20 are rare. (For common values on some standard tests, see Fiske, 1966*b*.) (2) The correlations between pairs of tests purporting to measure the same trait (i.e., with the same or synonymous labels) are typically moderately low. Common values may be .50 to .60 for intelligence tests but only .30 to .35 for measures of personality. When two measures of personality utilize different modes of observation (see Chapter 5), a much lower relationship or no relationship is often found. Even when the attenuating effects from the unreliabilities of the two measures are eliminated, the relationships generally indicate more distinctness than overlap, and only very rarely approach congruence. (3) The correlations of a test are also low with outside variables that are theoretically related to it. If there is a nontest criterion for the variable involved in a test, as in job performance or clinical diagnostics, the values will be modest at best. In studies of construct validity, we determine the degree of correlation between a test and measures of other variables to which it should, in theory, be related. The magnitude of such expected relationships is rarely predicted in precise terms. Hence it is not possible to say that obtained values are consistently less than expected, but it can be said that few high values are consistently observed in such work.

Most psychologists would accept these statements as accurate or as close to the facts. Granting them, how are they to be interpreted? Do they indicate major weaknesses in psychological measurement generally, but especially in the measurement of personality constructs? Do they stem from the fact that test construction has been based on faulty conceptualizations of the constructs at which the measuring procedures are aimed? (I.e., would much more consistency and covariation be observed if only we had identified and described the right variables?) Or does the picture found among systematic observations in measurement work reflect quite accurately the levels of association existing in nature, outside the measuring place? All three interpretations seem correct to some degree. The first two have been considered in various earlier chapters. Here we shall look at the third. We shall also consider the implications of these generalizations for studies of construct validity.

Specificity in Behaviors

COMPLEXITY OF STIMULI

In studies of pitch or of loudness, it is possible to present the subject with two stimulus tones that differ only in the attribute under investigation. Having been instructed to attend to that attribute, S responds solely in terms of his perceptions of that attribute of the tones. In investigations of personality, much more complex stimuli are ordinarily used. It can be argued (as it was in Chapter 8) that the stimuli used in personality measurement should be homogeneous in quality, and ideally should differ from each other only with respect to the frequency of positive responses they elicit; i.e., items should vary only in their pull, in the strength of the variable that a subject must have in order to give a positive or keyed response. In practice, it is difficult to find items that use the same basic content but do not irritate subjects by being blatantly repetitious. To be sure, it may be possible to find several such stimuli that mean essentially the same thing to any one subject, and differ only in some property such as intensity or degree. But the set of such stimuli for that subject will usually be different from the set that is fairly homogeneous for some other subject. As we saw in the last chapter, there is interaction between a subject and an item, so an item does not have exactly the same qualitative meaning for all subjects.

The matter can be illustrated by considering responses to a Rorschach inkblot. One subject's response may be determined by the outline, another's by the texture, and that of a third by the color. The blot is a complex with many attributes, any one or two of which may influence S's response. Of course, one kind of information sought from such protocols is exactly that: What stimulus properties of the cards does a given subject attend to, react to, and utilize in creating his percept? Much Rorschach scoring is based on a relative frequency model (Model B in Chapter 8) rather than on a cumulative homogeneity model (Model C).

In other procedures, each of several stimuli is intended to be reacted to only with respect to a single common aspect: the dominance aspect of questions about behavior in interpersonal situations (regardless of the kinds of people indicated); the mechanical aspect of interest items dealing with machines, vehicles, and devices. Unfortunately, a subject might express interest in a machine because of the ingenuity of its design, in a car because of its prestige or symbolic value, or in a device because of its novelty. More usually, a person who is interested in some mechanical objects will also be interested in others, whatever the basis for such interests. Thus a person's dispositions may be quite consistent, his reactions to stimuli quite regular, provided that the stimuli are classified in accordance with similarity of meaning for him. The problem in measurement is to find stimuli that have common meanings for all subjects in the population to be measured, i.e., stimuli with one preeminent characteristic that is interpreted the same way by all subjects, other characteristics not having any effect upon responses. Even in the content of scales for one kind of intelligence, one often finds enough specificity of items to generate low correlations between them.

MULTIPLICITY OF DETERMINANTS

Stimuli are only one factor determining behavior. The situation is another. We have seen in the last chapter that even a single common measuring situation can have different meanings for different subjects. The situation can be analyzed into several parts: e.g., in the testing situation, there is the objective reason the subjects are there, there are the physical characteristics of the place, including the physical climate (humidity, etc.), and there is the examiner. Returning to the test itself, there is its response format. In Chapter 10 we have seen that subjects may determine some responses on the basis of the format—avoiding extremes, preferring the "yes" alternatives, etc. Hence in a total testing context, where everything is kept objectively constant, some features of the total stimulation confronting the subjects may affect the responses of some subjects but not of others. Once again, the investigator should work to minimize the influence of all determinants other than the stimuli themselves.

Behavior is, of course, not completely chaotic. The preceding paragraphs have emphasized the confounding influences intruding even into standardized situations. But there are also common and general reactions; e.g., subjects typically apply themselves to tests of capacities, trying to give right answers and to obtain high scores. In general, they tend to do as they are asked. Rarely will a subject refuse to take a test. Among those starting a test, most keep working on it until they have finished. Only once in a while will a subject give up and mark the remaining items arbitrarily.

The basic source of difficulty is not the multiple determination of behavior (which, by itself, would not pose serious obstacles) but rather the fact that, in terms of available measurements today, the determinants do not operate in a highly regular, consistent fashion over all subjects. Thus it would not cause much difficulty if a given change—e.g., in the situational aspects—increased all scores the same amount or the same proportionate amount. Unfortunately, the behavior of organisms does not show such regularity.

For contrast, consider the measurement of basic physical attributes. We can measure the length of several solid objects at one temperature and then change the temperature and measure again. Our new measurements will have consistent relationships to the first set. For each type of material, we can find a function allowing us to relate the two sets of measurements rather precisely, each value of the function being determined by the temperatures. Such regularity is possible because all other factors possibly affecting length can be kept constant.

More telling is the fact that the same attribute, such as temperature, can be measured by several independent procedures. By use of appropriate correlational techniques, we can obtain practically perfect correlations between the observations from two such procedures. (We can also go further, and write equations enabling us to predict from one instrument the readings that will be obtained on another, but such exactness in transformations is too high a goal for psychologists to seek today.) These operations and results are possible in this case because the attribute does not change between the applications of the two measuring procedures, because the application

of a measuring procedure has trivial or no effects on the values of the observations obtained, and because the context can be controlled so that it does
not interact with the attribute being measured. For example, only if a very
cold thermometer were plunged into a very small quantity of hot liquid
would the act of measuring affect the readings seriously.

In psychology, the situation is quite different. The attribute may change
somewhat between applications of measuring procedures and the act of
measuring may affect the attribute being measured, but these effects can be
studied and have generally been found to be relatively small. More central
and prepotent is our inability to isolate a single attribute, to devise a procedure such that responses are determined solely or mostly by that single
target attribute.

A difficulty peculiar to psychology involves the difference between natural
situations and experimental conditions. In everyday life, a person perceives
the total situation and determines how he will react, i.e., what changes in
his experience he will act to obtain. In a testing situation, we do not want
the subject to determine what effects he will try to attain. We ask him to
adopt the purpose we give him, namely, to carry out the task as we instruct
him to do so. Hence our observations are of specific acts within the larger
framework we have established for him. His natural, free responding is
constrained by our restrictions and directions. The consequence may be
that his responding in the test situation is not representative of his usual
behavior. The obvious implication is that we should design situations so
that the subject feels as free and natural as possible, so that his motivations come easily from within him rather than being imposed upon him by
the demands of the task.

The Specificity of Instruments and Their Scores

We opened the chapter by pointing out that behaviors are relatively specific and distinct even though they may share similarities with other behaviors and that such specificity is also found in psychometric data—separate items have very low correlations with other items; tests of the same
variable have low correlations with each other and as low or lower correlations with outside variables. We have attributed this set of generalizations
to several things: test and nontest stimuli are complex and reactions to
them may be determined by qualitatively different factors in different subjects; more broadly, any total constellation of stimulus plus context may
be reacted to in diverse ways, each determined by a particular pattern of
influences from aspects of that constellation. These involve interactions between person and environment, in the technical sense that the contributions
of identified aspects of that environment vary from one person to another.

The preceding paragraph implies that the score for one person is not strictly comparable to the score for another person, since each score is influenced systematically by variables with little or no effect on the other score. One can add here also the influence of the state of the person, a factor that reduces the consistency of his responses over time. But these interactions also contribute to low correlations between tests. Even though two tests may appear to the psychologist to be measuring much the same variable, the intercorrelation of their scores will be reduced by any interactions between a subject and one test which are different from those between that subject and the other test. I.e., any objective differences between two measuring procedures can generate differences in the individual subject's pattern of interaction with them. Such confounding effects are in addition to effects associated with the objective dissimilarities themselves. To illustrate at the item level, one test may ask, "Do you enjoy chocolate ice cream? Yes or no." The other may have the statement "I am fond of coffee ice cream. True or false." Some relationship would be expected between these items, since some people like many flavors of ice cream but others do not eat it at all. Yet the correlation will be reduced by the extent to which some people like one of these flavors but not the other. The correlation may be reduced further if some subjects interpret "enjoy" as intense pleasure and others as "like" more than "dislike," and similarly if "fond of" implies for some subjects a craving for or unusually pleasant associations with, but for others implies merely liking a little. It is also conceivable that "true" and "yes" may not have exactly equivalent meanings for some subjects.

I have argued in several earlier places that the correlations between two measures of the same variable may be reduced by differences in any one of several demonstrable features: response format, content, instructions, and the testing context. In particular, differences in the perspectives for the observations and in the modes used for measurement are especially likely to be associated with reductions in the magnitude of the intercorrelation, i.e., associated with correlations well below the anticipated level indicating essential interchangeability. It is now time to provide some details supporting these generalized statements. We shall dig into the data more minutely here than we have elsewhere in this text because the topic has not been examined in quite this way before.

SPECIFICITY IN GUILFORD'S MEASURES OF INTELLIGENCE

Tests of intelligence use the same mode (Mode 3, Capabilities). They are administered in such a way that the state of the subject is rather unimportant and the person-situation interaction plays a small role. While intelligence as ordinarily construed is not central to personality, it is useful to

examine its measurement for any light it may throw on the measurement
of other aspects of personality.

Guilford (1967) structures intellect according to the *operation* performed
on the *content* to obtain the *product*. Identifying 5 types of operations, 4
kinds of content, and 6 classes of products, he obtains 120 potential cells
or hypothetical abilities. See Figure 11.1. He warns us, however, that new
parameters may need to be added. There may also be additional categories
for each parameter, and therefore many more distinguishable entities.

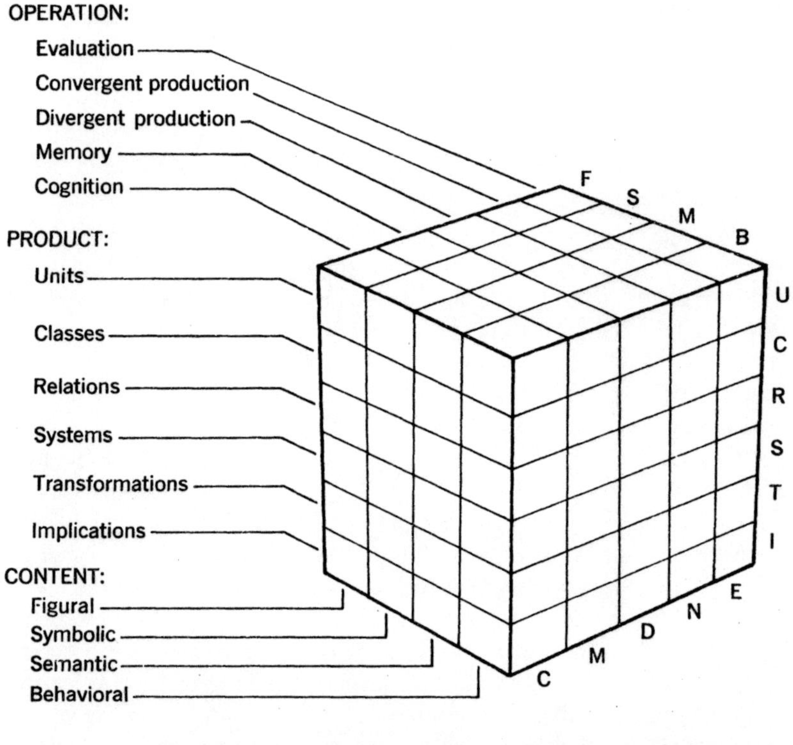

Figure 11.1. The structure-of-intellect model, with three parameters. From
The Nature of Human Intelligence *by J. P. Guilford. Copy-*
right 1967 by McGraw-Hill, Inc. Used with permission of
McGraw-Hill Book Company.

Guilford has identified tests for many of the 120 cells, and in his research program is systematically developing and checking on tests for additional cells. The following tentative statements are based on examination
of several reports from his project. Since each report deals with tests having at least one component in common (i.e., one category for one pa-

rameter, such as classes for the product parameter, the sample of reports cannot be taken as necessarily representative of the whole structure. The careful and intensive work on tests for each cell makes clear that, even with relatively explicit conceptualizations of the categories on each parameter, one cannot assume that one's *a priori* design of a test for such a specific ability will be found empirically to be largely free of influence from other abilities. For example, a test designed for one cell may appear empirically in the factor or set of tests that measure another cell—perhaps the cell differing only in product from the intended one.

From long experience, Guilford and his colleagues construct tests with quite satisfactory levels of reliability of the internal consistency type. Yet the several tests constructed for each ability, and even the two or three that he selects as the best representatives of the ability, have intercorrelations distinctly below the ceiling that their observed reliabilities would permit. For example, tests with reliabilities of .80 and .78 may intercorrelate .37 when the value could be .79, the geometric mean of the reliabilities. In a more favorable instance, tests with reliabilities of .69 and .61 correlate .51, which is not a great deal below the potential *r* of .65. These are about the worst and the best of several instances examined. They clearly indicate some specificity, more or less, for even the selected tests of a single ability among the 120.

(The reader with limited knowledge of the product-moment correlation coefficient, *r*, should be warned that, while the direct comparison of *r*'s is reasonable in this particular simple inspectional context, the comparison of *r*'s for other types of analyses may require some prior transformation; for example, to r^2.)

Guilford's Structure-of-Intellect is a model with great conceptual elegance, and one that he has shown to have considerable theoretical fruitfulness. Yet it may eventually be determined that differential assessment of certain abilities that are in the same category on one or two parameters is so difficult that it is doubtful whether practical discriminations between them are worth attempting. In some instances in the data from his project's reports, the two preferred tests for one ability correlate only a few points higher (e.g., .51 vs. .45) with each other than their median *r* with preferred tests from cells sharing two of the three parameters (operation, content, and product). With variation around that median *r*, an occasional correlation can be observed to exceed the one between the two tests of the same ability.

The reader should note that Guilford and his colleagues have been exploring the many cells in the model of the intellect, rather than intensively developing and refining each of the numerous tests they have tried out. Hence these observations do not indicate the extent to which it is possible to create tests measuring almost entirely one cell. It is also true that part of the apparent specificity or lack of close agreement among tests for the same cell is due to their different patterns of overlap with other cells. That is, one test may correlate somewhat with tests for cells A, B, and C while another has some correlation with tests for cells C, D, and E. Hence it is not always the distinctiveness or uniqueness of each of the tests in a cell that produces their limited degree of intercorrelation; the particular patterns of partial overlap with other aspects of intellect may also contribute.

Thus even in the domain of intelligence, pure tests of a narrowly conceptualized entity may have considerable specificity and such tests may overlap quite considerably with tests that are conceptually similar in some parameters but distinct in others. It may be that the several classes of each parameter can be differentiated more completely in theory than in practice. (Consider the developments proposed by Varela, 1969.)

SPECIFICITY IN OTHER TESTS OF INTELLIGENCE

Baughman and Dahlstrom (1968) have recently completed a careful study of racially segregated children in a rural, economically deprived area in the South. Among the many tests they used were the Stanford-Binet Intelligence Scale (1960 Revision), an individually administered test with roots going back to the first systematic testing of intelligence by Binet, and the Thurstone Primary Mental Abilities Test (1962 Revision), a group-administered test providing scores for Verbal Meaning, Perceptual Speed, Number Facility, Spatial Relations, and Reasoning, as well as a total score. The authors found that

> the average performance of the Negro children was much lower than that of the white children on each of the tests and subtests; however, the size of this gap was dependent upon the particular measures used as well as on the sex and ages of the children being examined [Baughman and Dahlstrom, 1968, p. 58].

They also report that their data

> show considerable inconsistency between the S-B and PMA data with respect to the age differences in the verbal capacities of the children. . . . One likely explanation for this disparity lies in the different modes of performance required in the two tests [*ibid.*, p. 60].

Although these authors are using mode to refer to differences in the task set for the subjects, all of which fall within the Capabilities Mode (Mode 3), their point is important: these two tests do not lead to the same pattern of relationships. If the parts of this study had been conducted by two independent investigators at different places, one using the S-B and the other the PMA, we might have wondered whether the different conclusions reached by these researchers from their dissimilar findings might stem from the samples used. But here the data from the two tests are from the same subjects, and hence the differences must be attributed to differencs in the capacities tapped by these tests and subtests. Such an interpretation would be quite readily accepted by those familiar with the instruments. For example, each of the several PMA subtests differs more or less from the others and also from most of the subtests in the Stanford-Binet with respect to contents, operations, and products. Even the total scores cannot be considered interchangeable.

SPECIFICITY IN MEASURES OF PERSONALITY

In the next sections, we shall look at correlations for pairs of tests with the same trait label. In some instances, both tests use the same mode, in others not. Our primary interest will be to determine whether the two tests have essentially similar profiles of correlations with measures of other traits. If two measures are actually measuring the same variable, they should have very similar profiles of correlations with measures of any other variables or traits. (Technically, if one of the two measures is clearly more reliable than the other, it can be expected to have a higher correlation in each comparison. We shall ignore this consideration since the reliabilities will usually be fairly similar and since we want to concentrate on the basic question of similarity in shape of the profiles: Do they have similar high points and low points?)

We shall also look at the similarity of such profiles as a function of the observed correlation between the two measures themselves. We can expect that the higher this correlation is, the more similar will be the profiles. In general, this expectation is supported by the data, but some notable exceptions occur.

What we are doing is asking in an approximate form whether the construct validities of the two measures are similar, i.e., whether the profiles indicate that the same construct is involved in the two measures. In more rigorous research on construct validity, one predicts from one's conceptualization and theorizing about the construct what will be the relative size of the correlations with each of a set of specified variables. (See Chapter 8.) For our present purposes, we are using whatever data are available. In the studies cited, the researchers tended to choose the variables forming the correlational profile for convenience (that is, they were measuring them anyway, and it is easy to obtain a complete intercorrelation matrix with a computer) or for purposes other than the study of construct validity. The relative frequency of studies using more than one measure of a single trait and obtaining correlations with several other variables is rather small; of these few, only a fraction were designed to assess the construct validity of the measures and hence use other variables selected on theoretical grounds.

SPECIFICITY IN PERSONALITY
TESTS WITHIN A SINGLE MODE

Karp (1963) and Goodenough and Karp (1961) provide examples from Mode 3 for measures not identified as intelligence. In these studies, factor analyses were carried out on batteries of tests that included several used to measure field independence. This term is construed by Witkin and his colleagues (1962) as referring to the capacity to overcome embedding contexts in perception; e.g., to identify a simple figure when it is embedded in a more complex design, as in the Embedded Figures Test. Karp identifies one of his factors with field independence. The tests with high loadings on this factor (loadings are correlations between tests and the abstract entity isolated as a factor) included those selected by Witkin as suitable indices of this capacity and several other aptitude scores, including the Object Assembly and the Block Designs from the Wechsler Adult Intelligence Scale. These latter two correlated .64 with each other. When we compare the patterns of correlations for each of these with the other sixteen tests in the study, we find very high similarity: for each correlate, the two values are within a few points of each other. This finding would not surprise a psychometrician who knew that, in this study, the reliabilities of these two tests were .64 and .65, and thus their intercorrelation was as high as it could be. In other words, the two tests, though a little different in task, are in this instance essentially interchangeable.

Two other tests that measure this same factor are the Rod and Frame Test and the Insight Problems. In the first, S confronts a rod and a rectangular frame that are tilted (nothing else being visible), and has to adjust the rod so that it appears vertical to him. The Insight Problems are designed to measure adaptive flexibility. They require S to restructure what is given him in order to reach a solution. Although each test had a reliability of about .90, their intercorrelation was only .30, a value that is not unexpected in view of the differences in the contents and tasks involved. Comparing their profiles of correlations with other tests, we find more dissimilarity than for the pair examined above. The largest discrepancy was for the Body Adjustment Test, which correlated .61 with the Rod and Frame Test but only .31 with the Insight Problems. (The reader may already have anticipated that the Body Adjustment Test requires the subject, seated in a tilted chair and surrounded by a tilted field, to adjust his chair to the upright.) Given such a large difference in correlation with a third variable, it can be concluded that the Rod and Frame and the Insight measures are more distinct and separate than equivalent or interchangeable.

Other examples with similar implications could be drawn from this study. Let us leave it with only one additional observation: in many instances, big differences between pairs of correlations are, like the one just noted, found with third variables also having large loadings on the factor. This finding is, of course, associated with two tendencies: tests with loadings on the same factor are likely to have high intercorrelations, and large differences between correlations are more likely when one of the values is high.

The study by Goodenough and Karp (1961) is of particular interest because they report factor analyses on two separate groups. Their samples are regrettably small—only 50 and 30, as opposed to the more adequate sample of 150 used in the Karp study above. In spite of the small sample and the consequent sampling fluctuation in obtained correlations, some consistency is found between the two sets of correlations: when a pair of tests have different correlations with a third variable in one group, they tend to have a similar pattern of r's in the other. One interesting difference occurs in both sets and also in the Karp study with older subjects (college undergraduates). The Embedded Figures Test and the Body Adjustment Test correlate .32 to .55 with each other, in the three groups. While these two tests have fairly similar correlations with most other tests, they have dissimilar correlations with the Block Design Test from the Wechsler Intelligence Scales: in each study, the value for the Embedded Figures Test is distinctly higher (as much as 36 correlation points). Here is an instance of two tests that are taken to be measures of the same concept, field independence, but which not only have rather limited intercorrelations but also have a different magnitude of association with an outside variable (Block Design) in each of three groups of subjects.

For an example from Mode 2 (Current Experiencing), we can note a study of the generality of cognitive complexity in structuring one's interpersonal environment. Cognitive complexity is the disposition to employ many dimensions or to make fine discriminations when perceiving and evaluating stimuli. Vannoy (1965) factor-analyzed twenty measures, including several designed explicitly to measure this disposition. These latter did not appear together on the same factor, so Vannoy drew the reasonable conclusion that cognitive complexity is not a single entity. The failure of these particular tests to emerge on the same factor is not surprising, since their intercorrelations were .43 or below. More pertinent to our purposes, they had rather dissimilar profiles of correlations with the other tests.

From Mode 1, let us look at some data on tests of dominance (Butt and Fiske, 1968, 1969). These data have the advantage of including three groups: female and male college students and basic airmen. Two scales, one developed by Thurstone and one by Gough and others, correlated .66

to .79 with each other, the values being a little below their reliabilities (.86 to .88 and .78 to .84, respectively). Their profiles of correlations with a score of other dominance measures and a dozen measures of theoretically relevant variables were quite similar. See Table 11.1. On the other hand, when each of these was compared to the dominance scale from Cattell's 16 PF test, the correlations were distinctly lower (.22 to .48) and the pattern of correlations relating the 16 PF measure to other variables was quite different from the pattern for the Gough or the Thurstone. Thus, even with moderate correlations between two tests such as the 16 PF and the Thurstone, the correlations with measures of other variables indicate that the constructs being assessed by these two tests must be seen as quite different. For example, in all three samples, a measure of impulsivity had a significant positive correlation with the 16 PF but not with the Thurstone, while a measure of neuroticism had a significant negative correlation with the Thurstone but not with the 16 PF. Inspecting the data for each of the three samples of subjects, we find that the conclusions about the distinctiveness or specificity of the tests tended to be very similar.

To provide an example from Mode 5, let us look at a study of conformity behavior by McDavid and Sistrunk (1964). They measured conformity by tendency to agree with a contrived majority of supposed fellow subjects on perceptual discriminations. They obtained separate scores for soluble tasks—discriminations that had been found easy to make—and insoluble tasks involving judgments between indiscriminable pairs of identical stimuli. Although the two scores had adequate reliability, they correlated only .20 with each other. Hence it is not surprising to find that these scores had dissimilar profiles of correlations with forty measures of personality. A difference in one feature of the task created quite distinct measures of conformity.

SPECIFICITY IN PERSONALITY
TESTS FROM DIFFERENT MODES

If tests given the same label and using the same mode often show marked dissimilarities in patterns of correlations with other measures, we should expect as much or more difference when the tests use different modes, and our expectation is supported.

In addition to ability tests, Baughman and Dahlstrom used a personality questionnaire (the MMPI), a projective or fantasy test like the TAT, teachers' ratings, interviews with mother and child, and several other procedures. They report differences between the characterizations obtained from the MMPI and those from other methods, such as teacher perceptions and interviews with the child, yet feel that, in such instances, both descriptions "may be reasonably accurate but may be presenting findings from different levels

Table 11.1. The correlations of three dominance scales with measures of other personality variables

Dominance scale	Group	Aggression	Verbal hostility	Impulsivity	Energy	Self-confidence	Need achievement	Superego control	Neuroticism	Unhappiness	Extraversion	Sociability	Socioeconomic status	Peer Ratings Succeed	Fail
Gough	IM[a]	.13	−.03	.04	.15	.44*	.33*	.11	−.36*	−.05	.50*	.40*	.04		
	IF[b]	.02	.24	−.01	.06	.49*	.43*	.29*	−.41*	−.27*	.53*	.38*	.19		
	L[c]	−.07	.08	−.26*	.36*	.50*	.44*	.38*	−.45*	−.27*	.55*	.45*	.26*	.43*	−.13
Thurstone	IM[a]	.04	−.02	−.02	.21	.46*	.37*	.08	−.30*	.01	.62*	.49*	.16		
	IF[b]	.03	.19	.18	.15	.36*	.33*	.32*	−.32*	−.23	.72*	.49*	.34*		
	L[c]	−.11	−.22*	−.20*	.10	.35*	.43*	.30*	−.37*	−.15	.58*	.38*	.18	.29*	.00
Cattell 16PF	IM[a]	.13	.28*	.33*	.32*	.14	.05	−.18	.08	.05	.13	.04	.24*		
	IF[b]	.22	.55*	.52*	.48*	.31*	.14	−.08	.02	−.09	.49*	.19	.22		
	L[c]	.34*	.21*	.20*	.29*	.22*	.14	−.10	−.05	.06	.20*	.09	.14	.14	.07

Source: D. S. Butt and D. W. Fiske, "Differential Correlates of Dominance Scales," *Journal of Personality*, 37 (1969): 415–28.
[a]Male students at University of Illinois Chicago Circle Campus (N = 77).
[b]Female students at Illinois (N = 61).
[c]Basic airmen at Lackland Air Force Base (N = 248).
*r is significant at .05 level.

of personality description" (1968, p. 258). For example, fantasy measures of achievement motivation were not related significantly to such motivation as rated by teachers, so it does not seem strange that these two methods yield dissimilar findings concerning sex differences. Measures of fantasy have frequently been shown to have little or no relationship with more overt measures for the same constructs. There is every reason to treat measures of these two levels or types of assessment as referring to separate constructs.

Comparisons between self-report inventories and a projective test are reported by Mosher (1966, 1968). The projective test was an incomplete-sentences instrument. Mosher's work is particularly interesting because he examined different aspects of guilt in these two studies, one with males and one with females. He presents multitrait-multimethod matrices (such matrices were discussed in Chapter 8) showing the correlations between three aspects as measured by the Mosher Incomplete Sentences Test (MIST) and by two forms of inventories.

The validity diagonals (containing the convergent validities) have quite high values, approaching or approximating the limits set by the reliabilities. Thus, for each form of guilt, the MIST measures essentially the same construct as the inventories. Furthermore, the three forms of guilt are rather well differentiated, especially by the MIST, both in the correlations within each instrument and in those between instruments. In the two studies, there is only one trivial exception to the pattern that Sex Guilt and Morality-Conscience Guilt correlate more closely with each other than either does with Hostility Guilt. (Mosher also included measures of social desirability and manifest anxiety, but these measures had correlations with the guilt measures too low to provide further evidence of differentiation.)

Mosher's studies indicate that different forms of guilt can be clearly discriminated, and that the construct of total amount of guilt feelings is too heterogeneous to be considered as a theoretically useful dimension of differences among subjects. The unusually high convergence between the projective test and the inventories might be taken as an argument against the importance of distinguishing modes: the inventories are Mode 1 and the Incomplete Sentences are presumably Mode 5, since the scoring is done by judges using a scoring manual. But in this instance, it seems likely that the Incomplete Sentences are more like a self-report instrument with free responses (rather than multiple choice). In examples Mosher provided in an earlier paper, the contents of the stems are topics about which one might feel guilt, and two of the stems are written in the first person. Hence the subjects were probably more aware that they were providing responses with self-reference than they usually are with less structured stimuli, such as inkblots.

Most studies permitting comparisons of procedures aimed at the same construct but using different modes provide tables of the multitrait-multi-method form and do not include correlations with external variables hypothetically related to the constructs under investigation. Such tables are more difficult to analyze for similarity of correlational patterns. For example, since measures using the same procedure tend to be intercorrelated more highly than comparable pairs of measures using different procedures, the matter of elevation or average level of each profile may have to be considered.

As an example, we can look at the intercorrelations of ratings on twenty-two variables made in connection with *The Prediction of Performance in Clinical Psychology* (Kelly and Fiske, 1951). In this research on assessment, students about to enter graduate training in clinical psychology were brought together for a week of interviews, projective and objective tests, situational tests, etc. (See Chapter 1.) At the end of that period, the clinical psychologists on the staff who had observed each subject and had studied all the protocols and scores for him rated him on a large number of variables. These ratings were pooled in a conference. Parallel ratings were also made by the three fellow subjects who not only had lived with him for that week but also had gone through the situational tests with him. (The median of the three was used in these analyses.) Each subject also rated himself. The ratings were all made on an eight-point scale, relative to a defined reference population, with suggestions as to the proportion of cases expected to fall at each of the eight points. The three sets of ratings, sixty-six variables in all, were intercorrelated. (Some of these correlations are given in Campbell and Fiske, 1959.)

Let us look at just one of the twenty-two variables, number 4: Depressed-Cheerful. This would seem to be a relatively overt characteristic and therefore easy to observe and rate. The interjudge reliability of the composite staff rating was estimated to be .85, and that for the median teammate rating was .76. (No estimate of the reliability of the self-ratings was possible from the data collected.) The staff and teammate ratings correlated .53, and these correlated .42 and .24 respectively with the self-ratings. In this sample, judgments of one's own cheerfulness did not agree closely with those of peers or experts.

The staff ratings and the teammate ratings of Cheerful were correlated with each of the twenty-two self-ratings. These two sets of correlations agreed very closely; the largest discrepancy was for their correlations with Cheerful, as seen above. In contrast, the two profiles for teammate and self-ratings as correlated with the twenty-two staff ratings were quite different: for eleven of the twenty-two variables, the discrepancy between the two correlations was greater than eighteen points. The teammate ratings of Cheerful had substantially higher correlations with staff ratings of Assertive and Unshakable Poise than did the self-ratings, while the self-ratings of Cheerful had higher correlations with staff ratings of Talkative, Adventurous, and Adaptable. Thus, while the staff and teammate ratings on Cheerful did not agree as well as they could and therefore had some specificity, these sets of ratings by others were functionally equivalent in terms of relationships with self-ratings. On the other hand, the teammate and self-ratings were quite differentiated and distinct, the nature of the two rather specific views being brought out by their separate profiles of correlations with various staff ratings.

The work of Zuckerman and his colleagues provides some interesting findings based on other kinds of methods. In one paper (Zuckerman *et al.,* 1961), they reported the measuring of dependency in a variety of ways, using three modes. Three forms of self-report intercorrelated significantly; of these, two with different questionnaire formats had quite similar profiles of correlations with other measures, with a discrepancy only for correlations with the Sentence Completion Test. The third, direct self-rating, had a profile fairly similar to the others but did correlate more highly with peer ratings (Mode 4). The Sentence Completion Test tended to fit the same pattern. On the other hand, the ratings based on Rorschach and on TAT did not correlate significantly with each other, with the Sentence Completion Test, or with anything else. Although their two profiles have some slight similarities, we cannot safely interpret comparisons of very low correlations. In contrast, the peer ratings had a profile fairly similar to those for three self-report measures, although peer ratings correlated only .24 and .28 with the two questionnaire measures. In this study of one variable, then, Mode 4 ratings by peers showed agreement with various Mode 1 self-reports almost as high as the correspondence among the profiles for these self-reports.

A more elaborate investigation was carried out on three affects (anxiety, depression, and hostility) with groups of patients and normals (Zuckerman *et al.,* 1967). Measures were derived from self-reports, from projective tests, and from ratings based on interviews. In general, the correlation between two measures of one affect was reflected in the similarity of correlational profiles, but not exactly; for example, two measures of anxiety, from interview and self-ratings, correlated only .17 in the control group, and yet their profiles were fairly similar. That study, however, provides some disturbing findings concerning the ratings from interviews. Both anxiety and depression were rated on the basis of several signs or aspects, these being averaged to obtain a composite rating for each variable. This rating by signs rather than by overall impression should have reduced any confounding effects from global or halo reactions. Yet for the patient group, anxiety and depression correlated .67 with each other. While their profiles of relationships to a number of autonomic variables were quite similar, their profiles with various tests were not as similar. But note that we are talking now about measures with different labels—about two different variables. Here is an instance in which measures of different traits by the same method show as much agreement with each other and over profiles of correlations as we find at best between measures of the same trait. In addition to agreement between measures of the same thing, we must be able to demonstrate differentiation of traits, especially when measured by the same procedure.

These various examples have been selected largely on the basis of ready accessibility. If anything, they may suggest a more favorable picture of convergence between measures of the same construct than seems to be typical. They do illustrate three important tendencies:

1. Two measures of the same construct generally have substantially different correlations with one or more other variables. This generalization is especially true for measures using different modes. Furthermore, in those instances where data are available from two or more samples, the differences tend to be consistent across samples, so that they cannot be written off as sampling fluctuations.

2. For pairs of such measures of the same construct, although important exceptions do occur, the degree of similarity between the profiles of correlation with outside variables is related to the correlation between the pair. If that correlation is high relative to their reliabilities, the profiles are likely to be quite similar. If that correlation is moderate or low, the profiles usually are dissimilar, with some marked discrepancies.

3. These discrepancies ordinarily indicate that the two measures are not indices of the same construct, but rather pertain to constructs that may overlap to some extent and yet clearly have aspects specific to one or the other. Hence, as a rule, measures of the same construct are not interchangeable empirically and must not be considered conceptually equivalent until a high degree of convergence in correlational patterns with other variables, or extrinsic convergent validity, has been demonstrated empirically.

It is important that the reader realize that specificity in measuring procedures is not confined to the personality domain. Different methods for measuring learning ability are not interchangeable, nor are those for hunger or for thirst. Pertinent references are given by Gulliksen in a technical paper (1968) on methods for determining equivalence of measures. Gulliksen also notes that reasonably high intercorrelations have been reported for measures of hunger drive and for measures of sex, though he does not warn the reader that such measures may show limited discrimination between one drive and another, and that measures of different drives derived from the same apparatus may show even higher correlations than measures of the same drive using separate methods (see Campbell and Fiske, 1959).

Other Views on Test Specificity

The reader should know that my deep concern about test specificity and its apparent implications seems not to be shared by all my colleagues working in the field of personality measurement. It is sometimes argued that the situation is not as bad as it has been presented here. For example, suppose that the common variance that generates the modest correlation between two tests is variance associated with the target construct, and suppose further that the specific variance in each test is not part of the construct. Then we could obtain highly satisfactory indices by combining scores from a number of such tests, the common variance building up with the additional tests and the specific variances tending to cancel each other out. This possibility is, of course, essentially the model of obtained test scores in classical psychometric theory (e.g., Gulliksen, 1950), the specific variance being labeled as error variance. Unfortunately, there is a substantial body of evidence indicating that test scores generally contain much systematic variance that is not associated with the target construct, variance associated with other traits or with response sets. As discussed in Chapter 10, such systematic variance is likely to be introduced from the reactions of the subject to the testing situation and to the test itself. It seems quite unrealistic today to hope that we can develop instruments that do not contain systematic variance from irrelevant sources. When such variance is present, it is highly likely that it will contribute to the scores of more than one test, so that the shared variance and the correlations between tests do not stem solely from construct-relevant sources.

It can also be argued that the low correlations between tests of one construct and their apparent specificity come from the fact that the tests are measuring different parts of the construct. If each test of a construct is itself psychometrically adequate in terms of its internal properties, and if each has some demonstrated validity, then again a useful composite score can be obtained from the several tests taken together. Such a score should have some reliability and good validity as an index of the total construct.

This orientation is, in principle, reasonable and worthy of consideration. In practice, the several tests must be expected to have the same limitations with respect to systematic irrelevant variance mentioned in the preceding paragraph. A fundamental objection to pursuing this orientation is its neglect of conceptual specifications. For example, one might consider combining scores from several tests of dominance that had low intercorrelations, the rationale being that they tapped different aspects of that trait. But usually these several tests were designed by researchers with somewhat different notions of dominance, and hence the composite would represent a polyglot, an amalgam with no conceptual core. In addition, the investigator pursuing this orientation would have no guidance as to which tests should be combined, and how many tests should be included in order to cover the construct completely, to say nothing of covering it evenly and systematically. Test specificity is more than a methodological problem to be overcome by technical developments. It is a reflection of specificity in behavior, and as such it raises crucial substantive problems for those conceptualizing and operationalizing the variables in the personality domain.

Implications of Test Specificity for Construct Validation

The specificity so widespread among measures of personality clearly indicates that no one measure of a construct can be taken as a sufficient index of it until substantial empirical support has been obtained for that decision. In addition, the typical correlation between two measures of purportedly the same construct does not give much promise for the hope that we can eventually devise procedures that can be calibrated so that indices from one can be transformed to equivalent indices on the other. (See the discussion of "The Modes and Their Differentiation" in Chapter 5.) The only possibility of such calibration suggested by current evidence would be a pair of procedures within the same mode, using the same format and task, and having highly similar content. For example, some questionnaire measures of dominance do have intercorrelations that approach the limit set by their own internal consistencies, as mentioned earlier in this chapter in connection with the findings of Butt and Fiske (1968).

If we can find at least two and preferably three procedures using the same mode which intercorrelate highly in spite of differences in content, format, or task, we can assume that we have a good operational hold on the construct as observed from that perspective. If we can find two other measures using a different mode which correlate highly not only with each other but also with the tests from the first mode, we can begin to think about a construct that has some generality beyond a single mode.

Suppose a researcher wishes to determine the construct validity of a test. If he limits himself to just that test, he will have difficulty in interpreting any observed departures from the correlational pattern he has predicted from his conceptual framework for that construct. He may have construed the construct incorrectly, he may have designed his test defectively, he may have overlooked some bias in his testing procedure, or his theoretical hypothesis may be wrong. If, however, he employs two tests that correlate well with each other, he can usually feel more confident that any failures to confirm hypotheses stem from conceptual rather than methodological weaknesses. The degree of such confidence will, to be sure, depend upon the apparent differences between his methods: two inventories with the same format and similar content may be interchangeable only with each other, but not with other measures of the construct at issue, and therefore provide no real basis for confidence in their congruence with the construct.

In many cases, it will be desirable to have three or four measures of the construct, each of which can be defended as having some validity even though the intercorrelations are only moderate. If the whole set, or all but one, correlate substantially as predicted with outside variables, then the investigator can feel he has support for his theoretical propositions. Whether such tests should be from the same or from different modes will depend on whether the conceptual framework in which the construct is embedded is seen as restricted to one mode or as holding for several modes. While some theorizing is clearly intended to deal with just one kind of observation (e.g., expert observation of present behavior), it will often be unclear to what modes or perspectives the conceptual work applies.

Summary

This chapter goes intensively and with concrete illustrations into the fundamental fact of specificity in behaviors both outside and inside the testing room. Two tests of the same construct typically have a moderate to low correlation between them, the level of relationship depending on whether the mode, the situation, the task, and the stimuli for one test are similar to or different from those for the other. Stimuli in general and test stimuli or items in particular are complex entities eliciting differential perceptions and interpretations from different people. A response may be determined primarily by any one or any subset of the multiplicity of influences potentially present in a situation. It is difficult to isolate a single attribute of human behavior, to obtain responses varying only on that attribute.

The great majority of psychological tests have considerable specificity. Their scores tend to correlate far less than perfectly with other tests of the same variable. Even when an ability is defined within a model such as Guilford's Structure-of-Intellect, each test of that ability will usually have some specific determinants not shared by other tests of that aspect of intelligence. Moreover, such a test is likely to correlate almost as well with tests of other similar abilities as with tests of its particular one. Similarly, even when two tests of a personality construct use the same mode, their intercorrelation is rarely so high that they can be considered interchangeable; more commonly, such tests show major differences in their patterns of correlations with other variables, indicating that they are not conceptually equivalent. Such dissimilar correlational profiles are more common when the measures use different modes; e.g., fantasy measures typically are differentiated from self-report or observations by others.

When two or more tests agree closely with each other and have similar profiles of correlations with other variables, we can feel with some confidence that they are measuring the same construct, although we must consider the contributions to their congruence that may have been made by similarity in such components as task and content. Such measures can profitably be employed in basic research to test theoretical propositions. More usually, several such tests with the same label will have correlations with each other and with other variables which indicate that they are not interchangeable. In such instances, we cannot consider a proposition to be supported empirically unless the predicted relationship is obtained with all or most of the measures.

CHAPTER TWELVE

Measuring a
Personality Construct
Today

The preceding chapters have emphasized the difficulties encountered in attempts to measure a concept of personality. Those critical analyses have pointed out the elusiveness of the phenomena or processes that we wish to study scientifically; they have also brought out limitations in current procedures, with particular attention to their inadequacies as indices of the concepts in which we are interested.

It is to be hoped that this exposition provides a basis for constructive action. It has been said that a major part of any scientific advance is identifying the right question, an axiom that might be restated for the present topic as isolating the sources of the difficulties in personality measurement. If the major weaknesses have been designated and described, personologists can focus their efforts on correcting them.

Criteria for Measurements of Individual Differences

To be effective, any basic research on individual differences requires adequate measurements. While many potential sources of inadequacy have been discussed in earlier chapters, the notion of an adequate procedure can be summarized as one that meets three criteria.

1. The responses from which indices are obtained must be determined as completely as possible by one important construct. Here we are consider-

250

ing the problem from a broad perspective: we are simply asking whether it is possible to measure some important constructs well. Once we have demonstrated that we can accomplish this objective, we can work on the extension of our methodology to provide techniques for most or all important constructs. For the moment, the question concerns the theoretical importance of the construct measured, its role in conceptual frameworks, and its range of interconnections with other constructs.

2. The indices must differentiate dependably among subjects. This requirement is there by definition: we have said already that we are interested in problems of differences among subjects on particular dimensions; we are assuming that such differences exist and we therefore must have procedures that produce a range of scores over subjects.

3. The indices must indicate the degree of the construct characterizing each subject during the present period in his life. Again, this requirement is part of the task we have specified. We are concerned here with measuring a trait rather than the state in which S happens to be (see Chapter 9). Using just one point in time for reasons of economy and convenience, we want to obtain an index closely approximating the mean index that would be obtained if we could measure the person a number of times, each such measurement not being affected by the preceding measurement operations. We have seen in Chapter 9 that on repeated trials stable responses are obtained when the setting, the task, and the stimuli have clear psychological meaning for S, when they have sufficiently strong impact on him so that they determine his responses and eliminate substantial contributions from momentary states or from other variables, and when S has a definite method for coping with the demands made of him.

We are of course saying that we want to measure validly some individual difference construct. These three criteria overlap to some extent in that they all pertain to that aim. They are stated separately to emphasize particular aspects of validity in this context. As we have seen in Chapter 2, the objective is somewhat different from that of measurement in experimental work to determine effects from specific conditions, work that has somewhat different requirements: it is aimed at state, or strength of the construct at just one point in time; it also seeks indices maximally affected by the common experimental condition and therefore minimally affected by all variables on which the subjects show individual differences, variables specific to the total experimental situation or more generalized over a range of situations, such as traits. In other words, the experimentalist wants all subjects to react the same way and to the same degree to each condition he introduces; such a situation would yield the clearest empirical findings.

There is also the special case in which the researcher wants to measure individual differences in a variable which may fluctuate over time. One instance is, of course, the measurement of mood. This is an important construct and we can readily differentiate subjects in terms of degrees from sadness to happiness, or better still, degrees of positive affect and degrees of negative affect separately. Tension-relaxation and energy-fatigue can also be differentiated. Such instances are from a class of constructs for which the third criteria, stability over time, is not appropriate: the conceptualization of mood specifies that it changes over time.

MEETING THE CRITERIA

It is noteworthy that it is quite possible and easy to obtain measurements that satisfy some pairs among these criteria. It is easy to elicit responses that are highly dependable and characteristic of subjects and which differentiate among them, thus meeting the second and third criteria. We can simply ask them to give their names, to state their heights, or to describe what they usually eat for breakfast. There are a number of attributes of people that can be measured quite adequately, but which have little interest for us. They simply do not provide indices for variables that are important to theories of personality.

Another important class of responses meeting these two criteria are responses to single items. It is possible to identify items on various personality instruments that differentiate subjects (at least into two groups) and which elicit highly stable responses. But it is not possible to find any one such item that provides adequate indices for an important construct, any item that yields scores reflecting the totality of such a construct. (Even if our construct were quite narrow and specific, we would have trouble designing a response format that differentiated subjects reliably into more than two or three classes or levels of strength on that attribute.)

It is also possible and rather easy to obtain responses that are determined by important constructs and which indicate stable characteristics of subjects, meeting the first and the third criteria. Practically everyone will react to a painful stimulus, to an unexpected loud noise, to news of the assassination of the President. Similarly, practically every subject can be induced to conform minimally to a simple procedure in a testing room: he will follow instructions to write the date in the indicated place on an answer sheet and he will make some mark on the answer sheet opposite each question. Many other examples can be given to show that most people are socialized to the extent that they conform to what is expected of them in many social situations. The more complete the conformity, the less the individual differences.

Are there measuring procedures in which the responses are determined almost wholly by an important construct and which yield indices showing individual differences (the first and second criteria)? One instance would be reports of last dreams. Such reports are qualitatively quite distinct from subject to subject and do not provide data on the same motive for all subjects. We should also consider fantasies of the kind created in response to a TAT card. From Chapter 1, the reader may recall that, in the TAT or Thematic Apperception Test, the subject is presented with a number of cards, one at a time, and asked to make up a story for each one. (See Murray *et al.*, 1938.) Such stories tend to be different from one time to another and thus do not meet the third criteria. (While the same construct may be reflected in different content, two such sets of stories do not yield consistent and stable ratings on any one variable.) They do differ from subject to subject, and so meet the second criteria. But such protocols do not really satisfy the first criterion: granted that these fantasy responses are often determined by important constructs, namely, the needs of the respondents, different responses are determined by different needs.

A possible exception might be the use of rather structured TAT cards depicting content that many subjects would bring into their stories in one way or another; for example, the cards used by McClelland *et al.* (1953), Atkinson (1958), and others to assess fantasy need for achievement. It has been found possible to rate stories to such cards with reasonable interrater agreement. But other motives also contribute to the stories. Even more important, it has been found that the average level of achievement rated on successive cards alternates (Reitman and Atkinson, 1958). It is as if a subject who tells a story with a central theme of achievement for one card is most likely to tell a story with a different theme for the next card. (Each of a number of variables can, of course, be determined for all subjects from such protocols: length, many linguistic characteristics, number of characters introduced, amount of affect, etc. But the utility of such indices for research purposes would depend largely on their stability over time. If their adequacy in reflecting constructs varies with their stability, they do not fit into this category of measurements meeting just the first two criteria.)

FULLY ADEQUATE MEASUREMENTS

Are there any measurements that meet all three criteria quite fully? The only major class is tests of Capabilities (Mode 3). There are a number of procedures that measure important abilities, which differentiate people, and which yield stable indices. In each of the other five modes, no procedure can be proposed which most personologists would agree met the criteria. Typically, the disagreements would center on the first criterion: in each such case, some psychologists would insist that the available evidence did not establish that the measurements obtained by the procedure were determined almost completely by a single important construct.

One possible exception may be sociometric techniques. For example, we can take a group of persons who know each other well, a group such as a small military unit or a fraternity. We can ask each person to rate every other person on talkativeness, sociability, or some other easily observable trait. The average perception of an S by his peers is a significant aspect of his personality, especially when the trait being rated is selected for its theoretical importance. The measurements obtained by sociometric techniques do differentiate subjects and are quite stable over time, so the three criteria are met well. It is probably significant that such procedures use Mode 4, observations of Prior Behavior, the subject not knowing that such measurements are to be made.

It should also be noted that, in this instance, we have essentially an operational definition; e.g., we may define popularity as the proportion of peers who report that they like S. The construct of popularity has little surplus meaning beyond the operation by which it is assessed. It seems likely that other possible exceptions, other procedures that might be advanced as meeting the three criteria, will also be instances in which the construct is defined by the operations utilized, and even here, the importance of the construct will typically be questioned.

This assertion that there are few fully adequate measurements should not be taken as an argument that all other measurements of personality are of little or no value. We do rather well in a number of areas. We can assess interests fairly effectively although our lengthy interest inventories may not be much more useful than direct questioning of subjects about their interests (see Dolliver, 1969). We can also measure values and attitudes with some success. We have procedures for observing important perceptual tendencies and cognitive style. More generally, we have many techniques that yield fairly stable individual differences among subjects and which appear to be determined largely by dispositions of the kind at which the instrument is aimed. But, as stated throughout this book, rarely if ever do we have consensus that any one procedure or any set of procedures is completely congruent with a target construct. We measure well many specific variables that appear to be portions of important constructs, the degree of overlap and the degree of irrelevancy being quite uncertain. The lack of coordination between a construct and its measuring operations is the major obstacle to be overcome.

These three criteria are not the only relevant considerations. Unfortunately, there are also practical requirements that many personologists would also like to set for measuring procedures. We want procedures that can be applied economically to most people. (Recall the discussion of ideal measurement in Chapter 7.) Sociometric techniques do not meet these practical requirements. It is rarely possible to apply them to each of a large group of people. For example, it is hard to get the necessary cooperation from a sizable group of peers, and any group less than all such peers is likely to be biased in some way. Under most circumstances, it would also be quite expensive to apply such methods.

But perhaps we have been too reluctant to spend the time, effort, and money necessary to obtain highly adequate measurements of personality. Our colleagues in the natural sciences do not stint themselves in these respects when they are convinced that such expenditures are necessary. We might advance personology by following their example.

In summary, it is technically possible to measure some attributes of people very well, especially abilities and traits that are defined essentially by the measuring operations. When we have stable and differentiating measurements, we rarely have consensus on the importance of the construct being measured. And on top of these basic methodological specifications, there are the matters of feasibility and economy.

Feasible Programs of Personological Research

We take it as axiomatic that the ultimate goal of personology is to have a set of constructs that help us to understand personality and its functioning, a set of constructs in a nomological net (Cronbach and Meehl, 1955); i.e., a set of constructs that are held to be related to each other and to variables outside of the personality domain, such as sex and education. Such a conceptualization is a theory of personality.

The viewpoint of this volume requires that there be subconstructs subsumed under each of these constructs. First, there are subconstructs associated with distinct perspectives or modes of observing personality phenomena. Second, there are lower order, more specific subconstructs designating the various forms in which the construct may be manifested within each mode. In addition to these elements in a behavioral facet, it will usually be necessary to delineate other facets and their elements (see Chapter 6). In particular, one or more situational facets are required.

These constructs and subconstructs would ideally be linked to measuring instruments using appropriate modes of observation. Such procedures would yield scores or other measurements, each of these indices being coordinated with a subconstruct. The obtained scores would satisfy pertinent psychometric criteria of dependability or generalizability and would have appropriate levels of correlation with each other.

In our research program during recent years, intensive studies of single variables have pursued this general approach for some part of the way. While the work on some variables has been largely exploratory, to gain experience with the strategy, work on other variables has led to published papers indicating the feasibility of the approach (Butt and Fiske, 1968, 1969; Pearson, 1969, 1970). I am convinced that fruitful programs of personological research can be executed along these lines.

The success of such programs will depend on several qualifications. The researcher must be able to work effectively with both conceptual and empirical materials, or the research must be conducted by a well-integrated research team that includes both kinds of competence. The key to effectiveness seems to lie in the researcher's style and direction of thinking. The natural tendency of the human mind is to deal with simple ideas, with one thing at a time. It is all too easy to develop an abstract conceptual analysis of a construct and then, turning to empirical procedures, to become preoccupied with psychometric considerations. What is difficult is to cope with both sides of the problem simultaneously. The researcher will be helped if he thinks about constructs as processes initiated by stimuli and affected by the context and the state of the person, processes that lead to products he can observe and record. Similarly, measuring procedures are schemes for producing processes in subjects. The challenge, the object of the game, is to produce in each subject the process delineated for the construct (by the method of simulated stimuli discussed toward the end of Chapter 6) or a process that has *a priori* relation to that process. A process is harder to think about than a fixed attribute of an object or person or a permanently recorded response on a piece of paper. But processes with antecedent conditions of external or internal stimuli (both focal and background) and consequent effects on S's experience or behavior provide the content of the personality phenomena we seek to understand, and in fact yield the content of all phenomena in psychology.

Even the most highly motivated researcher may be discouraged by the magnitude of the task when he contemplates the systematic and comprehensive study of a single concept that the literature indicates is important. He can maintain his morale by setting more modest, intermediate goals for himself. Within the broad domain of the general construct that intrigues him, he can select a small part, a subconstruct referring to one form of the process occurring under conditions that are easy to create and modify. For example, he might choose to study dominating behavior between pairs of peers who did not know each other before entering the experimental room. He might limit himself just to the internal-cognitive variety of novelty-seeking. The structure of science is built on the work of many people, each making his own contribution by doing his own thing in his own way.

For the craftsman applying his competences to his task, what methodology is available to him? Following consideration of that topic, let us review the sequential steps that are involved in measuring a personality construct today.

Methodologies

EMPIRICAL APPROACHES

One technique for developing measuring procedures has been thoroughly tried, tested, and refined: the group difference method. For instance, the Strong Vocational Interest Blank has keys for many vocations, each key being based on responses that differentiated those in the vocation from those in other vocations. Similarly, the MMPI has clinical scales based on responses distinguishing patients with a particular psychopathological diagnosis from normal people.

In each instance, the score obtained with such a key is taken to indicate the degree to which the subject resembles the criterion group. The method has also been used widely in applied work; for example, in personnel selection, one can determine which responses made at the time of application for a job or for a training program are given more frequently by persons who are later successful than by those who fail later, and then use that set of responses for a key to predict the likelihood of success for future applicants.

This actuarial technique is not quite as simple as it sounds. It has been found necessary to check or cross-validate the key derived from one pair of groups by applying it to another pair. If this is not done, one may find that the key includes items that are unique to the original groups, as a function of sampling fluctuations, rather than typical of the populations from which these samples were drawn. It is also true that the method is never fully effective. Under favorable conditions, it can be used to identify a small group with high probability of falling in the criterion group (e.g., those who will be successful at the job); yet it will contribute little to the prediction of the later classification of many other subjects. Part of the difficulty lies in the content used: the groups originally identified as high or low on the criterion are ordinarily different from each other in several respects, such as particular abilities, interests, motivations, and background or biographical data, and it may not be possible to devise instruments that include all relevant dimensions.

When our interest is in a construct, this empirical method can be employed only when it is possible to identify clear-cut criterion groups, such as those definitely high or low on the construct. In other words, if we already have a measuring procedure (diagnostic judgment, employer rating, or expert appraisal) which differentiates such extreme groups, we can use this method to develop a more economical but less effective instrument with some criterion-related validity (see Chapter 8). Under some conditions, the method may be useful as a starting point. For example, Binet originally validated his innovative scales for intelligence by comparing the responses with teacher ratings. After further work on the construction and refinement of intelligence tests, such a criterion was no longer used. It was apparent that the improved tests were more accurate measures of the target abilities than the judgments of the teachers.

Another important empirical method is factor analysis. This is a complex mathematical method of identifying a few abstract dimensions that will account for much of the observed correlation among a set of scores or other measurements. For example, a set of tests that includes some with verbal content and some with quantitative or numerical content might yield two broad factors, one for each type of content. Tests using words tend to correlate with each other more highly than they do with tests using numbers, the latter in turn correlating highly among themselves. The scholastic aptitude tests given for admission to college usually yield a verbal score and a mathematical or quantitative score.

Verbal ability is not, however, homogeneous. If a set of verbal tests is factor-analyzed, one may obtain several factors: vocabulary knowledge, verbal fluency (ability to think of words rapidly), memory for words seen, ability to reason with words, etc. The factors actually obtained from a factor analysis depend on many things. Primarily they are a function of the variables included in the analysis. E.g., unless a factor is represented by at least two and usually three or more of the tests or other variables being analyzed, it cannot be identified. The findings also depend on the form of factor analysis used; over the past decades, several technical approaches to the problem have been devised, usually serving somewhat separate purposes or answering different questions (see Nunnally, 1967, Chapters 9 and 10; Harman, 1960). If one assumes that the factors themselves may be correlated, it is possible to analyze tests so that correlated factors can emerge, with the correlations between them then being subjected to a second analysis to identify second-order factors. Anxiety often emerges as such a factor.

Figure 12.1 will give the reader some idea of the products of a factor analysis. The data are extracted from an analysis of the staff ratings in the assessment study (Kelly and Fiske, 1951) discussed in the preceding chapter. The analysis (Fiske, 1949) yielded five factors, of which three are shown in the figure. Factor B was labeled "conformity," Factor C was called "emotional control," and Factor D the "inquiring intellect," the names being created to identify what appeared to be the cores of the factors. The variables with high loadings on Factor B were Conscientious, Serious, and Trustful (numbers 17, 5, and 9, respectively). Those high on Factor C were Unshakable Poise, Placid, and Self-Sufficient (numbers 7, 16, and 15). The two high on Factor D are Imaginative and Broad Interests.

The reader with good aptitude for visualizing in three dimensions can imagine a three-dimensional representation of these two-dimensional figures. Imagine a third axis running out from the origin in the upper left figure, at a

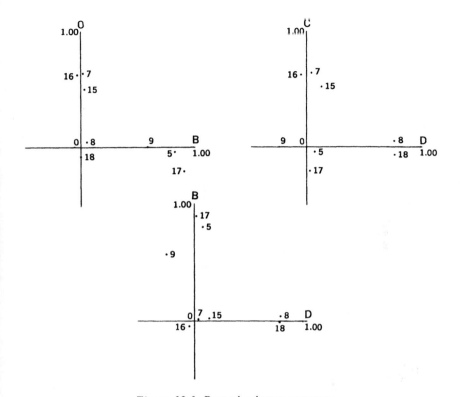

Figure 12.1. Part of a factor structure

right angle to the page, with variables 8 and 18 close to it, toward its end. This structure would then depict all three factors simultaneously.

This figure was drawn to provide a relatively clear picture: if the positions of the other fourteen variables had been indicated, the results would not have appeared so neat. It is hoped, however, that these data will indicate how the correlations among variables can be analyzed to obtain abstract dimensions based on what the variables have in common.

Factor analysis can be used for a fishing expedition, for purely exploratory work aimed simply at seeing what factors will appear. Such strictly empirical work rarely contributes to clarification of concepts. It is usually much more profitable to design studies with some tentative expectations or hypotheses based on preliminary theorizing or capitalizing on interpretations of prior research. For instance, one can factor analyze a multitrait-multimethod matrix by the special technique devised by Jackson (1969) to determine whether the several scores for each trait do relate to the same factor, as one would obviously assume they should. Factor analysis can also be used to determine which miniature scales belong together in higher order, more comprehensive variables, and to examine overlaps of empirical variables developed by various investigators (e.g., Comrey and Jamison, 1966; Comrey and Duffy, 1968).

There are a number of types of factor analysis, as well as techniques with somewhat similar objectives, such as cluster analysis (Tryon and Bailey, in press). Very promising is three-mode factor analysis for dealing not only with persons and stimuli but also with a third mode such as situations or observers (Tucker, 1964). Methods for isolating types or clusters of persons (e.g., McQuitty, 1968) also have their utility. Several techniques, including canonical regression analysis, were used in a study of the comparability of the Rorschach and Holtzman inkblot techniques (see Chapter 1 and Bock and Haggard, 1963). A number of other techniques for statistical analysis or for hypothesis-testing can also be employed in building and refining measuring instruments. Each of this wide range of methods was, of course, designed for a particular objective other than the strategy advocated in this book. Yet, as suggested in preceding paragraphs, they can often serve this strategy.

During his training, the serious student of measurement becomes familiar with the existence and functions of these various techniques; subsequently, from intensive study, he acquires a deeper understanding, and from practical experience with their application he develops sound judgment about their relevance and applicability to particular problems.

PSYCHOMETRIC TECHNIQUES

A few psychometric concepts and methods were sketched in Chapter 8. While psychometrics and test theory are among the more highly developed aspects of psychology, the concerns of such work were rather narrow during the first decades. Attention was concentrated on the analysis of test responses almost to the exclusion of other topics (see the comprehensive presentation of classical test theory in Gulliksen's *Theory of Mental Tests,* 1950). While such work continues (Lord and Novick, 1968), the emphasis has more recently been extended in both directions. In *A Theory of Data,* Coombs (1964) analyzes in formal terms the kinds of tasks that can be given to subjects, the kinds of data obtained, and techniques suitable for working with each. Although validity had always been of much concern, the concept was first analyzed systematically by the committee producing the *Technical Recommendations for Psychological Tests and Diagnostic Techniques* (American Psychological Association *et al.,* 1954), and was further elucidated in the subsequent *Standards for Educational and Psychological Tests and Manuals* (American Psychological Association *et al.,* 1966). Two members of the first committee, Cronbach and Meehl, published the invaluable paper on construct validity (1955; see the section on it in Chapter 8) which made explicit the basic steps in allowing a test and a construct to affect each other by carefully planned validational research. A few years later, Campbell and Fiske (1959) demonstrated the necessity of establishing convergence or agreement between measures of the same trait by different methods. This volume is, in essence, aimed at further development of methodology for validational work, i.e., for linking even more closely the instrument and the construct. Most of the entire range of psychometric concepts and techniques can be brought to bear, at one point or another, on this problem.

The Measurement of a Construct

To indicate where personality measurement is today, let us outline a program that can be followed by an investigator seeking to develop highly satisfactory procedures for research involving a particular construct. Note that, even though such work is primarily instrumental in that it is intended to provide means for a more distant goal of testing propositions about constructs, the endeavor must be recognized as programmatic: an adequate instrument cannot be devised and tested completely in a single study or a few weeks. In the philosophy of science, it has been stated that a science progresses as a function of advances in instrumentation and measurement. The researcher who is discouraged by the work necessary to develop adequate measuring procedures can take heart in the realization that the quality of his later experimentation (and that of others) will be greatly enhanced by his effort devoted to developing and refining instruments.

The preceding paragraph implies that the available techniques for measuring personality are not satisfactory. While such an evaluation is a judgment on which qualified people may differ, there is close to unanimous agreement that what is available is not completely satisfactory, even for the concepts on which the most research has been done.

To a large extent, this section will bring together and organize a number of topics considered separately in earlier chapters. It will be an attempt to fit the pieces together.

CONSTRUCTS, PERSPECTIVES, AND MODES

The starting point is the conceptualization of the target construct, the topic of Chapter 6. No matter how well the investigator thinks he knows his construct, he must prepare a full and explicit statement about it, for himself and others. In doing so, he will find that there are many aspects of the construct and its conceptual surround which he has not examined carefully before. This framework is, of course, not to be seen as a definitive, fixed, and final formulation. Unlike an architect's blueprint, which the contractor is expected to follow precisely, it is more a sketch of the terrain to be explored, a sketch that is as detailed and as accurate as his insight and available empirical knowledge can make it, and which will be modified as further information and insights are obtained.

An early decision concerns the perspective or perspectives that are pertinent. Is the construct embedded in a theory with the perspective that a person's personality is his social stimulus value? If so, ratings by others and observations of present behavior are the relevant modes to be used (Modes 4 and 5). Does the construct refer to motivation of which the subject is typically unaware? Perhaps it is part of psychoanalytic thinking or some other dynamic theory. If so, the most useful perspective will be that of the expert observer, and the observations will fall in Mode 5. Suitable modes are related to the perspectives selected.

Each of the modes has its strength and weaknesses. Mode 1 (reports of Self Description) is so widely used because it is economical and convenient. It also has the merit of being a direct approach to the person's views of himself and his behavior. It is therefore the mode of choice for studying constructs within self-perception. Its numerous potential liabilities have been detailed in many places in this book. They center around the likelihood that S's report will be determined in part by his reaction to the situation of making such a report, i.e., to the act of stating his perceptions. Other limitations involve S's individualistic interpretations of items.

Mode 2 (reports of Current Experiencing) has the advantage that the experiencing can be made so vivid that it is easy for S to respond appropriately. In most instances, the design and content of the procedure can be selected so that S will not experience any apprehensiveness about being tested and can cooperate fully with the examiner. It has the limitation that the substance of some constructs do not readily permit them to be studied by use of this mode. It is better for characteristics of perceiving, cognizing, and valuing than for attributes of performance or capacity.

The full potentialities of this mode have not been determined. While some may feel that asking a person about his usual behavior or feelings (as in Mode 1) will yield more dependable and useful information, it may be that we can obtain more standardized and pertinent responses by asking a subject to imagine a set of conditions and tell what he would feel or be inclined to do. The latter approach (Mode 2) may be easier and less threatening for the subject.

Mode 3 includes measures of Capabilities. It shows what the person can do under favorable circumstances. It is clearly the best mode for that important but restricted set of constructs referring to abilities and optimal cognitive functioning. It can only set an upper limit for estimating the sub-

ject's level of performance in everyday circumstances, with their distractions, conflicting motivations, and assorted other influences.

The great advantage of Mode 4 (Prior Behavior) is based on its defining
characteristic: measurements can be made on the basis of behavior that
the subject does not know will be used for this purpose. It is limited by
the fact that prior products may not be relevant to the construct being
studied and the fact that reports from others are always based on restricted
types of observation. A wife does not ordinarily observe her husband at
work and a supervisor does not observe him at play.

Indices from Mode 5 are based on the subject's responses while coping
with meaningful and more or less realistic tasks, such as an interview, a
projective technique, or a situational test, as in a leaderless group discussion. The distinguishing feature of this mode is that the final scores or measurements are based on judgments, usually by experts who have directly
observed the subject's behavior during these tasks. Its main advantage is
that it can be used to measure constructs that require considerable sophistication on the part of the observer or rater. Another advantage is the
possibility of making the tasks realistic and meaningful for the subject,
so that he becomes deeply involved. For example, the OSS assessment program used a "construction test" in which the subject was assigned the task
of directing two men who were actually staff members playing assigned
roles (Office of Strategic Services Assessment Staff, 1948). In spite of the
patent artificiality of the conditions and in spite of the observers sitting
nearby, the personal interactions with the stooges could not be treated ca-
sually by the subject.

The disadvantages are of two kinds. To some degree that may be hard
to assess, the subject's behavior is determined by his awareness of the fact
that he is being measured. It is also true that each observer or rater is to
some extent a unique measuring instrument and his ratings will agree only
fairly closely, and never perfectly, with those of another rater. Note that
the observed sample of behavior is long enough so that it includes a number of specific acts; the rater has to arrive at a single value for each attribute which combines the information in each of the various behaviors.

The advantage of Mode 6 is that psychophysiological indices are essentially beyond the voluntary control of the subject. The disadvantages are
of three kinds. Physiological recordings are lengthy and laborious to score.
Such reactions have individual patterning: one subject may react to anxiety
with pronounced palmar sweating, another with sharp acceleration of heart-
beat, and a third by change in respiration. Perhaps more serious is the
question whether it is possible to distinguish more than a few broad kinds
of reaction, such as pleasure or positive interest, anxiety or apprehension,
preparation for coping with stress, and preparation for action.

At the present stage of progress in personality measurement, it seems essential to work separately with indices from different modes. The concepts of perspective and mode are based on the postulated and empirically supported assertion that the different views and modes of observation yield qualitatively different information. As a usual practice, and at least until experimental findings indicate otherwise, the researcher should process and interpret data from each mode as distinct from, though possibly somewhat related to, data from other modes.

Within a mode, the investigator should ordinarily use more than one procedure. If he has no conceptual reason for treating the several scores for his construct as separate aspects, he may wish to pool them to arrive at some kind of composite score. Different methods of pooling such scores can be adapted from the models for combining item scores in the early part of Chapter 8.

Steps in Developing and Evaluating a Measuring Procedure

In this section we shall outline the several steps by which an investigator can check out the procedure he is developing, to determine its adequacy and potential weaknesses. Having conceptualized his construct explicitly (see Chapter 6), he has selected an appropriate class of observations among the six modes considered in Chapter 5. Usually he will have developed his measure to index one or more elements within a facet of his subconstruct. From the theoretical context of his construct, he will also have derived experimental propositions to be tested empirically, statements that take into account the perspective (see Chapter 4) he has selected as most suitable to that context. His goal is to create a measuring procedure that is optimal for testing the propositions, since it has maximum congruence with the designated subconstruct.

For convenience, we shall talk as if he were working on only one measure at a time, even though he may be simultaneously developing two or more procedures from one mode and may even be constructing procedures using other modes. In view of the pervasiveness of the test specificity examined in Chapter 11, such coordinated attacks seem essential and, in the long run, economical. In some instances, the ambitious investigator with substantial assistance and resources may wish to work on parts of two constructs concurrently, especially if both can be measured by appropriate items combined in a single instrument. If so, he must be careful not to spread his attention too thin so that the quality of his methods suffers through oversight.

Each of the following steps requires a decision about the answer to a question.

1. CONTENT VALIDITY

Is the content of the test appropriate to the specified construct? Are the items of the kind specified in the formulation of the construct, or explicated in deductions from that construct which have been made as guides to operationalizing it? While it may seem quite unnecessary to review the content in this way, this step is spelled out here because it is all too easy to shift one's attention from descriptions of pertinent behavior in the everyday world to content convenient for use in tests. Thinking about such concrete illustrations, the investigator or experimenter (E) may overlook any qualitative changes unwittingly introduced. While the evaluation of content validity is the responsibility of E, he should obtain the judgments of qualified associates on this matter. They will often point out difficulties or omissions overlooked by him. Ultimately, he expects his conceptualization and his instrument to be understood by others and accepted by them. It is well for him to seek consensual agreement at this early stage (see also Chapter 8).

2. PROCESS VALIDITY

When each subject takes the test, does he use the process intended by E? Recall that within the general process of coping with E's expectation that S will complete the test, there are shorter processes associated with each item. S encounters the item, perceives and interprets it, reacts to that interpretation, and then selects and marks his response. In Chapter 6 it was noted that the process intended by E may be one of three kinds: a process with simulated stimuli, in which the test elicits the same process as that specified in the conceptualization (e.g., S perceives the stimulus as he perceives similar stimuli outside the testing room and utilizes a broad class to categorize it); an *a priori* related process in which, for instance, S shows he knows the meaning of a word now, from which E can infer that he went through a process of acquiring and retaining that meaning at an earlier time; or an empirically related process, as in answering an item in the way that those with interest in a particular vocation have been found to answer it.

Given the kind of process intended, one must also consider the specific form of the process. For multiplication items, E expects S to perform the arithmetical operations and then mark the answer he obtains. With preference for designs, E expects S to decide which appeals more to him. For a question about how he behaves in a particular situation, E expects S to recall some instances and answer accordingly.

But suppose that, instead of carrying out the arithmetical operation, S makes a rough calculation and guesses; or he may consistently mark the second figure in each pair of designs; or he may restrict the situations he considers in some way. Such subjects are not experiencing the process that E intended. In the first case, E may be able to detect it by including alternatives that are approximately right (e.g., which other subjects give when asked to estimate the answer very quickly and approximately). With the designs, E can readily detect that S's regularity of response is unrelated to any parameter (such as complexity) which he built into the items. The determination of S's process on a questionnaire item is much more difficult: E must somehow inquire of S just what he did, and S may not be able to recall well (see Chapter 10). One partial solution is to have a group of subjects indicate which items they could not answer readily and perhaps also time their responses unobtrusively—longer times usually indicating some problem in interpreting the question or in selecting the answer.

If there appears to be some opportunity for response sets to intrude (see Chapter 10), E should score the tests for such sets. He can, for example, determine whether there are systematic individual differences in the number of "yes" responses chosen. While he should, of course, have designed his tests to control for such possible biases, he should also check the effectiveness of such efforts.

3. INTERJUDGE AGREEMENT

Is the agreement between scorers sufficiently high? When the scoring requires human judgment, as in all free-response tests (in which S produces his own response content rather than checking a choice presented to him), the reliability of the scoring must be established, as pointed out in Chapter 8. Ideally, the scoring procedure should be sufficiently explicit so that any qualified judge can code or score the responses with a high degree of objectivity and agreement with other scorers.

It is also necessary to determine the agreement between raters when Modes 4 and 5 are used. How closely do others agree on their perceptions of S, based either on his past behavior or his behavior in a current testing situation? Experts must agree closely with each other; less agreement need be demanded of lay raters in Mode 4. Low agreement between raters may not require E to discard his procedure if he can use enough ratings so that the average rating itself has satisfactory reliability. Under such circumstances, however, E should ponder the implications stemming from marked individuality in the ratings. Is the variable poorly defined? Does the rating require too large an inferential leap? Do the raters stress different clues or evidence?

4. HOMOGENEITY

If the score is based on responses to several items, to what extent do the items measure the same thing in each subject and to what extent do the subjects' patterns of response indicate that the items have similar meanings for them? Several homogeneity indices were discussed in Chapter 8. If it is evident that the generalizability of the test is not satisfactory, E can examine the item-test correlations and other data, eliminating poor items and perhaps adding new ones. He may want to factor the items to see whether some are associated with some small, unwanted factor.

Some complementarity between steps 3 and 4 can be seen. In considering interjudge agreement, each judge is in a sense an item: each provides a subscore that is combined with others to obtain the final score, and the concern is with agreement or correlation between such subscores.

5. STABILITY

E should obtain data on the stability of the scores derived from his procedure so that he can judge whether the degree of this stability corresponds to what was anticipated in the conceptualization of the construct (see Chapter 9). To refer again to the most clear-cut illustration, a measure of mood should not be completely stable from day to day. Too high stability should suggest that the responses were determined not by mood but perhaps by some reaction to the situation, such as an interpretation that others may think it is undesirable to have a number of moods, and especially undesirable to feel discouraged or depressed. In contrast, too low stability for a measure of ability might suggest that the test was too difficult for most of the subjects, and they had to guess frequently. If E finds the stability of his measure is not congruent with his expectations, he may revise his thinking about the construct. More likely, the difficulty lies in the instrument, and he should seek another way to measure the construct.

These five steps in evaluating a measuring procedure use primarily the responses obtained by that procedure itself. E examines only the consistency of part scores from items, the agreement between scores from separate scorers or judges, or the congruence between content and construct and between observed and expected stability. The next four steps consider agreement or convergence between the measure under study and measures for the same general construct.

6. CONVERGENCE OVER MEASURING CONDITIONS

Are the conditions suitable for the construct? In developing a test, E ordinarily decides in advance what conditions are most appropriate for its administration. This may be all that is feasible for E: it may be quite difficult to determine empirically what set of conditions is optimal. E should give the matter serious consideration. It may be that the test can be used only under special circumstances. Certainly an obvious measure of antisocial tendencies cannot be given profitably in a situation where a superior known to S requires him to sign his answer sheet. Again, a measure of creativity or of productivity of ideas may need to have a context in which S feels relaxed and at ease with E, perhaps without any felt need to achieve well, to compete, and certainly without any fears of being evaluated.

On the other hand, is there anything detrimental about the conditions used? This question can be answered only by administering the procedure under several sets of conditions to obtain evidence as to the effects of the conditions and the set that seems to work out best.

7. CONVERGENCE OVER FORMAT

To what extent are the obtained scores affected by the format used? Does the measure correlate highly with measures using the same or very similar content but different response alternatives? E.g., "yes" and "no" might be compared with "yes," "uncertain," and "no." In ratings, an unbroken line with only the ends labeled might be compared with six graduated steps, each one defined in words. It is rather expensive and difficult to make empirical comparisons between various pairs of possible formats. E should, however, study what has been learned about various formats so that he can at least make an informed decision about the one he will use. Moreover, if his measure is found to have inadequate indices of homogeneity or stability, he may want to reconsider the format employed. (Curiously, there is no standard text integrating the scattered studies on format and other topics involved in constructing personality tests. The discussion of rating scales in Guilford's *Psychometric Methods* [1954, Chapter 11] has points that the thoughtful reader can apply in work on other techniques.)

8. CONVERGENCE WITHIN MODE

Does the measure agree closely with other measures of the construct using the same mode? The only available data may be those collected by E with other measures he has devised; it is unlikely that any available measure developed by others will be aimed at exactly the same construct. Correlations between tests with the same label were examined in Chapter 11. In view of the specificity so rampant among personality tests, E can have no confidence that his test does not suffer from such specificity unless he demonstrates its correlations with other measures from the same mode. This, of course, is a major reason for developing several measures of a construct concurrently.

9. CONVERGENCE BETWEEN MODES

If E has some expectations about the degree of agreement among various kinds of observations for his target construct, he will want to determine whether his measures conform to his expectations in this respect. Here is one place where E is likely to change his expectations rather than his measures when his predictions are not confirmed. If his measures are satisfactory by each of the preceding evaluative steps, he may well accept the empirical findings and alter his conceptualization, or he may reserve judgment until further evaluation has taken place.

The final three steps involve correlations with measures of other variables, as in studies of construct validity and of convergent and discriminant validation.

10. DISCRIMINANT VALIDATION WITH CONSTRUCTS FROM THE SAME SUBSTANTIVE AREA

Is the measure differentiated sufficiently from measures of somewhat similar variables? Measures of dominance should be differentiated from measures of aggression or hostility toward others. Affiliation or desire to share with others would ordinarily be construed as separate from dependence upon others. When E has developed measures of several somewhat similar traits, he should determine the degree to which they are differentiated both within any one general type of technique (such as questionnaires) and across different techniques from the same mode (e.g., within Mode 1, questionnaires, adjective checklists, and ranking procedures). His analysis can be based on a multitrait-multimethod matrix in which all scores from all methods are intercorrelated (see Chapter 8).

Unfortunately, E may not have measures meeting his needs optimally. He will probably have to use his own measures of his construct together with measures of other constructs developed by other people. The possible difficulty here is that there may be format or other differences among his measures and others', such differences producing better apparent discrimination than that which he would obtain if each of several constructs were measured by each of several procedures, each procedure being the same for the several constructs it measured, except for obvious differences in content.

If E is simultaneously developing measures for several elements within a facet of his subconstruct, he will want to demonstrate appropriate discriminations among them. This is a demanding requirement that may be more difficult to meet than many of the others. It is, however, essential if the subscores, the indices for elements, are to be considered separately. (See the account in Butt and Fiske, 1968, of partial success in differentiating the elements in a behavioral facet for dominance.)

11. DISCRIMINANT VALIDATION WITH CONSTRUCTS OF OTHER KINDS

One part of construct validation is establishing that a measure does not correlate too highly with measures of other constructs. In Step 10, such measures were conceptually similar ones. Here the question is: Is the measure sufficiently independent of quite different variables that often confound personality measurement? Measures derived from such free-response products as TAT stories should ordinarily be designed to be unrelated to vocabulary and verbal fluency. Measures of interest in an area as reflected in knowledge of facts about it should be minimally related to measures of memory and other aspects of intelligence. (See Campbell, 1960.)

E will often not have an exact prediction for the relationship between his construct and some other potentially confounding one. He should nevertheless obtain the correlation between his measure and each of a number of standard variables: measures of various kinds of intelligence, of education, socioeconomic status, sex, and perhaps such common response sets as acquiescence and social desirability.

12. CONSTRUCT VALIDATION

The final and major evaluation of a measure is the assessment of its construct validation (see Chapter 8): Does the measure have the pattern of correlations with measures of other variables which was predicted in the conceptualization of the construct as embedded in a theoretical framework with other constructs? If the obtained pattern is quite unlike the expected one, there is probably something wrong with the design of the measure. It may have been evaluated favorably in each of the preceding steps, and yet be defective because of some error in its original conception. If the predicted relationships are found for some variables but not for others, the difficulty may lie in the measure, in the conceptualizaiton, or even in the measurement of the other variables. It is unfortunately true that we have no starting point on which to build. We devise our procedures as well as we can, and then must evaluate them against other measurements that may have their own weaknesses. If we predict our construct to be related to anxiety, which one or ones of the dozens of anxiety tests should we use? I.e., which one best represents the concept of anxiety involved in our theoretical framework? Perhaps no one measure is fully appropriate. Perhaps some combination of scores can be formed to represent that concept.

When a study of construct validity produces generally negative findings, the entire design of the research must be reexamined critically. Were the testing conditions appropriate? Was an appropriate population sampled? We often theorize implicitly about a particular segment of mankind, such as people with backgrounds similar to our own. Limiting our attention to a specified group is quite desirable, provided we make this restriction explicit so that it enters our thinking and can be communicated to others. Trouble arises when we unwittingly theorize about one group and then attempt to confirm our predictions on a different group.

The research trainee should know that research studies rarely yield exactly the predicted findings. If the researcher suspects that the results were somehow affected by the population of subjects sampled, he can select a more appropriate population. If some predictions are upheld and others are not, the researcher will obviously examine the latter. He may decide that his measures of the theoretically related variables are unsuitable for the particular application, and design a subsequent study with other measures of those variables. He will certainly want to reexamine his predictions very critically: Was he correct in predicting that his construct as measured by the measure on which he has worked so long should be related to these other concepts as indexed by the measures employed? In effect, he must devote some attention to the conceptualization and operationalization of these other variables.

Clearly, the wise investigator will not confine himself to just one measure of his construct at a time. The discussion in this section has been presented in such terms solely for clarity of exposition. As noted at the outset, the desirable strategy is to work concurrently on two or more distinct measures of the target construct. Ordinarily only a little extra effort is involved in utilizing such multiple measures, and the potential advantages are great. For example, multiple measures permit determination of extrinsic convergent validation from comparisons of profiles for relationships with outside variables, of the kind examined in Chapter 11. If no measure of the target construct correlates appreciably with any of the outside variables as measured, then the difficulty is likely to reside in the conceptualization and the inferred relationships. If one measure shows fair to good construct validation and the others do not, then E may consider refining and modifying his hypothesized relationships to specify that they hold for one aspect of his construct (the one measured by the successful procedure), and not for the aspects measured by the other procedures.

The researcher may find that none of his several measures for the target construct show any association with one outside variable. If so, the fault lies either in the prediction or in the measure of the outside variable. The patterning in the other results may suggest where the trouble lies.

The active reader may have seen that running through these comments on identifying the reasons for failure to confirm predictions there is the fundamental scientific notion of consistency. Science is always searching for consistencies. In the present context, the regularity may be the overall conformity among the relationships obtained for a given measure, or their regular intransigence about coming out in the desired way. The consistency may be among the patterns of findings for the several measures of the target construct. Even when some predictions are confirmed and others are not, E will certainly want to see what is common to the first set, what to the second, and how they differ. Of course, the more critical kind of consistency is between findings from similar studies, especially when conducted quite independently by separate researchers. When E tries to diagnose the ailment of his latest studies, he is really making a prognosis of his findings in the next study of that series.

Construct validational work proceeds from one study to another, programmatically. After E has carried out his first study and interpreted his findings, he will want to change some things and execute another study. He may alter his research plan and use the same measures again. He may modify his conceptual framework and predict relationships with other variables. If he modifies his picture of his construct, he will have to develop new measures or modifications of his original ones. In this way, concepts guide empirical research and experimental findings alter concepts. This interaction is the essence of science. Yet it cannot be effective unless measuring procedures are well coordinated, if not closely congruent, with the concepts being studied.

Summary

To measure individual differences on a personality construct, three criteria must be met: (1) the measure must yield responses determined primarily by an important construct, (2) the responses must vary over people, and (3) the responses must serve well to characterize each person. The problem in measurement is to satisfy all three of these criteria simultaneously. While pairs of these criteria can be met, it is difficult to meet all three in the testing room. Practical and economic requirements must also be considered.

The comprehensive and fully adequate measurement of a whole concept in current personality theory is an awesome task. Most such concepts are complex and can be analyzed into subconstructs for pertinent modes of observation, each such subconstruct subsuming others that designate separate manifestations and situational aspects. A feasible objective for the individual investigator is the delineation and measurement of some integral portion of this total framework. At the investigator's command are empirical methodologies that may at times be helpful, as well as psychometric and statistical methods that are quite powerful when used with understanding.

In the development of a measure for a construct, a number of evaluative hurdles must be leaped. The measure must obviously have appropriate content. It must elicit in subjects the process we intend: the subject must go about his task in the way we expect. The scoring must be reliable. If raters or judges are used, they must agree closely with each other. The measure must be internally consistent: from indices of homogeneity and generalizability, we must be able to demonstrate that the several items are measuring the same variable. Measures or scores must have appropriate stability over trials. The procedure should be administered under optimal conditions; at the least, we should have some information about the effects of the conditions on the scores. The format should be appropriate and not bias the measurements. Ordinarily, we may seek agreement with other measures of the construct that use the same mode, though we are likely to be disappointed here. Agreement with measures from different modes should also be examined. The measure should discriminate the target construct from similar constructs. Its scores should not have sizable contributions from irrelevant variables: intelligence and verbal facility are usually not seen as pertinent. Finally, we hope that the measure will have a pattern of correlations with other variables somewhat similar to the profile predicted from our prior conceptualization. Discrepancies between the obtained and the expected must be studied to determine what must be changed: The theory? The construct? The measure? The design for the empirical research on validity of the construct?

While much effort is required to develop a measure approaching these high standards, the labor is unavoidable. If personology is to advance, we must improve the quality of our measuring procedures.

CHAPTER THIRTEEN

Prospects and Issues

"What's Past is Prologue"

After a brief look at the history of personality measurement, this book has examined the content of the field today. It has indicated what is available to the investigator pursuing basic research in personology. It has considered methodological concepts, techniques, and tools, and the diverse kinds of measuring procedures that are available. A major emphasis has been placed on what can and should be done, with exhortations to researchers to roll up their sleeves and do it. An underlying objective has been to challenge investigators in personology to avoid the path of least resistance, the easy tactical decision to accept some term current in conceptual thinking as if it were an adequate scientific construct and to employ accessible measuring procedures simply because others have used them and they seem rather applicable to the investigation being planned.

This chapter will consider the prospects ahead for measurement in personology. What are the directions in which progress will be made? Any such prediction entails the classical dynamic of wishful thinking: the prognosticator prophesies that which he hopes will happen. Would that the phenomenon of self-fulfilling prophecy should also occur!

Following the discussion of prospects, we shall examine some of the issues whose resolution cannot be foreseen. In view of what has been achieved to date, personology is distinctly a young science. We hope we can appropriately consider it well beyond infancy and carefree preschool days; it is a child entering adolescence, beginning to introspect, to be self-conscious. We trust it will cope maturely with this developmental task.

Several basic notions have been presented and examined in the preceding chapters: personality phenomena as processes, the value of full delineation of constructs, the specificity of behaviors and observations, and perspectives and modes as integral components in measurements. Another thesis has been the contribution of the data producer, especially the aware and reactive subject. A brief recapitulation at this point will serve as a framework within which the prospects for the future can be considered.

Figure 13.1 is a schematic view of personality measurement. Central in it is the ongoing stream of processes within a person which provide not only the phenomena that personology seeks to understand but also the particular phenomena used in empirical observations. On the upper side are the observations of actions resulting from this stream of processes. It is these observations as stored in the memories of those interacting with the subject or as concretized in physical artifacts that provide the basis for measuring in Mode 4 (observations of Prior Behavior) and the indices obtained from its procedures.

On the lower side of the figure, another approach to measurement is schematized. It is intended to indicate the features common to the other five modes of observation, and hence may not optimally represent each of these procedures. (The arrows indicate some major directions of effects.)

E has a general construct he wishes to investigate. From this construct, he extracts a subconstruct, such as the construct as it can be observed by an appropriate mode. Within that mode, he designs a measuring procedure to yield indices of some element or elements within a facet of the subconstruct. In application to our subject, the setting and the instructions impinge on S, affecting the stream of processes, which in turn affect the way he perceives the stimuli. The stimuli as he experiences and interprets them initiate processes that, among other effects, influence his perception of the response alternatives, which then influence the response recorded for measuring purposes. The data producer may be S himself or another person as O. From these data, indices are obtained in some one of the ways considered in earlier chapters.

The figure is, of course, incomplete in several respects. It does not, for example, depict the naturally occurring stimuli that impinge constantly on S. Also, there is no attempt to indicate the state of the subject, either as it naturally occurs or as it has been affected by prior manipulations of E. (In this discussion, the term "natural," as opposed to "experimental," refers to aspects of the interactions that are not produced by E.)

Prospects

One prospect ahead of us is the further development and utilization of these basic notions. This prediction is based on current trends. Starting

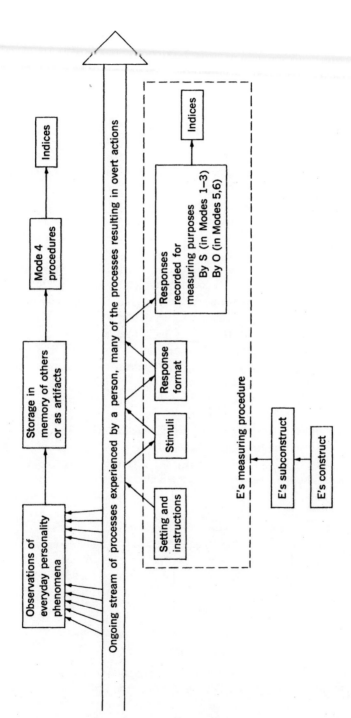

Figure 13.1. A schematic view of personality measurement

with the bottom of the figure, the notions of perspectives and modes are gaining prevalence. Five modes used in attitude measurement have been identified (Cook and Selltiz, 1964). Emmerich (1966) considers the processes characterizing appraisals of personality, each total process or perspective involving a transactional relation between the observer and the observed. (His use of process and of perspective differ somewhat from mine.) For the study of the whole life span, Neugarten states the necessity of using two perspectives: that of the clinical psychologist, who "tries to put himself into the frame of reference of his . . . client and to see the world through that person's eyes," and that of the observer, who "brings his own frame of reference to the data and interprets according to his own theories" (Neugarten, 1969, p. 129). The necessity of plural perspectives in evaluating psychotherapeutic change is becoming generally accepted (see Fiske *et al.,* 1970).

The need for better conceptual specification is being reiterated (for some recent references, see Fiske and Pearson, 1970). As one aspect, the compound or even heterogeneous nature of common substantive concepts is receiving explicit theoretical and empirical attention. While it is particularly true for such global terms as "creativity" (Jackson and Messick, 1965; Tryk, 1968) and "anxiety" (McReynolds, 1968), it is not limited to these. The empirical dissection, by factor analysis or other techniques, of almost any personality instrument, especially questionnaires, yields relatively distinct dimensions within the domain of the trait at which the total instrument was originally aimed.

The prospect of increasingly more systematic analysis and delineation of concepts is certainly desirable and to be encouraged. Without suitable concepts, we cannot have useful theory. It has been stated that a highly developed body of theory is necessary for fruitful measurement in the physical sciences (Kuhn, 1961). Systematic theory is equally necessary for fruitful measurement in the social sciences. Such measurement leads to dependable empirical generalizations and to definitive testing of theoretical propositions, permitting an appraisal of the understanding provided by the theories.

Another prospect is for closer coordination of concepts and measurements (represented in Figure 13.1 by the arrow between the boxes for subconstruct and measuring procedure). Up to perhaps the early 1950s, personality workers fell into two groups: the giant theorists and the toilers in the psychometric vineyard. Subsequently there have been those who are at home in both realms. George Kelly (1955) constructed his own approach to measurement compatible with his theoretical position. Dynamic psychologists with training in experimentation are devising techniques and measuring procedures for studying cognitive behavior as part of reality contact (e.g., Holzman, 1966). Experts in pure measurement are applying their skills to the construction of methods for measuring important theoretical variables (e.g., Loevinger, 1966, Gleser in Gottschalk and Gleser, 1969).

INDIRECT MEASURES

There are good prospects for developing methods that are free of subject interaction with the measuring procedure. While most of these follow the scheme indicated at the top of Figure 13.1 representing Mode 4, pupillometry seems to be an exception. The use of pupil size as an index of positive interest (Hess, 1968) was mentioned in Chapter 1. A whole book (Webb *et al.*, 1966) has been devoted to unobtrusive measurement. Indirect methods of assessing personality have been reviewed recently (Hermann, 1968). The picture is more one of promise than of actuality. Many of the possibilities await further replication and confirmation. As with pupil size, a number of techniques appear useful for identifying general variables—such as interest, arousal, tension, or anxiety—but may be less valuable for measuring more narrowly specified concepts. Furthermore, many indirect methods provide signs rather than indices. I.e., they may yield data enabling us to conclude that, in certain subjects, variable X is present in clear and strong form at a particular moment, but the absence of the sign may not justify the inference that X is absent, since X may be manifested in some other way in those in whom the particular sign is missing. Clearly this would involve a set of simultaneous recording procedures (like a polygraph) which can detect the presence of X (say, tension or anxiety) in whatever form it may appear in each of the several subjects. The technical problem of obtaining comparable indices for all subjects from their peaks on profiles of such a battery of measures has not been fully solved.

The future of such indirect measurement is difficult to foretell. We may find that it cannot readily be used in studying most standard constructs, or subconstructs that have been delineated in explicit detail, or constructs whose definition includes a specification of particular stimuli as antecedents for the critical behaviors. In defense of indirect measures, we should note that they have clear methodological advantages and can be based on natural behavior rather than experimentally elicited reactions. Perhaps we shall find that they are excellent as auxiliaries, rather than as major methods coordinate with the more direct techniques, and that they can be used to measure some particular kinds of variables that experimenters must measure, at least as experimental controls.

COLLABORATIVE MEASUREMENT

Consider the opposite extreme of subject awareness. Some subjects try to beat the experimenter by figuring out what he is after and may even try to prevent him from achieving it, at least as far as they personally are concerned. Perhaps we have been drawn unwillingly into playing that game with subjects. One promising direction for the future of personality measurement is eliciting the full collaboration of the subject in the work. We can ask subjects to imagine that they are in a particular situation and to tell us how they would feel and act (as discussed in Chapter 6). The possibility of actually conducting experiments in this fashion has been proposed (Kelman, 1967) and tried out (Greenberg, 1967) with promising results. If psychologists can learn to be comfortable with such strategies and can learn how to enlist the wholehearted cooperation of subjects, they may be able to explore quite effectively some topics that are now difficult to study empirically.

We cannot claim that simulation can replace actuality. I am simply indicating that the possibilities of this type of experimenter-subject relationship have not been adequately investigated. Of course we must expect that simulation can be used most effectively with a rather limited segment of the general population. Yet it may prove fruitful for indicating leads, for revealing confounding influences that were previously unsuspected.

What the future holds with respect to realistic experimental manipulations is uncertain. Some recent work (to be considered later in this chapter) suggests that we can involve subjects in situations that are quite meaningful to them and which provide good approximations to naturally occurring situations. A related possibility is the utilization of more vivid stimuli. Obviously the experimenter must enter such work with great attention to the rights of the subject, with concern about any possibility of harming him in any way. Yet thoughtful investigators may be able to create methodologies that elicit the willing and informed collaboration of subjects and still carefully protect them.

THE EXPERIENCING AND BEHAVING SUBJECT

Another prospect is greater understanding of the measuring process as S experiences it and reacts to it, as suggested in Figure 13.1 Extended discussions earlier in this book delineate the problem and the need for further study of it. To learn about personality phenomena, about the processes within those phenomena that go on in human beings, personologists devise testing procedures and experiments that permit the recording of reactions and behaviors during the brief periods when subjects are in these situations. They believe that an understanding of these particular behaviors will enable them to learn to understand the other behaviors classified within the personality domain.

Yet of course the functioning of subjects in testing situations is not just functioning under more sterile laboratory conditions in which many potential influences are eliminated or at least reduced in strength. It is also experiencing and reacting to the laboratory equipment that imposes constraints on subjects. To use another analogy, subjects in personality testing are like wolves confined in a zoo. On the one hand, they are no longer able to search out and pursue their normal prey; on the other, they react to their keepers and to the visitors who come to view them through the bars of their cages. It is reasonable to expect that personologists can develop intensive knowledge about subjects as they function in the testing room or experimental laboratory. It is less certain how soon they will develop a methodology permitting them to make accurate inferences from these conditions to those of life outside those walls.

Much of the history of personality measurement can be seen as concern with the effects produced by the measurement process itself. Several decades ago, it was recognized that raters tend to rate inaccurately because of the bias introduced by the halo they attribute to subjects. It has long been recognized that subjects might conceal material sought by an interviewer and that subjects can slant their responses to questionnaires to avoid an unfavorable self-portrayal or to effect a positive picture. The conceptualization of response sets and styles more than two decades ago has led to intensive study of them and vigorous debate about the extent of their influence. Certainly personologists should devise or select tests that minimize the possible intrusion of these unwanted variables.

A major development in recent psychology is the recognition that human beings are active organisms, not just entities that react to the application of stimuli. The concept of process has been given much attention in this volume, and this concept carries with it the notion that much is going on within a living person, that a person is in different states at different times. Pertinent to this emphasis and its implications for measurement are some theoretical notions recently proposed in the general literature. Smith (1968*b*, p. 368) has called attention to momentary self-perceptions that may be inconsistent with the more enduring concept of self. Building on a neglected concept of regnant processes introduced by Murray (1938), Klinger (in press, Chapter 7) has developed the idea of regnant subselves in his efforts to conceptualize the process in eliciting fantasy need for achievement. In the same paper he has discussed the concept of current concerns as one potentiating determinant of themes in fantasy, dreams, and play. Such a concern is seen as lasting over periods of time of much greater duration than the brief, almost ephemeral regnancies of the subselves. All of us can recognize such concerns in our own experience: preoccupation with an exam coming up tomorrow; plans for a trip; working through the memory of a disturbing interaction with another person; assimilating the significance of a minor success. These concepts, current concern and subself, refer to that section of the ongoing stream of processes in S (Figure 13 1) taking place while the measuring occurs.

This new line of conceptual work is important not only in its opposition to a strictly behavioral and observational approach to personality, but also because it begins to give us a handhold on the way a person changes from minute to minute, from hour to hour, and from day to day. Beyond the obvious implications for general theory of personality, this work has implications for our understanding of measuring processes that last only a few minutes or perhaps an hour or two. For some purposes, we may wish to tap these current concerns, recognizing full well that they are transitory. But when we are seeking to estimate enduring dispositions in subjects, we must design our measuring procedures to override the effects of these temporary preoccupations. The task and stimuli provided by the test must be preemptive without evoking resistance from the subjects.

The prospect, then, is for a better understanding of S as he is at the moment he enters the measuring situation. He comes in not only with various dispositions, interests, and values that have existed for months, years, or decades, but also with a current mood and with current concerns. Once in the situation and introduced to the requirements of the measuring procedure, he begins to interact with the test and its stimuli. In the future we must develop a better understanding of these brief interactions, going well beyond the initial efforts considered in Chapter 10.

Issues

THE TARGET CONSTRUCTS FOR PERSONALITY MEASUREMENT

This section will consider a number of questions and problems for which the prospective answers are not at all clear. Many of these involve the nature of the constructs at which we aim our measures of personality. The quite human tendency to attribute responsibility to others is very widespread, and hence the personologist concerned with measurement must be cautious about blaming the personality theorists for the present limitations of personality measurement. Undoubtedly both sides have some responsibility for the present state of affairs. Certainly the conceptualization of personality is still in an immature stage of development.

One basic question is the level of abstraction at which nomothetic dimensions of personality should be conceptualized. Broadly inclusive types have been proposed, such as Jung's introversion vs. extraversion, but any such type has been found to be too heterogeneous to be fruitful, even with Jung's original additional dichotomies of thinking and feeling, judging and perceiving, sensing and intuiting. Instincts and other global attributes have not worked well. Even Murray's list of needs and Cattell's array of trait-factors offer multifaceted variables. Yet any taxonomy that is more specific and concrete would involve hundreds of discrete variables to be conceptualized, measured, and studied experimentally.

It will probably be found that the appropriate level of abstraction depends upon the purpose of the theorizing, and that personology requires concepts at several levels. Whatever the outcome, it is certain that the theorist must be explicit about the level at which each concept is pegged, and the measurer must take the level into account in designing his procedures for obtaining response data and for producing indices. This whole problem may be resolved when personology gets its Newton or its Mendeleev.

Perhaps personology is still basically dependent on the experience of the personologist. Most personality concepts refer to behaviors or manifestations that can be observed in other people, or occasionally to experiences that are best appreciated when they happen to us. It may be that personology will really come into its own as a science when its concepts are tied to operations and to values calculated from observations. A provocative article on approaches to teaching thermodynamics (Dixon and Emery, 1965) provides many stimuli for thoughtful analogizing and speculating about the possible future of the very different field of personology. Perhaps personology has been approached from the macroscopic, experiential orientation and needs to have a more abstract and microscopic approach, as soon as we can develop appropriate theoretical models.

Yet it has been held that the philosophy of science and the theory of measurement developed for the physical sciences may not be sufficient for some other sciences such as psychology and especially personology. Have these latter fields been held back by naïve attempts to imitate the physical sciences? For instance, a theory of measurement was developed by N. R. Campbell (1928) from his knowledge of the physical sciences. His work included the concepts of fundamental and derived measurement, with which a number of psychologists were preoccupied three or four decades ago. But it may be that Campbell's theory, while quite appropriate for the physical sciences, is only one form of a more general theory from which a theory of measurement for the behavioral sciences could be derived as a parallel special case.

It is hard to determine to what extent the methodology of the physical sciences should guide the methodologist in the behavioral sciences, and especially in psychology and personology. Neither the extreme of blind imitation nor that of provincial rejection is wise. Certainly the behavioral methodologist should gain familiarity with the methodology in other fields, to achieve a perspective from which he can see his own field somewhat objectively, and to stimulate his own thinking. Any decision to borrow experimental designs, methods, or concepts of measurement should be based upon careful judgment of suitability to the phenomenologically different subject matter in his own field.

To return to a question closer to the topic of this book, exactly what is a nomothetic personality dimension? Is it something that varies in amount, as the voltage increases when batteries are hooked up in series? Or can the same dimension involve steps of more than one kind, just as adding batteries wired in parallel yields higher amperage and not higher voltage? Taking a psychological example, we have the impression that increasing steps of intelligence are associated with qualitative changes. Is this true, or is this simply a function of our ineptness in test construction? When an aspect of intelligence is adequately delineated, it often seems possible to build an instrument that has increasingly difficult items of pretty much the same kind. And of course some abilities are assessed not in terms of presence or absence, but in terms of speed of functioning.

This problem has been mentioned at several earlier points in this book. For instance, if the personality variable refers to reaction to a class of stimuli, the measuring procedure may yield several kinds of indices based respectively on speed, strength, or duration of reaction, or alternatively on the intensity of stimulus necessary to effect a reaction. Additionally, the index may be based on one or another attribute of the reaction itself, or on some particular quality of reaction.

A related question is the homogeneity of reactions at different levels of assumed strength. Jones (1958) has published data suggesting that some traits have an attribute of polarity such that measurement data for them are more internally consistent at the more psychologically meaningful pole. Subjects scoring toward the Internal pole of Rotter's scale of perceived locus of reinforcement have been found by Hersh and Scheibe (1967) to be more homogeneous than subjects scoring toward the External pole. While these findings make intuitive and psychological sense, they may simply be artifacts of the measuring procedures themselves.

There is also the question whether it is possible to measure most personality variables without considering their place in the subject's personality structure. Do traits that are strong tend to be more central to a subject's personality? Centrality means the psychological significance of the trait for the person: the degree to which manifestations of it affect his sense of well-being or his feelings of tension; the number of other traits to which the given trait is connected in some way. (See Sanford, 1956.) If a trait is central to a person's personality, is the quality different from its quality in other people? Or can we simply measure each trait separately, and obtain serviceable indices without regard to the place of the trait in each subject's personality?

PERSONALITY CONSTRUCTS IN CULTURAL SETTINGS

This book has been restricted to a rather provincial outlook on personality as it appears in the United States today, or perhaps only as it appears in middle-class American culture. Do personality constructs and their inter-relationships take different forms in other cultures? This is a question for the future to answer. The amount of relevant research is quite small. For example, Tsujioka and Cattell (1965) indicate that similar factors are found for American tests when translated into Japanese and given to sub-jects in Japan. But consistency of patterning across demographic groups in one country was not found in the work of Ernhart and Loevinger (1969). When the methodological problems of translation of personality items (see Werner and Campbell, in press) have been overcome, we may be in a po-sition to use different cultural settings as naturally occurring experimental conditions for studying the development and determination of personality attributes.

MULTIPLE DETERMINATION AND
RESULTANT SPECIFICITY OF SCORES

One central and unresolved problem has close relevance to both measuring and conceptualizing. The pervasiveness of specificity has been repeatedly noted in the preceding chapters (especially Chapter 11)—specificity in systematic measurement and presumably also in observed behavior occur-ring outside the testing room. (The specificity of a set of measurements is the degree to which their systematic variance and its determinants are not shared by other sets of measurements of the same construct. The interac-tion between processes in S and the components of the particular measur-ing procedure are schematized in Figure 13.1.) Responses vary regularly with conditions. When a change is made in instructions or in format, for ex-ample, there is likely to be a change in the responses, such that the new set of indices do not correlate so highly with the old set that they can be taken as interchangeable.

The behavior of interest to the personologist is determined by multiple influences. Personologists await the creative insight of some exceptional in-novator who can show us the strategy that will be most fruitful, which will make possible a giant step in our understanding of personality phenomena. Are we trying to explain too much? Should we limit our attention to the strongest bonds between situation and reaction which can be found for each person under some particular circumstances? Or should we continue to pursue the seemingly endless task of identifying and assessing the contribution of each of the many components contributing to the variation in our indices? This systematic analysis is confounded by complex interactions and by the probable variations in the contributions of such components from one person to another.

Consider, for example, the measurement of the need for achievement. Close to two decades ago, McClelland (McClelland *et al.*, 1953) initiated his own sustained program of research on this variable, a program that has proliferated into programs of his students and many other investigators. This major body of experimentation was based originally on a rather simple testing procedure. In this particular form of the Thematic Apperception Test, a series of pictures is presented to subjects with instructions to tell a story about each in turn. The pictures were selected for their capacity to elicit achievement fantasy. A detailed scoring manual permits good agreement between scorers in their indices for the variable of fantasy nAch, as it has come to be called.

From the first studies of nAch, it was found that scores could be elevated by such experimental manipulations as verbal instructions. But what else affects these scores? Among other workers, Klinger (1966; in press) has reviewed the literature and studied the matter empirically. He notes that the scores can be elevated by exposure to purely nonverbal communications from achievement-oriented models or even by simple observation of such models in action. But exposure to films of such models has effects that vary with or interact with other aspects of the procedures: the use of an experimental cubicle; the introduction of a prior rest period and a subsequent task before the storytelling, etc. Klinger makes it clear that fantasy production is highly sensitive to situations and immediately prior experiences. If these factors affect group means, it is most probable that they affect individual indices differentially. So what one set of conditions should an experimenter use in his basic research involving individual differences in nAch? No confident answer can be offered at this time.

The need for describing and measuring situations has been pointed out by many writers (e.g., Sells, 1963; Rotter, 1954, 1955; Magnusson, 1969), some of whom have sought to fill that need by *a priori* or empirical work. How well can it be done? Can we measure situations in respect to their meaning for individual subjects? Can we do so without initiating a whole new set of procedures based on self-report? Is that one mode of observation sufficient in this context? Can we separate, conceptually and empirically, indices of S's perception of the situation and indices of his reactions within it? The possibilities here are probably not restricted by the availability of suitable statistical methods or by feasibility of processing the complex data (given the capacities of current computers). The limitations most likely to hamper this work lie in the courage and mental capacity of the experimenter and the resilience of the subjects, who would have to apply themselves actively and seriously to very extensive test batteries.

IS TRAIT A FALSE CONCEPT?

Much of this volume has dealt with the measurement of traits as dimensions along which individuals differ in a consistent and stable fashion. As indicated earlier, the most simple trait approach involves the ascription to individuals of dispositions: this person is outgoing, that one is hostile, these others are dominating. But it has been noted for many years (e.g., Allport, 1937) that manifestations of traits vary with the situation: a man may show one trait at the office and an almost opposite one at home. Murphy (1964) suggests that half of what is determining personality at any given time is situationally defined, and that may be an underestimate.

Even if we take situations into account, and even if we allow each person to manifest the given trait in his own way, the concept of trait may simply be a misleading one. Its simplicity has made it highly attractive, but perhaps the phenomena of personality cannot be understood adequately by means of such simple notions. Consider also the material on specificity examined in Chapter 11. If an advancing science develops increasingly sharp concepts coordinated to continually more precise measuring operations, then personology must anticipate an infinitely expanding lexicon of attributes on which people differ.

But what other options are open? The use of qualitative designations has already been tried in typologies, and they provide even less precision of description measurement. A more refined kind of typology has been developed by people working with the Minnesota Multiphasic Personality Inventory. Some have classified subjects into categories according to peaks in their profiles on the clinical scales. Marks and Seeman (1963) have obtained a set of sixteen personality types, based on test configurations, which they find represent about 80 percent of adults seen in a psychiatric setting. They have provided typical actuarial descriptions for each type. Perhaps some such typological system will prove to be the best that can be done with present methods and approaches, although the theoretical fruitfulness of this strategy has yet to be demonstrated.

Another option is to seek methods for identifying the several personality dimensions most characteristic and pervasive in each person's experience and behavior. A long list of potential dimensions might be prepared, from which those best fitting each subject would be drawn. In order to understand a particular person, a set of six to ten dispositions may prove sufficient. Allport (1961, p. 366) reports that students, when asked to describe another person they know well, typically list about seven or eight "essential characteristics."

It is even possible that personology may, as it matures, conclude that the description of the individual person is not a fruitful objective. It is certainly questionable whether intensive studies of individuals have added substantially to the science of personality. More often, the study of a case or a life history yields a fascinating account that is intriguing, as insights into other personalities always are, but which merely demonstrates that certain influences can operate in determining an adult personality, or that certain motivational patterns can exist. For clinical service to a patient, we do not need to know everything about his personality. It may be sufficient to identify the sources of his distress, maladaptation, and ineffectiveness on the one hand, and to locate and assess his potential strengths on the other. For other applied work, it is the fit of the person to the specifications of the job or training position that is needed. (See Stern, Stein, and Bloom, 1956.) For basic research on the mechanisms and dynamisms of personality, it may be sufficient to measure the dispositions operating in the particular experimental setting.

A MORE MODEST STRATEGY

Perhaps personology has set for itself too difficult a goal: perhaps it is trying to run before it can walk. Instead of directly attacking personality as a whole, instead of trying to measure well each of the many postulated constructs along which people seem to differ in their everyday lives, perhaps personology should seek to understand fully how personality functions in quite restricted settings. A considerable amount of research today fits into this orientation. Reactions to pain and other stress have been studied in experimental settings (e.g., Schachter, 1959). Janis (1958) has investigated the real stress of impending operations. This may be the best route to major progress in personology. Yet it is not ideal: tolerance for pain has been observed to vary with the warmth of the experimenter's manifest personality. In the clinical study of persons confronting realistic stress, the subject may still be aware of the fact that he is being assessed and may try to put on a strong, cool front.

Optimal situations would be ones that were commonly met in the outside world, and ones that would allow observation and data gathering without affecting S's behavior. The design of such research would be challenging. Moreover, the ethical problems of studying persons without their knowledge or permission would have to be suitably resolved.

In pursuing this strategy, it would be best to work with more than one setting so that the effects of the situation could be assessed. In addition, the delineation of each setting must be quite explicit. The adequacy of the measurement of the situation could be determined by demonstrating that it could be replicated elsewhere by other researchers.

It is noteworthy that, in the discussions in this chapter and in several earlier chapters, the matter of the setting for the observations and measurements keeps recurring. Somewhere in this topic may be the key to problems of personality measurement. As indicated earlier, the measurement of ability and aptitude owes much of its success to the use of a setting that tends to maximize performance, so that we can assess the capabilities of subjects. We have also mentioned (in Chapter 6) Wallace's proposal (1966, 1967) that we turn our attention to measuring response capabilities in the personality domain. Along similar lines, Wallach and Kogan (1965) have shown great insight in measuring creativity in children under optimal conditions for eliciting such dispositions, conditions carefully designed to eliminate evaluation apprehension (see Rosenberg, 1969). These approaches indicate that one option for studying many variables is to design settings that maximally facilitate their appearance and expression.

For other variables, it might be fruitful to determine the most extreme manifestations that each subject has ever displayed, or has displayed in the past year. Such a procedure would have to be designed to be fully permissive, encouraging justifications and rationalizations for manifestations of undesirable dispositions. It should work well for neutral or favorable traits. It would capitalize on the fact that extreme instances of phenomena are sometimes easier to observe and understand.

Both of these possibilities depart from the conventional aim of measuring the typical dispositions of subjects, and perhaps we should. It is extremely difficult to specify what we mean by "typical," especially if we try to state it in a manner conducive to practical operationalizing of it. Such a shift in emphasis might lead more directly to an understanding of personality phenomena than the current correlational study of individual differences. Until their potentialities are better known, both strategies should be pursued by personologists.

IS THE SINGLE-VARIABLE APPROACH VIABLE?

This book has concentrated on the narrow objective of measuring personality variables one at a time, an approach that has the value of making the problems in personality measurement somewhat easier to grasp. It can also be defended on the grounds that we cannot hope to obtain adequate measurement of several variables simultaneously until we are able to measure each one in isolation from the others. (See the discussion in Chapter 7.) It can also be advocated on the practical grounds that the single-variable approach allows the investigator to concentrate his cognitive productivity and to consider carefully the many influences that may affect just that one dimension.

The single-variable approach and presumably all nomothetic orientations are hounded by the problem of psychological equivalence, with which the reader should be quite familiar by now. With respect to the particular variable, are the several stimuli (such as the items of a scale) psychologically equivalent for each subject? And even more troublesome is the question whether any one stimulus is psychologically equivalent across subjects. There is the additional matter of equivalence between two stimuli or two responses that are different in surface or phenotypical appearance. While it is quite clear that such apparently dissimilar stimuli or responses may be psychologically interchangeable for some one person, they may not be for all persons, and hence they cannot be included in standardized measuring procedures. Are watching football and watching baseball the same, psychologically? And what about playing football and playing baseball? To take a more extreme example, some people scale mountains, some race automobiles, some parachute from planes. If no one tries all these risky activities, are they psychologically interchangeable, or just somewhat similar?

But would these matters be taken care of if we attempted to assess more than one variable at a time? We are ready to agree that naturally occurring behavior is highly complex. At any one point in time, a person is coping with several stimuli and is expressing more than one personality disposition. (Consider the appearance of the elaborate diagram, like Figure 13.1, which would have to be drawn to represent even a brief section of a subject's experience and behavior in a natural setting.) Should we attempt to set up realistically complex situations and assess several variables at once? The great advantage would lie in the possibility of observing how variables interact with each other, and even how one disposition might take the place of another. E.g., a subject might seek to gain some gratification from one source if he felt that the gratification he usually received from another source was less likely to be obtained at that moment.

It may be a matter of courage, but I do not feel ready to attempt such a strategy. I also wonder whether a personologist can reasonably expect to comprehend and interpret the complex interactions involved in such an approach. Is the example of the physicist relevant here? He does not ordinarily investigate such an elaborate situation if he can help it. In principle, he could study a hydrogen-filled balloon with the objective of learning how to predict its course. Theoretically, he could measure wind direction and speed at every level and at every moment, the relative pressure inside and outside the balloon, its rate of expansion from the heat of the sun, etc. Practically, physicists have approached such problems by working with one variable at a time, controlling other influences by eliminating them or keep-

ing them constant. While arguing from analogy with another science may
be misleading (as discussed above), the rate of progress in the natural sciences indicates that it would be wise for us to check carefully the appropriateness of borrowing their strategies. It is possible that the kinds of interactions and interrelationships among variables are qualitatively different
in the physical and behavioral sciences, sufficiently so to justify a search for
a distinctively appropriate strategy. Still, I remain convinced that we
should try to understand simple things first, usually concentrating on just
one concept at a time.

Some Possible Strategies

The development of personology has reached a stage at which personologists may well pause to reexamine their current strategies and consider
other possibilities. The strategy that has been advocated in this book is,
from a wider viewpoint, only a relatively slight (but significant) variation
on a strategy being followed in much research today. The advocated strategy emphasizes the selection of theoretically important dimensions, the
thorough analysis and conceptualization of each such construct, the development of measuring procedures coordinate with that formulation, and the
use of these procedures in empirical tests of propositions. This strategy
builds on the best current theorizing, by others or by the investigator. It
ignores the question of degree of overlap among such constructs, requiring
only that the overlap correspond with *a priori* expectations and not stem
from contamination or impurity in the products of the measuring operations.

That strategy contrasts rather sharply with the empirical search for dimensions within the responses of some one type of instrument or those from
a single mode of observation. Those pursuing this strategy by such methods
as factor analysis often seek independence or minimal overlap among dimensions, implicitly hoping that each such mathematical abstraction will
correspond with a psychologically homogeneous dimension.

Some of the preceding sections have raised questions about both these
strategies, e.g., questions about the postulation of traits and about the study
of single variables. Another kind of question concerns the logical organization of personality constructs. Perhaps we should not start either with current constructs or with covariation among scores, but should attempt to
establish a systematic taxonomy of personality attributes. We might seek
parameters on which attributes can be categorized. Does Guilford's Structure-of-Intellect (see Chapter 11) provide any guidance or suggestions?
Like intellectual processes, personality processes perform operations on
contents, although the kinds of products are not neat, coordinate categories. Of course, since intellectual processes in psychological tests are con-

strained and directed by the instructions, they represent a very specific kind of psychological functioning, unlike the relatively unrestricted processes subsumed under personality functioning. Guilford (1959) has some suggestions about possible cross-classification schemes within the domain of personality, but they have much less intuitive appeal and fruitfulness than his model for intellect.

There is also the "modest strategy" proposed earlier in this chapter, the attempt to understand personality functioning within a standard or controlled situation. This is the strategy of much experimental work on personality today. It has the merit of studying immediate processes rather than attempting to estimate average dispositions of subjects. While tests designed to elicit target-relevant processes (by simulated stimuli) or *a priori* related processes (see Chapter 6) also utilize immediately relevant processes, the experimenter often has the advantage of being able to make his stimuli more compelling and hence may be able to minimize contamination from reactions to being in a laboratory. Perhaps the ideal for the experimenter is lifelike simulation by confederates. A higher proportion of bystanders in a subway car went to the aid of someone in simulated trouble (Piliavin, Rodin, and Piliavin, 1969) than the proportion observed in a similar medical emergency within a psychology laboratory (Darley and Latané, 1968). Although the two studies differ in many aspects, the physical and psychological locale may be the factor accounting for the difference in findings.

Most of this section, and much of this chapter, has been concerned with the basic issue of how to classify into theoretically fruitful categories the infinite variety of behavior. It may be that the nature of personality phenomena simply do not lend themselves to classification according to standard simple rules, such as the rules that the classes be mutually exclusive (nonoverlapping) and exhaustive (covering every instance). Certainly these phenomena are not like the blocks used in clinical testing of cognitive functioning: they are not permanent objects that differ from each other in a very few physical properties on which consensus can readily be obtained, such as color, shape, and height. Perhaps we must learn how to use a more complex classification scheme more appropriate for the complicated nature of the phenomena, a scheme that specifies multiple and alternative criteria for assignment to each class.

Much hard theoretical and metatheoretical work is required to straighten out some of these matters. Perhaps we need to be more clear about the objects of the entire enterprise of personology. Exactly what are we trying to do? In particular, what are the functions of the constructs we want to delineate and investigate? Should the ground rules for personology and perhaps for other social sciences be different from those of the natural sciences?

Major progress in personality and its measurement may be awaiting the explication of the philosophical foundations of personology.

> ". . . what's past is prologue, what to come,
> In yours and my discharge. . . ."
>
> The Tempest

Whatever strategy a personologist may adopt, for whatever personal or rational reasons, he must accept the necessity for producing sound data, data that meet the criterion of intersubjective agreement, which Popper (1959) indicates to be essential in science. The data must be both sound and conceptually significant, two requirements that are often difficult to meet simultaneously in research on personology. The adequacy of the observations and indices must be demonstrated by internal evidence as specified by psychometric concepts and by external relationships as called for by theoretical statements. Ultimately, personality measurements must also be shown to function appropriately under manipulations controlled by the experimenter. In the future, personology will be an experimental science.

Summary

What are the directions in which personality measurement is likely to progress? The simultaneous use of multiple perspectives and modes of observation will become more prevalent. Concepts will be analyzed into subconstructs and both will be more explicitly delineated. In the next generation of personologists, each investigator will work, perhaps alternately, at both the conceptual and the operational levels, maximizing the coordination between concepts and data.

Indirect measurement will be developed further to fill an ancillary but valuable role. In a contrasting strategy, the subject will be brought into the experiment more as a partner than as an antagonist. The psychology of the subject as he functions in the experimental laboratory or testing room will be better understood. More will be known about the flow and constant changing of his mental processes.

Questions still to be resolved are many. At what levels of abstraction should we peg our constructs to make theoretical progress? Should the constructs of personology have an experimental rather than an experiential basis? Can we extract significant quantitative dimensions along which people do not differ in the quality of their experience or behavior? Will homogeneous dimensions be found to be universal or culturally specific? Can we find conceptual dimensions that are systematically linked to measurements in spite of the manifest specificity of each test as a function of its particular determinants?

Are we misguided in searching for common nomothetic dimensions? Should we, instead, seek to understand the functioning of people in particular standard situations? Will some new simultaneous multivariate strategy supersede the single-variable approach? Sooner or later, these questions will be answered, personality measurement will reach adulthood, and it will be realistic to talk about personology, the science of personality.

Glossary

(Phrases are alphabetized by their first word. For terms not included in the Glossary, see the Index.)

AFFECT: a feeling or a feeling state.

a priori RELATED PROCESS: a test design in which the test itself is intended to elicit in S a process theoretically related to the process specified for the construct that the test is attempting to measure.

ASSESSMENT: (1) a loose general term for measurement; (2) (as in assessment program) a complex measuring procedure in which several subjects are observed in a sequence of unstructured and structured activities (lasting for hours or days) and are rated by trained observers.

CATEGORICAL SCALE. *See* nominal scale.

CATEGORICAL VARIABLE: a variable using a categorical or nominal scale; i.e., a series of unordered classes into one of which each object or person is placed. A distinctive quality identifies each such class.

CONCEPT: an abstract term identifying a class or an attribute. Here it is usually used to refer to a dimension of personality phenomena in early stages of theorizing. *See* construct.

CONCURRENT VALIDITY: the correlation between a test and a criterion when the two are measured at approximately the same time.

CONSTRUCT: a formal concept, a concept that has been systematically defined, delineated, and perhaps related to other constructs. (The term may also be used to emphasize the fact that the concept has been created or construed by a scientist.)

CONSTRUCT VALIDITY: the extent of agreement between (1) the obtained relationships for a test with other variables and (2) the relationships expected on the basis of the conceptualization developed for the construct that the test is intended to measure.

294

CONTENT VALIDITY: the validity of a test as judged from analysis of its contents I.e., how well do the task set for S and the content of the items sample the universe of the concept that the test is intended to measure?

CONVERGENT VALIDATION: the extent of positive correlation between two or more measures of the same concept, using separate methods of measurement.

CORE: the unique quality to which a construct refers, the essence common to all manifestations of the construct.

CORRELATION: the degree of association or relationship between two variables. (It is usually stated in terms of a correlation coefficient. The most common of these coefficients is the Pearson product-moment correlation, which can vary from $+1.00$ for maximum positive relationship through $.00$ to -1.00 for maximum negative relationship.) The verb form, "correlate," means to determine the association between, when used in the active voice ("E correlated the two tests"), and means associated or related to each other, when used in the passive voice ("X was highly correlated with Y").

CRITERION: in test construction, a variable assumed to measure adequately that which a test is intended to measure, and hence used in evaluating the test. (The term is also used here in the more general sense of a standard for judging.)

CRITERION-RELATED VALIDITY: the extent to which a test correlates with a criterion. (The form may be concurrent or predictive, depending on whether the test is administered at about the same time as or earlier than the criterion measure.)

CUMULATIVE HOMOGENEITY MODEL: a psychometric model in which the score is based on the subject's responses of a designated type (i.e., correct or keyed responses) to a series of stimuli that can be ordered in accordance with the proportions of such responses elicited by the several stimuli.

DATUM: a fact, observation, or classification. Here, datum usually refers to the score or categorization assigned to the response made to one item or stimulus. (Strictly speaking, this scoring is based on one attribute of the response, the attribute selected by the experimenter as relevant to his variable.)

DIFFERENTIAL HOMOGENEITY MODELS: a psychometric model in which a subject's score is based on the applicability to him of items falling within a range or segment on a scale (in contrast to items higher or lower on the scale).

DISCRIMINANT VALIDATION: the extent to which the correlation between two measures of the same concept, based on separate methods, exceeds the correlations between measures of different concepts obtained by those same methods.

ELEMENT: a form or class within a facet.

EMPIRICALLY RELATED PROCESS: a test design in which the test elicits in S a process that has been shown empirically to be related to the process specified for the construct being measured.

ENDORSEMENT VALUE: a numerical index for an item indicating the proportion of subjects who make the keyed response to it (answer it positively, attribute it to themselves, etc.).

EQUAL INTERVAL SCALE. *See* interval scale.

FACE VALIDITY: the apparent validity of a test as determined by inspection.

FACET: a basis for classifying a set of complex observations or data pertinent to a construct, as obtained by one mode. E.g., a behavioral facet referring to the specific forms of the behavior; a situational facet for categorizing the types of situation in which the relevant behaviors occur.

FACTOR ANALYSIS: a statistical procedure for obtaining, from the correlations among a set of variables, a smaller set of abstract dimensions, each of which is found to be common to an indicated subset of the original set of variables.

FREE RESPONSE TEST: a test in which S produces his own response (as in writing out his answer), as opposed to selecting one of several response options provided by the examiner.

FREQUENCY MODEL: one of several psychometric models in which the index or score utilizes the frequency of S's responses of a specified kind to the several stimuli, the stimuli being treated as interchangeable, as undifferentiated from each other.

GENERALIZABILITY: this comprehensive term refers to the confidence with which an experimenter can generalize from a set of scores to other data. The term is used here to include both reliability and validity. Reliability is generalizability from responses to one set of items to those made to a set of similar items, or from one point in time to another, etc.; validity is generalizability to different measures of the target construct or to the construct itself.

HOMOGENEITY COEFFICIENT: a homogeneity index that is a correlation coefficient; e.g., r_{ii}, r_{pp}, r_{tt} (which see).

HOMOGENEITY INDEX: an index of the sameness among subjects or items, obtained from responses of the subjects to the items. E.g., are the items differentiating the subjects in the same way? Are the subjects differentiating the items in the same way?

IDIOGRAPHIC: pertaining to the particular; e.g., to an individual personality.

INDEX: (noun) a quantity or score assigned to a person on the basis of several responses and taken to represent the degree to which he possesses an attribute; (verb) to assign to a person a score for an attribute.

INTERJUDGE RELIABILITY: the type of reliability estimating the generalizability of a procedure over raters or judges, determined from the correlation between their ratings.

INTERNAL CONSISTENCY: the type of reliability or generalizability estimated from the correlations among the items or other parts (e.g., halves) of a test. The form of this coefficient used here is identified as r_{tt}; it is commonly labeled as Kuder-Richardson 20, or simply K-R 20. A more general form is known as coefficient alpha.

INTERVAL SCALE: a measurement scale with equal intervals between its designated points (so that the distance between two objects or persons can be stated); sometimes called an equal-interval scale.

INVENTORY: a paper-and-pencil test of personality with verbal content (practically synonymous with "questionnaire," but "inventory" implies inclusiveness of coverage and typically measures more than one variable).

ITEM VARIANCE: that part of the total variance in a matrix of responses which is contributed by the variance among the means for items. (Note: Here, this is a short term for variance of item means. In other psychometric writing, item variance is the variance of the distribution of responses to a single item.)

MEASUREMENT: generally, the assigning of numerals to objects in accordance with certain rules. More specifically, the assigning of scores or indices to persons on the basis of their responses as elicited by a standard procedure. (Occasionally used as a synonym for "score" or "index.")

METHOD: a class of measuring procedures having in common several components (such as mode, context or conditions, task, data producer, stimuli).

METHOD VARIANCE: that part of the variance in a set of measurements which is attributed to the method involved in the measuring procedure used.

MODE: one of six classes of procedures for measuring personality.

MULTIPLE CHOICE: a test format in which two or more response options are provided for each item, and S is instructed to mark one.

MULTITRAIT-MULTIMETHOD MATRIX: the matrix of correlations among all the scores when two or more traits have been measured by two or more methods, each trait having been measured by each method.

NATURALISTIC OBSERVATION: an observation made under naturally occurring conditions, as opposed to conditions set up by an experimenter in a laboratory or testing room.

NOMINAL SCALE: a measurement scale composed of qualities or classes with no order (also called a categorical scale).

NOMOTHETIC: the general, as opposed to the particular or individualistic; e.g., a nomothetic attribute of personality is a property applicable to most or all people.

ORDINAL SCALE: a measurement scale on which objects or persons are just ordered or ranked.

PERSON VARIANCE: that part of the total variance in a matrix of responses which is contributed by the variance among the means of persons.

PERSONALITY: the way a person characteristically is observed to interact with his environment—external, somatic, and intrapsychic.

PERSONOLOGY: the scientific study of personality.

PERSPECTIVE: a viewpoint from which personality phenomena can be observed; e.g., a friend's observation of S's behavior or S's observation of his own experience and behavior.

PHASE: a stage or segment of a psychological process; e.g., perceiving, evaluating, or intending.

PREDICTIVE VALIDITY: the correlation between a test and a criterion measure obtained at a later point in time.

PROCESS: a hypothesized sequence of internal activities, initiated by a stimulus and sometimes concluding with an action or overt response.

PSYCHOMETRIC MODEL: a set of rules for obtaining an index or score from the data for several responses.

QUESTIONNAIRE: a paper-and-pencil test of personality, the content being questions or implied questions. (Practically synonymous with "inventory.")

r_{ii}: the average intercorrelation between the items of a test.

r_{pp}: the average intercorrelation between persons, over the items of a test.

r_{tt}: the standard index of the internal consistency of a test.

RATIO SCALE: a measurement scale with intervals specified in terms of distance from an absolute zero or natural origin.

RELIABILITY: the extent to which two or more sets of measurements (using essentially the same procedure) agree with each other or, more strictly, covary over people. *See also* generalizability, homogeneity, internal consistency, stability, interjudge agreement.

REMAINDER VARIANCE: that part of the total variance in a matrix of responses which is not contributed either by person means or by item means. It is the variance of the obtained responses around the responses expected on the basis of the pertinent item mean and person mean.

RESPONSE: this very general term is used here primarily to refer to an act following presentation of a stimulus or item. In measurement, "response" usually means the act as recorded, i.e., the category into which the response is placed. (Note that the term is also used loosely for an alternative provided for S in a multiple-choice test.)

RESPONSE SET: the consistent tendency to select responses with some common property other than one related to the substantive variable the test is intended to measure; e.g., the tendency to mark the "yes" or "true" alternatives, regardless of the content of the item.

RORSCHACH: a test composed of ten inkblots, presented singly to S with the instruction to tell what the blot looks like or might represent. (Named after its creator, Hermann Rorschach.)

SCALE: the abstract form of the system of numbers into which observations are mapped, as in the measurement scales (nominal, ordinal, etc.). The term is occasionally used to refer to a measuring procedure, as in attitude scale.

SCORE: a number assigned to a person on the basis of his response to one item or his responses to several items (usually restricted to test responses, and hence more specific than index).

SIMULATED STIMULI: a test design in which the test is intended to elicit in S the process as specified for the construct. (The name derives from the fact that, for practical or methodological reasons, the items or stimuli used in the test are typically not those involved in the process as it occurs naturally, but are selected to simulate such stimuli as closely as possible.)

SOCIAL DESIRABILITY: a set to respond by choosing the more socially desirable or socially approved response alternative.

SPECIFICITY: the extent to which an act or a test score is distinctive, rather than correlated with other acts or scores.

STABILITY: the type of reliability or generalizability estimated from the correlation between scores on a test obtained from two separate administrations at different times.

STATE: the psychological condition of a person at a moment in time. (It may be influenced by physiological processes as well as by recent psychological events.)

STIMULUS: anything that affects a sense organ and thereby modifies behavior. The term is frequently used here to refer to an item, a unit in a test to which S is expected to respond, a usage intended to emphasize the fact that personality is embedded in the total field of psychology.

SUBCONSTRUCT: a portion or form of a construct, usually one designated as a target for measuring procedures; e.g., the construct as observed in one mode.

SUBJECT VARIABLE: a characteristic of subjects which affects their test-taking behavior and their responses to tests.

TEST: a standard set of operations for measuring. Most psychological tests include instructions to S telling him what he is expected to do and a set of stimuli or items, to each of which he is expected to respond.

TEST DESIGN: the relationship intended by the experimenter between the process occurring in S as he responds to an item in a test and the process involved in the construct as conceptualized. (Three designs are: simulated stimuli, *a priori* related process, and empirically related process.)

THEMATIC APPERCEPTION TEST (TAT): a technique in which S is presented with a set of pictures, one at a time, and asked to make up a story about each.

TRAIT: a lasting characteristic attributed to persons in varying amounts or strengths (as opposed to a temporary state).

TYPOLOGY: a psychometric model in which each person is placed in one of two or more qualitatively different types (the types forming a nominal or categorical scale).

VALIDITY: the extent to which a test measures the variable (or concept) it is intended to measure. *See also* concurrent validity; construct validity; content validity; criterion-related validity; face validity; generalizability; predictive validity.

VARIABLE: a quantity that varies; here, a general term for an aspect of personality, usually one that varies over people. The term is used when the emphasis is on the observations or the data rather than on the attribute indexed or reflected by the data.

VARIANCE: technically, the mean of the squared deviations of a set of observations from their mean. (The study of individual differences and correlational psychology seek to determine the sources of this variation among people.)

References

ADORNO, T. W.; FRENKEL-BRUNSWIK, E.; LEVINSON, D. J.; and SANFORD, R. N. 1950. *The authoritarian personality.* New York: Harper.

ALEXANDER, F.; FRENCH, T. M.; and POLLOCK, G. H. 1968. *Psychosomatic specificity,* vol. 1. Chicago: University of Chicago Press.

ALLPORT, G. W.
  1937. *Personality: a psychological interpretation.* New York: Holt.
  1942. *The use of personal documents in psychological science.* Social Science Research Council bulletin no. 49, New York.
  1961. *Pattern and growth in personality.* New York: Holt, Rinehart & Winston.
  1965. (Ed.) *Letters from Jenny.* New York: Harcourt, Brace & World.

AMERICAN PSYCHOLOGICAL ASSOCIATION. 1968. Ethical standards of psychologists. *American Psychologist* 23: 357–61.
——— *et al.*
  1954. Technical recommendations for psychological tests and diagnostic techniques. *Psychological Bulletin Supplement* 51: 201–38 (pt. 2 of no. 2).
  1966. *Standards for educational and psychological tests and manuals.* Washington, D.C.: American Psychological Assn.

American Psychologist.
  1965. Special issue: Testing and public policy. 20: 857–989.
  1966. 21: 401–78.
  1967. 22: 345–99.

ATKINSON, J. W., ed. 1958. *Motives in fantasy, action, and society.* Princeton, N.J.: Van Nostrand.

AVERILL, J. R., and OPTON, E. M., JR. 1968. Psychophysiological assessment: rationale and problems. In *Advances in psychological assessment,* ed. P. McReynolds, vol. 1, pp. 265–88. Palo Alto: Science & Behavior Books.

BARKER, R. G., ed. 1963. *The stream of behavior: explorations of its structure and content.* New York: Appleton-Century-Crofts.
——— and WRIGHT, H. F. 1951. *One boy's day: a specimen record of behaviors.* New York: Harper.

300

BARRON, F.
1953. An ego-strength scale which predicts response to psychotherapy. *Journal of Consulting Psychology* 17: 327–33.
1968. *Creativity and personal freedom.* Princton, N.J.: Van Nostrand.

BASS, B. M. 1954. The leaderless group discussion. *Psychological Bulletin* 51: 465–92.

BAUGHMAN, E. E., and DAHLSTROM, W. G. 1968. *Negro and white children: a psychological study of the rural South.* New York: Academic Press.

BECK, S. J. 1954. *The six schizophrenias: reaction patterns in children and adults.* American Orthopsychiatric Assocation research monograph no. 6.

BLOCK, J. 1961. *The Q-sort method in personality assessment and psychiatric research.* Springfield, Ill.: C. C. Thomas.

BLOOM, B. S.
1956. (ed.) *Taxonomy of educational objectives: the classification of educational goals. Handbook I: Cognitive domain.* New York: David McKay.
1964. *Stability and change in human characteristics.* New York: Wiley.

BOCK, R. D., and HAGGARD, E. A. 1963. *A comprehensive psychometric study of the Rorschach and Holtzman inkblot techniques.* Chapel Hill: Psychometric Laboratory, University of North Carolina.

BOLGAR, H. 1965. The case study method. In *Handbook of clinical psychology,* ed. B. Wolman, pp. 28–39. New York: McGraw-Hill.

BRADBURN, N. 1969. *The structure of psychological well-being.* Chicago: Aldine.
———— and CAPLOVITZ, D. 1965. *Reports on happiness: a pilot study of behavior related to mental health.* Chicago: Aldine.

BRIM, O. G., JR., and HOFF, D. B. 1957. Individual and situational differences in desire for certainty. *Journal of Abnormal and Social Psychology* 54: 225–29.

BUROS, O. K., ed.
1961. *Tests in print.* Highland Park, N.J.: Gryphon Press.
1965. *The sixth mental measurements yearbook.* Highland Park, N.J.: Gryphon Press.

BUTCHER, J. N., and TELLEGEN, A. 1966. Objections to MMPI items. *Journal of Consulting Psychology* 30: 527–34.

BUTLER, J. M.; RICE, L. N.; and WAGSTAFF, A. K. 1962. On the naturalistic definition of variables: an analogue of clinical analysis. In *Research in psychotherapy,* ed. H. H. Strupp and L. Luborsky, vol. 2, pp. 178–205. Washington, D.C.: American Psychological Assn.

BUTT, D. S., and FISKE, D. W.
1968. A comparison of strategies in developing scales for dominance. *Psychological Bulletin* 70: 505–19.
1969. Differential correlates of dominance scales. *Journal of Personality* 37: 415–28.

BYRNE, D. 1964. Repression-sensitization as a dimension of personality. In *Progress in experimental personality research,* ed. B. A. Maher, vol. 1, pp. 169–220. New York: Academic Press.

CAMPBELL, D. P. 1968. The Strong Vocational Interest Blank: 1927–1967. In *Advances in psychological assessment,* ed. P. McReynolds, vol. 1, pp. 105–30. Palo Alto: Science & Behavior Books.

CAMPBELL, D. T.
1957. A typology of tests, projective and otherwise. *Journal of Consulting Psychology* 21: 207–10.
1960. Recommendations for APA test standards regarding construct, trait, or discriminant validity. *American Psychologist* 15: 546–53.
—— and FISKE, D. W. 1959. Convergent and discriminant validation by the multitrait-multimethod matrix. *Psychological Bulletin* 56: 81–105.
—— and STANLEY, J. C. 1963. Experimental and quasi-experimental designs for research on teaching. In *Handbook of research on teaching*, ed. N. L. Gage, pp. 171–246. Chicago: Rand McNally.
CAMPBELL, N. R. 1928. *An account of the principles of measurement and calculation*. London: Longmans, Green.
CARNAP, R. 1966. *Philosophical foundations of physics*. New York: Basic Books.
CARR, H. A., and KINGSBURY, F. A. 1938. The concept of traits. *Psychological Review* 45: 497–524.
CARSON, R. C. 1969. *Interaction concepts of personality*. Chicago: Aldine.
CARTWRIGHT, D. S.; KIRTNER, W. L.; and FISKE, D. W. 1963. Method factors in changes associated with psychotherapy. *Journal of Abnormal and Social Psychology* 66: 164–75.
CATTELL, R. B.
1946. *Description and measurement of personality*. Yonkers, N.Y.: World.
1957. *Personality and motivation structure and measurement*. Yonkers, N.Y.: World.
1966. The data box: the ordering of total resources in terms of possible relational systems. In *Handbook of multivariate experimental psychology*, ed. R. B. Cattell, pp. 67–128. Chicago: Rand McNally.
—— and SCHEIER, I. H. 1961. *The meaning and measurement of neuroticism and anxiety*. New York: Ronald Press.
—— and STICE, G. F. 1957. *The Sixteen Personality Factor Questionnaire*. Champaign, Ill.: Institute for Personality and Ability Testing.
—— and WARBURTON, F. W. 1967. *Objective personality and motivation tests: a theoretical introduction and practical compendium*. Urbana: University of Illinois Press.
CHAPMAN, L. J., and CHAPMAN, J. P.
1967. Genesis of popular but erroneous psychodiagnostic observations. *Journal of Abnormal Psychology* 72: 193–204.
1969. Illusory correlations as an obstacle to the use of valid psychodiagnostic signs. *Journal of Abnormal Psychology* 74: 271–80.
——; ——; and BRELJE, T. 1969. Influence of the experimenter on pupillary dilation to sexually provocative pictures. *Journal of Abnormal Psychology* 74: 396–400.
COMREY, A. L., and DUFFY, K. E. 1968. Cattell and Eysenck factor scores related to Comrey personality factors. *Multivariate Behavioral Research* 3: 379–92.
—— and JAMISON, K. 1966. Verification of six personality factors. *Educational and Psychological Measurement* 26: 945–53.
COOK, S. W., and SELLTIZ, C. 1964. A multiple-indicator approach to attitude measurement. *Psychological Bulletin* 62: 36–55.

COOMBS, C. H.
  1952. *A theory of psychological scaling.* Engineering research bulletin no. 34. Ann Arbor. University of Michigan.
  1964. *A theory of data.* New York: Wiley.
CRONBACH, L. J.
  1946. Response sets and test validity. *Educational and Psychological Measurement* 6: 475–94.
  1950. Further evidence on response sets and test design. *Educational and Psychological Measurement* 10: 3–31.
  1955. Processes affecting scores on "understanding of others" and "assumed similarity." *Psychological Bulletin* 52: 177–93.
  1957. The two disciplines of scientific psychology. *American Psychologist* 12: 671–84.
  ———— and GLESER, G. C. 1965. *Psychological tests and personnel decisions.* 2nd ed. Urbana: University of Illinois Press.
  ———— and MEEHL, P. E. 1955. Construct validity in psychological tests. *Psychological Bulletin* 52: 281–302.
  ————; RAJARATNAM, N.; and GLESER, G. C. 1963. Theory of generalizability: a liberalization of reliability theory. *British Journal of Statistical Psychology* 16: 137–63.
DAHLSTROM, W. G. 1971. The theory of types and some exemplification in psychopathology. In *Handbook of modern personality theory,* ed. R. B. Cattell. Chicago: Aldine.
  ———— and WELSH, G. S. 1960. *An MMPI handbook.* Minneapolis: University of Minnesota Press.
DARLEY, J. M., and LATANÉ, B. 1968. Bystander intervention in emergencies: diffusion of responsibility. *Journal of Personality and Social Psychology* 8: 377–83.
DAVIDS, A. 1955. Comparison of three methods of personality assessment: direct, indirect, and projective. *Journal of Personality* 23: 423–40.
DEMENT, W. C. 1965. An essay on dreams: the role of physiology in understanding their nature. In *New Directions in Psychology II,* pp. 135–257. New York: Holt, Rinehart & Winston.
DIXON, J. R., and EMERY, A. H., JR. 1965. Semantics, operationalism, and the molecular-statistical model in thermodynamics. *American Scientist* 53: 428–36.
DOLLIVER, R. H. 1969. Strong Vocational Interest Blank versus expressed vocational interest: a review. *Psychological Bulletin* 72: 95–107.
DUBOIS, P. H. 1970. *A history of psychological testing.* Boston: Allyn & Bacon.
EATON, A. M., and FISKE, D. W. In press. Item stability as related to implicit set and subject-item distance. *Journal of Consulting and Clinical Psychology.*
EDWARDS, A. L. 1957. *The social desirability variable in personality assessment and research.* New York: Dryden.
EDWARDS, W. 1961. Costs and payoffs are instructions. *Psychological Review* 68: 275–84.
EMMERICH, W. 1966. Personality assessments conceptualized as perspectives. *Journal of Projective Techniques and Personality Assessment* 30: 307–18.
ENDLER, N. S., and HUNT, J. McV. 1968. S-R inventories of hostility and comparisons of the proportions of variance from persons, responses, and situa-

tions for hostility and anxiousness. *Journal of Personality and Social Psychology* 9: 309–15.

———; ———; and ROSENSTEIN, A. J. 1962. An S-R Inventory of Anxiousness. *Psychological Monographs* 76 (17, whole no. 536).

ENGLISH, H. B., and ENGLISH, A. C. 1958. *A comprehensive dictionary of psychological and psychoanalytical terms.* New York: Longmans, Green.

ERNHART, C. B., and LOEVINGER, J. 1969. *Authoritarian family ideology: a measure, its correlates, and its robustness.* Multivariate Behavioral Research Monograph no. 69–1.

FISKE, D. W.
  1949. Consistency of the factorial structures of personality ratings from different sources. *Journal of Abnormal and Social Psychology* 44: 329–44.
  1957. The constraints on intra-individual variability in test responses. *Educational and Psychological Measurement* 17: 317–37.
  1961a. Effects of monotonous and restricted stimulation. In D. W. Fiske and S. R. Maddi, *Functions of varied experience*, pp. 106–44. Homewood, Ill.: Dorsey Press.
  1961b. The inherent variability of behavior. In *ibid.*, pp. 326–54.
  1963a. Homogeneity and variation in measuring personality. *American Psychologist* 18: 643–52.
  1963b. Problems in measuring personality. In *Concepts of personality*, ed. J. Wepman and R. Heine, pp. 449–73. Chicago: Aldine.
  1966a. On the coordination of personality concepts and their measurement. *Human Development* 9: 74–83.
  1966b. Some hypotheses concerning test adequacy. *Educational and Psychological Measurement* 26: 69–88.
  1967. The subject reacts to tests. *American Psychologist* 22: 287–96.
  1969. Subject reactions to inventory format and content. *Proceedings of the 77th Annual Convention of the American Psychological Association*, pp. 137–38.

——— and BUTLER, J. M. 1963. The experimental conditions for measuring individual differences. *Educational and Psychological Measurement* 23: 249–66.

———; CARTWRIGHT, D. S.; and KIRTNER, W. L. 1964. Are psychotherapeutic changes predictable? *Journal of Abnormal and Social Psychology* 69: 418–26.

———; HUNT, H. F.; LUBORSKY, L.; ORNE, M. T.; PARLOFF, M. B.; REISER, M. F.; and TUMA, A. H. 1970. The planning of research on effectiveness of psychotherapy. *Archives of General Psychiatry* 22: 22–32.

——— and PEARSON, P. 1970. Theory and techniques of personality measurement. *Annual Review of Psychology* 21: 49–86.

——— and VAN BUSKIRK, C. 1959. The stability of interpretations of sentence completion protocols. *Journal of Consulting Psychology* 23: 177–80.

FOA, U. G. 1965. New developments in facet design and analysis. *Psychological Review* 72: 262–74.

FORER, B. R. 1949. The fallacy of personal validation: a classroom demonstration of gullibility. *Journal of Abnormal and Social Psychology* 44: 118–23.

FRENCH, J. W. 1965. The relationship of problem-solving styles to the factor composition of tests. *Educational and Psychological Measurement* 25: 9–28.

GARDNER, R.; HOLZMAN, P. S.; KLEIN, G. S.; LINTON, H.; and SPENCE, D. P.

1959. Cognitive control: a study of individual consistencies in cognitive behavior. *Psychological Issues* 1(whole no. 4).

GETZELS, J. W. 1953. Methods used to study personality. *Journal of the National Association of Deans of Women* (June), pp. 154–58.

GOLDBERG, L. R.
1968a. The interrelationships among item characteristics in an adjective checklist: the convergence of different indices of item ambiguity. *Educational and Psychological Measurement* 28: 273–96.
1968b. Seer over sign: the first "good" example? *Journal of Experimental Research in Personality* 3: 168–71.
——— and JONES, R. R. 1969. *The reliability of reliability: the generality and correlates of intra-individual consistency in responses to structured personality inventories.* Research monograph 9, no. 2. Eugene: Oregon Research Institute.

GOLDSTEIN, K., and SCHEERER, M. 1941. Abstract and concrete behavior: an experimental study with special tests. *Psychological Monographs* 53 (2, whole no. 239).

GOODENOUGH, D. R., and KARP, S. A. 1961. Field dependence and intellectual functioning. *Journal of Abnormal and Social Psychology* 63: 241–46.

GOTTSCHALK, L. A., and GLESER, G. C. 1969. *The measurement of psychological states through the content analysis of verbal behavior.* Berkeley: University of California Press.

GOUGH, H. G. 1968. An interpreter's syllabus for the California Psychological Inventory. In *Advances in psychological assessment,* ed. P. McReynolds, vol. 1, pp. 55–79. Palo Alto: Science & Behavior Books.

GREENBERG, M. S. 1967. Role-playing: an alternative to deception? *Journal of Personality and Social Psychology* 7: 152–57.

GUILFORD, J. P.
1954. *Psychometric methods.* 2nd ed. New York: McGraw-Hill.
1959. *Personality.* New York: McGraw-Hill.
1967. *The nature of human intelligence.* New York: McGraw-Hill.

GULLIKSEN, H.
1950. *Theory of mental tests.* New York: Wiley.
1968. Methods for determining equivalence of measures. *Psychological Bulletin* 70: 534–44.

GUTTMAN, L. 1965. The structure of interrelations among intelligence tests. In *Proceedings of the 1964 Invitational Conference on Testing Problems,* pp. 25–36. Princeton, N.J.: Educational Testing Service.

GUTTMAN, L. 1970. Integration of test design and analysis. In *Proceedings of the 1969 Invitational Conference on Testing Problems,* pp. 53–65. Princeton, N.J.: Educational Testing Service.

HAKEL, M. D. 1968. How often is often? *American Psychologist* 23: 533–34.

HALL, C. S., and LINDZEY, G. 1970. *Theories of personality.* 2nd ed. New York: Wiley.

HARMAN, H. H. 1960. *Modern factor analysis.* Chicago: University of Chicago Press.

HARTSHORNE, H.; MAY, M. A.; and SHUTTLEWORTH, F. K. 1930. *Studies in the organization of character.* New York: Macmillan.

HAYS, W. L. 1967. *Quantification in psychology.* Belmont, Calif.: Brooks/Cole.

HERMANN, M. G. 1968. *Indirect methods of assessing personality.* Research bulletin 68–9. Princeton, N.J.: Educational Testing Service.

HERSCH, P. D., and SCHEIBE, K. E. 1967. Reliability and validity of internal-external control as a personality dimension. *Journal of Consulting Psychology* 31: 609–13.

HESS, E. H. 1968. Pupillometric assessment. In *Research in psychotherapy,* ed. J. M. Shlien, vol. 3, pp. 573–83. Washington, D.C.: American Psychological Assn.

HOLT, R. R. 1958. Clinical and statistical prediction: a reformulation and some new data. *Journal of Abnormal and Social Psychology* 56: 1–12.

———— and LUBORSKY, L. 1958. *Personality patterns of psychiatrists,* vol. 1 New York: Basic Books.

HOLTZMAN, W. H.; THORPE, J. S.; SWARTZ, J. D.; and HERRON, E. W. 1961. *Inkblot perception and personality.* Austin: University of Texas Press.

HOLZMAN, P. S. 1966. Scanning: a principle of reality contact. *Perceptual and Motor Skills* 23: 835–44.

HUMPHREYS, L. G. 1962. The organization of human abilities. *American Psychologist* 17: 475–95.

JACKSON, D. N. 1969. Multimethod factor analysis in the evaluation of convergent and discriminant validity. *Psychological Bulletin* 72: 30–49.

JACKSON, P. W., and MESSICK, S. 1965. The person, the product, and the response: conceptual problems in the assessment of creativity. *Journal of Personality* 33: 309–29.

JAHODA, M. 1958. *Current conceptions of positive mental health.* New York: Basic Books.

JANIS, I. L. 1958. *Psychological stress.* New York: Wiley.

JENKINS, J. G. 1946. Validity for what? *Journal of Consulting Psychology* 10: 93–98.

JONES, M. B. 1958. The polarity of psychological tests. *Journal of Consulting Psychology* 22: 25–29.

JONES, L. V. and THURSTONE, L. L. 1955. The psychophysics of semantics: an experimental investigation. *Journal of Applied Psychology* 39: 31–36.

JOURARD, S. M. 1969. The effects of experimenters' self-disclosure on subjects' behavior. In *Current topics in clinical and community psychology,* ed. C. D. Spielberger, vol. 1, pp. 109–50. New York: Academic Press.

———— and LASAKOW, P. 1958. Some factors in self-disclosure. *Journal of Abnormal and Social Psychology* 56: 91–98.

KAPLAN, A. 1964. *The conduct of inquiry: methodology for behavioral science.* San Francisco: Chandler.

KARP, S. A. 1963. Field dependence and overcoming embeddedness. *Journal of Consulting Psychology* 27: 294–302.

KELLY, E. L. 1967. *Assessment of human characteristics.* Belmont, Calif.: Brooks/Cole.

———— and FISKE, D. W. 1951. *The prediction of performance in clinical psychology.* Ann Arbor: University of Michigan Press. (New York: Greenwood Press, 1969.)

KELLY, G. A. 1955. *The psychology of personal constructs,* vol. 1: *A theory of personality.* New York: Norton.

KELMAN, H. C. 1967. Human use of human subjects: the problem of deception in social psychological experiments. *Psychological Bulletin* 67: 1–11.

KLINGER, E.
1966. Fantasy need achievement as a motivational construct. *Psychological Bulletin* 66. 291–308.
In press. *Structure and functions of fantasy.* New York: Wiley.

KLOPFER, B.; AINSWORTH, M.; KLOPFER, W.; and HOLT, R. 1954. *Developments in the Rorschach technique,* vol. 1. New York: World.

KLOPFER, W. G. 1968. Current status of the Rorschach test. In *Advances in psychological assessment,* ed. P. McReynolds, vol. 1, pp. 131–49. Palo Alto: Science & Behavior Books.

KLÜVER, H. 1936. The study of personality and the method of equivalent and non-equivalent stimuli. *Character and Personality* 5: 91–112.

KOHLBERG, L. 1963. The development of children's orientations toward a moral order. I. Sequence in the development of moral thought. *Vita Humana* 6: 11–33.

KRATHWOHL, D. R.; BLOOM, B. S.; and MASIA, B. B. 1964. *Taxonomy of educational objectives: the classification of educational goals. Handbook II: Affective domain.* New York: David McKay.

KRAUSE, M. S. 1961. The measurement of transitory anxiety. *Psychological Review* 68: 178–89.

KROGER, R. O.
1967. Effects of role demands and test-cue properties upon personality test performance. *Journal of Consulting Psychology* 31: 304–12.
1968. Effects of implicit and explicit task cues upon personality test performance. *Journal of Consulting and Clinical Psychology* 32: 498.

KUHN, T. S. 1961. The function of measurement in modern physical science. In *Quantification: a history of the meaning of measurement in the natural and social sciences,* ed. H. Woolf, pp. 31–63. Indianapolis: Bobbs-Merrill.

LACEY, J. I. 1956. The evaluation of autonomic responses: toward a general solution. *Annals of the New York Academy of Science* 67: 123–64.

LANDIS, C., and HUNT, W. A. 1939. *The startle pattern.* New York: Farrar & Rinehart.

LEARY, T. 1957. *Interpersonal diagnosis of personality.* New York: Ronald Press.

LOEVINGER, J.
1948. The technic of homogeneous tests compared with some aspects of "scale analysis" and factor analysis. *Psychological Bulletin* 45: 507–29.
1965. Person and population as psychometric concepts. *Psychological Review* 72: 143–55.
1966. The meaning and measurement of ego development. *American Psychologist* 21: 195–206.

LORD, F. M., and NOVICK, M. R. 1968. *Statistical theories of mental test scores.* Reading, Mass.: Addison-Wesley.

LOVELL, V. R. 1967. The human use of personality tests: a dissenting view. *American Psychologist* 22: 383–93.

LUBORSKY, L. 1962. Clinicians' judgments of mental health. *Archives of General Psychiatry* 7: 407–17.

McCLELLAND, D. C.
1951. *Personality.* New York: William Sloane.
1961. *The achieving society.* Princeton, N.J.: Van Nostrand.

————; ATKINSON, J. W.; CLARK, R. A.; and LOWELL, E. L. 1953. *The achievement motive.* New York: Appleton-Century.

McDAVID, J. W., and SISTRUNK, F. 1964. Personality correlates of two kinds of conforming behavior. *Journal of Personality* 32: 420–35.

MACKINNON, D. W. 1965. Personality and the realization of creative potential. *American Psychologist* 20: 273–81.

McNEMAR, A. 1962. *Psychological statistics.* 3rd ed. New York: Wiley.

McQUITTY, L. L. 1968. Improving the validity of crucial decisions in pattern analytic methods. *Educational and Psychological Measurement* 28: 9–21.

McREYNOLDS, P. 1968. The assessment of anxiety: a survey of available techniques. In *Advances in psychological assessment*, ed. P. McReynolds, vol. 1, pp. 244–64. Palo Alto: Science & Behavior Books.

MADDI, S. R., and ANDREWS, S. L. 1966. The need for variety in fantasy and self-description. *Journal of Personality* 34: 610–25.

————; CHARLENS, A. M.; MADDI, D.-A.; and SMITH, A. J. 1962. Effects of monotony and novelty on imaginative productions. *Journal of Personality* 30: 513–27.

MAGNUSSON, D. 1969. *An analysis of situational dimensions.* Psychological Laboratories report no. 279. Stockholm: University of Stockholm.

MANDLER, G., and KESSEN, W. 1959. *The language of psychology.* New York: Wiley.

MARKS, P. A., and SEEMAN, W. 1963. *The actuarial description of abnormal personality: an atlas for use with the MMPI.* Baltimore: Williams & Wilkins.

MASLING, J. 1966. Role-related behavior of the subject and psychologist and its effects upon psychological data. In *Nebraska Symposium on Motivation, 1966*, ed. D. Levine, pp. 67–103. Lincoln: University of Nebraska Press.

MASLOW, A. H. 1954. *Motivation and personality.* New York: Harper.

MEEHL, P. E.
1954. *Clinical vs. statistical prediction: a theoretical analysis and a review of the evidence.* Minneapolis: University of Minnesota Press.
1965. Seer over sign: the first good example. *Journal of Experimental Research in Personality* 1: 27–32.

MEHRABIAN, A. 1968. *An analysis of personality theories.* Englewood Cliffs, N.J.: Prentice-Hall.

MESSICK, S. 1965. The impact of negative affect on cognition and personality. In *Affect, cognition, and personality*, ed. S. Tomkins and C. Izard, pp. 98–128. New York: Springer.

MISCHEL, W. 1968. *Personality and assessment.* New York: Wiley.

MORGAN, C. D., and MURRAY, H. A. 1935. A method for investigating fantasies. *Archives of Neurology and Psychiatry* 34: 289–306.

MOSHER, D. L.
1966. The development and multitrait-multimethod matrix analysis of three measures of three aspects of guilt. *Journal of Consulting Psychology* 30: 25–29.
1968. Measurement of guilt in females by self-report inventories. *Journal of Consulting and Clinical Psychology* 32: 690–95.

MURPHY, G. 1964. Shall we ever really understand personality? *Journal of Projective Techniques and Personality Assessment* 28: 140–43.

MURRAY, H. A. 1959. Preparations for the scaffold of a comprehensive system.

In *Psychology: a study of a science,* ed. S. Koch, vol. 3, pp. 7–54. New York: McGraw Hill.

———, et al. 1938. *Explorations in personality.* New York: Oxford University Press.

MURSTEIN, B. I., ed. 1965. *Handbook of projective techniques.* New York: Basic Books.

NEUGARTEN, B. L. 1969. Continuities and discontinuities of psychological issues into adult life. *Human Development* 12: 121–30.

NEWCOMB, T. M. 1959. Individual systems of orientation. In *Psychology: a study of a science,* ed. S. Koch, vol. 3, pp. 384–422. New York: McGraw-Hill.

NUNNALLY, J. C. 1967. *Psychometric theory.* New York: McGraw-Hill.

OFFICE OF STRATEGIC SERVICES ASSESSMENT STAFF. 1948. *Assessment of men.* New York: Rinehart.

ORNE, M. T. 1962. On the social psychology of the psychological experiment: with particular reference to demand characteristics and their implications. *American Psychologist* 17: 776–83.

PALMER, F. 1970. Socioeconomic status and intellective performance among Negro preschool boys. *Developmental Psychology* 3: 1–9.

PAUL, G. 1969. Outcome of systematic desensitization. II. Controlled investigations of individual treatment, technique variations, and current status. In *Behavior therapy: appraisal and status,* ed. C. M. Franks, pp. 105–59. New York: McGraw-Hill.

PEARSON, P. H.
1968. A conceptual and methodological study of three Rogerian concepts. Unpublished Ph.D. dissertation, University of Chicago.

1969. Openness to experience as related to organismic valuing. *Journal of Personality* 37: 481–96.

1970. Relationships between global and specified measures of novelty-seeking. *Journal of Consulting and Clinical Psychology* 34: 199–204.

In press. Differential relationships of four forms of novelty-experiencing. *Journal of Consulting and Clinical Psychology.*

——— and MADDI, S. R. 1966. The Similes Preference Inventory: development of a structured measure of the tendency toward variety. *Journal of Consulting Psychology* 30: 301–8.

PILIAVIN, I. M.; RODIN, J.; and PILIAVIN, J. A. 1969. Good Samaritanism: an underground phenomenon? *Journal of Personality and Social Psychology* 13: 289–99.

POPPER, K. R. 1959. *The logic of scientific discovery.* New York: Basic Books.

RAPAPORT, D. 1959. The structure of psychoanalytic theory: a systematizing attempt. In *Psychology: a study of a science,* ed. S. Koch, vol. 3, pp. 55–183. New York: McGraw-Hill.

RASCH, G. 1960. *Probabilistic models for some intelligence and attainment tests.* Studies in Mathematical Psychology no. 1. Copenhagen: Danish Institute for Educational Research.

RECHTSCHAFFEN, A. 1967. Dream reports and dream experiences. *Experimental Neurology,* supplement 4: 4–15.

REITMAN, W. R., and ATKINSON, J. W. 1958. Some methodological problems in the use of thematic apperception measures of human motives. In *Motives in fantasy, action, and society,* ed. J. W. Atkinson, pp. 664–83. Princeton, N.J.: Van Nostrand.

RICE, L. N. 1965. Therapist's style of participation and case outcome. *Journal of Consulting Psychology* 29. 155–60.

ROGERS, C. R. 1959. A theory of therapy, personality, and interpersonal relationships, as developed in the client-centered framework. In *Psychology: a study of a science*, ed. S. Koch, vol. 3, pp. 184–256. New York: McGraw-Hill.

RORSCHACH, H. 1942. *Psychodiagnostics*, trans. P. Lemkau and B. Kronenberg. New York: Grune & Stratton.

ROSENBERG, M. J. 1969. The conditions and consequences of evaluation apprehension. In *Artifact in behavioral research*, ed. R. Rosenthal and R. L. Rosnow, pp. 279–349. New York: Academic Press.

ROTTER, J. B.
1954. *Social learning and clinical psychology*. New York: Prentice-Hall.
1955. The role of the psychological situation in determining the direction of human behavior. In *Nebraska Symposium on Motivation, 1955*, ed. M. R. Jones, pp. 245–69. Lincoln: University of Nebraska Press.
1960. Some implications of a social learning theory for the prediction of goal-directed behavior from testing procedures. *Psychological Review* 67: 301–16.
1966. Generalized expectancies for internal vs. external control of reinforcement. *Psychological Monographs* 80 (1, whole no. 609).

SANFORD, N. 1956. Surface and depth in the individual personality. *Psychological Review* 63: 349–59.

SARASON, S. B. 1954. *The clinical interaction: with special reference to the Rorschach*. New York: Harper.

SAWYER, J. 1966. Measurement *and* prediction, clinical *and* statistical. *Psychological Bulletin* 66: 178–200.

SCHACHTEL, E. G. 1945. Subjective definitions of the Rorschach test situation and their effect upon performance. Contributions to an understanding of Rorschach's test. III. *Psychiatry* 8: 419–48.

SCHACHTER, S. 1959. *The psychology of affiliation*. Stanford, Calif.: Stanford University Press.

SCHOENFELD, W. N., and FARMER, J. 1970. Reinforcement schedules and the "behavior stream." In *The theory of reinforcement schedules*, ed. W. N. Schoenfeld. New York: Appleton-Century-Crofts.

SCHUBERT, D. S. P. 1969. Factors influencing change on retest. Unpublished Ph.D. dissertation, University of Chicago.

SCHULTZ, D. P. 1969. The human subject in psychological research. *Psychological Bulletin* 72: 214–18.

SCOTT, W. A. 1968. Conceptions of normality. In *Handbook of personality theory and research*, ed. E. F. Borgatta and W. W. Lambert, pp. 974–1006. Chicago: Rand McNally.

SELLS, S. B. 1963. Dimensions of stimulus situations which account for behavior variance. In *Stimulus determinants of behavior*, ed. S. B. Sells, pp. 3–15. New York: Ronald Press.

SHAW, M. E., and WRIGHT, J. M. 1967. *Scales for the measurement of attitudes*. New York: McGraw-Hill.

SIMPSON, R. H. 1944. The specific meanings of certain terms indicating differing degrees of frequency. *Quarterly Journal of Speech* 30: 328–30.

SINCLAIR, E. J. 1956. The relation of color- and form-dominance to perception.

Unpublished Ph.D. dissertation, University of Chicago.
Sᴍɪᴛʜ, M. B.
1968a. Competence and socialization. In *Socialization and society*, ed. J. A. Clausen, pp. 270–320. Boston: Little, Brown.
1968b. The self and cognitive consistency. In *Theories of cognitive consistency: a source book*, ed. R. P. Abelson and M. J. Rosenberg, pp. 366–72. Chicago: Rand McNally.
Sᴏsᴋɪɴ, W. F., and Jᴏʜɴ, V. P. 1963. The study of spontaneous talk. In *The stream of behavior: explorations of its structure and content*, ed. R. G. Barker, pp. 228–81. New York: Appleton-Century-Crofts.
Sᴘɪᴇʟʙᴇʀɢᴇʀ, C. D., and Lᴜsʜᴇɴᴇ, R. E. 1971. Theory and measurement of anxiety states. In *Handbook of modern personality theory*, ed. R. B. Cattell. Chicago: Aldine.
Sᴘɪᴛᴢᴇʀ, R. L.; Eɴᴅɪᴄᴏᴛᴛ, J.; and Cᴏʜᴇɴ, G. M. 1966. *Psychiatric Status Schedule*. Albany: Biometrics Research, New York State Department of Mental Hygiene.
Sᴛᴇᴘʜᴇɴsᴏɴ, W. 1953. *The study of behavior*. Chicago: University of Chicago Press.
Sᴛᴇʀɴ, G. G.; Sᴛᴇɪɴ, M. I.; and Bʟᴏᴏᴍ, B. S. 1956. *Methods in personality assessment*. Glencoe, Ill.: Free Press.
Sᴛᴇᴠᴇɴs, S. S.
1958. Measurement and man. *Science* 127: 383–89.
1968. Measurement, statistics, and the schemapiric view. *Science* 161: 849–56.
Sᴛʀɪᴄᴋᴇʀ, L. J. 1969. "Test-wiseness" on personality scales. *Journal of Applied Psychology* monograph 53, no. 3, pt. 2.
———; Mᴇssɪᴄᴋ, S.; and Jᴀᴄᴋsᴏɴ, D. N.
1967. Suspicion of deception: implications for conformity research. *Journal of Personality and Social Psychology* 5: 379–89.
In press. Conformity, anticonformity, and independence: their dimensionality and generality. *Journal of Personality and Social Psychology*.
——— and Ross, J. 1964. An assessment of some structural properties of the Jungian personality typology. *Journal of Abnormal and Social Psychology* 68: 62–71.
Sᴡᴇɴᴇʏ, A. B. 1967. Designing effective motivation instruments to measure motivation components. In *Objective personality and motivation tests: a theoretical introduction and practical compendium*, R. B. Cattell and F. W. Warburton, pp. 127–148. Urbana: University of Illinois Press.
Sᴢᴀsᴢ, T. S. 1960. The myth of mental illness. *American Psychologist* 15: 113–18.
Tʜᴜʀsᴛᴏɴᴇ, L. L. 1953. *The development of objective measures of temperament*. Psychometric Laboratory report no. 1. Chapel Hill: University of North Carolina.
Tʀʏᴋ, H. E. 1968. Assessment in the study of creativity. In *Advances in psychological assessment*, ed. P. McReynolds, vol. 1, pp. 34–54. Palo Alto: Science & Behavior Books.
Tʀʏᴏɴ, R. C. 1957. Reliability and behavior domain validity: reformulation and historical critique. *Psychological Bulletin* 54: 229–49.
——— and Bᴀɪʟᴇʏ, D. E. In press. *Cluster analysis*. New York: McGraw-Hill.
Tsᴜᴊɪᴏᴋᴀ, B., and Cᴀᴛᴛᴇʟʟ, R. B. 1965. Constancy and difference in personal-

ity structure and mean profile, in the questionnaire medium, from applying the 16 PF Test in America and Japan. *British Journal of Social and Clinical Psychology* 4: 287–97.

TUCKER, L. R. 1964. The extension of factor analysis to three-dimensional matrices. In *Contributions to mathematical psychology*, ed. N. Frederikson and H. Gulliksen, pp. 109–28. New York: Holt, Rinehart & Winston.

———; DAMARIN, F.; and MESSICK, S. 1966. A base-free measure of change. *Psychometrika* 31: 457–73.

TUPES, E. C., and KAPLAN, M. M. 1961. *Similarity of factors underlying peer ratings of socially acceptable, socially unacceptable, and bipolar personality traits.* AFSC, ASD-TN-61-48. Lackland Air Force Base.

TURNER, C. B., and FISKE, D. W. 1968. Item quality and appropriateness of response processes. *Educational and Psychological Measurement* 28: 297–315.

TYLER, T. A. 1968. Response stability, person-item distance, and homogeneity. Unpublished Ph.D. dissertation, University of Chicago.

UNDERWOOD, B. J. 1957. *Psychological research.* New York: Appleton-Century-Crofts.

VANNOY, J. S. 1965. Generality of cognitive complexity-simplicity as a personality construct. *Journal of Personality and Social Psychology* 2: 385–96.

VARELA, J. A. 1969. Elaboration of Guilford's SI model. *Psychological Review* 76: 332–36.

VERNON, P. E.
1953. *Personality tests and assessments.* London: Methuen.
1964. *Personality assessment: a critical survey.* New York: Wiley.

WALLACE, J.
1966. An abilities conception of personality: some implications for personality measurement. *American Psychologist* 21: 132–38.
1967. What units shall we employ? Allport's question revisited. *Journal of Consulting Psychology* 31: 56–64.

WALLACH, M. A., and KOGAN, N. 1965. A new look at the creativity-intelligence distinction. *Journal of Personality* 33: 348–69.

WEBB, E. J.; CAMPBELL, D. T.; SCHWARTZ, R. D.; and SECHREST, L. 1966. *Unobtrusive measures: nonreactive research in the social sciences.* Chicago: Rand McNally.

WEINSTEIN, M. S. 1969. Achievement motivation and risk preference. *Journal of Personality and Social Psychology*, 13: 153–72.

WERNER, O., and CAMPBELL, D. T. In press. Translating, working through interpreters, and the problem of decentering. In *A handbook of method in cultural anthropology*, ed. R. Naroll and R. Cohen. New York: American Museum of Natural History.

WIGGINS, J. S. Forthcoming. *Personality and prediction: principles of personality assessment.* Reading, Mass.: Addison-Wesley.

WIGGINS, N. 1966. Individual viewpoints of social desirability. *Psychological Bulletin* 66: 68–77.

WINDLE, C.
1954. Test-retest effect on personality questionnaires. *Educational and Psychological Measurement* 14: 617–33.
1955. Further studies of test-retest effect on personality questionnaires. *Educational and Psychological Measurement* 15: 246–53.

WITKIN, H. A.; DYK, R. B.; FATERSON, H. F.; GOODENOUGH, D. R.; and KARP, S. A. 1962. *Psychological differentiation* New York: Wiley.

WITTENBORN, J. R. 1961. Contributions and current status of Q methodology. *Psychological Bulletin* 58: 132–42.

ZUCKERMAN, M.; LEVITT, E. E.; and LUBIN, B. 1961. Concurrent and construct validity of direct and indirect measures of dependency. *Journal of Consulting Psychology* 25, no. 4; 316–23.

———— and LINK, K. 1968. Construct validity for the Sensation-Seeking Scale. *Journal of Consulting and Clinical Psychology* 32: 420–26.

————; PERSKY, H.; ECKMAN, K. M.; and HOPKINS, T. R. 1967. A multitrait-multimethod measurement approach to the traits (or states) of anxiety, depression, and hostility. *Journal of Projective Techniques and Personality Assessment* 31, no. 2: 39–48.

Index

Abelson, R. P., 311
Ability, see Intelligence; Mode 3
Achievement, need for (nAch), 12, 64, 171, 241n, 253, 280, 285
Acquiescence, 213–15, 217n
Actuarial technique, 18, 176, 257
see also Empirical approach
Adorno, T. W., 95, 300
Affect, 40, 244, 294
Affiliation, 98
Ainsworth, M., 69, 307
Alexander, F., 173, 300
Allport, G. W., 6, 12, 65n, 74, 77, 108, 124, 191, 286, 300
Alpha, see Reliability, coefficient alpha
American Educational Research Association, 168, 171, 300
American Psychological Association, 168, 171, 225, 260, 300
Andrews, S. L., 92, 308
Anxiety, 11, 86n, 168, 244, 277
see also S-R Inventory of Anxiousness
A priori related process, 114–118, 265, 291, 294
Assessment, 294
program, 7–9, 11, 14, 243, 263
Atkinson, J. W., 64, 253, 285, 300, 308, 310
Attitude scale
Likert, 147
Thurstone, 133, 146n
Autobiographies, 12
Averill, J. R., 79, 300

Bailey, D. E., 260, 312
Barker, R. G., 179, 300, 311
Barron, F., 9, 11, 301

Bass, B. M., 78, 125, 301
Baughman, E. E., 236, 240, 301
Beck, S. J., 69, 301
Behavior
multiple determination of, 230–32
observations of, see Mode 5
prior, see Mode 4
specificity of, 34, 36, 228–49
variability of, 33n, 36, 49
see also Stability
Binet, A., 167, 236, 257
Block Designs Test, 238n
Block, J., 77, 301
Bloom, B. S., 106, 190, 287, 301, 307, 311
Bock, R. D., 260, 301
Body Adjustment Test, 76, 238n
Bolgar, H., 301
Borgatta, E. F., 310
Bradburn, N. M., 201, 301
Brelje, T., 213, 302
Brim, O. G., Jr., 147, 301
Buros, O., 7, 301
Butcher, J. N., 224, 301
Butler, J. M., 27, 51, 57, 75, 130, 225, 301, 304
Butt, D. S., 98n, 104, 221, 239, 241, 247, 256, 269, 301
Byrne, D., 11, 91, 301

California Psychological Inventory, 77
Campbell, D. P., 77, 301
Campbell, D. T., 86, 88, 164n, 167, 198, 243, 245, 261, 270, 278, 284, 302, 312
Campbell, N. R., 282, 302
Capabilities, see Mode 3
Caplovitz, D., 201, 301

314

Carnap, R., 43, 302
Carr, H. A., 32, 302
Carson, R. C., 108, 302
Cartwright, D. S., 149, 165, 197, 200, 302, 304
Case study, 25
Cattell, R. B., 14, 45, 58n, 66, 109–11, 114, 180, 240n, 282, 284, 302n, 311
Change
    from experimental treatment, 191–94
    and initial level, 197–99
    measurement of, 197–201
    from psychotherapy, 194–97
    by self-report, 200n
    substantive aspects, 200
    and unreliability, 199n
Chapman, J. P., 174, 213, 302
Chapman, L. J., 174, 213, 302
Charlens, A. M., 21, 308
Civil Service Selection Boards, 8
Clark, R. A., 64, 253, 285, 308
Clausen, J. A., 311
Cluster analysis, 58, 260
Code of Ethics, 225
Cognitive complexity, 239
Cognitive style, 9, 41, 71, 76, 254
Cohen, G. M., 78, 311
Cohen, R., 312
Collins, A., 20
Comrey, A. L., 260, 302
Concepts, personality, 3, 11, 294
    see also Construct
Conceptualization
    guidelines for, 92–110
    and modes, 101n
    as working definition, 94, 96
Confidentiality, 224, 227
Consistency, in science, 271n
    situationally determined, 178–80
    see also Stability
Construct(s), 14, 30n, 294
    centrality of, 283
    context for, 96–98
    core of, 98–101, 117, 295
    definition of, 28–30, 36
    interaction among, 130n
    level of abstraction, 281n
    specification of, 90–118
    and subconstructs, 102, 255n, 299
    validation, 247n, 270
    see also Concept
Content validity, 265
Context for measuring, 84n
Context of discovery, 26
Context of justification, 26
Convergence of scores, 267–69

Convergent validation, 88, 267–69
Convergent validities, 242
Cook, S. W., 86, 277, 302
Coombs, C. H., 139, 260, 303
Core, see Construct, core of
Correlation, product-moment, 100, 235, 295
Creativity, 9, 267n, 277, 288
Criterion, 8, 18, 28, 36, 53n, 167n, 229, 295
    group, 115, 257
Cronbach, L. J., 18, 127, 153n, 160, 168, 189, 213, 215, 255, 260, 303
Cumulative homogeneity model, 230, 295
Current concerns, 280
Current experiencing, see Mode 2

Dahlstrom, W. G., 77, 108, 236, 240, 301, 303
Damarin, F., 199, 312
Darley, J. M., 291, 303
Data
    matrix, 155n
    producer, 68–72, 174n, 275
Data box, 45
Datum, 131, 137, 295
Davids, A., 206, 303
Deception, 204
Dement, W. C., 39, 303
Dependability, 46
    see also Reliability
Dependency, 244
Depression, 243n
Desensitization, 194n
Design
    a priori related process, 114–18, 265, 291, 294
    empirically related process, 115–18, 265, 295
    simulated stimuli, 114–18, 256–65, 291, 298
Desire for Certainty Test, 147
Discriminant validation, 269n, 295
Distance, person-item, 163, 187n
Dixon, J. R., 282, 303
Documents, personal, 12
Dollard, J., 12
Dolliver, R. H., 254, 303
Dominance, 98–100, 104, 133–35, 239–41
DuBois, P. H., 4, 9, 303
Duffy, K. E., 260, 302
Dyk, R. B., 65, 73, 76, 238, 313

Eaton, A. M., 130, 193n, 207, 303
Eckman, K. M., 244, 313
Edwards, A. L., 12, 216, 220, 303

Edwards Personal Preference Schedule, 12
Edwards, W., 200, 303
Ego-Strength Scale, 11
Elements, 30, 103–06, 117, 295
Embedded Figures Test, 66, 76, 238n
Emery, A. H., Jr., 282, 303
Emmerich, W., 277, 303
Empirical approach, 58n, 109, 257, 390
    see also Actuarial technique
Empirically related process, 115–18, 265,
    295
Endicott, J., 78, 311
Endler, N. S., 105, 115, 125, 179, 303
Endorsement values, 49, 154, 295
English, A. C., 137, 304
English, H. B., 137, 304
Environment, 37–39, 45
    see also Setting
Ernhart, C. B., 284, 304
Evaluation apprehension, 204, 288
Examiner, subject reaction to, 212n
Experiencing, current, see Mode 2
Experiencing, stream of, 177–80
Experimenter effects, 212n
Extraversion, 11, 107, 146, 241, 281
Extrinsic convergent validation, 245, 271

Facet, 30, 103–06, 117, 128, 296
Factor, 14, 58, 109n
Factor analysis, 13n, 58, 239, 258–60,
    277, 296
    three-mode, 260
Farmer, J., 57, 310
Faterson, H. F., 65, 73, 76, 238, 313
Field independence, 238n
Fiske, D. W., 8, 20, 27, 29, 35, 49, 51, 57,
    88, 91, 98n, 104, 111, 130, 142n,
    149, 154, 157n, 162, 164n, 178,
    183, 185n, 193n, 196n, 200, 205,
    207, 228, 239, 241, 243, 245, 247,
    256, 258, 261, 269, 277, 301–04,
    306, 312
Foa, U. G., 103, 304
Forced-choice format, 219
Forer, B. R., 174, 304
Franks, C. M., 309
Frederikson, N., 312
Free response test, 55, 143, 296
French, J. W., 208, 304
French, T. M., 173, 300
Frenkel-Brunswik, E., 95, 300
Freud, S., 10n, 26, 107

Gage, N. L., 302
Gardner, R., 42, 66, 304
Generalizability, 154, 175, 193, 255, 267,

296, 298
    from data, 131
    over judges, 173
    from laboratory, 195
    over producers, 152n
    beyond a test, 163–72
    for a test, 150–163
    unity of, 171n
    see also Reliability, Validity
Getzels, J. W., 66, 305
Gleser, G. C., 18, 154, 160, 278, 303, 305
Goldberg, L. R., xiv, 160, 173, 186, 305
Goldstein, K., 12, 305
Goodenough, D. R., 65, 73, 76, 238n,
    305, 313
Goodman, G., 144
Gottschalk, L. A., 278, 305
Gough, H. G., 77, 239–41, 305
Graphology, 10
Greenberg, M. S., 279, 305
Guilford, J. P., 13, 75n, 99, 105, 110, 128,
    140, 167, 233–36, 248, 268, 290n,
    305
Guilt, 11, 242
Gulliksen, H., 159, 245n, 260, 305, 312
Guttman, L., 30, 103, 305

Haggard, E. A., 260, 301
Hakel, M. D., 222, 305
Hall, C. S., 11, 305
Harman, H. H., 258, 305
Hartshorne, H., 7, 305
Hays, W. L., 305
Health-Sickness Rating Scale, 166
Heine, R., 17, 304
Hermann, M. G., 278, 306
Herron, E. W., 5, 181, 306
Hersch, P. D., 283, 306
Hess, E. H., 9, 76, 79, 131, 278, 306
Hoff, D. B., 147, 301
Holt, R. R., 9, 69, 173, 306n
Holtzman Inkblot Technique, 5, 181, 260
Holtzman, W. H., 5, 181, 306
Holzman, P. S., 42, 66, 277, 304, 306
Homogeneity
    of items, 154
    model, see Model
    of persons, 154
    of scales, 142–46
    see also Reliability
Homogeneity coefficients, 160–62, 296
    and variances, 161n
Homogeneity indices, 153–63, 175, 266n,
    296
    computation of, 157–62
Hopkins, T. R., 244, 313

Hull, C., 12
Humphreys, L. G., 128, 306
Hunt, H. F., 196n, 277, 304
Hunt, J. McV., 105, 115, 125, 179, 303
Hunt, W. A., 45, 307

Idiographic, 24n, 108, 296
Impulsivity, 20, 97n, 240n
Incomplete Sentences Test, Mosher, 242
Index, 43, 46, 48, 50, 53, 56, 121, 296
  defined, 137
  producer, 69–71, 174n
Indices, evaluation of, 137–76
  models of, 137–76
  potential, 133–35
Individual differences, criteria for measurements of, 250–55
Individual person, description of, 17n, 287, *see also* Idiographic; Case study
Insight Problems, 238
Institute for Personality Assessment and Research, 9
Intelligence, 99, 128, 233–37
  measurement of, 41, 51, 11, 113, 128, 140, 171, 233–37
  see also Structure-of-Intellect
Interaction, person-item, 155, 159, 230
Interchangeability of tests, 232–49
Interjudge agreement, 266, *see also* Reliability, interjudge
Internal consistency, 151–54, 175, 296, *see also* Reliability
Intersubjective agreement, 292
Interview, 5n, 8n, 71, 78, 240, 243n, 263
Introversion, 11, 107, 146, 281
Inventory, 6, 12, 14, *see also* Questionnaire
Items
  ambiguity in, 221n
  correlations between, 35, 54, 228, *see also* r_{ii}
  reactions to, 207
Izard, C., 308

Jackson, D. N., 100, 204, 259, 306, 311
Jackson Personality Research Form, 12
Jackson, P. W., 106, 277, 306
Jahoda, M., 28, 306
Jamison, K., 260, 302
Janis, I. L., 287, 306
Jenkins, J. G., 167, 306
John, V. P., 123, 311
Jones, L. V., 56, 222, 306
Jones, M. B., 283, 306
Jones, M. R., 310

Jones, P. P., 186, 305
Jourard, S. M., 144, 213, 306
Judges, generalizability over, 173
Judgment
  clinical, 173n
  expert, 172–75
Jung, C. G., 10n, 107, 146, 281

Kaplan, A., 306
Kaplan, M. M., 100, 312
Karp, S. A., 65, 73, 76, 238n, 305n, 313
Kelly, E. L., 243, 258, 306
Kelly, G. A., 8, 31, 65n, 97, 277, 306
Kelman, H. C., 279, 306
Kessen, W., 90, 94, 308
Kingsbury, F. A., 32, 302
Kirtner, W. L., 149, 165, 197, 200, 302, 304
Klein, G. S., 42, 66, 304
Klinger, E., 280, 285, 307
Klopfer, B., 69, 307
Klopfer Prognostic Rating Scale, 69
Klopfer, W. G., 69, 78, 307
Klüver, H., 54, 307
Koch, S., 309n
Kogan, N., 288, 312
Kohlberg, L., 146, 307
Krathwohl, D. R., 106, 307
Krause, M. S., 86, 307
Kroger, R. O., 130, 191–93, 207, 307
Kronenberg, B., 310
Kuder-Richardson 20 (K-R 20), 153, 296
Kuhn, T. S., 277, 307
Kuncel, R. B., 223

Lacey, J. I., 200, 307
Lambert, W. W., 310
Landis, C., 45, 307
Lasakow, P., 144, 306
Latané, B., 291, 303
Leaderless Group Discussion Test, 78, 263
Leary, T., 86, 307
Lemkau, P., 310
Levinson, D. J., 95, 300
Levitt, E. E., 244, 313
Lewin, K., 12
Lindzey, G., 11, 77, 305
Link, K., 92, 313
Linton, H., 42, 66, 304
Loevinger, J., 143, 146, 152, 278, 284, 304, 307
Lord, F. M., 260, 307
Lorenz, K., 26
Lovell, V. R., 85, 212, 307
Lowell, E. L., 64, 253, 285, 308

Lubin, B. 244, 313
Luborsky, L., 9, 166, 196n, 277, 301, 304, 306, 308
Lushene, R. E., 114, 180, 311

McClelland, D. C., 64, 66, 86, 253, 285, 308
McDavid, J. W., 240, 308
MacKinnon, D. W., 8n, 308
McNemar, Q., p, 47, 308
McQuitty, L. L., 260, 308
McReynolds, P., 277, 300n, 305, 307n, 311
Maddi, D-A., 21, 308
Maddi, S. R., 21, 23, 73, 92, 304, 308n
Magnusson, D., 285, 308
Maher, B. A., 301
Mandler, G., 90, 94, 308
Marks, P. A., 286, 308
Masia, B. B., 106, 307
Masling, J., 212, 308
Maslow, A. H., 66, 308
Matrix, multitrait-multimethod, 88, 165, 242, 259, 268, 297
May, M. A., 7, 305
Measurement,
    conditions for, *see* Measurement, setting for
    defined, 131, 297
    effect of measuring on, 231n
    as experimentation, 56
    fundamentals of, 122–36
    of height, 47, 144n
    ideal, 122–24
    indirect, 278, 292
    non-reactive, 127
    personality, *see* Personality measurement
    in physics, 27, 143, 231n, 289
    public nature of, 26
    scales, *see* Scale
    setting for, 17–19, 50n, 57, 106, 206, 267n, 288
    specificity in, 228–49
    subject awareness of, 47, 70n, 85n
    and substantive theory, 10–15, 108n
    in testing situation, 127–29
    theory of, 282
Measurements
    comparability of, 51
    stability of, 183–86
Meehl, P. E., 69, 168, 173n, 255, 260, 303, 308
Mehrabian, A., 65, 308
Mendeleev, 10, 282
Menninger Foundation, 9, 166

Messick, S., 100, 106, 152, 199, 204, 277, 306, 308, 311n
Method, 89, 165n, 297
    of measuring, 88n
    variance, 88n, 165n, 297
Miller, N., 12
Minnesota Multiphasic Personality Inventory (MMPI), 6, 69, 77, 114, 162, 215–17, 224, 240, 257, 286
Mischel, W., 308
Mode(s), 68–89, 233, 237, 261–64, 268n, 277, 297
    and constructs, 84
    defined, 72
    differentiation of, 81–84
    of observations, 32
    and perspectives, 87n
    and process, 81n
Mode 1, 70–74, 77, 82, 85n, 124, 127, 130, 185, 190, 197, 204, 210, 214, 239, 242, 244, 262, 269, 275
Mode 2, 70–74, 76n, 82n, 85n, 125, 127, 166, 185, 194, 204, 209, 214, 239, 262, 275
Mode 3, 70–74, 76n, 80, 82n, 86n, 125, 127, 184, 190, 197, 204, 210, 214, 233–38, 253, 262, 275
Mode 4, 70–76, 80, 82n, 85–87, 124, 126, 130, 152, 166, 183, 197, 204, 214, 244, 262n, 266, 275, 278
Mode 5, 70–74, 77, 80–83, 85–87, 124n, 127, 152, 172, 184, 197, 204, 240, 242, 262n, 266, 275
Mode 6, 70n, 73n, 79, 82–84, 86, 127, 166, 172, 184, 194, 197, 204, 263, 275
Model, cumulative homogeneity, 142–45, 149, 151, 154
    differential homogeneity, 146, 149, 151, 295
    frequency, 140, 296
    psychometric, *see* Psychometric model
    relative frequency, 142, 149
    specific relative frequency, 142
    typology, 146, 150
Mood, 129, 252, 267
Morgan, C. D., 5, 308
Mosher, D. L., 11, 242, 308
Motivation, 41
Mowrer, O. H., 12
Multiple choice format, 55, 297
Multitrait-multimethod matrix, 88, 165, 242, 259, 268, 297
Murphy, G., 286, 309
Murray, H. A., 5, 8, 12, 22, 65, 97, 104, 107, 124, 191, 253, 280, 282, 308n

Murstein, B. I., 79, 309

nAch, *see* Achievement, need for
Naroll, R., 312
National Council on Measurement in
    Education, 168, 171, 300
National Opinion Research Center, 205
Naturalistic observation, *see* Observa-
    tions, naturalistic
Needs (Murray), 6, 22, 282
Neugarten, B. L., 277, 309
Newcomb, T. M., 66, 309
Newton, 282
Nomothetic, 24n, 36, 108, 281, 283, 289,
    293, 297
Novelty, 21, 92
Novick, M. R., 260, 307
Nunnally, J. C., 258, 309

Object Assembly Test, 238
Observations of behavior,
    classes of, *see* Modes
    naturalistic, 7, 26, 61, 122–27, 191, 297
    subject awareness of, 123
    see Mode 5
Observer, 68–71, 75, 77–89
    psychology of, 126n
    variables, 85n
Office of Strategic Services Assessment
    Staff, 8, 78, 263, 309
Openness to experience, 98, 169
Operational definition, 254
Opton, E. M., Jr., 79, 300
Organismic valuing, 169
Orne, M. T., 80, 196n, 209, 277, 304, 309

Palmer, F., 212, 309
Parloff, M. B., 196n, 277, 304
Paul, G., 194, 309
Pearson, P. H., 12, 22n, 73, 91n, 98, 125,
    169, 217, 256, 277, 304, 309
Peer ratings, 64n, 71, 240, 243n, 253–55
Persky, H., 244, 313
Personality, 3, 297
    abilities conception of, 66, 95n, 128,
        288
    complexity of, 26
    and culture, 284
    definition of, 16n, 35, 37–39
    natural history of, 61n
Personality measurement
    applied, 4, 18
    defined, 203
    expert judgment in, 172–75
    history of, 5–10
    issues, 281–93

prospects, 274–81
    schematic view of, 275n
Personality phenomena, classification of,
    286–93
Personality tests, reactions to, 210–12
Personology, 18, 28, 56, 177, 274, 282,
    291–93, 297
Persons, homogeneity of, 283
Perspective, 3, 31, 62–67, 233, 261n, 277,
    297
    and indices, 64n
    and modes, 87n
    and theories, 65–67
Phases, *see* Process, phases in
Piliavin, I. M., 291, 309
Piliavin, J. A., 291, 309
Polarity, 283
Pollock, G. H., 173, 300
Popper, K. R., 292, 309
Primary Mental Abilities, 13
    Test, 236n
Prior behavior, *see* Mode 4
Privacy, 224n, 227
Process, 3, 32, 36, 44–46, 275, 280, 297
    construct-relevant, 129
    general, 38–43
    implications of concept of, 41–43
    item, 111n, 265n
    in measuring, 42, 110–18
    phases in, 3, 40–42, 297
    in responding to item, 222–24
    task-reactive, 130
    test, 111n, 265
    validity, 265
Prediction, clinical, 173n
    statistical, 173n
Press, 124
Projective test, 9, 71, 78n, 243, 263
Propositions, axiomatic, 24–28
Psychiatric Status Schedule, 78
Psychological equivalence, 289
Psychology
    applied, 4, 12, 18
    clinical, 5, 11, 18, 65
    correlational, 19, 27, 36
    experimental, 19, 27, 36, 251
    see also Selection
Psychometric model(s), 140–51, 175, 295n,
    298n
    critique of, 149n
    and measurement scales, 148n
    and qualities of responses, 150
    see also Model
Psychometrics, 140, 260
Psychophysiology, *see* Mode 6
Psychotherapy, measurement in, 194–97

Pupillary reaction, 9, 79, 278

Q-sort, 77
Questionnaire, 30, 35, 71, 298, *see also*
    Inventory
  items in, 221n

r_{gg}, 160–62
r_{ii}, 160–62, 298
r_{pp}, 160–62, 298
r_{tt}, 160–62, 298
Rajaratnam, N., 154, 160, 303
Rapaport, D., 65, 309
Rasch, G., 187, 309
Rechtschaffen, A., 39, 309
Reichenbach, H., 26
Reinforcements, control of, 12, 91, 283
Reiser, M. F., 196n, 277, 304
Reitman, W. R., 253, 310
Relative frequency model, 230
Reliability, 46, 54, 128, 171, 296, 298,
    see also Generalizability; Homo-
    geneity
  coefficient alpha, 153, 160–62, 296
  interjudge, 124, 152n, 296
  internal consistency, 151–54, 175, 296
  K-R 20, 153, 296
  stability, 152, 183–86
Remainder variance, 298
Repression-Sensitization Scale, 11, 91
Response(s), 298
  aspects of, 55
  attributes of, 132n
  capabilities, 288
  classification of, 57, 131n
  equivalence of, 56
  potentialities, 95
  qualities of, 150
  stability of, 121, 251–55
  startle, 45
  variance of, 52
Response sets, 213–20, 226, 266, 270,
    280, 298
  control of, 219n
Rice, L. N., 75, 301, 310
Rod and Frame Test, 66, 76, 238
Rodin, J., 291, 309
Rogers, C., 12, 66, 169, 310
Rorschach, H., 5, 298, 310
Rorschach Inkblot Test, 5n, 14, 29n, 69,
    78, 80, 131–33, 141n, 151, 230,
    244, 260, 298
Rosenberg, M. J., 204, 288, 310n
Rosenstein, A. J., 105, 115, 125, 304
Rosenthal, R., 310
Rosnow, R. L., 310

Ross, I., 146, 311
Rotter, J. B., 12, 91, 108, 283, 285, 310

Sanford, (R.) N., 95, 97, 283, 300, 310
Sarason, S. B., 28, 208, 310
Sawyer, J., 69, 174, 310
Scale, 138–40, 298
  categorical, 138, 294
  information in, 139
  interval, 138–40, 149, 151, 296
  measurement, 138–40, 175
  nominal, 138, 150, 297
  ordinal, 148, 150, 297
  and psychometric models, 148n
  ratio, 138n, 149, 151, 298
Scaling, 187
Schachtel, E. G., 207, 310
Schachter, S., 287, 310
Scheerer, M., 12, 305
Scheibe, K. E., 283, 306
Scheier, I. H., 14, 59, 180, 302
Schoenfeld, W. N., 57, 310
Schubert, D. S. P., 188, 310
Schultz, D. P., 209, 310
Schwartz, R. D., 127, 278, 312
Score(s), 298
  specificity of, 232–49
Scoring, dichotomous, 159, 161
  multi-step, 147n
  scaled, 147
Scott, W. A., 106, 310
Sears, R., 12
Sechrest, L., 127, 278, 312
Seeman, W., 286, 308
Selection, personnel, 4, 6n, 12
Self description, *see* Mode 1
Self-disclosure, 144, 211
Sells, S. B., 285, 310
Selltiz, C., 86, 277, 302
Sentence Completion Test, 73, 242, 244
Setting, *see* Measurement, setting for
Shlien, J. M., 306
Shaw, M. E., 77, 310
Shuttleworth, F. K., 7, 305
Simpson, R. H., 222, 311
Simulated stimuli, 114–18, 256–65, 291,
    298
Simulation, 279, 291
Sinclair, E. J., 76, 131, 311
Single-variable approach, 14, 288
Sistrunk, F., 240, 308
Situation, analysis of, 285
Situational test, 8, 71, 78, 243, 263
16 PF Test, 58, 109, 240
Skinner, B. F., 13, 57
Smith, A. J., 21, 308

Smith, M. B., 78, 280, 311
Social desirability, 213–20, 242, 298
Sociometric techniques, 8, *see also* Peer
    ratings
Soskin, W. F., 123, 311
Specificity, 298
  of behaviors, 228–49
  of instruments, 232–49
  of measurements, 228–49
  in personality measures, 237–49
  of scores, 284n
Spence, D. P., 42, 66, 304
Spielberger, C. D., 114, 180, 306, 311
Spitzer, R. L., 78, 311
Spranger, 6, 12
S-R Inventory of Anxiousness, 105, 115,
    125, 179n
S-R Inventory of Hostility, 180
Squares Test, 29
Stability, 152, 298, *see also* Consistency;
    Reliability; Variability
  of behavior, 121, 184–86
  conditions for, 180–83
  long-term, 189
  of measurements, 183–86
  and person-item distance, 187n
  of responses, 49, 121, 186
  of scores, 267
  short-term view, 177–88
Stanford-Binet Intelligence Scale, 28, 236n
Stanley, J. C., 198, 302
State, 40, 42n, 45, 48–50, 106, 117, 299
Stein, M. I., 287, 311
Stephenson, W., 77, 311
Stern, G. G., 287, 311
Stevens, S. S., 158, 311
Stice, G. F., 58, 109, 302
Stimulus, 299
  complexity of, 229
  kinds of, 206–08
  in tests, 52–55
Stricker, L. J., 100, 146, 188, 204, 220,
    311
Strong Vocational Interest Blank, 7, 77,
    115, 191, 257
Stroop Test, 76
Structure-of-Intellect, 13, 76, 105, 128,
    234–36, 248, 290
Strupp, H. H., 301
Study of Values Test, 6, 12, 77
Subconstruct, 102, 255n, 275, 299
Subjects, motives of, 209–12, 278n
  psychology of, 206–12, 279–81
  reactions of, 34, 121, 203–27
  rights of, 224n
  variables, 85n, 220n, 299

Subsolvent, reagent, 280
Sullivan, H. S., 108
Swartz, J. D., 5, 181, 306
Sweney, A. B., 114, 311
Szasz, T. S., 28, 311

Task, 51n, 57, 207
TAT, *see* Thematic Apperception Test
Taylor Manifest Anxiety Scale, 29
Tellegen, A., 224, 301
Temperament, 41
Terman-Miles test, 77
Test(s), 299
  construction, 53n, 57, 229
  designs, 113–18, 265, 299
  development and evaluation, 264–72
  format, 268
  ideal, 154–56
  interchangeability of, 232–49
  projective, 8n, 243, 263, *see also* Ror-
    schach; Thematic Apperception;
    Sentence Completion
  simulated, 205
  situational, 8, 78, 243, 263
  subject perception of, 79–81, 203–05
  subject reactions to, 121, 203–27, *see*
    also Subjects
  task set by, 51n
  theory, 246, 260
  ways of taking, 208
Testing, conditions for, 44
  ideal, 129, *see also* Test, ideal
  layman's view, 204–06
  positive motivation in, 225n
  preferred conditions for, 211
  subject awareness of, 70n, 75, 206–08
Test-wiseness, 188, 220n
Thematic Apperception Test (TAT), 5n,
    55, 64, 69, 78, 106, 108, 197, 244,
    253, 270, 285, 299
Therapy, behavior, 194
Thorpe, J. S., 5, 181, 306
Threshold, 186n
Thurstone, L. L., 13, 56, 131, 222, 236,
    239–41, 306, 311
Tomkins, S., 308
Tracy, R., 185
Trait, 88, 299
  concept of, 286n
  factors, 282
Tryk, H. E., 277, 311
Tryon, R. C., 153, 260, 312
Tsujioka, B., 284, 312
Tucker, L. R., 199, 260, 311
Tuma, A. H., 196n, 277, 304
Tupes, E. C., 100, 312

Turner, C. B., 223, 312
Tyler, I. A., 49, 163, 187, 194, 233, 312
Typology, 107, 146, 148, 151, 286, 299

Underwood, B. J., 29, 312

Validation, 163–72
  convergent, 164–66, 267–69, 295
  discriminant, 164–66
  extrinsic convergent, 245, 271
  see also Validity
Validity, 46, 54, 128, 171, 175, 296, 299
  concurrent, 166, 294
  construct, 167–71, 173, 175, 229, 237,
    261, 294
  content, 164, 171, 295
  criterion-related, 166n, 171, 173, 257,
    295
  face, 164, 167, 296
  predictive, 166, 297
  see also Generalizability; Validation
Van Buskirk, C., 185, 304
Vannoy, J. S., 239, 312
Varela, J. A., 236, 312
Variability of behavior, 33n, 36, 49, *see
    also* Stability
Variable(s), categorical, 108
  defined, 94n, 299
  interactions among, 288–90
Variance, 46n, 50, 299
  artifactual, 159
  common, 246
  error, 246
  item, 162, 297

of item means, 155, 157–59
method, 88n, 165n, 297
person, 153, 162, 297
of person means, 155, 157–59
remainder, 157–59, 162
specific, 246
total test, 157n
Viewpoint, *see* Perspective
Vernon, P. E., 6, 77, 312

Wagstaff, A. K., 75, 301
Wallace, J., 66, 95n, 106, 128, 288, 312
Wallach, M. A., 288, 312
Warburton, F. W., 111, 114, 302, 311
War Office Selection Boards, 8
Webb, E. J., 127, 278, 312
Wechsler Adult Intelligence Scale, 80,
    238n
Weinstein, M. S., 64, 312
Welsh Figure Preference Test, 76
Welsh, G. S., 77, 303
Wepman, J., 304
Werner, O., 284, 312
Wiggins, J. S., 312
Wiggins, N., 218, 312
Windle, C., 188, 312
Witkin, H. A., 65, 73, 76, 238, 313
Wittenborn, J. R., 77, 313
Wolman, B., 301
Woodworth Personal Data Sheet, 5
Woolf, H., 307
Wright, H. F., 179, 300
Wright, J. M., 77, 310

Zuckerman, M., 92, 244, 313